Whitewashed Adobe

Whitewashed Adobe

THE RISE OF LOS ANGELES
AND THE REMAKING OF ITS MEXICAN PAST

William Deverell

UNIVERSITY OF CALIFORNIA PRESS

BERKELEY   LOS ANGELES   LONDON

Frontispiece. The "city of the future" in
the late 1880s. Courtesy of the Huntington
Library, San Marino, California

University of California Press
Berkeley and Los Angeles, California

University of California Press, Ltd.
London, England

First paperback printing 2005
© 2004 by the Regents of the University of California

Library of Congress Cataloging-in-Publication Data

Deverell, William.
    Whitewashed adobe : the rise of Los Angeles and the
remaking of its Mexican past / William Deverell.
        p.   cm.
    Includes bibliographical references and index.
    ISBN 978-0-520-24667-6 (pbk : alk. paper)
    1. Mexican Americans-California—Los Angeles—
History.   2. Los Angeles (Calif.)—Ethnic relations—
History.   3. Los Angeles (Calif.)—History.   I. Title.

F869.L89M515   2004
979.4'94046872-dc22   2003065066

Manufactured in the United States of America
14   13   12   11   10   09   08   07
10   9   8   7   6   5   4   3   2

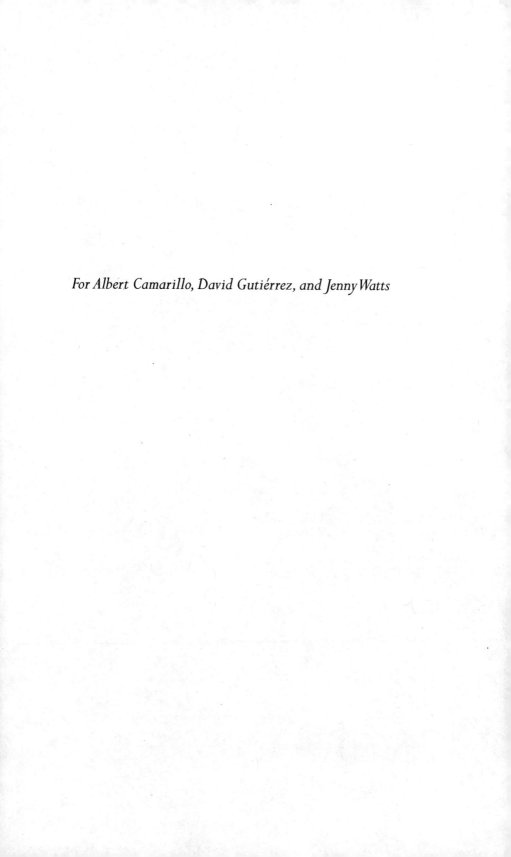

For Albert Camarillo, David Gutiérrez, and Jenny Watts

The publisher gratefully acknowledges the generous contribution to this book provided by the Lisa See Fund in Southern California History.

*Americans have their leveling ways: La Ciudad de Nuestra
Señora la Reina de los Angeles de Porciuncula has
become, in one hundred years, L.A.*

RICHARD RODRIGUEZ
Days of Obligation: An Argument with My Mexican Father

CONTENTS

LIST OF ILLUSTRATIONS AND MAPS / xi

ACKNOWLEDGMENTS / xv

INTRODUCTION: CITY OF THE FUTURE / 1

1 / THE UNENDING MEXICAN WAR / 11

2 / HISTORY ON PARADE / 49

3 / REMEMBERING A RIVER / 91

4 / THE COLOR OF BRICKWORK IS BROWN / 129

5 / ETHNIC QUARANTINE / 172

6 / THE DRAMA OF LOS ANGELES HISTORY / 207

CONCLUSION: WHITEWASHED ADOBE / 250

NOTES / 253

INDEX / 321

ILLUSTRATIONS AND MAPS

Frontispiece: The "city of the future" in the late 1880s / ii

1. Sonoratown, the "Spanish part" of Los Angeles, ca. 1870s / 16

2. The corner of Aliso and Los Angeles Streets in downtown, 1886 / 27

3. Racial types of "Life in the Feudal Era" of nineteenth-century Los Angeles / 33

4. A page from an early twentieth-century diary of a mission-to-mission tour / 35

5. Building Los Angeles, ca. 1910 / 37

6. Mexican workers in downtown Los Angeles, early twentieth century / 38

7. "A Typical House-Court" / 39

8. "Greasers in Embryio": Early twentieth-century tourist photograph of Mexican boys in Los Angeles / 40

9. Troops marching in La Fiesta de Los Angeles, 1894 / 51

10. Float at La Fiesta de Los Angeles parade, 1894 / 55

11. Local royalty, La Fiesta de Los Angeles, 1894 / 56

12. Children marching in La Fiesta parade, 1894 / 57

13. Representing old Spain: "Caballeros" / 61

14. La Fiesta poster, 1896 / 63

15. Representing Aztecs? Native Americans and La Fiesta's revival of a mythic regional past / 67

16. The Chinese dragon parading at La Fiesta / 69

17. The river that was: The Los Angeles River, late nineteenth century / 95

18. The Los Angeles River flowing next to the Elysian Hills, late nineteenth century / 96

19. The Los Angeles River in flood, 1880s / 104

20. Flood damage in the 1880s / 105

21. Los Angeles River, north from the Seventh Street Bridge, February 19, 1914 / 112

22. Salt Lake Railroad at Macy Street and the Los Angeles River, February 20, 1914 / 112

23. Photographer Charles Puck adrift following 1916 floods / 113

24–26. 1930s channelization of the Los Angeles River / 124–125

27. Mexican workers, Simons brickyard, early twentieth century / 131

28. Making adobe, early twentieth-century Los Angeles / 134

29. The Simons Brick Company's Yard No. 3 in Montebello / 140

30. The Simons company band / 157

31. Ernestina Macias on the lap of Walter Simons, 1920s / 159

32. Building industrial Los Angeles together / 165

33. Trucks ready to haul at Simons Brick Yard No. 3 / 167

34. Growing up in Yard No. 3: The young Walter Malone Jr. / 170

35. A "typical" postcard view of early twentieth-century Southern California / 174

36. A photographic representation of supposedly "typical" ethnic traits, early twentieth-century Los Angeles / 175

37. 742 Clara Street, Los Angeles / 177

38. 741 Clara Street, with siding removed to trap rats / 180

39. Plague survivor Raul Samarano / 181

40. The Baptist Mission church, plague abatement headquarters / 185

41. Plague abatement wrecking crew / 188

42. Mexican shack in rear of tortilla factory, 612 N. Alameda / 189

43. Looking west on E. 6th Street from Imperial / 189

44–45. Wrecking crew at work, back of 2039 E. 7th Street / 190

46. "Negro shack in business section, near 2039 E. 7th Street" / 192

47. Plague abatement as erasure, 2039 E. 7th Street / 192

48. Plague eradication destruction in the Utah Street district east of the Los Angeles River / 193

49–50. Vernon *colonia* burning / 194

51. John Steven McGroarty / 213

52. Act 1 of *The Mission Play*: Return of Portolá from Monterey / 218

53. Act 2 of *The Mission Play*: Fiesta scene / 221

54. Progress as linear tableau: A *Mission Play* advertisement / 222

55. *Mission Play* window advertisement, ca. 1920 / 227

MAPS

1. Southern California, ca. 1850 / 20

2. Los Angeles River, stream flow over time / 102

3. Bird's-eye view of Los Angeles / 107

ACKNOWLEDGMENTS

I have had an enormous amount of help with this book. I never would have finished it otherwise. I am most grateful to the dozens of friends and colleagues who have been so generous with their time, patience, and knowledge. This project also received significant institutional support, for which I am also very thankful.

Parts of *Whitewashed Adobe* have appeared elsewhere. My thanks go to David Wrobel and Mike Steiner for soliciting an essay in which I tried out many of the ideas from several of the following chapters; that essay appeared in the *Many Wests* volume they brought out with the University of Kansas Press. Portions of this work also appear in early form in a piece I co-wrote with Doug Flamming in John Findlay and Richard White's *Power and Place* volume on the North American West published by the University of Washington Press. I'd like to thank Blake Allmendinger and Valerie Matsumoto for helping me refine ideas about the 1924 plague outbreak in Los Angeles; chapter 5 is a newer version of an essay that first appeared in their coedited volume *Over the Edge: Remapping the American West*, published by the University of California Press.

Several institutions have generously aided in the research and writing of this book. I'd like to thank the Getty Research Institute, where I spent a period as a visiting scholar during the "Perspectives on Los Angeles" thematic year. The Institute staff and other visiting scholars made my time there extremely stimulating and enjoyable. I am grateful to the Office of the

President of the University of California system for generous support in the form of a President's Fellowship in the Humanities, 1994–1995. With my friend and colleague Doug Flamming, I spent an extremely productive period as a visiting scholar at the Clark Library during its yearlong investigation of the American West. My thanks extend to UCLA's Center for Seventeenth and Eighteenth Century Studies for support during that year, as well as to the Ahmanson Foundation, for its support while I was at the Clark and at the Getty Research Institute. The first full draft of *Whitewashed Adobe* was completed while I was a Fellow at the Center for Advanced Study in the Behavioral Sciences during the academic year 1998–1999; the Center, the California Institute of Technology, and the Andrew W. Mellon Foundation made that year possible, for which I am exceedingly grateful. Neil Smelser, former CASBS Director, and Robert Scott, former CASBS Associate Director, deserve special mention for their collegiality and congeniality.

It is a pleasure to acknowledge the support of my friends in the history department at the University of California, San Diego, where this project first began a long time ago. I continue to be grateful for the tremendous support I have received from the Division of the Humanities and Social Sciences at Caltech. John Ledyard, former chairman of the division, and division administrator Susan Davis deserve special thanks in this regard. My thanks to the members of the social history workshop at the University of Chicago, particularly Gabriela Arredondo (now of UC Santa Cruz), who invited me to present some of my work before the group. I am grateful to the students and faculty of the history department at the University of California, Davis, whose response to a paper I presented helped me rethink a number of points in the book. I also thank the members of the Los Angeles History Group, a collegial collection of the "usual suspects," who can always be relied upon to offer good words, good questions, and good ideas. The tragic death in 2003 of Professor Clark Davis, co-convener of this group, robbed the history profession of a talented scholar and teacher, and his passing stole from us all a man of abiding decency.

Research assistants George Ingersoll and Stacy Kamehiro helped me track down valuable sources. Helga Galvan and Victoria Seas of the Division of the Humanities and Social Sciences at Caltech assisted me at several junctures. Professor Ralph Shaffer provided research help on the Los Angeles River and its flood cycles. George Miles, Curator of Western Americana at the Beinecke Library, Yale University, helped me locate terrific sources that I would otherwise never have encountered. Patti Murray,

Walter Malone, Gene Chávez, Ray Ramirez, Ernestina Macias, and Jess Garcia opened my eyes to the world of Simons Brick Yard No. 3. Historian Charles Montgomery's perceptive thoughts and writings, especially his book *The Spanish Redemption: Heritage, Power, and Loss on New Mexico's Upper Rio Grande*, pushed my thinking forward in a number of ways.

My thanks to Howard Markel of the University of Michigan, who shared with me work that shaped my ideas about ethnicity and illness. Dace Taub of the Regional History Center at the University of Southern California offered her usual generous research help and equally generous kindness. Monsignor Francis Weber, Andrew Sherman, Kevin Feeny, Sister Mary Rose Cunningham, and Viola Carlson offered me help at a number of junctures. Caltech's Interlibrary Loan staff, especially Shadye Peyvan, saved my research life on innumerable occasions. Thanks, too, to the entire Readers Services staff at the Huntington Library, the librarians of the Center for Advanced Study, and Janet Clemmensen of the California State Library.

Others in the community of scholars deserve thanks for sharing ideas with me: Jared Orsi, Jane Apostol, the late Martin Ridge, Jennifer Tucker, Kevin Starr, Kevin Gilmartin, Alan Taylor, Roy Ritchie, Anne Hyde, Doug Sackman, Michael Bellesiles, Laura Edwards, Jim Scott, Natalia Molina, and Becky Nicolaides. Insightful readings by Virginia Scharf, Philip J. Ethington, and Robert Dawidoff improved this book. Miriam Feldblum and Doug Smith reminded me to think about things in different ways and to pose different questions. Kate McGinn, formerly of the Fuller Theological Seminary Archives, helped me with my research. Philip Goff, Director of the Center for the Study of Religion and American Culture at Indiana University–Purdue University, Indianapolis, also aided me in many ways. Alan Jutzi, Avery Chief Curator of Rare Books at the Huntington Library, helped me track down materials and deserves general credit for his unstinting support of scholarship. Blake Gumprecht helped me understand the Los Angeles River better. Janet Fireman never failed to offer a good idea or smart question. Dr. Ellen Bogen Alkon helped me with questions about her father, public health physician Emil Bogen. My friends in the Social History Reading Group helped me sharpen ideas about 1920s Los Angeles. Special thanks to David Igler, Philip Goff, Doug Smith, and Alan Jutzi for putting in long hours helping build our informal institute for the study of the American West.

At the University of California Press, Monica McCormick's good cheer, good ideas, and patience buoyed this project. Also at the Press, former Director Jim Clark and Director Lynne Withey deserve my gratitude for their insights and loyalty to this book. Randy Heyman and Marilyn Schwartz, both of the Press, aided me in the process as well. It has been my good fortune to work with copyeditor Kay Scheuer once again, and I am grateful as well to David Peattie of BookMatters for his help in shepherding this book from manuscript to hard covers. Friends and colleagues Ben Johnson, Roberto Lint-Sagarena, Shana Bernstein, Michelle Nickerson, Daniel Hurewitz, Clark Davis, and Mark Wild offered many ideas on the chapter addressing Simons Brick Yard No. 3. I owe a scholarly debt of no small proportion to the two outside readers who commented on *Whitewashed Adobe* for UC Press. The great western historian Robert Hine was one of these readers, and I am grateful for his encouragement and advice. Historian Edward Escobar lugged the manuscript around twice. I admit that I was at first reluctant to recast the book along the lines he suggested. His second reading (and second set of comments) convinced me that I was being stubborn at the book's expense. While disagreements yet remain between us, I know that his insights and care strengthened this book. I am also grateful to Professor Vicki Ruiz of the University of California, Irvine; Professor Ruiz read the book as a member of the editorial committee of UC Press, and her detailed report offered a number of excellent scholarly and editorial suggestions.

It has been more than decade's worth of privilege to work with talented graduate students at UC San Diego. I want especially to thank former students Phoebe Kropp, Mark Wild, and Sarah Schrank, whose fine work on the history of Los Angeles has shaped my own in lasting ways. Doug Flamming of the Georgia Institute of Technology, my former Caltech colleague and research partner at the Getty and the Clark, helped shape this book more than he knows. His patient, insightful reading of draft chapters improved them immeasurably. My friend Bryant Simon of the University of Georgia is a font of penetrating insight, historical and otherwise. David Igler of the University of California, Irvine, offered constant encouragement and support to the project; he also read the draft with care and wisdom. Mike Davis has taught us all a great deal about Los Angeles, and I'm pleased to acknowledge his unstinting support and generosity here. My thanks as ever to friend and valued collaborator Tom Sitton of the Los Angeles County Museum of Natural History, who read the manuscript and reminded me that I really ought to get the thing published. I hope someday to know as much about Los Angeles as Tom does, but I know I'm only kidding myself. David Gutiérrez gave this study the kind of sustained and critical read that only he can provide; his ideas and uncompromising insistence on sharpening aspects of the book's structure and argument were of great help. Had I not started work on this book, I probably wouldn't have gotten to know Greg Hise of the University of Southern California as well as I have, and I'd be the lesser person for it. Greg has taught me an enormous amount about Los Angeles and other topics, scholarly and not, and I'm proud to collaborate with him on a number of projects.

My mother, my father, and my sister have always stood alongside me in what I do, what I teach, and what I think. As I have gotten older, the extent of their patience and unwavering support become even clearer to me. I want especially to acknowledge the expertise of my father, Dr. William F. Deverell, who helped me locate and interpret medical documents related to the 1924 plague outbreak in downtown Los Angeles.

This book is dedicated to three remarkable people. For more than twenty years, the historian Albert Camarillo of Stanford University has helped shape me as a scholar and a person. The same is true of two decades of friendship with David Gutiérrez of the history department at the University of California, San Diego. Jenny Watts came up with this book's title. For that, for sharing in the joy of Helen Watts Deverell, and for countless other reasons, my river runs to thee.

City of the Future

Tomorrow shall be the flower of all its yesterdays.

MOTTO OF THE SOUTHWEST MUSEUM,
FOUNDED 1907, LOS ANGELES

The adventurous pioneers, who were the warp and woof of that pueblo, even in the early days had a curious prophetic feeling about the destiny of Los Angeles. Always one of their favorite sports, indoor and outdoor, was to make bold prophecies about the future of California.

BOYLE WORKMAN, *The City That Grew,* 1935[1]

I am a foresighted man, and I believe that Los Angeles is destined to become the most important city in this country, if not in the world.

HENRY E. HUNTINGTON, ca. 1920[2]

Can there be any *doubt* but what Los Angeles is to be the *world's greatest city* . . . greatest in *all* of the annals of history? Can there be any doubt but what MAN *wants* her to so become . . . or doubt that she *has touched the imagination of general public opinion* as no *other* city in history has touched the millions?

SHERLEY HUNTER,
Why Los Angeles Will Become the World's Greatest City, 1923[3]

Los Angeles has been the city of the future for a long time. Even as far back as the 1850s, at the moment of California statehood, people thought and spoke and wrote about Los Angeles as urban destiny in the making. Seventy-five years ago, John Steven McGroarty, journalist, playwright, and poet, wrote that Los Angeles was "the old new land of promise." "The City of Destiny," McGroarty called it.[4] Indeed the city seems almost able to bend time, at least in the ways people described it and talk about it even today. Los Angeles, they say, forges a relationship between the past and the present that makes every tomorrow unnaturally close by. Even more audacious, something about the place made people believe that their Los Angeles present was the rest of America's, if not the world's, future. Los Angeles as crystal ball.

How else to explain the signs? Readers of the city's dominant newspaper, glancing at its masthead eighty years ago, couldn't possibly miss the clues. A ship glides across the top of the paper, just above the relentless urging to "Sail on, sail on, sail on, and on." Starker and more telling was the tiny yet unmistakable printer's bug at the upper left corner of the *Los Angeles Times* masthead: a bright star encased in a circle, with a band spelling out "DESTINY" strung across its middle.[5] Los Angeles has always been a city on the make. And Los Angeles' destination and Los Angeles' destiny have always been the same: the future. *Sail on, sail on, sail on, and on.*

Prophecy and its symbols sprang from relentless ambition. A century ago, calculating city builders looked across the Los Angeles basin, even across the Pacific Ocean, and saw their personal destinies inextricably linked to the future of a then-small city. They explained Los Angeles' distinctiveness simply by suggesting that it already existed in a space ahead of the temporal curve. The rest of the state, nation, and world would watch, copy, and catch up. The city as time machine: *come aboard and try out the future.* Eighty years ago, real estate tycoons and booster wannabes reminded everyone of the city's steep demographic trajectory, proud of the equation that made population increase into the very definition of progress. "In 1901," an advertisement chided, Angelenos "laughed" at projections of the city's 1910 population. But Los Angeles hit that projected 350,000 mark with room and years to spare. By 1911, the city had exploded and had thereby grown full of true believers. A million people would be in the basin by 1920, "and it will come true."[6] Thus it was. "Here will be the greatest civilization the world has ever known," promised the usually taciturn John Fredericks, district attorney of Los Angeles, with all the unquestioning conviction of one of the chosen.[7]

In the early 1920s, Los Angeles realtors trying to outboost one another entered the "City of Los Angeles" poetry contest sponsored by their trade magazine. In one breathless stanza after another, they described the city "of eternal youth—a city without slums," an "inspirational vision of destiny," "the fulfillment of history's prophecy," "the most famous city in the entire world." Los Angeles: a place where "the best blood, intelligence and man-power from every state in the Union, crystallized into a composite loyalty for one city."[8]

Even great poets felt the fever of the future. A dazed William Butler Yeats, wandering around Los Angeles in the mid-1920s, wrote, "Here if anywhere in America, I seem to hear the coming footsteps of the muses." "Ask the older congested cities of our country if *they* can *parallel* such a promise," a representative booster pamphlet of the period queried—"whether or not their greatness lies in the *future* or in their proud achievements of the past. Los Angeles has everything in the future."[9] "Greater Southern California," declared the slogan printed on Los Angeles newspaperman, power broker, and real estate mogul Harry Chandler's 1920s stationary, complete with an arrow aimed at the future "Straight Ahead."[10]

Prophecy, faith, and wide-eyed optimism, shot through with presumptions of the racial superiority of self-identified Anglo Saxons. Los Angeles sailed on, through the 1920s and into the Great Depression, through the Second World War and postwar suburbanization, and on through the upheavals and violence of the 1960s, even unto today. Time only rephrased the in-evitable as the slightly questionable. Thirty years ago, scholars and policy wonks gathered at the Los Angeles campus of the University of California for a symposium called "Los Angeles: Metropolis of the Future?" The question mark only took up space, only made an academic conference slightly provocative. Of course Los Angeles and the future worked together, the notion insisted. The metropolis would *inherit* the future and other places would grow to resemble Los Angeles. The future belonged to Los Angeles, the future *was* Los Angeles. Or so presumption promised.

Prophecy in the city of destiny, like all prophecy, can have its portents of darkness, even apocalypse. We need look no further for a recent version of this than Mike Davis's tremendously influential book *City of Quartz*, with its provocative subtitle "excavating the future in Los Angeles," not to men-tion its back cover suggestion that in Los Angeles "we may glimpse our own future, mirrored with terrifying clarity."[11] Los Angeles just may be the city of destiny, Davis argues, but that future is hardly a pretty one.

Yet myths die hard. Dire predictions—which in the case of the Davis book came all too true in 1992—seem not to dispel faith in Los Angeles as some kind of prophetic urban quilt, a fabric optimistically suggestive of what America or the world could be, might be, will be. Associations of place and time include assessment of the city's ethnic and racial diversity as somehow a precursor, anticipating what other cities, other places will be or look like. In this way, Los Angeles trends supposedly become templates for urban futures everywhere. A book like David Rieff's *Los Angeles: Capital of the Third World* suggests, even predicts, as much. Immigration trends, coupled with the region's already stunning ethnic, racial, and national diversity, will create a multicultural Los Angeles of the near future that global cities will eventually come to mimic. Of course the question always remains, posed either implicitly or explicitly, whether demographic complexity alone can encourage peaceful interactions between people.[12]

But even this expectation, that the racial future of Los Angeles has special meaning for other places, that ethnic and demographic features of the city's neighborhoods somehow foreshadow an "everyurban" tomorrow, is not really new, at least not in its broadest characterizations. On the contrary, an old theme in the city's history posits, even expects, an explicit and intertwined relationship between *race* and *time*. Gone, however, are the social mathematics in the old equations associating ethnicity with prophecy; they have been reformulated in ways that render a different, a very different, sum. In days past, fortune-telling about Los Angeles commonly equated the promise of the twentieth century with Anglo Saxon ascendancy and white ethnocentrism. In the words of one representative booster from the 1920s, sentiments unabashedly published in the region's premier business journal, it was merely grade school figuring that in Los Angeles "Anglo-Saxon civilization must climax in the generations to come."[13]

One of the winners in the 1924 poetry contest spelled out the racial logic. Los Angeles was the spot—city leaders of the 1920s liked to call it, without a trace of irony, the "white spot"—where prophecy met history, where a place inherited millennial destiny. The poetry was tortured, but the gist is concise: "Dominion over land and sea of this enduring Race— Supreme Historic Prophecy—is now in final consummation."[14] It was not hard to imagine a world in which all this came to pass. We should not be surprised that such pronouncements could be made. We may cringe at such racial and racist determinism, but we should not think of it as happenstance or merely the wishful thinking of bigots. On the contrary, such visions are but the expected product in a city constructed *precisely* around racial categories and racial exclusion. Los Angeles is not so much a city that got what it wished for. It is a city that wished for what it worked diligently to *invent*. And that inventing in part entailed what this book is about, the whitewashing of other stories, other cultures, and other people's memories on the landscape.

Yet now, in much popular discourse, associations between city, future, and ethnicity have fundamentally changed. On one hand, the "Los Angeles as End of the World" race war phantasmagoria has been and remains, as Mike Davis reminds us in his book *Ecology of Fear*, an important historical and cultural expression of the city's darkest visions.[15] Will such characterizations accelerate in the twenty-first century?

But there exists another temporal thread that extols Los Angeles (often in neo-booster breathlessness) as the one place in America, if not the world, where the "multicultural future" exists now. Somehow—no one seems too inclined to offer the social blueprint—Los Angeles will by sheer example pave the way for a rainbow coalition future. Now it must be that this future works or will work precisely because that older futurist vision of Anglo Saxon ascendancy never got fully realized, derailed by second thoughts or by collisions with civil rights activism or the hard facts of demographic change. The same kind of language that once described Los Angeles as the best urban example of eugenic hygiene is now supposed to conjure up images of multicultural harmony. The Los Angeles future now is championed as diverse for, it seems, diversity's sake. As the notion goes, the region has been brought fast to its egalitarian ethnic senses by the hard lessons of Rodney King, the spectacle of the O.J. trials, or complacent acceptance that majority and minority populations will soon (at least by census reckoning) change places.

Yet a future foretold is not a future come true. Optimistic forecasts about ethnic and racial common ground, about a common future for the city of destiny, evince worthy aims. But as a historian, I am obliged to suggest that the city of the past deserves concentrated study before that leap to the city of the future is possible. It is imperative to continue digging into the soil of the Los Angeles past. What we find is a city that, even in its expressions of institutional and infrastructural growth, adhered to patterns of racial privilege and ethnocentrism. Pronouncements about a multicultural future that works may only be so many naive words and empty phrases. Or they may be lies, deliberate ones at that. We should be suspicious of the elasticity of language to defy the concrete reality of social problems. In other words, it was not at all that long ago that similar language and optimism promised a very different Los Angeles of the future. Los Angeles was once to be the world's urban beacon because racial supremacy *worked* here, because Anglo Saxons in charge worked so diligently to maintain particular lines of racial and ethnic privilege. If latter-day suggestions of racial and ethnic harmony in the future are to prove at all feasible, it seems to me important that we better understand the former expressions of racial singularity and supremacist triumphalism. Wrestling with memory and history in this way just might be socially therapeutic. It certainly is overdue.

This book is about the interplay between cultural authority and ethnic stratification in Los Angeles from the 1850s until the coming of the Second World War. It is primarily concerned with how processes of urban maturation reveal patterns of ethnic relations. In particular, *Whitewashed Adobe* focuses upon ideas and behavior of whites toward Mexicans. To narrow the focus even more, the following chapters concentrate especially on those whites with social, political, economic, and cultural power at their disposal. It is the web of their actions and perceptions that concern me most in this book. An earlier generation of scholars called them "city builders," and that description fits here as well.

At the heart of *Whitewashed Adobe* are two assumptions. This book's scholarly objective is to make a convincing argument that Los Angeles came of age amidst (and in part because of) specific responses to Mexican ethnicity and Mexican spaces. This "ethnic stance," one of the American Southwest's most important and troubling cultural markers, often attempted to isolate Mexicans in time and space. Understanding Los Angeles requires grappling with the complex and disturbing relationship between whites, especially those able to command various forms of power, and Mexican people, a Mexican past, and a Mexican landscape. The broader point at the core of *Whitewashed Adobe* is that coming to terms with these historical patterns—and thence, we can hope, deviating from them—is critical to the forging of a city true to a *different* Southern California future.

Modern Los Angeles is an urban phenomenon unlike any other in the history of the United States. It has prompted numerous scholarly investigations of its rise to metropolitan prominence. The city and region have also generated numerous historical analyses of the resident population of Mexicans and Mexican Americans. Both scholarly patterns are of great importance. The city's booming rise out of the 1880s, roaring on through the 1920s, is a historical marvel. And there can be little doubt that the region's complex and very often troubling history of ethnic relations, of which the history of Mexicans and Mexican Americans is of course a major part, makes up an important urban chapter in the story of race relations in

America. My discussion starts from an assumption that these two themes might analytically be joined or at least examined side by side. The chapters analyze the growth of Los Angeles through prisms of ethnic relations, ethnic contact and conflict, and ethnic representations. *Whitewashed Adobe* is an exploration of the deep implications of what prominent Angeleno Joseph P. Widney meant when he wrote that "the Captains of Industry are the truest captains in the race war."[16]

How did Los Angeles grow? Better yet, how did Los Angeles mature? How did it reach a level of urban self-consciousness, and what are some of the forms that urban identity took? *Whitewashed Adobe* examines the maturation of Los Angeles by paying attention to ideas about race and ethnicity, to ideas whites, particularly elite, city-building whites, held about Mexicans. Its pages also explore the ways in which Los Angeles, once part of Mexico itself, came of age through appropriating, absorbing, and occasionally obliterating the region's connections to Mexican places and Mexican people. Six chapters investigate these processes from 1850 through the Great Depression. At the dawn of California statehood, Los Angeles yet seethed with the racial enmity characteristic of the recent war with Mexico. Within a generation, Los Angeles business interests, looking for a commercially viable way to establish urban identity, hit upon a way to borrow Mexican cultural tradition in a brilliant public relations maneuver, an urban carnival called La Fiesta de Los Angeles. Faced with environmental catastrophe in the shape of an unreliable and occasionally unyielding Los Angeles River, early twentieth-century city leaders found themselves forced into a brief history lesson that demanded they listen to the Mexican voices in the Los Angeles landscape, if but for an instant, if but for memory's sake alone. What Los Angeles of the 1910s and 1920s had rather do with the resident Mexican population, as we especially see in chapter 4, was put them to work on the job of literally fashioning modern Los Angeles by shaping millions upon millions of clay bricks. When the resident population of Mexican laborers became unruly, as a very few did by crossing paths with a deadly disease vector in the 1920s, the city of Los Angeles responded with a ferocious campaign that obliterated Mexican homes and neighborhoods. But restraining the region's ethnic history and ethnic peoples could be done in ways more subtle than fire and destruction, as we will see in the final chapter.

Los Angeles matured, at least in part, by covering up places, people, and histories that those in power found unsettling. Los Angeles became a self-conscious "City of the Future" by whitewashing an adobe past, even an adobe present and adobe future. That whitewashing was imperfectly, even crudely, accomplished—adobe yet showed through—but it was nonetheless a way by which white Angelenos created distance (cultural or personal) between themselves and the Mexican past and the Mexican people in their midst.

Thanks to the pioneering efforts of a collection of talented scholars, we know a great deal about the Mexican and Mexican American history of Los Angeles. In the early twentieth century, sociologist Emory Bogardus and economist Rockwell Hunt of the University of Southern California sent dozens of graduate students into the field, and by so doing, into Mexican Los Angeles. These young scholars returned with studies rich in social detail, detail still relevant these many decades later.[17] Soon thereafter, anthropologist Manuel Gamio and his assistants collected ethnographies and oral histories of ethnic Mexicans in the region.[18] Then came the historical morality tales of the great Carey McWilliams. Later, the burst of intellectual and political energy erupting from the civil rights movement and infant Chicano studies programs in the 1960s and 1970s produced insightful analyses of the social and political history of Mexicans and Mexican Americans in Southern California.[19] In recent years, scholarly investigations of the ethnic history of Southern California (as well as the entire Southwest) have grown increasingly sophisticated. We have a baseline understanding of ethnic community and cultural development, to which has been added a more complicated story of intra-community and inter-generational fissures, conflicts, and divergence.[20]

Such scholarship, to which this book is deeply indebted, is rich and important. It confirms Los Angeles as a site from which to gauge national attitudes and behavioral response to both Mexicans and Mexico. After all, Los Angeles was once part of the Republic of Mexico: the abrupt transitions of the 1840s and 1850s offer case-study insights into national opinion. What is more, Anglo Americans in nineteenth- and early twentieth-century Los Angeles exhibited the common tendency to use Mexico and Mexicans as interchangeable identifiers and metaphors. Lastly, Los Angeles encountered, again during the period from just prior to California statehood forward into the new century, those various geographic and demographic imperatives that forced the city to address what white Angelenos stubbornly persisted in describing as "the Mexican problem."

Whitewashed Adobe has a slightly different purpose and a different historical angle to pursue than most of these other studies. It is a book less about the resident Mexican population than about white (or, as this book generally refers to the class, Anglo) perceptions of and behavior toward the ethnic Mexican population of Los Angeles. A model for this study is found in the work of the historian Alexander Saxton. As Saxton described it, his classic 1971 monograph *The Indispensable Enemy* examined "the Chinese confrontation on the Pacific Coast, as it was experienced and rationalized by the white majority."[21] This book proceeds from a similar vantage, examining contact between white Los Angeles, especially elite white Los Angeles, and the resident Mexican population, even the Mexican landscape, over the course of several critical generations. These perceptions, attitudes, and behaviors are themselves woven in important ways into the very fabric of the modern city of Los Angeles.

Along with a grateful nod to Saxton, this perspective owes a heavy debt to the writings of the journalist, lawyer, and historian Carey McWilliams, a scholar whose work seems to grow in importance with each passing year. In his many books, McWilliams presaged much of modern western American and California history. The single theme of McWilliams's multifaceted work that most informs this book is his analysis of changing ethnic representations in the transition from Los Angeles village to Los Angeles metropolis.

A full half-century has passed since McWilliams wrote about Southern California's preoccupation with what he termed the Spanish Fantasy Past and the ways that preoccupation fostered ethnic assumptions and presumptions.[22] I'd like to think that this book takes up where McWilliams left off in describing and explaining the role of institutional racial prejudice in the maturation of metropolitan Los Angeles.

Like McWilliams, especially in his classic *Southern California Country*, I am convinced that narratives about Mexico and Mexicans are integral to the city's cultural and economic rise during the period between the Mexican American War and World War II. Woven into a particular Los Angeles identity, these narratives can reveal an urban and institutional anatomy of prejudice. Through an exploration of the roots and ramifications of ethnic bordering—the construction of cultural categories in which ethnic others get placed—a great deal can be learned about the history of this city. Lest that sound too academic, let me suggest that one cannot miss these containers on the historical landscape of Los Angeles. They are everywhere, and Los Angeles grew up around them. These categories might take shape as labor segmentation, as with the prevailing tendency to view Mexicans as the region's ever-present supply of unskilled (always unskilled) labor. They might be the residential restrictions expressed at the boundaries of a Mexican neighborhood. They might be the containers of school or religious segregation. They might also be the bonds of memory or history, as in the ways in which Los Angeles enshrined particular visions of the Spanish, as opposed to the Mexican, past. If the city of the future is to work, we must look more closely at how these categories and containers were built, who built them, and how they got filled. Then we have to take them apart.

By this approach, I do not mean to suggest that ethnic Mexican resistance to such practices, however expressed, was not present and sometimes effective on the historical landscape of Los Angeles, ca. 1850–1940. At the same time, I do not wish to underestimate or deemphasize the power of the dominant society to limit and proscribe forms of class or ethnic resistance to discriminatory representations or behaviors. The following chapters concentrate almost exclusively on that latter phenomenon.[23]

Nor is my contention in these pages that powerful Anglos in Los Angeles rendered Mexicans invisible by insisting that they inhabit these particular cultural or other containers. It is the opposite view: borders created from discriminatory wage systems, from public memory, and from political exclusion all had to do with rendering Mexicans *expressly* visible, lest they disappear into the polity, into the neighborhoods, into the city of the future. Put simply, one important feature of the "Los Angeles future," at least as old as the city's American rebirth in the middle of the nineteenth century, has long been about race and keeping race in check. That is a common feature throughout the grim history of racial exclusion, discrimination, and segregation in American history, and the history of Los Angeles proves no different.

In pursuing this line of inquiry, we turn first to the 1850s and the bloody aftermath of the United States war against the Republic of Mexico. It was a little war, a war supposedly over only two years after it started. My purpose in chapter 1 is to examine the ways in which an Anglo and newly American Los Angeles grew amidst the brutal violence of Mexican-hating, and in consequence furthered a fateful trajectory into the city of the future.

ONE

The Unending Mexican War

The Mexican race now see, in the fate of the aborigines of the north, their own inevitable destiny. They must amalgamate and be lost, in the superior vigor of the Anglo-Saxon race, or they must utterly perish. They may postpone the hour for a time, but it will come, when their nationality shall cease.

Democratic Review, February 1847[1]

We accuse Californians and Sonorenos of being enemies to us—they are so in fact and in detail. And what wrongs are theirs? Where are their lands, their cattle and horses, and their money? Gone! They are nearly all paupers. And the mercenary avarice of American gamblers has made them such.

WILLIAM WALLACE, diary entry, 1857

The cut-throats of California and Mexico, naturally met at Los Angeles, and at Los Angeles they fought.

HORACE BELL[2]

Ugly reflexive characterizations about Mexicans are deeply rooted in the California past. The expressions of 1820s and 1830s American visitors such as the sailor Richard Henry Dana anticipate the racial and ethnic presumptions of later generations. Once imperial designs upon Mexico had been put into motion (exactly what Dana meant by his California commentary, "In the hands of an enterprising people, what a country this might be!"), it became an act of patriotism to refer to Mexicans in explicitly racist terms.[3] The 1846–1848 war against the Republic of Mexico—a nasty, brutal affair—drove home Manifest Destiny's darkest assumption that racial and national supremacy went hand in glove.

Scholars have disagreed about the chicken and egg quality to such a perspective: was racial hatred followed by expansionist determinism or vice versa? Tensions within this binary could seem subtle given the euphemistic language of Manifest Destiny rising in the early-to-mid-1840s. Softened by references to God's hand in all this, expansionist aggression could be painted in phrasings of divinity, glory, and the inevitability of Christian (read Protestant) triumph. But any blessed sweetness fell away as the project was rendered stark and grim by warfare and the lusty "All Mexico" cries of antebellum expansionists. "The truth is," declared one U.S. senator in 1847, "the Mexicans are a rascally, perfidious race."[4]

Taken as mere fact, such perceptions of a nation, a place, and a people had obvious ramifications in the far West. California, after all, was dragged to the brink of statehood by Manifest Destiny's crude racial determinism. First came the quixotic Bear Flag Rebellion against Mexican California by John C. Frémont and confreres, followed by outright warfare between the United States and the Republic of Mexico. But surrenders and treaties hardly put a stop to the violence of racial enmity—not General Robert Stockton's capture of Los Angeles in early 1847 nor the 1848 signing of the treaty of Guadalupe Hidalgo.

For one thing, territorial aggrandizement continued, not limited to the 1853 Gadsden Purchase, with its addition of 29,000,000 acres to what would become lower Arizona and New Mexico. Not long after peace, the adventurer and land pirate William Walker rehearsed his later invasion of Nicaragua with paramilitary campaigns in Baja California and Sonora. Walker was hardly alone. The Mexican Republic faced invasion by land and sea numerous times after 1848, and these expeditions often began in California and continued, oddly enough, well into the latter part of the century. As historian Robert May has written, "the racialist strains of Manifest Destiny survived the peace with Mexico and helped inspire post-war filibustering." Californian Horace Bell, a follower of Walker in Nicaragua, fondly recalled the postwar era: "What wild schemes, what adventurous plans were concocted overnight in those early years of the Golden State!"[5]

What happens to our understanding of California or Los Angeles history if we suggest that, diplomatic or treaty assurances to the contrary, the Mexican War did not end in 1848? "Poor Mexico!" an Angeleno confessed in his diary between filibustering raids in the mid-1850s. "It is supposed that she will now be permitted to breathe freely several times, before the next heel is placed upon her neck."[6]

It had all seemed so direct and simple, California moving step by step toward its rightful American future. "The war between our government and Mexico, in a short time after, ceased to exist," the California chronicler Benjamin Truman wrote. "California became a Territory of the United States, and, legally, Los Angeles was no longer a Mexican pueblo, but a 'burg' of the great Yankee nation."[7] But as early Los Angeles historian James Miller Guinn wrote in 1901, in a phrase succinct and on target, the "process of Americanizing the people was no easy undertaking." Laid atop the Mexican War and its violent, racist exuberance were the postwar brutalities of the Gold Rush, the beatings, the criminalization, and the lynchings of resident Mexicans, most of whom had, at least by treaty, become Americans. "To shoot these Greasers ain't the best way," declared one California vigilante in the Gold Rush period. "Give 'em a fair trial, and rope 'em up with all the majesty of the law. That's the cure."[8]

What's more, the none-too-subtle extortions imposed by the "foreign miner's tax" stood as frontier-era precursors of more recent California public referenda aimed at ethnic others. Such legal expressions of racial malice make the ever-widening ripples of ugly discriminatory ideas and behavior even easier to spot and track on the historical landscape. They also suggest a posture that the Mexican American War had made all too obvious to whites in California. Mexicans and Mexico were to be approached with arms and martial readiness. "This southern California is still unsettled," wrote field scientist William H. Brewer in 1860. "We all continually wear arms—each wears both bowie knife and pistol (navy revolver), while we always have for game or otherwise, a Sharp's rifle, Sharp's carbine, and two double-barrel shotguns," hardly the paraphernalia of peacetime. Did the Mexican War end?[9]

Horace Bell, soldier of fortune, rancher, journalist, and memoirist all rolled into one, remembered 1850s Los Angeles as an immensely violent place. First came vigilante action aimed at the sons of prominent rancher José del Carmen Lugo (the vigilantes came up on the short end of that deal). Then in 1851, with the lynching of a Mexican man named Zavalete, again the "Los Angeles mob raised its horrid head." Things only worsened with time, as Bell notes with irony unchecked.

Such was the plane of civilization to which our people had attained in the early period of the city's American history. . . . American rule had certainly demonstrated to the benighted sons of Mexico the superiority of our civilization. We had evolved a very simple rule for the classification of the population. A man was either a manhunter, or he was one of the hunted. That is, if he amounted to anything at all. If in neither classification, then he was a mere nonentity. The decent minority—for there was such a group of nonentities—wondered when and where it would all end. It was barbarism gone to seed.[10]

By the middle of the decade, tensions between "Americans" and Mexicans threatened to explode. Judge Benjamin Hayes, whose Los Angeles diaries offer an especially illuminating glimpse into the years he called "a transition state to better order and more perfect security," felt the pressures of his times and judicial duties. In sentencing a Mexican man to death for murder, Hayes made certain to have his remarks translated into Spanish, read aloud, and then published. This was not for the condemned, he argued, so much as for "his young countrymen, who are betraying too many signs of hostility to *Americanos.*" Yet wasn't such hostility justified, given the legal system's propensity for racial profiling, ca. 1850? After all, as an attentive journalist of the period noted, "punishment seems to be graduated by the color of the skin, and not the color of the crime."[11]

Itinerant schoolteacher and newspaperman William Wallace traveled three times from New England to Southern California in the 1850s. His journal, kept with meticulous care in small leather-bound books, is a barometer of the social and ethnic tensions of the period. Looking out across the expanse of the Los Angeles basin in the early spring of 1855, Wallace could barely contain his excitement at being back in the West. His entries foreshadow the later effervescence of Los Angeles boosters. "I love the country, the climate is incomparable, the scenery is grand, the plains are beautiful, the flowers are everywhere." Yet natural beauty could not fully mask the difficulties and the violence, "the dangers, the vices, the self-sacrifices, the cold-blooded crimes through which the pioneers have guided this unformed and malformed community."[12]

Wallace felt the social hangover brought about by the recklessness of American occupation, warfare, and statehood. "We are now like fast boys upon their travels, and our imprudences have brought us into trouble," he mused. Rapid change marked everything. "The California of ten years ago is not the California of to-day," he noted. "The old country, with all its simple manners and customs, [has] all departed; everything has become new, and is as yet unformed." Riding out from the village center to teach school near the San Gabriel Mission, Wallace encountered Gabrielino Indians trying to maintain some semblance of their former lives and folkways. But the racial future of Los Angeles would not likely tolerate such appeals to tradition, he figured. "Fashion and folly are working their way in here—and by and by all these Indians will be shaped like white folks."[13]

William Wallace feared the power of these mysterious social and racial forces which could recast ethnicity, just as he admitted that he was afraid of Divine Retribution revealed in the earthquakes that occasionally threw him to the ground. He believed that the vengeance of God would offer rebuttal to the blood sports of 1850s ethnic conflict. All the signs pointed in that direction. Social niceties, which had seemed so much a part of everyday life, now went unperformed and unsaid. Many of the genteel *Californios*, those Latino rancho elites grappling with seismic marketplace changes and quickening political obsolescence, displayed unusual, though largely unspoken, hostility toward Americans. It was rumored that they washed their hands after touching American money, "to wipe away the stain from them before they are laid away." "The curses upon the Americans are deep and bitter," Wallace noted, and "there is little sympathy between the races."[14]

In the summer of 1856, a Los Angeles deputy marshal named William Jenkins killed unarmed Antonio Ruiz over "a petty two dollars." In the ensuing turmoil, William Wallace expected civil war to erupt as the companion to natural disaster, a full-blown resumption of the Mexican American War. The incident provoked thoughts on Wallace's part of the propensity of Anglos to cast Mexicans as enemies and to use such categorizations to justify the wrenching transitions of the era. "We accuse Californians and Sonorenos of being enemies to us—they are so in fact and in detail. And what wrongs are theirs? Where are their lands, their cattle and horses, and their money? Gone! They are nearly all paupers. And the mercenary avarice of American gamblers has made them such."[15]

Wallace no doubt agreed with contemporaries who described Los Angeles in the first years of California statehood as wracked by race war.[16] The place also witnessed a curious conflict over names—wherein disputes over naming reveal deeper antagonisms. What had been the Mexican American War only a few years earlier became a war against Mexican Americans. The treaty that ended the U.S.-Mexico War had been explicit about the citizenship consequences of peace. Mexicans who stayed would become Americans.[17] But diplomatic assurances have rarely meant less on the ground. As the historian David Gutiérrez has noted, Guadalupe Hildago "could do little to

Figure 1. Sonoratown, the "Spanish part" of Los Angeles, ca. 1870s. Courtesy of the California History Room, California State Library, Sacramento.

transform the biased views of Mexicans that Americans continued to entertain." In some ways, enmity only increased, as "Americans" and "Mexicans" still existed worlds apart, treaty or no treaty.[18]

Despite de jure citizenship status, Mexicans could not exercise the franchise with anything close to the same ease as lighter-skinned Angelenos. On the contrary, the poorest among the Indians and Mexicans of the village might get literally corralled and violently coerced into casting bought votes, as Wallace's diary for 1857 detailed. "All shades of dark colors (the 'piebald classes') were there, half breeds, Indians, Soñorenses. . . . They were plied with bad whiskey, and when they became riotous were knocked on the head." Such civic obscenities further emphasized a paradox. Mexicans were not Americans, even though they were.[19] Mexicans, as Figure 1 suggests, did not even live in Los Angeles. Mexicans still lived in Mexico, in Sonora or Sonoratown, in "homes for the defeated." Both logic and geography argue that 1850s Sonoratown, north of the plaza, not far from the banks of the Los Angeles River, was in fact *in* Los Angeles, *in* California, *in* the United States. But logic and social reality do not of course always operate in tandem. Sonora and Sonoratown *were* Mexico in the popular perceptions of many an Anglo Angeleno, a Mexico gradually becoming surrounded by an Americanizing Los Angeles (which, as the dominant spatial and political category, did not need a corresponding "Anglo town" reference).[20]

Words again. Weren't the 1850s all about exchanging one Californian, the elite Mexican, for another, the Anglo?[21] Who would become the Californians of the new state? Californian, *Californio*: these *had* had specific contextual meanings. They had once been direct references to the region's Latin population in the vernacular of the pre-American period and just afterwards (the references were even class coded, the latter being the elite designation). By decade's end, the sad conclusion could be offered: *Californios* "have passed away like our foggy mornings. There is nothing to show for their existence." William Wallace's diary entry might have been premature: *Californios* would continue to exercise some authority, mostly social, in Southern California for another generation. But his instincts were right; the transition had begun and little could stop it.[22] Within a few short decades, drought, legal entanglements, intermarriage, the imposition of a new political economy, outright thievery, and the removal of *Californios* from positions of political power had turned the world upside down. California, the spoils in both place and name, belonged now to the victors. Nor could these former elites play much of a role or profit by the nostalgic renderings of the California past (which, ironically, placed them at the center of much of the romance). "Contained by Anglo newcomers and cut off from a reservoir of native folk traditions," the historian Charles Montgomery has observed, the *Californio* gentry "was forced largely to cede California's Spanish revival to the imagination of Anglo promoters." "Perhaps never since Adam fell from Eden," wrote a sympathetic visitor to nineteenth-century California "has there been a sadder realization of Paradise Lost than is afforded by these native Californians."[23]

Not long after William Jenkins killed Antonio Ruiz, friends of the murdered man gathered at his fresh grave. The *Los Angeles Star* called them "among the lowest and most abandoned Sonorians and Mexicans." When they filled the streets, threatening violence against the Americans in the village, William Wallace must have thought his fears of civil unrest prophetic. Nor was he alone in such trepidation. Judge Benjamin Hayes, the same man who had recently ordered a hanging as a public deterrent to ethnic violence (despite the fact that his act was precisely that which he hoped to curtail), fairly quaked with fear. "It must be admitted that about midnight a deep apprehension of disastrous consequences did settle upon the minds of the people," he wrote.[24] Trouble broke out. A melee, a horse shot and killed, Marshal William Getman wounded. Rumors flew: three hundred or more armed Mexicans had gathered to lay siege to the town. Whites mobilized. Ozro Childs, a local tinsmith, volunteered to ride east about ten miles to El Monte, local capital of anti-Mexican word and deed, for help from the El Monte boys, ruffians always spoiling for a fight.[25]

With the arrival of several dozen heavily armed El Monte reinforcements, white Angelenos quickly organized a Committee of Safety. William Wallace lamented what he saw as the final breakdown of a society pinned between the retributions of nature and the havoc of racial enmity. "It would seem as if heaven and hell were in league against us. The drought is increasing on the plains and by the roads we are almost cut off from the world except by water or across almost impassable deserts. But the worst feature of all is the moral depravity and the propensity to fight which increases among all classes. . . . the rifle and revolver are our trust."[26]

"Blood flows in the streets—justice weeps," Wallace wrote in his neat hand. "All is anarchy." Matters got even worse. In the early months of 1857, Wallace penned eyewitness accounts of two critical moments in village history, powerful symbols of the period's ethnic turmoil and violence. In late January, the steamer *Sea Bird*, anchored off the coast at San Pedro, dropped off one hundred men under the command of one Henry A. Crabb. Crabb arrived in Los Angeles by way of Northern California and a recent failure to win a seat in the U.S. Senate (he had been in the California statehouse representing the San Joaquin Valley). "Colonel" Crabb's band of men included what were likely underemployed and unlucky gold miners from the northern mines, as well as a smattering of former members of the California legislature. They came to Los Angeles with a plan as ambitious as it was misguided, having something to do with recently vanquished Mexico.

"What do these men want in Sonora?" Wallace asked himself. Soon all became clear. Crabb aimed to take a big chunk of what remained of northern Mexico after the territorial surgery performed by the Treaty of Guadalupe Hidalgo and the Gadsden Purchase. The men of the little army wished, as did many of their filibustering contemporaries, to then turn their prize into a slave-holding region. Crabb had tried, impotently, the same thing a year or so earlier. Now he and his band meant business.[27]

Crabb and his soldiers (the harmlessly euphemistic "Arizona Colonization Society"), rumored to be just the advance team of a force twelve to sixteen hundred strong, simply refused to believe that the Mexican American War had ended nearly ten years earlier. Chronology's truths meant nothing against adventuring promise. Heeding Manifest Destiny's earlier "All Mexico" rallying cry, they went about stockpiling weapons, wagons, and supplies in Los Angeles and the nearby hamlet of El Monte. There they were delayed for several weeks, tending to the wounds of one of their own who had been shot by his comrades aboard the steamer coming south from the Bay Area. Hindsight suggests this as an apt omen of things to come for Crabb and company.

Local men itching for glory, or those with nothing to lose, signed up for the fateful journey, joining one of the various infantry "companies" (A, B, C, etc.) or the "artillery." Confidence ran high. Judge Hayes noted that one of the filibusters had neglected to inform his wife back in Kentucky what he was up to; he preferred that she know of his plans after Crabb and his followers had attained glory in Mexico. The judge was less sanguine. "I knew more of Sonora and Sonoranians then he did," he later wrote.[28]

"They gained no sympathy here," declared William Wallace, adding that "the community felt relieved at their departure." An official comment from the United States government offered the succinct assessment that the "expeditionists have certainly chosen an unfortunate time for their movements as regards the interests of the United States in their relations with Mexico." Once encumbered with weapons and supplies, most of the would-be heroes inexplicably refused to purchase horses or mules, apparently preferring the more spectacularly martial, not to mention exhausting, alternative of marching to Mexico all the way from Los Angeles. Once there, Crabb and his "pedestrian crowd" expected, as Wallace delicately phrased it, "to arrange the internal dissensions of the people," albeit "at the sword's point." Again, hindsight suggests this as dangerously wishful if not downright stupid. Wallace hinted as much in his descriptions of the civilian army. "Though gentlemanly in their manners, they did not appear like men accustomed to Hardship." Time would prove that assessment prophetic. For now, though, Wallace surmised that the "fact that they find it unprofitable to remain longer in California is pretty good evidence that our social condition must be improving; although at our neighbor's expense."[29]

But William Wallace was wrong. Even Crabb-less, the Los Angeles social condition showed little sign of improvement. The local ramifications of heightened ethnic tension revealed themselves in newspaper headlines only a day after Crabb's departure. The bodies of Los Angeles County sheriff James R. Barton and several of his constables had turned up south of Los Angeles near Mission San Juan Capistrano. Barton and his men had been murdered by a roving band of outlaws under the leadership of Juan Flores, a recent escapee from San Quentin. Despite the shock, Wallace thought

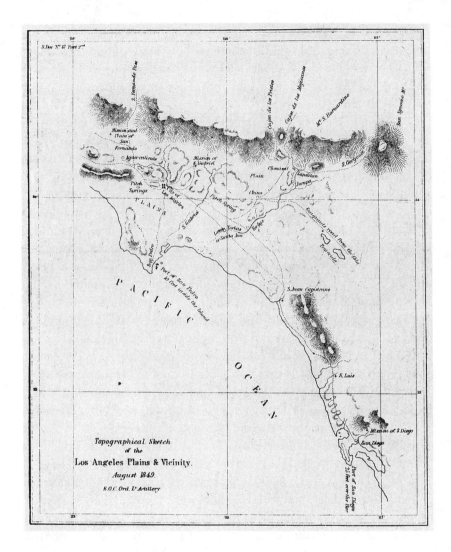

Map 1. Southern California, ca. 1850.

that the murders, said to be done from ambush, might just be the tonic Anglo Los Angeles needed in order to spring to life and claim the region once and for all. "It is fortunate that Barton and confreres were killed—it needed as great a calamity to move the selfish Anglo blood, that is here only greedy for money."[30]

"Will the people rise in their might, and sweep the villains and murderers from the face of the earth?" asked the *Los Angeles Star*. "Or will the present deep feeling be allowed to exhaust itself in idle complainings? Time will tell." Authorities trundled the coffins containing the bodies of the martyred lawmen back toward Los Angeles. A large crowd met the cortege at the banks of the Los Angeles River. The blood of the victims, the *Star* mourned, "cries from the ground for vengeance."[31] No surprise: violence begat violence. At the San Gabriel Mission (as much a regional central place in this era as the plaza in Los Angeles), four men, supposedly members of the Flores band, soon faced a hanging judge. At a hastily arranged hearing, the judge asked those present if they believed the men in custody should be hanged. Hands shot up all round, including that of the judge himself. Justice will be done. But the grim affair was quickly botched. As one execution went forward, the hangman's rope broke, whereupon the judge himself attempted to shoot the man who tumbled to the ground. The gun misfired, prisoner seized both judge and gun, fired a harmless shot, and was shot dead by the phalanx of well-armed bystanders.

Then another rumor. Local Indians in league with the Mexican population had mounted a violent conspiracy against the whites of the basin. "Lock the doors and bolt the windows," warned one frightened man, firm in the belief that the bandit Flores and company "were on their way to Los Angeles, to murder the white people."[32] The darker races supposedly had a plan of violence, rape, and destruction. Horace Bell had no doubts about the ambitions of Flores; he believed the Mexican War to have flared anew. Flores would "go to Los Angeles, raise the standard of revolt and rid the country of the hated gringos."[33]

Dusk brought dire predictions of impending doom. "All the [white] women and children at dark were seen rushing into central houses," William Wallace wrote. Four paramilitary companies, themselves ethnically delineated, formed to defend Los Angeles whiteness: the Dutch (the Dutch!), the British, the Irish, and the French. They spent time cleaning, loading, and firing their weapons. "There were very few calm men," Wallace noted. "Some cursed their guns. . . . others wanted guns. Some blustered and cursed the Californians." Word went quickly to Fort Tejon in the mountains to the north: *send soldiers.*

The four companies of white sentinels, after leaving behind a detachment to guard women and children in the center of town (twelve men hurriedly answered the request for six guards), marched in formation to the Montgomery Hotel, "where we expected to be sent directly against the enemy." Nothing happened. Los Angeles remained quiet under a bright moon.

Within a day, the men, sagging under the weight of their pistols, rifles, muskets, and knives, organized themselves into a military cordon. Some now feared that the little town would be attacked by an armed force of as many as six hundred Mexicans bent on retribution. With pickets stationed thirty paces apart, they surrounded the entire upper (white) portion of Los Angeles. The standoff, Wallace noted, was ethnically explicit, between "the Americans" and "the Californians."

In eerie foreshadowing of the notorious Zoot Suit affair during the Second World War, house-to-house searches in the lower part of the city and down at the Los Angeles River revealed hiding Mexican men and boys who, some forty in number, were detained, jailed, and then visited by frightened and tearful Mexican women. "There is much anxiety among the Californians," Wallace noted. "What a joyous time we will have hanging the rascals!" With the arrival of Fort Tejon's United States troops, the "thirst for blood" only increased. "If human sacrifices can give rest to the unquiet souls of the dead, they will soon be at ease, for a hecatomb of victims are in readiness," Wallace somberly predicted.[34]

White leaders convinced *Californio* Andres Pico to chase down those "ruffians" left in the countryside, because "it was believed by many that . . . the face of a Californian was the only one that could operate." Armed improbably with lances, Pico's men went out into the hills, determined to demonstrate to Anglos that a difference between "Californians" and "Mexicans" yet existed. Pico, at the head of this "show of California force," did his work well, with, according to Wallace, biblical efficiency. "He came upon them in their fastnesses, and slaughtered them and captured them in detail." Pico killed some of his prisoners and chopped off their ears as trophies. Others lived and told of the ambush of Barton. The sheriff had been shot from his horse, they said; he had fallen into a sitting position and continued to fire his weapon. Juan Flores had yelled out, using both Spanish and English, "We have got you now. . . . God damn you." Barton fired his pistols and a shotgun until his ammunition was exhausted. He threw the empty pistols at his attackers and returned the insult, "Now kill me God damn you." They did.

With the capture of Flores, who was marched to the city jail tied hand and foot, a rope around his neck, calls for retribution only increased. "Americans are not amenable to the people," Wallace wrote, while admitting that "there are as many villains among them as the others." Vigilante posses fanned out across the Los Angeles basin and north toward Santa Barbara, and "a broad distinction is made between Californians and Americans." Posses hanged captured men from whatever height convenience offered. Others were beheaded. Estimates of the body count ranged to well over a hundred. Vigilante Louis Mesmer claimed that seventeen men were hanged in seventeen days. A rumor swirled about that the El Monte boys had been seen bowling with the head of a murdered Mexican.[35]

With the aid of the curate at Mission San Buanaventura, one of the captured signed a confession before he and ten others were executed for the Barton murders. Teenager Jose Jesus Espinosa, "fully convinced that after a few hours I shall have ceased to exist, and shall appear before the presence of God," stated that, the rumors notwithstanding, there were only a handful of "thieves and murderers" loose in the region. From Espinosa's confession, it was unclear if the band of men so described even took part in the murder of Barton and his deputies.

The martyred sheriff took it upon himself to clear up some of the confusion. Wallace, a devoted table-rapping spiritualist, noted in his journal that "we have had several spiritual meetings at which Barton appeared and related his inward life." It had taken the sheriff about six hours to realize that he was indeed dead and had "passed into the world of shadows." "His condition is much better than when here, but his feelings of revenge are so powerful that he regrets death. He is strongly excited because he was killed by such worthless outlaws. . . . Barton, like all spirits, advises decent men to leave this country."[36] The Los Angeles future looked grim to both the quick and the dead.

On Valentine's Day, 1857, a triangle rung in the downtown plaza summoned people from Los Angeles and its hinterlands to the trial of Juan Flores. Officials read aloud the charges against him in three languages (presumably English, Spanish, and French), and the presiding judge, dispensing with legal niceties, declared that the will of the majority would prevail. The vote was for hanging. "This, I think, was one of the most magnificent spectacles ever witnessed by man," Wallace wrote. "The whole people, of all colors, rose up together as one man, and shouted: 'Let him be hung.'" The crowd marched to the city jail, seized Flores (who had been "expecting this visit"), and hanged him "like a dog" on gallows overlooking the village.[37] The hangman did his job poorly. Flores struggled with the rope, had his arms restrained, and strangled to death.

Meantime, Henry Crabb and his filibustering associates (the *Star* called them, perhaps tongue-in-cheek, the "Gadsden Purchase settlers") successfully navigated the desert, made it to Fort Yuma, and punched into Mexico. They soon found themselves in deep trouble. The trip across the desert had been harsh and taxing. Of course, Crabb brought the travails upon himself. In a letter to a Mexican official, he wrote disingenuously (and perhaps a bit nervously?) of his surprise at the hostile reception he had received from the Mexican people. He came in peace, he said, "with the intention of finding most happy firesides with you . . . with the intention of offending no one." Crabb shrugged off concerns about the weapons that weighed heavy on the arms and shoulders of him and his men. "You know that it is not common for Americans, or any other civilized people, to go unarmed." Indians were about, Crabb wrote, so his men were naturally well armed. "I learn with surprise that you are adopting measures of indignation, and are collecting a force to exterminate me and my companions."[38]

That was true. Mexican authorities moved rapidly to repulse the Crabb invasion, drumming up support from the local citizenry by recalling the recent state of war between the United States and Mexico. "Let us fly, then, to chastise, with all the fury which can scarcely be restrained in hearts full of hatred of oppression, the savage filibuster who has dared, in an evil hour, to tread on the national territory, and to provoke—madman!—our anger. No pity, no generous sentiments for that rabble!"[39]

American consular officials in Mexico City had gotten wind of the incursion, and predictions regarding the fate of Crabb and the adventuring Americans were dire. John Forsyth of the United States delegation assumed that in "the natural course of the conflict between the invaders and the Mexican troops, some of our misguided countrymen will fall into the hands of the latter, and will, doubtless, be summarily dealt with." He was right. The "Arizona Colonization Society" got pinned down by a force of Mexican soldiers and citizens at Caborca who sang out "long live Mexico!" and "death to the filibusters!" Mexican authorities had insisted to the Mexican military that they, in the words of one official, "punish the audacity of those pirates who think to outrage with impunity the honor of the Mexican republic by taking possession of one part of it like bandits. . . . they will pay dearly for their rash enterprises."[40]

Crabb remained ever defiant. "If blood is to flow, with all its horrors," he wrote to Mexican official José Maria Redondo, "on your head be it, and not on mine. . . . I shall go where I have long intended to go, and I am only waiting for my emigrants. I am the principal head, and I intend to act according to the dictates of natural law and self-preservation." Events would soon prove Crabb's unfortunate choice of leadership metaphors— casting himself as principal head—particularly ironic.

Soon surrounded, cut off from their supplies, and with many wounded,

Crabb's men opted for a white flag. They tossed aside their daggers, pistols, and rifles. But surrender meant nothing without a state of actual war. Mexican authorities responded by lining up the captives ("some of California's brightest ornaments," wrote an American, "men of intelligence, refinement, and character") before a dawn firing squad. "The news from Sonora is not at all flattering to the revolutionists," Wallace noted with admirable precision. "All of this class are shot without mercy—the Soñorenses having no use for prisoners."[41] Hapless Henry Crabb ought to have remained a California office-seeker. Mexican authorities cut off his "principal head" and stewed it in a jar filled with vinegar. Some said that the grim totem was sent back to Los Angeles as a very tangible warning against further efforts at rearranging the Mexican border with the United States. Maybe Crabb, or part of him, did come back to Los Angeles, maybe not. The critical fact remained: Crabb brought the enduring Mexican War with him into Mexico.[42]

Hundreds of miles north in San Francisco, a young adventurer named Charles Edward Rand, out to make his California fortune, sent home word of Crabb's demise to his parents: "Poor fellows, they met a horrid death. It has caused a great deal of excitement here," he wrote. He then made a frightening prediction. The "feeling of revenge [though] smothered will break out sooner or later and then woe to [the] 'poor Mexican' 'mongst the crowd." As one vengeance-minded journalist wrote, "the blood of the martyrs is the seed of the church." [43]

Blood did flow in Los Angeles, the putative "city of angels." The place, historian James Guinn declared, was nothing but an "ungodly city." Morrow Mayo, following in Guinn's footsteps, suggested that the "town's angelic name was too ridiculous for such a hell-hole." More fitting yet was the sobriquet tossed about in the 1850s and 1860s. Los Angeles? No. Los Diablos.[44]

"A FOREIGN TOUR AT HOME": RECASTING HISTORICAL ROLES

The bloody 1850s sent Los Angeles spinning with such ethnic hatred that it has yet fully to recover. It may take some digging, some excavation beneath the city's contemporary social and political structures, but the 1850s are still with us. The murderousness of that decade slowly faded, the rage that Anglos adopted vis-à-vis Mexicans and, especially and overwhelmingly, against Indians lessened, softened by a variety of economic and demographic factors. Declining populations of nonwhites, in either absolute or proportional terms, rendered seeming threats less palpable. The region's Native American population, worked to death, chained to logs outside jails and places of labor, and struggling with unyielding demographic collapse, fared the worst. Not even in death could they expect respectful treatment. Mid-century Indian deaths, even if foul play was indicated, might be written off as the result of a mysterious "visitation by God." This did make grim sense, in a way, given Manifest Destiny's assurances that expansion and racial triumph went hand in hand, legitimated as if through holy writ.[45]

The number of Mexicans, too, fell off, at least in proportion to whites arriving in the Los Angeles basin. Whereas Mexicans in 1850s Los Angeles may have accounted for as much as 80 percent of the total population, the figure had plummeted to something like 20 percent in just a generation, a flip-flop of stunning magnitude and speed.[46] The American ascendancy in Los Angeles—represented by such diverse moments as the arrival of the Southern Pacific Railroad (1876) and simultaneous disappearance of Mexicans from electoral office (the last Mexican mayor of Los Angeles left office in 1872)—made the "boom of the eighties" an almost entirely racially specific affair.[47] These processes and benchmarks help to create a new version of both "the Mexican" and the "Mexican problem" in Los Angeles.

Part of the Los Angeles ascendancy came about through rewriting history. In other words, to create the language of American-era, skyward trajectory—in commerce, in outlook, in urban enthusiasms—some merely resorted to casting even the recent past as the dark ages. Anything, then, would be substantial improvement upon what came earlier. "A wonderful change has come over the spirit of its dream, and Los Angeles is at present— at least to a great extent—an American city," wrote Benjamin Truman in his exuberant *Semi-Tropical California*, typical of the genre.[48] Truman's use of the dream metaphor was also common; Los Angeles resembled nothing so much as Sleeping Beauty to legions of observers in the 1870s and 1880s. And versions of this fairy tale did the work of racial pedagogy along the way. Whereas white Los Angeles (always cast as feminine) would awaken to embrace her future, the Mexican presence of old had fallen comfortably asleep. Somnolence within the ethnic population occupied the attention of Los Angeles writers, as "sleepy" became the watchword historical descriptor of town, region, people, as if statehood and the transitions thereof simply exhausted everyone, man, woman, and child alike. And of course the adjective stood in for all manner of other descriptions: pre-capitalist, pre-modern, lazy, primitive, Catholic. A few examples should suffice. "I first vis-

Figure 2. The corner of Aliso and Los Angeles Streets in downtown, 1886. Author's collection.

ited Los Angeles in 1867," wrote Benjamin Truman. "Crooked, ungraded, unpaved streets; low, lean, rickety, adobe houses, with flat asphaltum roofs, and here and there an indolent native, hugging the inside of a blanket, or burying his head in a gigantic watermelon, were the, then, most notable features of this quondam Mexican town."[49]

Angeleno Andrew Copp noted in his autobiography that the "half Mexican" population of 1870s Los Angeles "were reported to walk in their sleep most of the twenty-four hours." Just like Richard Henry Dana long before him, Copp alluded to the promise and potential of the region, attainable if, and only if, "the people would ever wake up and develop them."[50] In accounts such as these, Mexican Los Angeles—"the lethargic going to and fro of a somnolent collection of human beings"—always gives way to Anglo Los Angeles sometime in the 1870s: "an awakening came, and behold a transformation appears."[51]

The Los Angeles problem was of course not sleepiness or some kind of weird village-wide narcolepsy. The "problem" was race and the nagging symptomatic persistence of the so-called Mexican problem. That is, there were too many of *them* for Anglo arrivistes, as yet uncertain in these pre-industrial years if Mexicans could be cast as permanent laborers, yoked to immutable Anglo presumptions about their place in the society.[52]

Demographic change could briefly recast that "problem" as an opportunity toward the end of the nineteenth century. During the boom period of the 1880s and 1890s, Los Angeles boosters championed the city to tourist and settler alike, and part of that lure was precisely the region's Latin past, or at least a carefully restricted version of it. As migrant Anglos became, Carey McWilliams writes, "obsessed" with the Spanish Fantasy Past, Mexicans became (if temporarily) picturesque in Anglo eyes—especially when they could stand in for those Spanish who had not lived on Southern California ground for nearly a century. This phase of Los Angeles history, critical to the growth juggernaut of tourism, allowed easterners to luxuriate in the Southern California so brilliantly advertised: exotic, semi-tropic, romantic. Los Angeles offered, as one tourist come-on promised, "A Trip Abroad in Your Own America," as well as all manner of chances to see the quaintness of ethnicity. In this imagery, a Mexican boy posed atop a burro selling flowers becomes less an indication of urban poverty than an unwitting actor in a period romance. "Here you will find true foreign color in your own United States." Come to Los Angeles, boosters insisted, and enjoy what one writer called "A Foreign Tour at Home."[53]

Demography certainly played a role in this recasting of Mexicans as something other than the violent threat that they had supposedly constituted in the 1850s. So, too, did Anglo expectation of further population dips. Mexicans were actually *supposed* to fade away, through both national deference and epidemiological determinism like that assigned to the region's Native American populations. First the Southern California Indians were to drift aside, then Mexicans, nodding silent and permanent good-byes to the audience of tourists and newcomer settlers now occupying the city's and history's center stage. The region, a booster pamphlet in search of Los Angeles investment capital proudly (if euphemistically) declared, "has less of the old California character than any other part of the State." Chronicler Jackson A. Graves devoted an entire chapter of his important autobiography to just this wishful expectation. "The Passing of the Dominant Race" explores exactly those transitions, both real and imagined, in local demography. And of course the assessment has more to do with the ascendancy of the Anglo Saxon than it does with the passing of the Latin.[54] It was, in the words of historian George Sanchez, the coincident coalescence of ideas into a nifty plan. "By depicting the city's Latino heritage as a quaint, but altogether disappearing element in Los Angeles culture, city officials [and others of similar status] inflicted a particular kind of obscurity onto Mexican descendants of that era by appropriating and then commercializing their history."[55]

Recall James Miller Guinn's comment that "the process of Americanizing the people was no easy undertaking." In other words, Guinn knew full well that one could date the American period of Los Angeles from early 1847, when Robert Stockton captured Los Angeles or shortly thereafter when Andres Pico capitulated to John C. Frémont. But, Guinn well understood, military or diplomatic "Americanization" was a blunt cultural marker, more indicative of process than culmination. The actual "transformation of the old pueblo from a Mexican hamlet to an American city continued through at least three decades after the conquest," Guinn suggested to his friends in the Historical Society of Southern California.[56]

The point is a subtle and important one, and it invites us to examine the transitions at about 1880 every bit as closely as those of the 1850s, when Los Angeles shuddered from the violence born of a sudden change in nationality. The signs are there: greater Anglo demographic presence to be sure; far less bilingual communication in the public sphere, in journalism, or in city documents; fewer, far fewer, Latino municipal officials; less intermarriage of elite Anglos into the once-elite *Californio* families, who had run out of land, money, and prestige at a fast clip.

There are other ways to judge the transitions. The mere presence of the Historical Society of Southern California, a distinctly white enterprise, is testament to some kind of transition in local culture, some maturation of a sort. Begun rudely in a dank police court office, the Historical Society nonetheless went about its work in earnest. *Save everything*, the society's president urged the membership in 1884, everything that will create a physical memory that the *1880s* were important. No need to concentrate on earlier periods, another society official advised. After all, the future did not belong to the Mexicans of those early years. They had lost in the blood sports of war and politics, and thus deserved their place as quaint occupants of an ancient past. "A score or two of names, a few crumbling adobes, and all is told," offered the society's president in pithy dismissal. "Our civilization developed along the lines of early England, and still earlier Angeln [*sic*], and Saxony; from the tribe and its chosen leader, not by the transmission from a superior to an inferior race." A publication of the era put the matter even more bluntly. Los Angeles had been founded by the "very scum of Mexico." Why celebrate that past and those founders, except when the strains of make-believe and fantasy could render the racially unpalatable somehow romantic?[57]

By the 1880s, with the real estate boom and swelling population of Anglo arrivistes, that imagined past had started to exhibit its soothing potential.

What had been once only "sleepy" was now attractive, mysterious, even exotic. "The City of the Angels is a prosperous city now," wrote Helen Hunt Jackson. "It has business thoroughfares, blocks of fine stone buildings, hotels, shops, banks, and is growing daily. Its outlying regions are a great circuit of gardens, orchards, vineyards, and corn-fields, and its suburbs are fast filling up. . . . But it has not yet shaken off its past. A certain indefinable, delicious aroma from the old, ignorant, picturesque times lingers still, not only in byways and corners, but in the very centres of its newest activities." One would not, could not, truly know Los Angeles, Jackson declared, unless one could penetrate the outward reserve of the "few remaining survivors of the old Spanish and Mexican *regime*."[58]

There is the merest suggestion of racial mixing in but a few of such observations, a notion that the diversity of peoples in Los Angeles might provide a bulwark against unforeseen evil. This is perhaps carrying the notion too far, especially since little mention is ever made of the violence of the 1840s and 1850s. But E. W. Jones, president of the Historical Society in 1889, felt it. "The blending of the races here is a theme of great significance. It seems at first sight as if the pioneer race, who brought the arts of civilization to these shores, is being extinguished by the flood of immigration which has prevailed for the last few years." But this was not the case, Jones said. "The blood of these adventurous people, strong in body and mind, still coursing through the veins of thousands among us, will not fail to tell powerfully upon the final homogenous race which is to occupy this region." Perhaps it was all an exercise in dissonance and deliberately poor memory. Yet read one way, Jones's comments are a radical call for miscegenation. He later congratulated Southern California's "mixed and fraternized races" for creating a population marked by "manhood, patriotism and ability."[59]

This is a rare observation to be sure, intellectually tantalizing precisely because it stands out in such sharp relief from the record. Others, Historical Society stalwarts among them, remained perfectly content in their belief that the non-Anglo races could not compete and would just slip silently away. As one tourist saw it, Mexicans lurking in the "obscure corners" on "the edges of the displacing civilization" were disappearing, "as if a blight had fallen upon them."[60] Or at least they would be outnumbered and hence rendered quaint in the process of becoming a less visible minority. "The old-time Spanish settlements found here and there appear like islands in the sea of modern American progress," sighed one representative tourist pamphlet.[61]

But the emphasis was on *complete* disappearance, wishful though it might have been. Thomas Kenderdine, who had first come to Los Angeles in the 1850s, discovered forty years later that the "one time Mexican tenants" of the plaza district had "mainly died away."[62] By 1900, according to Angeleno Mary Mooney, one could look "in vain, and in vain!" for Mexicans on the streets of the city. "One by one they faded away," wrote Jackson Graves in his autobiography. Yet the requiems of course came too early. Mexicans in Los Angeles and the Southwest did not disappear from history's stage. Even someone like Graves knew it. On the contrary, the pull effects of an expanding industrial economy in Southern California, as well as the push effects of early twentieth-century revolutionary turmoil in Mexico, reversed population and demographic downturns. "Their children," Graves writes of the land grant class of *Californios*, "became day-laborers." He may not have been precisely correct, in that *Californios* maintained some social prestige and, in a few cases, money enough to live well even after their land was gone. But Graves knew enough to know that Mexicans had not melted away. "Largely written off as a 'vanquished' element," McWilliams writes, "the Mexican population of Southern California began to increase after the turn of the century," first through the labor demands of the agricultural hinterland and then in response to the workplace needs of early Los Angeles industrialization.[63]

The dominant Anglo society set about creating certain cultural and physical boundaries by which to contain this expanding population, the sheer size of which troubled whites. Labor segmentation, which welded class to ethnicity, had virtually assured a lasting Mexican presence in the roughest ranks of manual or agricultural labor. But even that was not enough to mitigate Anglo discomfort. "From 1907 to 1940," McWilliams reminds us (with concise though too-brief precision), "'the Mexican problem' was a hardy perennial in Southern California."[64]

Part of that so-called problem revolved around culture and cultural space. Anglos found it difficult to describe the growing population of Mexican workers who supplied much of the required labor in metropolitan Los Angeles as "picturesque" any longer. A single workman, a scattered few: these might be romanticized with relative ease. But the gathered dozens, hundreds, thousands of Mexican day laborers looked every bit the shape and size of a proletariat. How could that be pictured in the quaint rhymes and images of Los Angeles boosterism?

Weren't new categories thus required? Did Anglo Los Angeles have to recast Mexican space and Mexican stereotypes once again? We would be wrong to underestimate the dimensions and ambitions of the program that Anglo Los Angeles, consciously or not, embarked upon to answer such queries in the affirmative.

Following the crude mid-nineteenth-century period of explicit ethnic violence (which of course had its own imperatives regarding ethnic boundaries), a sort of cultural backing and filling took place. Some of this was undoubtedly related to changes in Anglo perspectives about Mexico. As such, we should briefly visit the heirs to Colonel Crabb's filibustering adventures. Later Los Angeles perspectives, narratives, and images about Mexico reveal ideas similar to those of the 1850s as regards Mexicans (on this side of the border or that). Territorial filibusters from Los Angeles would continue to raid northern Mexico, though no longer on foot, and presumably with more wariness and less hubris than Henry A. Crabb.[65] To be sure, as journalist Harry Carr pointed out in the 1930s, "Los Angeles has always been conscious of the fact that it is next door to Mexico," and that international proximity (as well as the definitions of that "door" and its placement) makes up an important part of the story told in this book. The ubiquitous early twentieth-century Chamber of Commerce term "Greater Los Angeles" takes on a whole new meaning if we consider it as a territorial description every bit as much as a qualitative one. Such Angelenos as those who sat in the Chamber of Commerce had long coveted Mexico, just as they expressed simultaneous discomfort with Mexicans on either side of the international boundary.[66]

In thinking of Mexico, elite Anglos deliberately muddied the distinctions between what is "ours" and what is "theirs." Much of this, by the turn of the century at least, was imperialism of a different stripe from Henry Crabb's quixotic incursion. But there are obvious semantic and cultural parallels to such possessiveness. For instance, the turn of the century marks the arrival of Southern California's somewhat startling geographic discovery: "Our Mexico." Nurtured in tandem by parlor writings and sophisticated appraisal of northern Mexico's raw land, raw minerals, and raw oil, this diplomatic fiction became a commonplace corollary to the regional conceit that painted Southern California as "Our Italy" or "Our Mediterranean."[67]

Ownership claims connoted by "Our Mexico" continued through the violent cycles of the Mexican Revolution of the early twentieth century, when many a Southern Californian thought little of the conceit (not to mention Crabbean danger) in ignoring the border to protect invested dollars. By the late 1910s and early 1920s, Southern California businessmen and their allied organizations firmed up the notion that what was south across the border might as well be considered part of Los Angeles. It was almost as if a kind of

Figure 3. Racial types of "Life in the Feudal Era" of nineteenth-century Los Angeles. From Boyle Workman's 1936 history, *The City That Grew.*

geographical fulcrum had been balanced. Los Angeles had once been Mexico (and, in parts, like downtown's Sonoratown, might be still); why not make Mexico into Los Angeles? After all, as one realty publication phrased it, "Western Mexico is in reality a hinterland to California." Not to be outdone, another agency heard its spokesman tell of his efforts to "solidify still further the supremacy of Los Angeles in the upbuilding of Mexico. . . . [Mexicans] know that Los Angeles is anxious to grasp their hand." Another representative business publication of the era, noting that Los Angeles would be "where western civilization is reaching its ultimate goal," declared that Mexican, even all of South American, commerce "belongs to Los Angeles by origin and heritage." In other words, Los Angeles was Latin enough to create cords of commerce, but the city would nonetheless see the ultimate conclusion of Manifest Destiny's racial promise! Topping the sentiment off, a powerful Chamber of Commerce leader offered his certainties regarding Mexican politics in the mid-1920s. Of the candidacy of Alvaro Obregon for president of Mexico, Chamber president William Lacy said that it was simply "impossible for him to lose" if the Chamber offered its weighty endorsement.[68]

And what of the Mexicans in, and continuing to arrive in, Los Angeles? Were they "ours," too? Much like darkroom alchemists, who fix and immobilize an image in time, place, and space, Anglos tried diligently to do the same to the Mexicans in their midst, to fix them in space and around a particular set of characteristics or traits tied ubiquitously to a social and ethnic category known as "the Mexican," or the even more reflexive "Our Mexican." The specificity of the reference revealed tacit Anglo American agreement about representation, about representativeness, and about typicality, and it was predicated upon distinct presumptions about ethnicity.[69]

How did these societal tendencies work? What did they mean? From the odd, brutal days of racialized adventuring in the 1850s, turn the years forward but a single lifetime and come meet some important characters in the drama of Los Angeles history. It is a weekday evening in the mid-1920s or thereabouts. Settled in for a quiet night in their Pasadena bungalow are the husband and wife whom journalist Harry Carr refers to as "Mr. and Mrs. Los Angeles."[70] Or maybe we are in Hancock Park or Glendale this evening, behind the wrought iron gates of a mission-style home, whitewashed stucco walls rising from a newly paved asphalt driveway. Arrivals of no more (and probably less) than a generation ago, the couple has on this particular evening been to din-ner, seen a show, or maybe a motion picture. Mr. and Mrs. Los Angeles are mildly prosperous. They are white. He is "a newspaper artist on a good salary" and works in a seven-story office building in downtown. Mrs. Los Angeles belongs to several clubs. They have many friends, three children, two cars. When they pronounce the name of their new home, Mr. and Mrs. Los Angeles say "Loss An Guh Leez." Mr. and Mrs. Los Angeles do not think much about Mexicans. But when they do, their thoughts are programmed by unexamined assumptions and reflexive representations.

These people are the city's Babbitts, not the "folks" as referred to by the bitter 1920s student of Los Angeles, writer Louis Adamic. They are more prosperous than the hardscrabble folks, more powerful, and less worn out. Adamic's "folks" were those people who turned 1920s Los Angeles into "a huge, exaggerated village; an Iowa or Kansas small town suddenly multi-plied by five hundred and some of its Main Street buildings grown twelve stories high." "Racially fatigued," Adamic called them.[71]

Mr. and Mrs. Los Angeles live above this weariness. They go to the the-ater with regularity. They drive to the Pasadena Playhouse on El Molino Avenue. When they have out-of-town guests, they like to venture across town to San Gabriel to see, for the fifth or sixth time, the *Mission Play*, the nation's most popular theatrical production in the years before the Second World War. Mr. and Mrs. Los Angeles sometimes drive out to the Little Theater of Padua Hills in Pomona. They especially like the Mexican Revue that the Padua Players put on once a month, which one of their acquain-tances recommended to them. "Every Mexican that I have ever known," he told them, "was born an artist and these shows are colorful, clever and delightful."[72]

San Fernando Rey de España
Founded September 8, 1797 by
Father Sitjar and Father Dumetz.

The quaint bell tower perched on the
corner of a row of buildings is the distinctive
feature of this Mission.
It was built in honor of Fernando
III of Spain and the first adobe chapel and
buildings were completed in 1806. The earthquake

Figure 4. A page from an early twentieth-century diary of a
mission-to-mission tour. Author's collection.

Mr. and Mrs. Los Angeles explore the Southwest. They read the Auto
Club's *Touring Topics* with interest. They drive to Palm Springs frequently
in the winter, where Mr. Los Angeles enjoys a round of golf or two. Mr. and
Mrs. Los Angeles drive an hour east to Riverside to spend weekends at

Frank Miller's famous Mission Inn, and they make exploring pilgrimages to "Ramona country" outside San Diego, where they take in the annual Ramona Pageant. They have seen a half dozen of California's missions, and they try to visit Mexico (Agua Caliente for car races, Tijuana for shopping and horse races) at least twice a year.

On the Fifth of May, Mr. and Mrs. Los Angeles go to Olvera Street "for the hilarities of Cinco de Mayo," and they also enjoy watching Mexicans celebrate September 16 and the revolutionary heroism of Miguel Hidalgo. When they think about the California past, and they do (they are barraged with mission motifs in everyday advertising, city signage, etc.), they think through the mist of romance. A cultural scrim hangs between them and the Southern California past, smoothing the painful edges of a sad and bloody history. The mission, they know, "was like one great family." If anything intruded on the myth, it was Mexicans themselves who, through anticlericalism or revolutionary zeal or both, destroyed the beautiful necklace of coastal missions. But even that ancient era of Mexican California shimmered with romance. Everyone was happy then, everyone carefree. This is what they believe. And they agree with their favorite *Los Angeles Times* reporter Harry Carr, the man who wrote that Los Angeles was "an epic— one of the greatest and most significant migrations in the long saga of the Aryan race."[73]

There are tens of thousands of such people in Los Angeles in the first decades of this century. Identified with the racial and growth trajectories of their city so much so as to share its name, Mr. and Mrs. Los Angeles constitute an apparently typical Anglo sensibility about culture, commerce, and the metropolitan landscape. They think they know the Mexican present, and they are sure that they know California's "Spanish" past. It is an era they think of as "a lost civilization."[74]

MEET JUAN GARCIA

My typical Juan Garcia knows no boundary. He does most of the manual labor of the Southwest, and unless the quota bars him, he will soon be standing beside the wheels in every industrial plant, working on every section of the railroads, and bending in toil on every farm. He is accomplishing a labor penetration of the United States.

ROBERT MCLEAN, *That Mexican!*, 1928[75]

Figure 5. Building Los Angeles, ca. 1910. Courtesy of the Huntington Library, San Marino, California.

> *It must be recognized . . . that the Mexican whom we find in Los Angeles is, as a class, of relatively low mentality; he is probably best fitted for work demanding ability of an inferior grade.*
>
> S. H. BOWMAN,
> "A Brief Study of Arrests of Mexicans," 1924[76]

There are other typical people in the Los Angeles of seventy-five or eighty years ago. They are a bit harder to find. Down flat against the banks of the Los Angeles River, adjacent to a grimy repair yard of the Southern Pacific Railroad, sits an old railcar on a rusted spur track covered by weeds. A small, neatly tended vegetable patch lies nearby. Smoke rises from a crude chimney pushed through the roof of the car. A steep five-step ladder drops from the wide freight door to the ground. So do, this same imagined evening in the late 1920s, several dark-eyed children, rushing to meet their father,

Figure 6. Mexican workers in downtown Los Angeles, early twentieth century.

who trudges toward them along the track after a day's work. A woman leans from the doorway, whispers a greeting to her husband. He smiles and climbs the ladder into his home.[77]

Meet Juan Garcia and family. Juan Garcia is a laborer and a Mexican. He works on a railroad section gang. The railroad allows him to live rent-free in the railcar home. Other laborers live nearby in small shacks and shanties. The railroad may move him to another section, another county, another state, at a day or two's notice. The railroad might just lay him off when the track work is finished. Juan Garcia works in a brickyard, molding clay into bricks, carrying heavy pallets into the sun to dry. Juan Garcia melts and pours asphalt on roads of dust. Juan Garcia does roadwork with pick and shovel. He cleans streets. His work is unskilled, hard, and hot.

Los Angeles laboring work, a 1920s report forthrightly declared, was "the occupation of the Mexican." "The drudgery of county and city has been his," in the words of a social worker. But fortunately for Southern California, Juan Garcia showed an "indifference to physical hardships and a supreme satisfaction in doing the menial." He works for the city's water department, clearing debris from waterways. Juan Garcia is "the unskilled laborer of the Southwest." He makes, if he's fortunate, between two and three dollars a day. Maybe he doesn't live with his family cramped into an old boxcar, though it is widely believed that Mexicans will "put up with

Figure 7. Early twentieth-century living conditions for Los Angeles Mexicans often resembled this collection of shacks and shanties, "typified" by the photographer as ethnically representative.

almost any sort of living quarters." The family might all live in a camp for unemployed Mexicans that the Catholic Church has set up over in Griffith Park (there's a white camp in the giant park as well, but the two groups are separated, "the great difference in diet necessitating such separation.").[78]

Social workers call the Garcias "peons" and "peasants" to drive home their non-American status and reinforce the perception of these people as "industrial assets." Or they make lists of people in Los Angeles, singling out Mexicans in taxonomies of visitors and Southern California types, as in "the Mexican, the tourist, the health seeker, the migratory laborer, the settler."[79] The Garcias live in a rusty boxcar or cheek by jowl in an overcrowded house or courtyard apartment (a "cholo court," they are often called). Their house court has one toilet for every six or eight families. Tuberculosis lives with them. Juan Garcia might live with other single men—some who have left their wives and families in Mexico—in a cheap boardinghouse. The ceilings are low. The walls are uncovered, maybe even unplastered. "What should be done for Juan Garcia?" wonder reformers of one stripe or another.[80]

Figure 8. "Greasers in Embryio": Early twentieth-century tourist photograph of Mexican boys in Los Angeles. Courtesy of the California History Room, California State Library, Sacramento.

The Garcias and people just like them do not have the same name as the city they live in. They could never be "Mr. and Mrs. Los Angeles," even though they helped build Los Angeles, paved it, cleaned it, made it. Legions of white Angelenos have never met, and will never meet, Juan Garcia, his wife, their family. Some try to forget that they share the same city, believing as one social worker described the prevailing attitude that "the Mexican is a problem of tomorrow."[81] Others judge "Juan Garcia" as a latter-day Juan Flores, the social bandit of the 1850s, with a racial propensity toward criminal behavior. Mexican boys are but "greasers in embryio," as far as many are concerned, just as they were to a young Anglo man who captioned his 1907 snapshot of Los Angeles Mexican boys with just this ugly flourish.[82]

A few whites, imbued with the optimistic Progressive-Era gospel of Americanization, reach out to people like the Garcias from complex motives mixed of compassion and enthnocentric nationalism. Perhaps someone had been to the railroad camp this same hypothetical day, one of the Americanization movement's front-line warriors, the home teacher. A woman teaching sewing or English stopped by, instructing in phrases such as "Swat the fly!" or "I scrub, I scrub." If they think about it at all, white Angelenos do not believe that the Garcias can be assimilated.[83]

Los Angeles in the 1920s is no less polyglot than it was in the 1850s. On the contrary, ethnic diversity had increased. But even more pronounced change had occurred in ethnic proximity over the intervening two generations. The strictures on ethnic behavior and place are such that the intimate ugliness of 1850s-era tensions has receded into segregated distances for the bulk of the Los Angeles population.[84] There are tens of thousands of Juan Garcias in early twentieth-century Los Angeles, most of them recently arrived from Mexico, but most Angelenos would not know it and would not care in the least.[85] The name—Juan Garcia—had by then become an accepted, unquestioned representation by Anglos of the *EveryMexican* caught somewhere between picturesque and proletarian. The identification of the Mexican laborer as Juan Garcia even suggested that individuation of Mexicans into persons need not take place. Three-fourths of the Juan Garcias in Los Angeles, in California, indeed in the entire American Southwest, work as unskilled laborers.[86]

What Juan Garcia and his family most assuredly are not is Californian, much less *Californio*. The former label had gone over fully to whites by now, the product of transitions in the political economy of the region dating back to the 1870s and 1880s. The latter identifier had ceased to mean much in the twentieth century: there just weren't many *Californios* around any longer. They'd long ago run out of land and power.

Nor is Juan Garcia white. Though the U.S. Census Bureau may persist in calling the Garcias white, few others do.[87] Nor is Juan Garcia a Spaniard. That descriptor has drifted away as well, victim of the twentieth century's belated realization that, lo and behold, few Spaniards called California home any longer. Of course, there could yet be Spanish features in the region, even typically so—places, roofs, buildings, or other nonpersons graced by romanticism and decidedly non-Mexican attributes. It was a game, in effect, an ugly game in which false definitional precision and arbitrary attachment of meaning carried real cultural weight. *That was Spanish, this is Mexican.* Juan Garcia was Mexican. A Mexican. *The Mexican.*[88]

Boosters got into the act, as boosters will. "In an effort to preserve the historical aspects of the Plaza and its immediate vicinity," the Los Angeles Chamber of Commerce decided in the 1920s "to establish a typical Spanish village surrounding the park, which was the birthplace of the pueblo that has come to be the biggest Metropolis in the Western Americas." Making the plaza Spanish, then, could make it less Mexican—by definition. Or so the logic of commercialism and racial typicality went.[89]

The possibilities were endless! Following the manufacture of the typical Chinese village, "China City," Chamber leaders set their sights on the next ethnic population. "Can we work with [the Japanese population of Los Angeles] to set up in their section a typical Japanese city wherein their native home life and artistic ability could be developed in their own interest and in the interest of the community?" the Chamber eventually wondered, as it contemplated a metropolis of theme-park ethnic subdivisions; an "it's a small world, after all" congregation imagined into being by notions of Los Angeles multiculturalism, 1930s-style.[90]

How does one group of people isolate and draw borders around another group of people? The constellation of behaviors and ideas that make up an Anglo cultural stance toward Mexicans (including legal, political, social, occupational, spatial, and other strictures) worked as a kind of cultural cryogenics. This allowed, even insisted, that the dominant society freeze Mexicans in time and space, and that it describe them in particular ways: childlike, simple, quick to anger, close to nature, primitive, hard-working, lazy, superstitious, possibly criminal.[91] They were, as a policeman put it with firmness, bathed in a "decidedly unfavorable light." It is instructive to consider how Anglo society made claims of ethnic Mexican representativeness and to remember how it profited by such arguments.[92]

By the early decades of this century, reliance upon a descriptive reflex (i.e., what was *typical*) had become an unquestioned trope in Los Angeles images and in the self-actualizing descriptions of Los Angeles growth.[93] The examples themselves are legion. Always, there was the weather: a typical day in Southern California, as depicted in photographs, on citrus crate labels or other ephemera: a clear vista, perhaps orange trees set against a snowy mountain backdrop. The built environment also attracted the "typical" label. Sprawling, luxurious tourist hotels became "typical tourist hotels." Palm- or oak-lined streets in wealthy neighborhoods became "typical Southern California boulevards." Postcard after postcard depicted lofty Tudors, giant bungalows, or stately mission revival mansions as "typical Southern California homes." And for each of these typical houses there existed an equally prosaic "typical garden," though one perhaps ambitiously landscaped, touched with expensive Japanese flourishes, or thick with transplanted cacti and succulents.

No better example of this reflex can be found than in the publications and ephemeral paperwork of the Los Angeles Chamber of Commerce in the first two or three decades of the twentieth century. A representative pamphlet—"Facts About Industrial Los Angeles, Nature's Workshop"— put out by the Chamber's Industrial Department in the 1920s aptly illustrates the typical appeal. Glossy pages and crisp black-and-white photographs invite the reader (investor, tourist, settler) into a world of redundant images, scenes, spaces, and places. Here we find in neat and stark representation the city's "typical skyline," its "typical textile plants," "typical views of clay products and glass plants," even the odd industrial juxtaposition of "oil and oranges—a typical refinery." Here, too, are "typical workingmen's homes," where, presumably, contented workers return after what could be nothing other than a "typical day."[94]

This is an important cultural tapestry that told a simple story. "Los Angeles is most typically American," wrote a booster reporter for the *Los Angeles Examiner* in 1922—but added the wishful, decidedly atypical declaration that "there are no poor in Los Angeles."[95] Southern California was, then, a paradise where everyone, men and "typical women" alike, could conceivably have a typical life.[96] To do so meant, of course, understanding the unstated in the images, especially those that associated great displays of wealth with the mundane and everyday. In Southern California, almost everyone could have workers working for them. There were, after all, apparently those typical workers who went to those typical worker jobs and lived in those typical workingmen's homes.[97] And there was also Juan Garcia, so typically a Mexican that he had an everyname synonymous with Mexican ethnicity. Of course his was not the "typical workingman's home" as much as it was what social reformers and others codified as the "typical Mexican home." And there was a profound difference: in housing quality, in regional geography, and most assuredly in the operation of local restrictive housing covenants. Even Olvera Street, that 1920s shops-and-stores invention complete with picturesque Mexican troubadours and pushcarts, can be found in the typical litany. An early promotional newspaper (the *"Olvera Street News*: The Magazine from the Birthplace of Los Angeles") proudly referred to the avenue as "probably the most typical street in America."[98]

Making Mexicans fit into explicitly racialized containers revealed not only what they *were* ("always the laborer, never the citizen," in the words of historian Mark Reisler) but also what they *were not* as well. And what Mexicans most decidedly were not were Anglo Saxon.[99] This is not to say that at certain points in its troubling history with Mexicans that Los Angeles did not try to remedy that supposed cultural and ethnic (i.e., genetic) failing. Los Angeles in the first decades of the twentieth century was one of the most important arenas of eugenics in the nation. Such attempts to de-Mexicanize the Mexican—socially, politically, biologically, culturally—help us to remember the kinds of boundaries constructed around typifying categories of what was or was not Mexican or a Mexican. The work could be pursued by all manner of Los Angeles Anglos, on the left as well as the right. After all, Americanization campaigns of the Progressive Era, at least in some respects, could be seen as a kind of social eugenics.[100]

Take the example of Progressive and reform-minded Rev. G. Bromley Oxnam. Like William Wallace fifty years before him, Oxnam kept a steady Los Angeles journal. A man whose brand of muscular Christianity made him something of a Theodore Roosevelt in broadcloth, Oxnam was one of the city's most energetic housing and social reformers prior to the First World War. It is a shame that Los Angeles has forgotten him. Mentored by Rockwell Hunt, James Main Dixon, and Emory Bogardus at the University of Southern California, and by the Rev. Dana Bartlett of the Bethlehem Institute, Bromley Oxnam entered Mexican Los Angeles armed with a few important, archetypal assumptions that he arranged into a kind of social chemistry. From his University of Southern California courses and professors he learned sociology's maxim that a problem defined was very nearly a problem solved. From the social gospel he drew Progressive insights about uplift and noblesse oblige. "Along with our social work," he wrote, "we must not forget the individual. A man is a man, has certain capacities and powers; these factors on the personal element will unite with your reagent of social reform and give a different compound every time."[101]

Bromley Oxnam also knew about Anglo Saxonism as a way to address what whites in Los Angeles, if they thought of it at all, unconsciously referred to as the Mexican problem. In the spring of 1913, Oxnam devoted every Monday to work in the Mexican house courts of downtown Los Angeles, east of Main Street. The district had tremendous problems: rampant poverty, high infant mortality, illiteracy, and disease. "Truly the problem almost overwhelms me," he admitted, if only to himself: "I hardly know what to do." Oxnam knew, too, of the Anglo tendency to essentialize Mexicans as implicated in their social position. He wrote of encountering a young Mexican boy at one of the courts, a youngster with "an artist's soul." The deck was stacked against the boy, Oxnam knew: "he was but a Mexican boy—fit for streetwork and nothing more—at least so some say." Nonetheless, Oxnam imagined one way to proceed, and "God helping me I'll make those people better."[102]

Within a few days of that private declaration, one of the city's local newspapers devoted a story to Oxnam and his expressly ethnic stratagem for addressing the Mexican problem. "G. Bromley Oxnam's Campaign in Mexican Quarter is Showing Results" ran the caption next to a photograph of Oxnam with four Mexican boys along with another heading: "Me An' Manuel's Knights'[;] Small Boys Foes to Dirt." Oxnam had started a club in a neighborhood where, according to the newspaper reporter, "an American housewife would have thrown up her hands at the floor and the flies." The club was called "The Order of Knights of The Round Table" with Oxnam as the young Arthur. "You believe in being very clean, don't you?" he asked his knights. "Yes, Mam," and "Di Signor" they responded, or so the reporter covering the exchange reported, no doubt somewhat linguistically confused himself.[103]

"I chose Arthur as a model," Oxnam told the reporter, "because he is somewhat of a hero and one that embodies principles of right living in his character." Thus, with Arthur, King of the Britons, and Bromley Oxnam entwined as their models, the Mexican boys of the Rhinehart Street Round Table set to work becoming less Mexican. This transition to an Anglo Saxon future required and was based upon rules: the boys (and they were all boys) would always do right, "because it is right"; they would be "kind to girls and ladies"; they would "not fight except for what is right, but when we fight we will never give up"; they would not lie; they would keep their bodies and their clothes clean; they would keep their houses clean ("Dirty houses make sick people"); and they would "love each other."[104]

This was Americanization hard at work, part of the reform juggernaut that hit early twentieth-century Los Angeles every bit as hard as it did Chicago or other better-known Progressive sites. Americanization is a complicated beast, some of it arising out of deep wells of humanitarian regard, and some of it, in Carey McWilliams's apt phrasing, "stupid, morose, and biased." Regardless of motive, certain groups and individuals alike in Los Angeles responded with a tremendously ambitious social and educational program of trying to understand (and "reform") "the Mexican." As Oxnam himself saw it, defining the problem was the critical first step on the journey to solution. As such, the Americanization program in Los Angeles was focused upon study after study of one "Mexican" trait or characteristic after another. Ethnic uplift was no doubt a goal, but so too was the simple scholarship of representation; as one 1920s report on Mexican families in Los Angeles declared, the case study of thirty-five Mexican families "represent[s], to a large extent, the entire group of Mexican families in Los

Angeles." Mexicans were easy, the logic went, to represent. They fit into boxes and stereotype because ethnicity was fate.[105]

As one University of Southern California instructor commented in 1916, "the burden of Americanization falls directly upon Los Angeles."[106] But this was a program without flexibility, already bounded at the start by the strictures of stereotype. Mexicans, read one early report on labor and housing conditions, were "quick to learn as children but slow when grown up. They are with us to stay; we can mold them as we will, and if we groom our horses, feed them, give them shelter and a bed when they have toiled hard for us at work which we would not do for ourselves—shall we do less for the hard-working stranger within our gates whose sons and daughters will soon be our American citizens?"[107]

Just as Bromley Oxnam imagined that substitution of Anglo for supposedly essential ethnic traits could move Mexicans along the path to progress, others opted for strategies more national (or at least semantic) in scope. To be sure, these went together in the larger scheme of things: even if the Mexicans in the house court were American citizens, they would not yet be "Americans." Birthright citizenship status was, in other words, meant to be earned and learned before it could be incurred. But some Americanizing Anglos apparently did believe that Mexicans could be uplifted simply by being renamed, in a gesture to the waning days of regional obsession with the ancient Spanish past. For instance, the Spanish American Institute, a Methodist vocational school for boys started early in the century in Gardena, ten miles south of Los Angeles, was assuredly not for the benefit of the region's Spanish Americans. The Institute, which some believed to be "the one great solution of the Border problem," performed its semantic and national sleight, first turning Mexican youths into Spanish boys, after which it became at least theoretically possible to commit more social chemistry and show off these "Boys as New Americans."[108]

Such sentiments were perhaps as coercive (or even cruel) as they were wishful, in that the dominant society had already organized the urban spaces where Juan Garcia and family lived into obvious architectural expressions of a Mexican periphery attached to an Anglo core. *Colonias* leaning against farmlands; barrios at water's edge; a railroad shack; the Mexican company town arrangements of a place such as Simons, just outside city boundaries, where Mexican workers ("our Mexicans") dug clay and made bricks at the world's largest brickyard. All these were Mexican spaces, and they held fast.

We should not forget the power of Anglo institutions to drive the point home. Company towns, like that at the Simons brickyard, the focus of chapter 4 of this book, were but one, albeit highly effective, way of creating and solidifying Mexican space. Unspoken local custom and codified real estate restrictions also helped etch Mexican space sharp on the landscape. "Race segregation is not a serious problem with us," a Whittier realtor proudly declared in the mid-1920s. "Our realtors do not sell [to] Mexicans and Japanese outside certain sections where it is agreed by community custom they shall reside." A fellow realtor not far away in Glendale mixed patriotism with exclusion, without even the slightest recognition of irony. Through enforcement of "suitable race restrictions, we can maintain our high standard of American citizenship," he wrote. This was, presumably, all the more critical in "an American town like Glendale."[109]

Should the crudeness of such redlining present any unlikely moral dilemmas to the community, one could always fall back upon the supposedly essential behavioral characteristics of the Mexican. Too many Mexicans in your neighborhood? "Advocate and push improvements," wrote realtor E. Spurlock of Compton, "and the Mexican will move." "The Mexicans can be well handled," wrote Charles Stewart of the Monrovia realty board, sounding ever so much like a plantation overseer, "and [they] are quite reliable." Barrioization allowed those concerned with segregation to offer that one could even count on the ethnic populations of Southern California to do the work of segregation themselves! "The Japanese, Mexican and colored population have segregated themselves in groups largely according to their own wishes," stated a satisfied realtor from Riverside. Such instances of blindness to the ugliness of exclusion must be examined not simply as indications of dissonance but as examples of the dominant society's conviction that there was such a static social and ethnic category as "the Mexican" ("the Japanese," "the Negro," etc.) which entailed certain traits and behaviors. It made it far easier to explain away barrios and colonias as a Mexican habit, than as a response to segregation's iron hand. "We have provided a section expressly for Mexicans and Negroes," wrote realtor R. P. Garbutt, as if the action was an example of community pride or progress, which, for many whites and many communities, it was.[110]

One "Mr. Los Angeles," an important officer of the city's Chamber of Commerce, said, "Juan Garcia has California agriculture and industry in the palm of his hand."[111] But no one really believed that: there were too many obstacles placed in their path for the "Juan Garcias" of Southern

California to have much, if any, power to confront the ambitions of the dominant society to keep alive that indispensable "Mexican problem."

Contemporary Los Angeles yet has its Mexican problem, expressed in continued labor segmentation, in vocal and electoral expressions of discrimination, and in anxious attempts to mitigate or even block the demographic inevitabilities of the twenty-first century. In paying close attention to the roots of that shifting problem, this book suggests that there may be promise embedded in the ethnic future of tomorrowland Los Angeles. But promise can be realized only as the result of difficult, even painful, history lessons. Digging beneath the surface of the city's present is the best way historians know to shape ideas into potential action for the future. It is an action—an excavation—predicated on remembering in hopes of forcing change. In continuing that work, we turn next to the ways Los Angeles tried to remake its troubled past as part of the effort to become the self-conscious city of the future. We turn to memory in and memory about Los Angeles, and the ways in which constructions of historical memory shaped the city's sense of self. We turn to the 1890s, to La Fiesta de Los Angeles, and to history on parade.

TWO

History on Parade

No other medium has so successfully advertised to the world the possibilities of Southern California as has La Fiesta.

FERD K. RULE, 1903[1]

[The] celebration . . . is peculiar to Southern California, and could not be so successfully carried on elsewhere. . . . By the middle of April comes a time of comparative leisure . . . everything is at its best. It is a very old institution introduced into California by the first Spanish settlers; some even think that the Indians held something of a fiesta as a token of appreciation of the bountiful conditions surrounding them.

A Business Venture in Los Angeles, or, A Christian Optimist (1899)[2]

Let us regard it as an established institution of Southern California, which means, experience and culture shall yet more fully perfect, and which shall become more and more fully in harmonious blending with the physical perfection and beauty of this modern Italy, this lovelier Greece of the New World.

Los Angeles Times, April 26, 1896

Our fiestas should conform more to the American than the Spanish idea of fiestas.

Los Angeles newspaper editorial, ca. November 1903[3]

It is a curious feature of the history of Southern California that the Los Angeles Fiesta belongs to the novelists more than the historians. Novelists often write about historical events of course, and they can do so with every bit as much accuracy as historians. But in the case of the Los Angeles Fiesta, historians have barely stepped into the ring. Fictional accounts abound which describe the citywide frenzy accompanying each springtime Fiesta in the last half decade of the nineteenth century. Taking their cues straight from the newspapers or their own eyewitness observations, writers and the occasional poet added characters, situations, and dialogue to the remarkable urban pageantry that made up this strange urban ritual called La Fiesta de Los Angeles.

Take for example the case of "Z.Z.," the author of the odd little 1899 novel *A Business Venture in Los Angeles, or, A Christian Optimist*. Z.Z. must have seen an April Fiesta or two, because the several days of parade and pageantry are important in her sentimental tale. The book's protagonists, sisters who run a small bookstore and curio shop in downtown Los Angeles, prepare for the coming of the Fiesta at the anxious urging of a knowledge-able friend. "Get out your best attractions to adorn your window," he tells them, "and make your store as alluring as possible." Money is at stake. Timed to coincide with spring citrus harvest, the Fiesta is "the harvest-time of the Los Angeles merchants." Thus encouraged, the expectant sisters spruce up their bookstore, add various items of bric-a-brac, and proceed to hit the jackpot of mercantile success. "Hurrah for stores in general, and this little bookstore in particular!" the happy sisters exult.[4]

As for the Fiesta itself, a processional parade of several days duration, the novel relays the courtly comings and goings in sequence. The Fiesta's Queen and court pass by in stately repose, the various military units march forward in precision, and float after float after float moves through the major streets of downtown Los Angeles in numbing repetition: "afterwards Chinese, Indians, the Fire department, Caballeros, prosperity floats, et cetera, et cetera."

But the effect could be spellbinding to nineteenth-century observers. People jockeyed for position on packed Los Angeles streets, elbowing one another aside as this or that float passed. Angelenos filled the second- and third-story windows of commercial buildings or homes lining the Fiesta route, craning their necks as the parade moved by. The diversity of the parade's participants was part of the event's excitement, something the novelist Z.Z. well understood. "The mixture of races and nationalities tak-ing part therein," she commented, "gave a flavor of originality to the whole,

Figure 9. Troops marching in La Fiesta de Los Angeles, 1894. Courtesy of the Seaver Center for Western History Research, Los Angeles County Museum of Natural History.

rendering it entirely distinct from ordinary processions, so that, from first to last, the interest was sustained, especially with those to whom the sight was a novel one." Indeed, La Fiesta transcended mere spectacle. It was "produced in such magnificence and with so much attention to detail, as not only to be beautiful to the eye, but valuable as object-lessons to young and old."[5]

La Fiesta certainly looks, from the vantage of more than a hundred years later, like spectacle. Exciting urban holiday, springtime ritual, harvest celebration, commercial boon, and tourist lure, yes, all wrapped up in the several days of exuberance. But object lesson? In what? For what purpose?

The Los Angeles Fiesta *should* attract those interested in the Los Angeles past at least as much as it once captivated audiences and fiction writers alike. There is much to explore, much to puzzle over about this striking rite of spring in the City of Angels. Little is known of La Fiesta today except that it was a parade. In the photographs in this chapter, La Fiesta looks ancient. It looks innocuous, even silly. But this is not the case at all, nor was it so a hundred years ago. On the contrary, the remarkably popular Fiesta was at the center of a number of contests over the Los Angeles future and how the city ought to get there. And the Los Angeles Fiesta, no matter how much its planners, participants, and observers wanted to think otherwise, was about ethnicity, too.

This chapter examines La Fiesta de Los Angeles from a number of perspectives. Most important to the analysis will be features alluded to in the passages culled from that hundred-year-old novel. What made the Fiesta important as mercantile harvest (and who was buying)? What else was at stake besides making money? What made it an object lesson? And how did all this relate, inexorably to "the mixture of races and nationalities taking part therein"?[6] Most important is the question of when and why elites in Los Angeles decided to utilize the past, particularly an unpleasant past now sanitized and whitewashed, as a cultural tool, an advertising gimmick, and a history lesson all rolled into one. Within the parade's representations of people and history, we can discern the outlines of prevailing ethnocentric notions that were themselves part and parcel of the growth of 1890s Los Angeles. By remembering La Fiesta, and remembering its literal place on the Los Angeles cityscape, we can reconstitute its important role in helping to build both the city and a particular regional identity. That will require pulling the parade out of the historical fog.

LA FIESTA IS BORN

To understand the rise of La Fiesta de Los Angeles, we have to go back at least as far as the founding of the Merchants Association at the end of 1893. A collection of local merchants, most of them with stores in downtown, sprinkled through with Los Angeles boosters and Chamber of Commerce stalwarts, came together to promote local commerce. Hardly an unusual act in cities across the nation, this melding was done largely as a wishful attempt to yank the city from the economic doldrums first produced by the collapse of the 1880s real estate boom and made all the worse by the woes of the depression of 1893. From such humble beginnings, the little Merchants Association would grow to become the Merchants and Manufacturers Association, or, as it was known colloquially, the M & M. By the early twentieth century, the M & M would be among the most vehement anti-union, open shop organizations in the entire nation.[7]

But prominence and notoriety were a long way off in the first years of the 1890s, though the success of the Fiesta undoubtedly helped the Merchants Association grow into the M & M bully it later became. The Merchants Association in the early months of 1894 had far simpler plans and goals than ferocious opposition to organized labor. The city had weathered, somewhat unsteadily, the frenzied years of real estate boom and bust. The good years of the 1880s had come and gone, leaving a depressed land and housing market in their wake, and the region's merchants faced problems making ends meet. Improved rail connections near and far had opened markets, but the transition also made certain that goods produced in Los Angeles now had to compete with those manufactured elsewhere. No longer could local commodities exist in the insulated bubble of far western commerce. The growing population of Los Angeles, which would crest 100,000 by the turn of the century—thus multiplying ten times in just two decades!—presented local merchants with an attractive market. Even better, at least to some industries and retail outfits, were those rail tourists from the East, people with real money to spend. Yet despite commercial promise and mercantile potential, the early 1890s were marked by the arrival of as much worry as hope. Business leaders pondered the city's economic future amidst falling prices and expectations. An outbreak of smallpox, with its attendant bad press, only made things worse.

The Merchants Association latched onto a clever idea. The city, the city's merchants, and the city's goods could all be boosted through the vehicle of pageantry and spectacle, with a healthy dollop of history tossed into the mix. The idea may have occurred to many in the infant businessmen's gathering. After all, similar urban productions, such as Mardi Gras in New Orleans, were by no means unknown. Even Pasadena's Tournament of Roses, without the football game yet, had been an annual event for several years by 1894. It soon became clear, however, that the driving force behind the Fiesta was downtown electrical fixtures merchant Max Meyberg. Meyberg pushed his plan of celebration and commercialization before his mercantile peers.[8]

The imagined event, whatever it was—carnival, pageant, parade, fandango—had first to be named. The Los Angeles City Council offered fifteen dollars to whichever local newspaperman came up with a suitable name for the fete. Out of forty entries, La Fiesta de Los Angeles was chosen the victor, thus marking the event as at least a tad unusual. *Los Angeles Times* journalist and regional booster Harry E. Brook, a man already proven good at naming things, proposed the event's Spanish name. That same year, Brook had named the region's ambitious new literary and region-booster journal *Land of Sunshine*.

Following the christening, La Fiesta momentum increased. Under the capable leadership of "Director General" Meyberg, assisted by Frederick Wood and Adolph Petsch, various committees made up of the city's elite worked diligently to make the first Fiesta a success. More than a dozen committees met regularly throughout the early spring of 1894 at the event's Board of Trade headquarters to work out the increasingly intricate program. These included committees devoted to Finance, Honored Guests, Public Comfort, Music, the Military, Advertising, Illumination (for the nighttime processionals), Invitations, Hotels, Amusements, and the "Committee on Transportation of School Children on April 12 for La Fiesta parade."[9] The Committee on Invitations designated two hundred and fifty VIPs across the nation for special notice of the impending bash.

Advertising La Fiesta was, of course, advertising Los Angeles, marketing the upstart city itself and doing so brilliantly. There's little doubt that the boosterism associated with the first Fiesta marked a coming of age for the city in this regard. Meyberg later recalled that it had been "our duty and our salvation to make La Fiesta our incentive for advertising Los Angeles," and he spoke fulsomely of mailings "to every city and hamlet in the United States."[10] The Finance Committee solicited Fiesta subscriptions, from businesses and individuals alike. The Southern Pacific Railroad, seeing perhaps a new tourist gambit in the Fiesta preparations, offered $500 to the infant venture. Few exigencies went unheeded or unnoticed. On the contrary, La Fiesta's planning moved with militarized attention to detail. Members of the Artistic Committee regulated the various float entries: they could not be "gross" or "unsightly," nor could they excessively advertise companies or products. Floats could not exceed strict height and length requirements (sixteen feet by twenty-five feet). Even the celebration's especially created musical theme—"the Fiesta March"—echoed the event's martial trappings.

From Meyberg's title of "Director General," down to the slips of paper— "circular orders" from headquarters—detailing directions to various Fiesta planners (slips which looked and read like battlefield dispatches), the Fiesta had very much the overtones of a military reenactment, a gathering where even the schoolchildren marched "with soldierly precision." Such overwhelming attention to discipline, which occasioned charges of overkill from surprising quarters, no doubt helped Fiesta officials consolidate their own regional influence as civic and commercial leaders.[11]

But Max Meyberg liked order, military order at that. With precise attention to minutiae, he continued planning the first Fiesta. Short of funds, he turned to the city government for assistance. He asked for help in making the grandstands along the Fiesta route, he received permission to use Los Angeles Park Commission horse teams and laborers, and he obtained the services of the vehicles and manpower of the Street Department to fetch

Figure 10. Float at La Fiesta de Los Angeles parade, 1894. Courtesy of the Seaver Center for Western History Research, Los Angeles County Museum of Natural History.

and tote and carry. Meyberg further requested that City Hall be appropriately decorated in bunting and flags (the Fiesta reimbursed the city $50 for doing so), and he urged the City Council to endorse a public announcement that the people of Los Angeles decorate their homes "for the coming carnival." "LET US ALL UNITE AND MAKE THE FIESTA A GRAND SUCCESS," the Council obliged in a message to the citizenry.[12]

As opening day approached, Los Angeles journalists took it upon themselves to further the spirit of civic sacrifice and boosterism. "Let us bury out of sight the mistakes of the past," the *Los Angeles Times* editorialized. "In place of looking to San Francisco for inspiration and example, it is time for the merchants to cut loose and start a new era of prosperity upon a broader plane. In the future the rotteness [*sic*] of San Francisco must shoulder her own responsibilities. Los Angeles is a new world formed with higher motives, broader principles, and greater ambitions. The Chicago of the West—the ambitious, prosperous city of the western Hemisphere."[13]

Sensing opportunity, the city's merchants got into the act. J. M. Hale & Co., a downtown store, took out big advertisements in the *Los Angeles*

Figure 11. Local royalty, La Fiesta de Los Angeles, 1894. Courtesy of the Seaver Center for Western History Research, Los Angeles County Museum of Natural History.

Times trumpeting "Two Great Attractions: La Fiesta de Los Angeles and J. M. Hale & Co.'s Grand Annual Muslin Underwear Sale." Similarly, Jacoby Brothers urged Angelenos to drop in for the "Great Fiesta Sale!" Shoppers could choose from such displays as the "Fiesta Sale of Boys' Short Pants Suits" and the "Fiesta Sale of Men's Hats and Caps."[14]

Planners divided La Fiesta into a week of specific daily events, Floral Day, Military Day, and Children's Day among them. On Floral Day, carnival carts and chariots brimming with children and flowers paraded downtown in the newer commercial districts of the city south and west of the original plaza. First came the "Angelitas" float, festooned with Anglo children dressed as floral angels. In quick succession came the desert float, covered in cacti and succulents; the floral ship, a Spanish galleon manned by schoolchildren; the missions, a float decorated with the flowers and vines brought to the New World by Franciscan padres; a mountain float of hilly terrain, complete with a rushing waterfall; the fruits and flowers of the irrigation float, showing the assembled crowds in Los Angeles streets "the actual results" of irrigation in helping to make the greater Southwest bloom; and the Flower Queen and her court, twenty or thirty young girls dressed as butterflies.[15]

Figure 12. Children marching in La Fiesta parade, 1894. Courtesy of the Seaver Center for Western History Research, Los Angeles County Museum of Natural History.

Other Fiesta floats included the "Busted Boom Float," a recreated interior from a real estate office, its broker and agent stalls empty, one sole and dejected realtor sitting with nothing to do. Adding to the exoticism of the affair was the Indian float, complete with fifty Yuma Indians brought to Los Angeles from Arizona, each paid a dollar to participate. Southern California Indian commissioner Francisco Estudillo, who had been contacted by Meyberg about Indian participation in La Fiesta, had at first balked at the suggestion, responding that he would "furnish Indians only on orders from the War Department at Washington." Meyberg persisted, assuring the commissioner that the Indians would be well taken care of and safeguarded from what Estudillo referred to as the city's "demoralizing associations." That these native peoples were imported from their pueblo to play ancient Aztecs only heightened the event's fantastic qualities.[16]

Fiesta planners worked to establish the pageant's diversity as a kind of racial *rapprochement*, up to a point. The presence of Native Americans bespoke inclusion, but mostly an attraction to exotic spectacle, as did Chinese marchers and floats. So, too, with the participation of African Americans. Fiesta planners were proud of this, boasting that "not many cities could produce representatives of four out of the five human races—

Caucasians, Mongolians, Africans, and red men from the residents of its immediate locality."[17] Also present were those representatives of the region's "Spanish American" population. These were most obvious as the "gay caballeros of the Spanish period" who "rode their fiery steeds with silver-mounted saddles and bridles and costumes of brilliant coloring," as one Fiesta planner later recalled.[18]

How many people witnessed this first Fiesta? There can be no sure way to know, but it seems likely that thousands gathered in the streets of down-town Los Angeles during the most popular events and processionals.[19] Contemporary accounts suggest that the crowds might have been as large as seventy-five thousand people, an impossible figure (that would have equaled the entire population of Los Angeles in the mid-1890s). Whatever the figure, it is probably true that the first Fiesta de Los Angeles witnessed the largest gathering in Southern California history to date.

But what did it mean? And what, exactly, were all these people celebrating? What did they get out of the affair? There can be little doubt that people thought La Fiesta important beyond the flowers, the bunting, the floats, and the crowds. For one thing, contemporaries thought that La Fiesta worked as an engine of Los Angeles growth, and they traced the city's upward trajectory from the spring of 1894 forward. In his important memoir, *Sixty Years in Southern California*, Harris Newmark wrote "that this first fiesta and the resulting strengthening of the [Merchants] Association have been among the earliest, and in some respects, the most important elements contributing to the growth and development of our city." Even a far-off newspaper concurred: the *Philadelphia Record* suggested that it was precisely events like La Fiesta that had transformed Los Angeles from a "sleepy Mexican town" into the rising metropolis of the Pacific Coast. Max Meyberg himself recalled, nearly forty years later, that "an immediate change in the condition of Los Angeles was created" in the wake of La Fiesta. "People forgot their troubles," he declared.[20]

Recent students of Los Angeles suggest that La Fiesta had been organized to occupy—or preoccupy—the city during the midst of railroad labor strife.[21] While it is true that tensions ran high during the 1894 Pullman strike, the nationwide rail boycott led by Eugene Debs began in June of that year and thus postdated the planning and execution of La Fiesta by a good six months. La Fiesta de Los Angeles owes its existence to more complicated circumstances and motives than attempts to distract the city from a rail strike or class strife (though planners would have thought this a good idea). La Fiesta sprang from deeper wells on the cultural landscape of Southern

California, and contemporaries often pointed it out as a natural continuation of patterns and traditions well established by the 1890s.

Certainly writer Charles Fletcher Lummis, who fell in love with La Fiesta de Los Angeles as much as he fell in love with Los Angeles and the entire Southwest, wished to see the event as continuity with the past. La Fiesta was no "parvenu," he claimed, for it was older than "the tallest palms beneath which it is enacted." "The Caucasian race has held fiestas in Southern California for over a hundred years," he insisted, and the revitalized event was "as much at home . . . as the chaparral on the hillside."[22]

But the irrepressible Lummis ought to have known better. The 1890s Fiestas were *different*, orchestrated by individuals and institutions far less willing than the often egalitarian Lummis to grant Caucasian status to any but themselves. La Fiesta offered the opportunity to further—in highly public fashion—the racial and ethnic distinctions Anglos wished to make between themselves and others. And it allowed these distinctions to be made in ostensibly peaceful, soothing, even celebratory ways. La Fiesta offered elite Anglos in Los Angeles the ideal vehicle by which to forget— whitewash—both the unpleasantness of recent decades as well as the entire bloody history of the Southwest throughout the eighteenth and nineteenth centuries. La Fiesta suggested, in name and practice both, that indeed a kind of *rapprochement* had been worked out between the white city-builders of Los Angeles and the Mexican past and people, and that it was time to celebrate. But the peace was a suggested, contrived peace.

This isn't to suggest that the event had no ties to the past whatsoever. But it was a past cloaked as nostalgia. Even vague understandings of regional history played a role in the coming and Harry Brook's naming of La Fiesta de Los Angeles. Anglos in Southern California had long been fascinated by the public and religious culture of the region's Mexican people. Rituals and events, both sanctified and secular, received Anglo comment, stares, and scrutiny from the early decades of the nineteenth century forward. Mexican or Catholic holidays, weddings, funerals, christenings: all came to represent part of the region's exoticism in the eyes of the white tourist and settler. Anglos evinced fascination with the springtime events leading up to Easter Sunday. Masked horsemen dashed about here and there, and effigies (most often of Judas Iscariot) hung from trees and fence posts. Catholicism, especially dark-skinned Catholicism, fixated new, lighter-skinned arrivals in Los Angeles.

But public celebrations and secular excitements garnered the most attention. Fandangos and fiestas feature prominently in Anglo commentaries from the mid-to-late nineteenth century, especially for what seemingly preoccupied the revelers. "The people of Los Angeles were a dancing people," remembered one pioneer journalist. "Indeed, everything but a funeral wound up with a dance." No less an authority than Helen Hunt Jackson wrote, in a moment of mindless fantasy, that the "Californian fought as impetuously for his old way of dancing as for his political allegiance." The spectacle and sheer energy of the fandango delighted non-Mexicans, many of whom relished (if from afar) the splendor of abundant food, drink, and what they clearly took as exotic, if not erotic, festivity.[23]

Carey McWilliams characterized Anglo perceptions of the Spanish Fantasy Past, and especially its inhabitants, in memorable imagery, as "one big happy guitar-twanging family." But the understanding of pre-Anglo or pre-statehood California rests as much on what people supposedly did while listening to all those twanging guitars, which was, from the perspective of Anglos, to sleep or dance. In other words, the Spanish Fantasy Past doesn't so much recognize dancing as require it. The sheer repetition of the dancing trope as a concise way to describe the region's post-mission period and its inhabitants is remarkable; it was almost as if dancing was itself organic, even vaguely biological. "It affected all, from infancy to old age," the nineteenth-century California historian Hubert Howe Bancroft noted, "grandmother and grandchildren were seen dancing together." Los Angeles journalist William Wallace left behind a similar account, made all the more ironic given his reportage of the 1850s as a seriatim litany of violent and bloody struggles. "How all our people are given to dancing. No matter what the occasion—in joy or sorrow—famine or plenty—drought or flood—the propensity is to dance. They dance when one dies and when one is born— they dance for politics and religion, for business and for pleasure—when one goes and when one comes. Happy the people who can illustrate all their sentiments by kicking!"[24]

Contemporary interpretations by whites of these affairs could do cultural work. Dancing imagery and language could easily play into notions of racial primitivism, as practiced in the white gaze upon of African Americans, for instance. Seemingly endless fiestas and fandangos could also be hitched to the indolence stereotype laid upon Mexicans in the post–Mexican War Southwest. A race of fandango-throwing people might be fun, Anglos imagined, but they weren't fit to take the region seriously enough to make much of it. Richard Henry Dana had suggested as much way back in the tallow and hide trade days of the 1820s and 1830s ("In the hands of an enterprising people, what a country this might be!"). Anglo public perceptions had not much changed sixty and seventy years later. The

Figure 13. Representing old Spain: "Caballeros." Courtesy of the California History Room, California State Library, Sacramento.

genius of La Fiesta was that it appropriated, enviously, celebratory aspects of regional Mexican culture for commercial and boosterish purposes of white Los Angeles. La Fiesta made it possible for whites simultaneously to borrow from and denigrate supposedly innate Latin cultural forms. Even more remarkably, La Fiesta's creators did so in a scripted atmosphere of presumed ethnic peacefulness, even progress.[25]

Though actual regional fiestas continued well into the American period, they clearly had begun to recede from the landscape, probably because there were fewer and fewer reasons to celebrate once statehood and its ethnic and other transitions took hold. A few locales, especially those less affected by transitions in the racial and political economy of Anglo Southern California, persisted. San Bernardino, the tiny hamlet east of Los Angeles, threw a big fiesta of its own in the mid-1890s, one far truer to regional culture and heritage than La Fiesta de Los Angeles. The San Bernardino fiesta included fandangos, a couple of bullfights, and the music of a Mexican band up from Sonora. The village's Spanish American society even went to Los Angeles to recruit, as a local paper phrased it, "Spanish American" spectators and participants. That kind of outreach to local Latinos would not take place in the Los Angeles version of tradition, not by a long shot.[26]

Max Meyberg and his partners figured that Los Angeles could go San Bernardino several times better, that their adolescent city could throw a fiesta of greater proportions, even one of lasting importance. Yet merely by insisting on a Spanish-language name for the event, these members of the Los Angeles elite signaled aspects of a cultural game plan. The great California literary critic Franklin Walker wrote brilliantly about the remarkable ability of Southern Californians to whitewash history and contemporary concerns with broad strokes of pageantry and romantic fiction. With particular reference to the 1890s, Walker noted that nascent exaltation of the Spanish past "also involved a painful association with the humble Mexican laborer . . . already consigned to his Sonoratown on the other side of the railroad track." Yet Angelenos could make the problems go away, or so they thought, by mixing together a cultural salve of equal parts dissonance and romance. "The Franciscans could be accepted as pious and picturesque, even when Catholics as a whole remained without the pale. The contemporary Mexican peon could be ignored by assuming that the leading figures of Spanish California had been of the best Catholic blood. And the drama of history could be made more intense by dressing up the more spectacular elements in the story and by refusing to see California as but a comparatively unimportant sector of the much richer Spanish empire to the south."[27] Thus it was with La Fiesta: invented tradition rolling by on the streets of downtown Los Angeles for thousands to enjoy and absorb.

Los Angeles, despite the recent real estate frenzy of the booming 1880s and an infant manufacturing sector, was still predominantly an agricultural center in the 1890s, devoted to growing, processing, warehousing, and shipping citrus and other fruits and vegetables. This farm economy can easily be discerned in the first Fiesta's color scheme. Planners festooned the streets of the city in red, yellow, and green, each to represent a different agricultural product upon which the growing prosperity of Los Angeles was founded: grapes, oranges, and olives. City residents complied with the suggestions of Fiesta planners to decorate their homes in these official agrarian hues, and city newspapers published a ditty about the Fiesta colors splashed across Los Angeles.

Mary had a little lamb.
Its fleece could not be seen,
For Mary had adorned it with
The yellow, red, and green.[28]

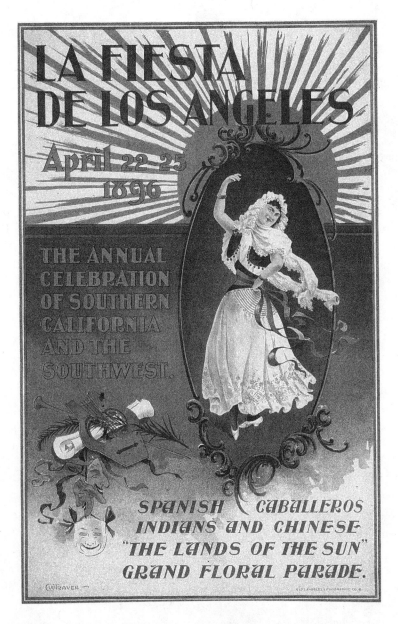

Figure 14. La Fiesta poster, 1896. Courtesy of the California History Room, California State Library, Sacramento.

The city responded in kind, wrapping municipal buildings and electric poles in bright tri-color bunting.

As the first day of La Fiesta 1894 arrived, planners engaged in a weird political farce, drawing on none-too-subtle historical allusions. Apparently it had been decided that the Fiesta, much like Mardi Gras in New Orleans, would suggest that the world had been turned upside down. Accordingly, the Fiesta Queen, Mrs. O. W. Childs, wife of a wealthy nurseryman in the city, would be granted the right to rule as mayor for the week of the Fiesta.[29] She would be assisted by her court, "well known society women" all, dressed in Spanish finery with *mantillas* draped across their faces. Fiesta planners, in costume and masked, engineered the farcical coup on April 8. Substituting a carnival mayor and council for elected city officials, the Fiesta-ites engaged in a kind of mock revolutionary spectacle that harkened back to the days of 1776. "Behold the beautiful citizens assembled to avenge your wrongs," one of the leaders shouted. "When a government, by its tyranny, becomes unbearable, there is nothing to destroy it but revolution. We prepare to destroy the tyranny of this government, and, in order that it may be fair, propose to try it by jury. Whether it is right or wrong don't make any difference. We propose to arrest it and bring to trial this municipal government and bury its officers one hundred and ten feet deep with their faces downward." With that, the mock government took over the reins of municipal power and stayed in charge through the week's events, and Southern Californians flocked to the streets of downtown to see what they often could not pronounce. Linguistic variations on the Fiesta theme included "fyesty," "fester," "fee-esty," "fee-estay," "fi-eestor," "feestay," "fiestor," "fer Easter," and "fi-ees-tor." The limits of white engagement with the region's Latin past, not to mention Latino residents, might be discerned in reference to these tongue-twisting bastardizations of a simple Spanish word.[30] What remains compelling about the spectacle, especially with its whimsical references to the traditionally lauded revolutionary past of the Founding Fathers, is that Angelenos were engaged in the creation of a public memory fitted to their region. George Washington had a place to play in this memory. But so too did the patriotism, a kind of exuberant, regional patriotism of the adolescent western city, that championed the neat progression of national and racial progress in the Southwest. From the vantage of a century later, La Fiesta looks like the party white Los Angeles threw to celebrate the triumph of Manifest Destiny in the Far West.[31]

La Fiesta leaders and urban boosters imagined that the several days would offer lessons as well as fun to the throngs assembled in the thousands on city streets. Meyberg himself characterized the Fiesta as a sensory extravaganza, complete with "sights beautiful to the eye and instructive to the mind." Part of that instruction was apparently in relation to the spirit inspired by the Revolutionary farce. The Fiesta ought to epitomize the democratic spirit of the urban West. Meyberg congratulated La Fiesta (and himself) for the ways in which it fostered such apparent togetherness: "people met on a common level and on equal terms." Or, as one Fiesta official put it a few years later, the Fiesta offered people "a chance to comingle with and study multitudes of their fellow creatures."[32]

But much of this democratic flavor and self-congratulation can be assigned more to wishful thinking and hindsight than to the ethnic or class realities of 1890s Los Angeles. The case of the Chinese participation in the first Fiesta is instructive. Apparently the decision to invite the Chinese to assemble a float or dragon entry for the parade had been met with great opposition. It had been, after all, slightly more than twenty years since the notorious massacre of a score of Chinese in downtown Los Angeles, and matters had not improved much since. One Fiesta planner recalled that the proposal to include the Chinese provoked "anything but enthusiasm on the part of many, some of the gentlemen going so far as to suggest that the mere idea of having the Chinese in the parade indicated failure, that their presence would lend nothing to the celebration and might result in a serious disturbance." The lengthy and heated debate about Chinese participation ended with an unusually egalitarian solution. The Chinese would be invited only if the organizers also included "all representatives of other nations within the city."[33] Lest that agreement sound too multicultural for the age—too in keeping with democratic ideals referenced in nods to the American Revolution—it was clear that wider ethnic participation in the parade could, in fact, drive home assumptions of regional progress predicated upon racial hierarchy. In other words, the Chinese participation had to fit the narrow confines of the parade's movement through time. As historian David Glassberg has astutely noted, in reference to a copycat Fiesta in turn-of-the-century San Francisco, civic celebrations of this sort "are representations of and for the [urban] collective but not necessarily by the collective. Such representations primarily serve as tools that some groups use to structure a common reality for others." In this, they become (in the absence or muting of counternarratives), "a framework for understanding the workings of urban social and political life at a level once removed from the immediate surroundings of neighborhood, workplace, or ethnic group."

La Fiesta offered a slice of Los Angeles society to interpret all of Los Angeles *to* all of Los Angeles.[34]

Charles Fletcher Lummis suggested that the Los Angeles pageant offered "a great deal more instruction" to its participants and viewers than did, for instance, Mardi Gras of New Orleans. In this he was echoed by others. Frank Van Vleck wrote in 1895 that the Fiesta was "such an object lesson as has never before been seen in the country; a pageant second to none in gorgeousness, and historically correct." This was not just any standard of correctness: all would be accomplished with "strict attention to historic and scientific accuracy of detail."[35]

What did that mean? On one hand, it meant simply that the progression of floats would be chronological—literally progress represented by movement and sequence. Most important to this was La Fiesta's Historical Day, the grandest processional of the entire week's events. Discrete historical periods, broken neatly into "divisions," worked their way through time, space, and downtown streets. It all began with a float of "angels" accompanied by Spanish cavaliers and moved through to those pueblo Indians who had been shipped in boxcars from Yuma to play the part of "Aztecs." From there the parade moved to and through the now trite historical periods: missions, the "drowsy pueblo," on through the peaceful ranchos, and into the American period. Every period had its own descriptive adjective, though La Fiesta had no space to give over to the mission period of genocidal consequences or the grim 1850s. That history had no role to play on Los Angeles streets. That past simply did not exist. All was neat, linear: history on parade, history that worked, step after step, float after float, each giving way to the next stage of an inevitably progressive future.

The only glitch came when a spectator took the show too much at its word and saw reality where there was only fantasy, or so an apocryphal tale recounted. An old soldier, glimpsing the Fiesta's Indian contingent, got transported back to frontier days. An eyewitness described his reaction: "There was a float bearing a genuine display of Indians imported from Arizona for the occasion. This was so realistic that an old soldier, who used to be with Custer, took off his hat after they had passed and felt for his scalp to see if it was still there. He said he supposed it was all right to have Indians in the parade, but all the same he didn't feel like trusting too far."[36]

Despite planners' attention to detail, the Fiesta careened off the highly organized track it had been placed upon at the end of the week. Drunken rowdies, including some of the city elite, celebrated long into the wee hours of the waning days of the event, and their excesses and revelries cast

Figure 15. Representing Aztecs? Native Americans and La Fiesta's revival of a mythic regional past. Courtesy of the California History Room, California State Library, Sacramento.

a sinister pall on La Fiesta's conclusion. Out-of-control revelers threw things at one another—handfuls of flour, pepper, even ammonia—and many tourists and locals alike believed that the Fiesta had fallen short of its promise of playful, peaceful fun. Another tense moment arose when men who had been promised a dollar to lead parade horses down the city streets appeared at Max Meyberg's store for their money. When Meyberg demurred, apparently because local banks had closed in honor of the Fiesta, there was potential trouble, so much so that Meyberg feared his store would be wrecked.[37]

Despite this bumpy conclusion, the initial Fiesta received much attention and fulsome praise. Joseph Crawley, a regional Southern Pacific railroad executive, loved it. It was, he wrote Director General Meyberg, "the greatest week of carnival, pleasure and, I am sure, of benefit to the city of Los Angeles and the surrounding country, than ever before, and [you deserve] the thanks of the people of Los Angeles and everybody."[38] Another observer got more to the point, noting how well Anglo Los Angeles had found a way to capitalize on Mexican culture. "Not only was our first attempt at the distinctive gaieties of the people of the Latin race a spectacular success, but it has had a pleasant pecuniary outcome."[39]

As time came round to plan the second Fiesta, the Merchants Association solidified itself into corporate status through state law. La Fiesta II accurately reflected the increasing bureaucratic nature of such change. An association attorney approved and modified Fiesta contracts and advertising, and Director General Meyberg utilized the organization's resources as he planned the second annual affair. As in the first Fiesta, Meyberg delegated the planning of all manner of events and exigencies to a series of committees. La Fiesta organization had evolved, in only a year's time, into a microcosmic version of Los Angeles city government itself.

The Chinese community balked at appearing in the second Fiesta; perhaps the overwhelmingly patronizing, even hostile, air that had accompanied Anglo commentary about their participation in the 1894 Fiesta exhausted their patience. But Fiesta planners recognized the touristic need for spectacle. They pleaded with the Chinese. An argument was made that the Fiesta was a table of multiple legs: one each represented by merchants, capitalists, manufacturers, and the Chinese, as if Asian ethnicity were itself an occupational category (which of course it very nearly was, given the restriction of Chinese to particular, and particularly feminized, jobs). According to this weird logic of civic balance, a Fiesta without the Chinese float would tilt toward chaos. The Chinese could help maintain order if they again joined the parade. They did, in grand style. The Chinese dragon in the 1895 Fiesta was eight hundred feet long; it took one hundred and fifty men, walking side to side, back and forth, to make it come to life.

As La Fiesta settled into its institutional form, fundraising took on an increasingly mercenary air. Businessmen who chose not to subscribe to the appeals for money received letters from the Merchants Association that spelled out the recalcitrant businessman's errors in not rising to support the cause. Meyberg and associates had less success the second time around with the City Council. Attempts at garnering a municipal appropriation for the Fiesta at first looked promising: Meyberg was able to get support for a council donation of $1,500. But when the matter was internally referred to the Council's own finance committee, Meyberg's proposal went down to defeat in a close vote.

Nor did everyone in Los Angeles embrace the Fiesta. More telling than the City Council's apparent reluctance to pony up a large donation was the opposition that the Fiesta garnered from Angelenos angry at the appropriation of any public funds at all. A February 1895 petition to the Council

Figure 16. The Chinese dragon parading at La Fiesta. Courtesy of the California History Room, California State Library, Sacramento.

spelled the matter out succinctly: "As true and loyal American citizens, [we] earnestly protest against the appropriation of one dollar of the public funds of this city at this time for any such unnecessary and useless purpose." The petition had been signed by dozens of Angelenos, their signatures lined up in two columns, four pages worth in all. Civic gaiety was apparently one thing; paying for it was another matter.[40]

In order to prevent a repeat of the previous year's chaotic conclusion, newspapers began a campaign calling for decorum throughout. Fiesta-goers were urged to keep an eye out for pickpockets, and they were likewise encouraged not to lower themselves into the ranks of the disorderly classes.

La Fiesta 1895 once again offered visitor and Angeleno alike an object lesson of historical progression, Victorian style. Chronological and cultural sequences again began early, with a representation of the El Dorado vision of five hundred years previous. The myth of El Dorado, the golden man, was enacted upon the Fiesta's first float, complete with a man dusted by gold and surrounded by ersatz Incas, "those wonderful aborigines of Peru." For accuracy, the planners of the El Dorado float studied the Bolivia and Peru photographs of Charles Fletcher Lummis (untroubled by the fact that his depictions were four hundred years later than the period conjured atop the float).

After the Incas came, not surprisingly, the Aztecs. Three tableau performances of Aztec life, scrupulously reproduced from available documentation, paraded before the spectators lining the streets of the city. History continued on by. The Aztec float came just before that upon which was depicted "our own southwest and its romantic historic peoples." Cliff-dwellers repulsed an attack of Apache; pueblo Indians ("actual Pueblos in their picturesque national costumes") stood or sat on their float as it slowly moved through time and space in downtown Los Angeles.

The neatness of such transitions, float to float, period to period, indicates the level of Fiesta planning. From the Indian float, time moved forward to the conquistadors and, quickly, to the mission period. Those missions of Franciscan construction, those "noble piles" which "are our most romantic possession," allowed Fiesta planners a site upon which to stage their version of the Spanish Fantasy Past. In the words of one observer and Fiesta supporter, the transition from Coronado's Southwestern search for mythic gold to the Franciscan search for souls meant the visual display of "the happy, patriarchal life of the Spanish occupation, with fair señoritas and dashing cavaliers, hacendados and vaqueros."[41]

From the mission era, the transition to the modern era was as seamless as it was swift. John Sutter and his fabled millrace earned a place, as did "a typical mining scene." Each of the latter-day floats offered to the assembled thousands the spectacle of "gorgeous allegorical tableaux of the New Era in this modern Garden of Eden." As a moving exclamation point to the whole affair, the Chamber of Commerce float, complete with Corinthian columns, rolled by: Los Angeles represented as the apex of European American civilization in the American West.

The success of the 1895 Fiesta prompted Charles Fletcher Lummis to wax eloquent about the cultural appropriateness of the event to the region. While admitting that the 1894 Fiesta had its share of problems ("a fruit picked half ripe, but it was no failure"), Lummis nonetheless figured that Los Angeles had hit upon the perfect vehicle for regional identification. "We have logically the keynote of Spanish America, with all its glamor and romance of the aborigine and the conquest," he wrote. "It is the intention to make the Fiesta de Los Angeles characteristic and significant; not to ape Italy or Greece, but to have it historically and logically our own. Which is as much as to say that it will be the only purely American affair of the sort in existence."[42] As telling a description of regional culture is that Lummis felt compelled to chastise readers in a brief story adjacent to his Fiesta praise. It was, he wrote, "thoughtless speech" on the part of educated Anglos to utilize the term "Greaser" in reference to Mexicans and Mexican Americans. Better to leave such bigotry "to the class whose epithets in general do not see print."[43]

La Fiesta II brought in some forty thousand visitors to the city, each of whom, on average, spent more than ten dollars while there. Even so, the event appears to have lost money, despite Meyberg's ability to raise nearly $20,000 in subscriptions.[44] A letter from Los Angeles educator John Francis to the Fiesta Finance Committee offered congratulations, as well as a contribution to help make up the shortfall. "I take pleasure in sending my check for an additional hundred dollars towards clearing up the shortage," Francis wrote. "If it were ten times greater, you would still be entitled to the warm thanks of every citizen, who has the interests of our city at heart. Truly it was 'A Magnificent Success,' and to the hard work and business ability of our merchants—the workers who 'scratched gravel'—Los Angeles must always remain heavily in debt. Hurrah for La Fiesta '95." Francis concluded his note with an enthusiastic endorsement for Fiesta III: "Dam the River and Paint the town Red, for '96."[45]

But, once again, not all shared in the enthusiasm. The *California Voice*, a "paper that dares to tell the truth," called the 1895 Fiesta a "relic of heathenism" and "great big nothing." Stitching together the usual list of targets employed by anti-Catholic bigotry, the paper attacked the Fiesta's tolerance of public drinking: "Every tin horn gambler, blackleg and pimp within a hundred miles of the city was here. . . . The closing night was disgraceful in the extreme. Streams of drunken men and women went in and out of saloons, and not a few girls were enticed to their ruin." It also editorialized that among the debauched event's strongest supporters were "foreign, liquor-guzzling, drunkard-making saloon [keepers] who can scarcely speak the English language." Perhaps what the editor disliked most was the Fiesta's mingling of races. "It is certainly not to the credit of such a gathering that . . . it was invariably admitted that the 'heathen Chinee' was far ahead in the display—that American heathenism was far inferior to Mongolian paganism."[46]

Criticisms notwithstanding, with two largely successful Fiestas under its belt, the Merchants Association felt justified in asking other civic organizations for help with Fiesta III. Consequently, the association appealed to the Chamber of Commerce and the Board of Trade for assistance. A new planning committee for Fiesta '96 was organized—the Committee of Thirty—with ten members from each of the three feeder business and commercial organizations with the most at stake in the annual Fiesta. Max Meyberg no longer would play a large role in the event he founded.

With the Fiesta now more or less ensconced as an annual affair—and with the concomitant rise of the Merchants Association to commercial and political prominence—larger and more powerful firms began to see the merit in associating with the pageantry. 1896 witnessed the arrival of Wells, Fargo and Company into the group of supporting businesses. The banking house offered to carry all the Fiesta flowers in from the outlying communities for use by the Floral Committee.

"LIKE RUNNING A CIRCUS AND A NEWSPAPER AT THE SAME TIME"

La Fiesta 1896 saw the inclusion of new faces into the planning operation, including some that *Land of Sunshine* magazine called "the foremost men of affairs in Los Angeles," and the *Los Angeles Express* termed "men long identified with the progress of Los Angeles."[47] These included Executive Committee president John Francis ("a well known capitalist and a large property owner"). Married to the daughter of Manuel Dominguez, Francis was part of a waning group in the region, that of Anglo men who had married into once-elite *Californio* clans.

None were as important in the day-to-day production of La Fiesta as inveterate city booster, writer, and publicist Charles Dwight Willard. Willard had started *Land of Sunshine* as a booster magazine and Chamber of Commerce organ in the mid-1890s, and he was never shy about claiming to personify the booster spirit in the Los Angeles basin. Sickly and sycophantic, Willard nonetheless brought to the task energy and organizational skills. "A new honor with an accompanying burden of . . . magnitude has been granted me," Willard wrote to his father in the fall of 1895.

I am secretary, which means general manager, of the annual celebration of So Cal that takes place in Los Angeles in April known as La Fiesta. It resembles the carnival at New Orleans. It attracts a great many thousand people from the East. It lasts four days and consists of processions games balls concerts etc. The whole business costing $30,000 or $40,000. A small army of people is employed including artists writers clerks collectors laborers costumers carpenters florests [*sic*] decorators typewriters etc. etc. until your brain reels to think of it all. It's a good deal like running a circus and a newspaper at the same time with social functions of all sorts and a few railway excursions on the side.[48]

Willard's busy schedule accelerated with the planning of the Fiesta, so much so that he wondered if his fragile health might break once and for all.

The work amounted to, in his words, "horrible strain," hardly worth the $600 or $800 he earned for it. "I expect to have the liveliest winter and spring I ever saw," he wrote, "and hope to live through to see the summer." The work likely did little to lessen Willard's pessimistic, even macabre, sensibilities, themselves decidedly unfestive. "If there is one thing in this world that I do believe clear to the bottom it is that we would all be much better off if we had never existed," he wrote. He nonetheless claimed to have single-handedly revitalized, in part through his Fiesta work and connections, the Chamber of Commerce, *Land of Sunshine* magazine, the Sunset Club (which he did start), the Free Harbor League, and the League for Better City Government.[49]

Charlie Willard clearly took the Fiesta work on as part of a booster plan and operation. His canary yellow Fiesta stationary referred to the event as "The Famous Annual Celebration of Southern California," and publicity flyers or postcards pointed out that a "pamphlet describing La Fiesta in detail and containing information about the City of Los Angeles and Southern California will be issued." Requests for more information about the event were efficiently funneled directly to the Los Angeles Chamber of Commerce.

As befits the Fiesta's conception of hierarchical racial progress, C. D. Willard was no racial egalitarian. His published work on the history of Los Angeles mirrors the same sort of progressions so obviously acted out in each Fiesta. To Willard, the Indians who once gathered at the plaza in mid-century Los Angeles were "idle, shiftless, and addicted to drink."[50]

His work on the Fiesta did break his health. To his sister, he wrote just prior to the opening that the "worst of all is yet ahead of me—probably the hardest month I have ever lived. . . . We have 12 events to handle—any one of them big enough to keep a good many people busy for many months. You can have only a faint comprehension of what it is like to manage such a menagerie of things all at once. I hope I don't go mad."[51]

Nonetheless, La Fiesta 1896 was much anticipated. "We need it," stated a *Land of Sunshine* writer (Willard, most likely, or maybe Lummis who had by then taken over as editor), "not only in business, but in our lives. The Saxon is too little a man of holidays." Despite anxious letters from easterners interested in seeing La Fiesta who wondered if "a person who speaks English [could] get around [in Los Angeles] without the aid of an interpreter," whether a tourist needed a passport, and whether Indians posed a threat, La Fiesta was of course a Saxon event. That was the whole idea. The parade had become part of a "racial experiment," according to *Land of*

Sunshine. Could Anglos thrive in the exotic region of Southern California? Could whites utilize the out of doors as a step toward further racial dominance, could they appropriate the landscape, even the very sunshine of the region? Could Anglos pull off a Fiesta? "La Fiesta de Los Angeles," the journal insisted, "is a step in the right direction."[52]

The same sort of farcical behavior that had characterized the two previous Fiestas was present in 1896. For instance, a body of the "Queen's Maskers" raided local stores and "looted" them of merchandise—mostly large advertising props in the shape of this product or that. Police or detectives who stepped in between the "looters" and their task were placed in a giant iron cage especially constructed for the purpose. Such highly ritualized behavior, which turned the world upside down in a moment of revelry, did not please all. The Minister's [*sic*] Association, for instance, protested that the looting by the Queen's Maskers did anything but set a high moral standard and tone for the youth of the city. They asked that it be discontinued as a Fiesta event, being thus "immoral and corrupting in its tendencies."[53]

Certain editorial commentators believed that the "Spanish features" of La Fiesta ought to be emphasized in the 1896 celebration far more than they had in the previous years. Trying, apparently, to do its part, the *Los Angeles Express* used a Latinized cartoon character (white cotton pants and shirt, sash, long hair and mustache) as illustration to its Fiesta stories and updates, at best a weak effort at inclusiveness and at worst a cheap-shot ethnic caricature.[54] The *Los Angeles Record*, a big Fiesta booster, pushed the issue. "It is particularly desirable that the Spanish features of La Fiesta—itself Spanish in name—should be made as prominent as possible. California abounds in reminders of the Spanish occupation, the nomenclature of the towns and all the points of consequence in the country being of Spanish origin." Tourists had learned to expect this flavor, the paper declared. "Let them not be disappointed."[55]

Yet even the *Record* evinced some discomfort with the Fiesta's flavor. Just prior to La Fiesta 1896, the paper ran a contest among its readers for the best Fiesta essay. Second prize went to a Dr. A. P. Miller of Los Angeles, no fan of the event. Miller's opposition to the springtime ritual sprang precisely from the Fiesta's preoccupation with those "Spanish features" some wished to accentuate. Miller's essay rehearsed standard Fiesta criticisms: it illustrated "foreign people, institutions, manners and customs." The event enshrined a "dead past much more than a living present;" it was, in short, "un-American, un-Republican, and un-modern." "If foreignism and the past predominate La Fiesta never can become our annual festival," he concluded. He had a solution, though, of sorts. Future La Fiesta events "should represent and illustrate the living American present, anticipating the splendid future which awaits Los Angeles and all California."[56] The editors of the *Record* apparently felt similarly. Worried that the Fiesta might not be doing its patriotic best, they insisted that the American eagle ought to be a regular feature atop one or more floats, and that copies of both the Declaration of Independence and the Monroe Doctrine ought to somehow be draped around the eagle for all to see (if not read).[57] In the eyes of such critics as Dr. Miller, the Fiesta no longer needed to flirt with a Latin past. Los Angeles had outgrown that infatuation, and the time had come—even just two years into the event's lifetime—to drop the Fiesta's "un-American" flavor.

How "Spanish" should La Fiesta become? Those that disagreed with Miller's perspective found the "Spanish features" of La Fiesta among its most attractive aspects. Even the *Chicago Evening Post* got into the act, writing a long story for its readers about La Fiesta opening ceremonies. "Mr. Francis and his beautiful Spanish wife will be dressed in yellow Spanish costumes," the paper commented, "and the native coachman, arrayed in sombrero and a caballero cape, will look like a picture from old Spain."[58]

The main parade event of 1896, which took place on April 22, was more elaborate than any in previous Fiestas. A giant banner—"VIVA LA FIESTA 1896"—hung across the main parade route. Three hundred United States Marines, anchored just off the coast aboard the man-of-war *Philadelphia*, marched alongside members of the California National Guard, the Spanish caballeros, and squadrons of local police. Fifty Native Americans, brought in from the California desert around Temecula, marched in native dress (described by one local paper as "one hundred Yuma Indians with G strings and paint").[59] The Chinese dragon, transported all the way from Marysville in the gold country, made its appearance, carried on the shoulders of "150 Celestials." The whole affair was graced by the music of the "La Fiesta March."[60]

As always, the parade emphasized historical progression through linear tableaux: savagery progressed to barbarism, barbarism became civilization. Ethnic group representation garnered, as always, special comment. The first day of the Fiesta featured the exhibition of "a Mexican aged 115 years" riding in a carriage with a city official. Lest parade goers doubt the authenticity of his ancient status, he supposedly carried his baptismal certificate with him as proof of his age. Such representations of the Latin past, as if to say "this is regional history personified," could hardly have been lost on Fiesta audiences: the past was brown, the future is white. Perhaps even more telling was the admittance that this aged man, who had ridden with the horsemen in La Fiesta 1895, "was forgotten till too late" in 1896, and thus had to ride in the carriage.[61] "The Tourist's Paradise," trumpeted a Pasadena paper in regard to La Fiesta and Southern California history in general. "Strange Spanish Scenes and Customs, the Happy Indolent Life of the Early Settlers of Southern California." Southern California history and life were different, the stories insisted, exotic, romantic, and harmless. History could be whitewashed, especially that history that directly contradicted La Fiesta's story line. "There were a few bloodless combats during the Mexican war," this same Pasadena paper commented, "before Los Angeles came permanently under American rule." La Fiesta enshrined that view of a pretty (sleepy, dancing) past, and added to it.[62]

Nor did the event traffic only in stock Mexican figures and the stock history of Mexican California. Blackface was omnipresent in 1896, including a parade skit in which a Simon Legree figure marched ahead of a slave (white in blackface, yet another whitewashing), complete with a rope around his neck. And while the "real Indians" might have lent an air of southwestern exoticism to the whole event, there was apparently room for improvement regarding those that faked it. "Those that represent Indians," the Los Angeles Record stated, "should secure a real Indian to assist in their make-up." Too many individuals had simply played "circus Indian," and their inattention to authenticity had been challenged. If only they would spend a bit more time on their representations of the ethnic other, all would be fine. Playing at or appropriating ethnicity itself was not the problem—that was a racial prerogative of Anglo Saxons in their city of the future. All that was required was a little care, a little regard for detail. The play had to be serious play.[63]

Did it work? As the ubiquitous Charles Fletcher Lummis himself saw it, La Fiesta 1896 "far surpassed its predecessors. The floats had a logical theme—the development of civilization in sunny climes."[64] The Los Angeles Times, the region's strongest Fiesta promoter, viewed the event with pride and expected that it would simply get better and better. "Let us regard it as an established institution of Southern California, which means, experience and culture shall yet more fully perfect, and which shall become more and more in fully harmonious blending with the physical perfection and beauty of this modern Italy, this lovelier Greece of the New World."[65]

In other words, the Fiesta wasn't foreign in a dangerous way (how could it be if many of the ethnic others weren't ethnic at all, only wearing makeup?). It existed as part of a master plan to render Southern California into "our Italy," to make Mediterranean allusions for an Anglo Saxon people riding the wave of the future alongside the Pacific. Ethnic difference and diversity could be quaint and charming. La Fiesta offered "the Anglo-Saxon race" the opportunity "to learn what the Latin races know by intuition, how to play."[66] As the legions of military escorts suggested, ethnic flavor and indulgence in non–Anglo Saxon behavior could easily be controlled. Flags were everywhere, observers remarked (and contemporary photographs make clear), as if to insist that the event's ethnic or non-American background was simple play. Omnipresent, too, was the militaristic flavor of La Fiesta, no doubt related to the patriotism of the event. In keeping with its Civil War sensibilities, La Fiesta 1896 even witnessed a Civil War reconciliation of sorts, when three former Union soldiers and three former Confederates raised the American flag together.

But merriment and nationalism came at a price. Some people just didn't appreciate La Fiesta, or perhaps they didn't quite understand that the parade's narrative really was a story of national and racial progress. Attacks continued. People, as essayist Miller had done, chastised La Fiesta for precisely the parade's allusions to a Latin California past—not that it was faked or romanticized, but that it was done at all. "Why the very name of the thing leaves a bad taste in the mouth," editorialized a paper in San Bernardino County. "It is foreign. Indeed the whole business is un-American, gotten up by an un-American crowd of adventurers in Spring Street." Calling the event "La Fake," the editors of the *Colton Chronicle* declared La Fiesta "an 'exotic' transplanted from foreign shores."[67]

The watchdog anti-Catholic America Protective Association (APA) went after La Fiesta as a dangerous throwback, a capitulation to "rags and rum." "Some day, when Los Angeles becomes civilized, our people will be ashamed of all this monkeyism, this relic of medieval Romanism; the original object of which was to amuse, and hold in check a people degraded and impoverished by robbery and superstition."[68] The *California Voice* agreed. Calling the Fiesta "unworthy of a christian people," the paper condemned the event for encouraging public drunkenness and debauchery. La Fiesta was but "a waste of time and money, and leaves few if any lessons of real value to anybody. It is a step backward toward heathenism rather than advancement toward a higher plane."[69]

Some clearly feared that the Fiesta was just going too far, that its mixture of races and ethnicities, scripted though it was, did more harm than good, especially as diversity might call into question certainties of racial hierarchy. The *Los Angeles Record* put one perspective quite succinctly. "Either bar the

Chinese altogether from participating in the parade lest spectators have another chance to say that the display of those 'heathens' was the most elaborate of all, while this very public is looking down on the same as inferior human beings, or acknowledge in other affairs their claim of rights and privileges enjoyed by all individuals of any other nationality living in this country."[70] The statement is striking for its allusion to the mere suggestion of equality, given that the experience of Chinese in Los Angeles had been anything but egalitarian.[71]

The objections raised by such groups as the Minister's Association, which attacked La Fiesta as "a remnant of a lower civilization than now prevails in Protestant Southern California," continued to dog Fiesta planners, even well after the week-long event had closed.[72] Local Protestant clergy disliked the end-of-the week carnival or All Fools' Nite, finding in it too many objectionable practices (if not objectionable people). Many resented the anonymity of the "maskers," feeling that concealment encouraged antisocial behavior, public drunkenness, and lewdness. Others struck out against the gender-bending cross-dressing tendencies of those celebrants in the final day of La Fiesta. The Woman's Christian Temperance Union lent its voice to objections. Others feared that mob action would be the natural counterpart to the Fiesta's ability to draw tens of thousands of people out of doors and into Los Angeles public space. Not a few suggested that La Fiesta, which had been seen as a different sort of festival than Mardi Gras, had in fact degenerated into just the sort of lawlessness and excess they imagined characterized events in New Orleans.

"Good boys who never before had drank, smoked, or had enjoyed women," complained the *Los Angeles Non Partisan*, "fell as much so as his sisters." What was more, La Fiesta's supposed beneficent effect in regard to the poor (especially at the time of national economic depression) rang hollow: "Great fun and the jails full of tramps and honest men, the streets full of men hungry and homeless. Where were the benefits from the La Fiesta for charity? No a cent, not a crust. To hell with the poor so long as we can make merry and enjoy ourselves."[73]

The result of such worry, pledged in public venues like meetings and newspaper stories, was a draconian Fiesta solution. Masks were forbidden unless the wearer was part of an official function or parade. No longer could everyday Fiesta-ites don masks to create anonymity, lest they court the unwanted attention of the authorities.

Despite the praise of such luminaries and regional commentators as Charles Fletcher Lummis, it is likely that the reception of Fiesta 1896 was less than the event planners and boosters would have liked. Only three years old, the Fiesta seemed to have run out of steam; perhaps, as many have suggested, city fathers could only focus so much attention on the event in the face of other pressing municipal issues. A sense of waning interest in La Fiesta prompted Lummis himself to, somewhat defensively, point out the Fiesta's benefits. The Fiesta marked an important racial and cultural transition, that proverbial "step in the right direction," in that it showed that Anglo Saxons could take recreational advantage of the open space and warm weather of the Southwest. As Lummis had stated before, by utilizing the cultural traditions of the region's Mexicans, Anglos could move racially forward themselves by displaying an uncharacteristic playfulness in the out-of-doors.[74]

By 1897, the Merchants Association had merged with the Manufacturers Association to form, logically enough, the Merchants and Manufacturers Association. The group, perhaps now weary of hosting the annual event, called a public meeting in the spring of 1896—the recent Fiesta fresh in their minds—to ask whether their sponsorship should continue into 1897. Opinions, generally favorable, nonetheless tended toward arguments about shortening the celebration to three, or even two, days. But most, if not all, considered that the Fiesta had become part and parcel of civic pride and should continue. One Angeleno put the matter simply when he suggested that Los Angeles moved forward with the Fiesta and moved backward without it.[75] The event was considered a public relations necessity, a great and powerful advertising magnet for capital and tourists both. It must continue.

Therefore, not long after the close of Fiesta 1896 came the plans for Fiesta 1897. A veritable who's who of local business elites, the Executive Committee met in La Fiesta rooms of the Chamber of Commerce. Led by the Committee of Thirty, planners sought to determine what commercial Los Angeles thought of the job they were doing. In a survey of local businesses, the Chamber asked whether or not the Committee of Thirty had adequately managed the Fiesta just held. Should it continue to be the major administrative body of La Fiesta de Los Angeles?

The survey relayed the local community's support, and the Chamber of Commerce added a plea for permanent status for La Fiesta, based on the fact that it was "of great benefit to Los Angeles and to all of southern California in attracting visitors to this section from the eastern states and in stimulating praiseworthy patriotism."[76] Accordingly, the "Fiesta Association" was incorporated under California law in the summer of 1896; this group became an arm of the Chamber of Commerce, complete with dedicated "Fiesta Rooms" at the Chamber building downtown.

Planning La Fiesta, despite the seemingly endless need to raise money, had become fairly straightforward by early 1897. The Committee of Thirty and Executive Committee listened to entrepreneurs wishing to cash in on the ethnic flavor of the event. For instance, they heard a plan offered by a Mr. Dunham to supply Indians for the 1897 event at $1 a piece, much as Lummis himself had done in earlier years. The Executive Committee tentatively agreed to let Dunham push forward with his plans but reminded him that any Indians must be "gotten up in a manner satisfactory to the Committee." Ethnicity was good, but only "satisfactory" ethnicity counted. The committee eventually contracted with a different purveyor, a Mr. Patton, "for the use of his Indians." Fiesta planners also contracted with local impresario L. E. Behymer to sell the official Fiesta program.[77]

Just before the 1897 Fiesta, planners, fearful that the event had become somewhat stale, tried to drum up interest. Creating a new category of Fiesta participant, the Executive Committee invented the "Sir Knights of La Fiesta." Three men would be selected each year, men who had distinguished themselves as great citizens of Los Angeles. The Knights would serve as special liaisons to the Queen, and they would be "gotten up" in outfits befitting their station.

The 1897 planners again had to fend off the organized opposition of such groups as the Woman's Home Missionary Society of Southern California and the WCTU, which vociferously objected to the masking practice and the drunken revelries of All Fools' Nite. Some journalistic entreaties against the event used All Fools' Nite to question whether or not Los Angeles deserved the title "City of Angels." Perhaps the days of Los Diablos had returned? Such complaints were received both by the Los Angeles City Council and the Fiesta's own Committee on Public Morals. The City Council responded by passing a municipal ordinance prohibiting "the wearing of masks, false whiskers, or otherwise disguising the person" between the hours of 11:30 p.m. and 6:00 a.m. Violators faced jail time or fines (or both). The police decided to enforce order by placing masked officers amidst the rowdies. Clearly the WCTU's vehemence over the matter had everything to do with drunken men's behavior toward women at the Fiesta; the organization decried the actions of men and boys who "grossly insulted and made outrageous advances on the womanhood of Los Angeles."[78] The *Evening Express* offered a rhyming prescription for level-headed behavior:

Sail in for fun
Don't wear a gun,
And to the rash give warning,
Not to get wild
Or be defiled
By a big head in the morning[79]

The 1897 edition went off much like previous La Fiestas. The Indians came again, camping at Second and Vine and using the streetcars to ride to and from the Fiesta grounds where they danced. Angelenos pushed and shoved one another trying to get good vantages to see the dancing. One tourist thought that only a handful of natives understood or knew the traditional dances, and he repeated the supposed truism regarding their sure disappearance from history's stage. "With their death," he wrote, "these dances will have become a tradition to lighten the pages of some future historian."[80]

Fiesta 1897 did not make very much money, at least not for its incorporated self. Receipts tallied just about $150 in the bank, with Fiesta property in the neighborhood of $6,500. Sniping in local papers increased. Maybe Los Angeles could do without an annual Fiesta? Maybe the city had outgrown its "saturnalia" and ought to concentrate instead on a more businesslike convention?[81]

With the close of 1897's Fiesta, the M & M again called a meeting to decide whether the event should continue into the next year. Many favored it, but some objected that the municipal expense was wasted on the celebration and ought be put to better use in civic improvements. It was felt that the Fiesta "demoralized" the studies of the city's schoolchildren, giving them an excuse to skip school and closing each year as it did with the "grand and glorious debauch" of All Fools' Nite. Yet one supporter countered that the Fiesta's balance sheet should consider not the impossible-to-figure bottom line, but rather the utility of "pleasure and education. We live for those things too, don't we?"[82] In the end, planners simply opted not to endorse "All Fools' Nite" at all; better, they thought, to just keep quiet about it.

In the fall of 1897, the Executive Committee decided that yes, there ought to be a Fiesta 1898. The theme would be wrapped around the Gold Rush, marking as it did the fiftieth anniversary of James Marshall's famed and fateful discovery of a gold nugget in John Sutter's millrace. Plans for the event, now scheduled for May, went ahead apace. Again, the worrisome aspects of All Fools' Nite became the focus of concerted action, prompting the City Council to toughen the anti-masking ordinance of the previous year (it was broadened to include certain hours throughout the week-long event).

By early 1898, funding had become a critical problem. Fiesta planners couldn't get the railroad corporations as interested as they had previously been. Postponement seemed the best option. But within a few weeks, by the end of February, optimism had risen anew, and the Committee of Thirty decided to push forward with La Fiesta '98. With only a month to go, the committee felt it necessary to get a pep talk from General Harrison Gray Otis of the *Los Angeles Times*. He came to the Fiesta rooms and addressed the group "on the general features of La Fiesta."[83] Would that there were notes from that address!

Other Fiesta opponents had more fierce objections. The *Porcupine* called the event the "Fiesta Farce," and suggested that it was childish, un-American, even shameful. The *East Side News* concurred: Los Angeles had progressed far enough from its ethnic roots. The Fiesta was unpatriotic. Flirtation with ethnic and racial cultures other than Anglo American had made it so. It should be changed or postponed or even eliminated. The staid Tournament of Roses in nearby Pasadena was a better celebration and more in keeping with Los Angeles' look to the future. Concentrate on that event, Fiesta bashers concluded. La Fiesta de Los Angeles had done its work well; it had advertised the city in a period when such publicity was necessary. Now, at the brink of the new century, the event's roots had proven embarrassing. It was, the editor of a small paper east of the city declared, the "Los Angeles Saturnalia," and "that jaundiced jowl of jack-assery." In short, the color of the city of the future was white, and the sooner the Fiesta organizers recognized and responded to that truism, the better.[84]

One paper continued, not surprisingly, to wave the banner of La Fiesta. The *Los Angeles Times*, by the late 1890s the preeminent paper of the region, had adopted the Fiesta as its own boosterism tool. Harrison Gray Otis of the *Times*, no shrinking violet he, championed the event as very Los Angeles, timely and appropriate. Even if the major rail companies, the Southern Pacific and Santa Fe especially, did not step up to the plate with their usual Fiesta contributions, Otis and his *Times* urged Los Angeles that the Fiesta must go on. He became a driving force behind the event, taking over, at least temporarily, as president of the Committee of Thirty. Needless to say, the support of the *Times*, and its liberal use of ink in the matter, earned the Fiesta the opposition of those papers and those editors in the labor camp.

Labor's reaction to the Fiesta does not seem to have been overtly political; rather, it seems that the *Times*'s support of the event, which clearly by 1897 had its problems, offered newspapers like the *Los Angeles Citizen* the chance to go after Harrison Gray Otis on a new front. This isn't to say that opposition was an empty vessel. On the contrary. As the decision whether to hold an 1898 Fiesta heated up, more voices arose in spirited reaction. Much was made, for instance, of Quaker opposition to La Fiesta, especially when the Friends colony in Whittier (out of which would emerge the young Richard Nixon some years later) condemned the event as "sinful and demoralizing." Such a perspective got further support when the *California Voice* declared the Fiesta a "debauch," representative only of "an effete civilization," immoral, horrible, and of danger to women. The city's Methodist ministers concurred, denouncing La Fiesta in group session.[85]

La Fiesta's supposed "multiculturalism," at least the 1890s version of the concept, did not hold water with the event's opponents. They attacked it for, as they claimed, its tendencies toward race mixing. "The heathen Chinee, Indians and Mexicans are appealed to join in the parade with their heathen, savage and semi-barbarous costumes, implements of war, etc., all of which are far from elevating in their character." If only, the *California Voice* seems to have pleaded, if only Los Angeles could have a good honest Anglo Saxon parade, something other than "this relic of the dark ages." This nod to other groups in the society, in the city, in the state, however mild, however calculated (however controlled!), was too much. Best just to squash, in the words of the good Quakers of Whittier, the "pernicious influence of this spectacular view of an antiquated civilization."[86] "Give us an American Fiesta," declared the *East Side News*.[87]

Then came the all-out attack on La Fiesta. In March 1898, amidst the *Times* assurances that all was copacetic with Fiesta 1898 (dates had been fixed for early May), the *Los Angeles Record* printed a bombshell of a story. Declaring that ninety-eight illegitimate births could be traced directly to All Fools' Nite in 1896, the paper went on record with the sharpest critique of La Fiesta yet. Implicitly associating the event's moral lassitude with outdated and uncivilized (i.e., ethnic) behavior, the paper insisted that the Fiesta had run its course of popularity and importance.[88] The *Times* tried to fight off the wild accusation, essentially pointing out in polite language that if the charge were true, Los Angeles fertility rates would exceed those of any other place on earth. "American girls are not brought up like hot-house plants," the *Times* declared.[89]

*The feeling is too anti-Spanish to enjoy caballeros or señoritas decked
in reds and yellows. It wouldn't surprise us to see the thing hooted
off the streets. The citizenship of this favored section advertise their
incompetency to entertain the public when they stoop to Spanish
models, such as mask carnivals and bull baiting, as on previous
occasions.*

Los Angeles Independent, March 12, 1898

Long before Los Angeles or California embraced Progressivism's initiative and referendum proposals, those electoral innovations that allowed citizens to make their voices heard above the chatter of the privileged, La Fiesta acted as a public referendum. That much is clear simply by the amount of attention it received, not only in the audiences that observed the springtime ritual but in the din surrounding each year's planning (or evaluating) as well. It would of course be too easy to say that La Fiesta operated as a referendum on any single issue or concern. The event crossed too many boundaries for that. It offered simultaneous discussion of any number of things: public drunkenness, monarchical hangovers, ritual, advertising, privilege, the place of the city in the region, etc.

But there's no question that La Fiesta was about race as well, or at least about the place of race and ethnicity in the agreed-upon fictions of regional history. From the parade's Whiggish presentation of floats moving through both space and time, to the ways in which people of color found themselves portrayed on those floats, La Fiesta co-mingled racial triumph and regional identity. Given organized planning that insisted La Fiesta honor so-called Spanish traditions in the region at the expense of the contemporary presence of Mexican people in Los Angeles, something was bound to give as the United States contemplated war with Spain. La Fiesta 1898 died a-borning.

Opposition to the event began to converge from several different vantages by the spring. Moral and religious outrage, especially at the supposed excesses and lack of decorum induced by All Fools' Nite—obviously inflamed by the charges of illegitimate births—made up one line of attack. Local politics ensured that the Fiesta cheerleading performed by Harrison

Gray Otis and the *Los Angeles Times* would provoke a negative response from labor and labor papers. Hinterland papers sniped at the Fiesta as too expensive or too tied to downtown Los Angeles merchants and mercantile ambitions. Atop all this came the rising tensions between the United States and Spain.

Rumors of war obviously created a big problem for Fiesta planners. Having tried to get La Fiesta 1898 onto solid footing, event planners found themselves caught up in a patriotic bind. How could a supposedly Spanish event remain overtly patriotic in the midst of jingoistic anti-Spain thought and behavior? It was one thing to do away with All Fools' Nite, which planners proposed to do (limiting masking to daylight hours), but what of the overall feel of the thing? How could La Fiesta's supposed "Spanish-ness" be seen as anything but the wrong sentiment at the doorstep of war? As a prominent U.S. Army officer offered, La Fiesta "being in name and other ways of Spanish origin makes the celebration especially in bad taste at this time."[90] Ever the critic of the event, the *Colton Chronicle* put that matter more succinctly, managing to take a swipe at La Fiesta's artificiality and patriotic shortcomings in one sentence. "That Los Angeles Fiesta may have to give way to a little real experience with the Spanish."[91]

Possible war between the United States and Spain prompted the postponement of Fiesta planning in late April 1898. The money already subscribed to the event was turned over to the local National Guard brigade, which was just then being outfitted for war. The United States declared war against Spain in late April, just about the time that the annual Fiesta would have taken place.

Fiesta planners and local elites explained their decision to call the event off, and they also took time to review the previous Fiestas. The organizing committee declared "that on account of war with Spain it was impossible to hold the celebration for the reason that the best judgment of all consulted was that a celebration at that time would be inappropriate." "La Fiesta Was Too Spanish," ran a fairly typical headline.[92] Then again, having but $51 in the bank might have had something to do with the postponement. Too, the retreat of the big railroad corporations so critical to the success of previous Fiestas did not help much. The committee suggested that the "moral effect of the refusal of these great corporations . . . produced a most depressing effect." [93]

Organizers figured that holding a celebration that was so self-consciously Spanish (as opposed, needless to say, to Mexican) would be, at best, ironic. At worst, La Fiesta 1898 could be deemed insultingly unpatriotic, what with its tribute to monarchy and Spain. Such "frolic under partially Spanish colors and a Spanish name would be not only ridiculous but an affront to the nation," wrote the editor of *Greater Los Angeles*. The Committee of Thirty felt that the "public mind would not be in harmony with the idea of a celebration, which, by precedent, partook in name and somewhat in character of a Spanish celebration, [and] determined that it would be inappropriate and unadvisable to hold a Fiesta of the usual character under the conditions then existing." Fiesta colors came under attack as un-American; they ought to be replaced with the red, white, and blue. Others felt that the Fiesta's posters and visual publicity were themselves un-American and inappropriate. Some, Harrison Gray Otis among them, thought that the show ought to be turned to overt patriotism (which, actually, it always had been), by restyling it into "La Reina Columbia." But in the end, the decision to donate money to the National Guard was deemed patriotic enough. "Those Fiesta funds will be spent Spanish after all," stated one paper. It probably didn't help matters much when a rumor began to circulate that the Fiesta caballeros (who were most likely about as Spanish as Harrison Gray Otis) had been called up for enemy duty in Havana.[94]

We should not ignore the ways in which patriotism was woven into the event, even into its postponement. Flags and expressions of nationalism had accompanied the various annual Fiestas since 1894; there is little doubt that the carnival met a need for enthusiastic displays of "Americanism," even as those displays were themselves touched with slight features of ethnic or national difference. With war threatened, and eventually arrived, La Fiesta had to respond or disappear. By spring of 1898, some in Los Angeles worried that the city's coastal defenses were not sufficient to repel a foreign assault. Such were the fears induced by affairs in Cuba. La Fiesta could not possibly withstand that kind of environment; not only was the event canceled, but Los Angeles mounted a campaign for a wildly patriotic Fourth of July parade and festival, one that removed allusions to Spain or the Old World. "This cruel war seems to be death to everything Spanish, even in name," was the surmise of the *Fallbrook Observer*.[95]

The Fiesta was likely not the only victim. Some believed that the region's Spanish street names ought to be changed to English. Rumor traffic about such things as the caballeros riding to Spain's aid no doubt offered others the opportunity to make a dig at the region's Latinos. For instance, Chamber of Commerce stalwart W. C. Patterson wrote that the frenzy of life in Southern California in the 1890s had prompted a community-wide need for relief. "As a result of this condition," he pointed out, "and influenced by the tendencies of the Spanish American citizens of Southern California, who are never so mercenary as to forego the opportunity of indulging in a frolic festival or fiesta, the idea was evolved of establishing in Los Angeles an annual affair." La Fiesta was, he said, "a breathing spell" from the hustle and bustle of life in the busy nineties. In other words, the sleepiness of 1830s Mexican Los Angeles, Patterson claimed in this nod to a traditional slur, could yet play a role in the Anglo Saxon city.

The city had put on four consecutive Fiestas, and W. C. Patterson found them each unique, each instructive in its own way, layer after layer of representation, each atop the other. "History, mythology and poetry have been drawn upon most freely for themes, to be represented by floats . . . rendered not only attractive and beautiful, but educational. The system of floats on each occasion represents a certain idea or connected series of ideas. Some of these representations have set many a person to renewed study of the literature of the ages."[96]

La Fiesta 1899 was also canceled, in favor of the Free Harbor Jubilee held in celebration of the federal appropriation to build a harbor in San Pedro. Fiesta officials and leaders loaned various items to the jubilee planners. In March 1899, the Fiesta Association disbanded. The association was in debt, and it had a fire sale of lumber, seats, and other Fiesta accoutrements in order to raise money. It looked as though La Fiesta de Los Angeles had run its course.

Charles Fletcher Lummis, ever a booster and fan of La Fiesta de Los Angeles, had written of the pageant in the mid-1890s that if "by any chance, it should be allowed to die out for a year or two, it would soon again be renewed, for the people would demand it."[97] Lummis was both right and wrong. In the fall of 1900, after a Fiesta hiatus of more than three years, it looked as though the event might be revived. After all, La Fiesta did have its fans. "Los Angeles made a great mistake when she abandoned her fiesta," wrote the *Los Angeles Herald*, "although the brush with Spain rendered its postponement imperative." Should the city bring la Fiesta back?

Yes, supporters believed. But the parade and pageant needed, for a variety of reasons, to look different. The celebration even needed a different name. "La Fiesta de Flores" was the first, grammatically clumsy choice, an event that, like Pasadena's Tournament of Roses, highlighted less the city's past than its floral present. The change, to a "new and improved Fiesta" pleased many, for it promised "to take the place of the old, European, un-American, monarchical affair which died out a few years ago," wrote the *East Side News*. "At last the merchants and business men are coming to their senses. The more sensible and more-American element having cried down and laughed down the medieval, Southern Europe, La Fiesta, with its mock queens and monarchical flummery, the city is now sobered and rational enough to inaugurate a Fair that will do as great credit, stimulate industry and art and benefit all branches of business as much as the fool La Fiesta injured legitimate traffic."[98]

To make the break with the past all the greater, Fiesta de los Flores (they got the name right in short order) lasted only a few days, as opposed to a week.[99] To top it off, they even planned for the visit of a special outside guest: President William McKinley, the man responsible for U.S. involvement in the Spanish American War. The symbolism was not lost on anti-Fiesta papers, who urged the event's organizers not to make McKinley "a side show to a week of bacchanalian festivity, that should have passed out of existence with the passing of Spanish influence in America." In short, it was time for an "American" fiesta as opposed to a "Spanish" event.[100] Thus it was: the *Los Angeles Times* "Fiesta number" of May 1901 utilized "American" themes in its cover. Gone were the Latin, albeit highly stylized, images of the last century. Just a few months shy of assassination, William McKinley did come to Los Angeles for the festival, where flags waved just as much as flowers.

The spring of 1902 saw open ethnic controversy. Apparently in response to unflattering remarks made by Caroline Severance, a prominent woman in Los Angeles civic affairs, a delegation of "Spanish American" women threatened to withdraw from that year's festival. According to the historian Gayle Gullett's thoughtful analysis, Severance, a well-respected women's rights activist and former abolitionist now in her eighties, had painted herself into a corner with comments about race. White women, she said, needed to learn to disregard race in social interaction in favor of respect for "education, character and good breeding." While obviously exchanging racial assumptions for class hierarchies, Severance's comments were nonetheless at least somewhat at the front edge of racial thought and behavior in 1902 Los Angeles. She ran into trouble, though, by pushing her arguments into very touchy racial territory. Why, she wondered, were white Americans so quick to draw the racial line between black and white when they interacted socially or otherwise with "representatives of other dark races," including "Spanish, Italian, East Indian, etc."?

At this, *Californio* women took great offense. Who did Caroline Severance think she was? How dare she call them black? As Gullett describes their angry response: "They were not white, as were Anglo-Saxons, but neither were they dark in the same sense as working-class Mexicans, Indians, or African Americans." "The Color Line Invades Fiesta" ran the headline in the *Los Angeles Times*. But of course it had always been part there, in precisely the terms that the Severance controversy had revealed. Racial and ethnic categories were all about history and hierarchy out here in the Far West, and being "white" or "Spanish" or "Mexican" mattered a great deal. All this had perhaps previously been expressed a bit more subtly or politely, or feebly disguised as playful fun. Convinced that the presence of "Spanish American" ties to the past were critical to not only the Fiesta but, by extension, regional understandings of race and racial hierarchy, the *Times* and Fiesta organizers convinced the *Californio* women to participate in the 1902 parade. But the parade was dying, and local controversy that struck at the heart of the event's assumptions could not have helped matters much.[101]

In the twentieth century, the city held intermittent Fiestas de Las Flores, up through the years of the Depression. While these flower festivals were popular, along with the increasingly popular Tournament of Roses, no celebration or pageant in the twentieth century matched the crowds and exuberance of the Fiestas of the late 1890s. Gone were those earlier days that saw

The City Fathers using all their power
To bring the past within the present hour
That their fair proteges might plainly see
The things that are, and things that used to be[102]

La Fiesta de Los Angeles, an important feature of the city's growth and increasing sense of identity, had done its work. As an icon in the invention of regional tradition, the ambitious spectacle urged Angelenos to think certain ways about the past and its inevitable transitions. Along the way, the event proved to be a brilliant advertising stroke, boosting the city it simultaneously explained. That part of the explaining had everything to do with interpreting the Mexican history of Los Angeles cannot be denied. In the events ordered, even militarized movement through the streets and crowds of excited observers, La Fiesta offered pedagogical insights to those who would pay attention.

Within less than twenty years of its founding, La Fiesta would be the model for another fascinating and iconic cultural phenomenon in the region, John Steven McGroarty's famed *Mission Play*. But that is getting ahead of the story. In chapter 3, our examination of the rise of Anglo Los Angeles focuses on an environmental subject, one that runs through the very heart of the city. We turn to the Los Angeles River and the role it plays in regional memory. At the same time, we consider the role regional memory plays in the life and times of the river itself.

THREE

Remembering a River

I went to the River Station for an hour, and crossed over into the dirt
and grime of Mexican Los Angeles.

G. BROMLEY OXNAM, diary entry, Los Angeles, 1913

No scientist will quarrel with [the] belief that the experiment in
Southern California will work out to the benefit of the Saxon.

CHARLES FLETCHER LUMMIS, 1896[1]

The Los Angeles River is best known by historians of California and
the general public for its great floods.

Los Angeles River Pollution Committee Report, 1949[2]

walkin' along by the l.a. river
stepping on broken glass, kicking cans
she's tellin' me i don't even know her
i guess there's some things i won't understand
i'd love to float away like old tom sawyer
i'd love to run away and be huck finn
poor river
empty river

E., "l.a. river," 1993[3]

In 1906, a Los Angeles settlement house worker named Amanda Mathews Chase published a book of stories about Mexicans called *The Hieroglyphics of Love: Stories of Sonoratown and Old Mexico*. She dedicated the little volume to her settlement house colleagues, offering that it was made up of sentimental tales of "the Mexican peonada . . . a dark and lowly people, who are yet rich with the riches of the poor, and wise with the wisdom of the simple."

Amanda Mathews Chase liked metaphors about Los Angeles Mexicans. She returned again and again in the book's stories to one in particular: water. The people in her stories lived close to water, down at the edge of the Los Angeles River. Within sight of Los Angeles, "a handsome, bustling, modern city," their neighborhood existed in a world apart: "dirty, peaceful, unprogressive." In Chase's eyes, the city's Mexican residents not only lived near water, they moved like water. Even one of her official reports as home teacher working with the Mexican families down near the river utilized watery images. She referred to a class of Mexican women (prior to instruction) as "a timid, sloppy, baby-submerged lot." It was clear from all these metaphors sailing by that Amanda Chase expected Mexicans to know about water, especially about the Los Angeles River, its courses, its movements. The river's temperament had become their own. It is as if the book's Mexicans were water themselves: elemental, each individual but a "drift from the tide of cheap Mexican labor . . . a tide which seeps continually through the ruinous adobe tenements of 'Sonoratown.' "[4]

Chase's naturalization of Mexicans as "river people" runs throughout the entire book. A woman in a story spoke in a "sluggish but endless current of conversation" that her husband—of course named Juan Garcia—"was not interested in damming," because he was lazy and drunk. The watery repetition flows on. "Señora Garcia would have liked to argue the matter further, and had quite a notion insisting on Teodota's giving up the paper, but there was no anchoring her conversational bark. She floated on to relating how the rats once ate the rent receipt, and before one could learn whether she had been obliged to pay the rent over again, she was adrift on Teodota's father's aunt's fear of the unpleasant rodents, and the paper was left far behind."[5] Rats and water. Was this Mexican Los Angeles?

Adrift in liquid inertia, the "old Mexican life" down at river's edge threatened to be "overflowed by the tide of American progress." One man in an Amanda Chase story even seeks an escape in the river. In doing so, Juan Gallardo changes the Los Angeles River, and he becomes one with it: "Juan turned in the direction of the river, thus giving time for escape. He was merely acting in unwilling obedience to a habit grown too strong for him.

The separate acts of unselfishness, the daily and hourly cherishing of his sulky little mistress, had dammed the current of his selfish passion and turned it into a new channel of loving."[6]

This chapter is an exploration not so much of metaphorical connections between people and water, Mexicans and the Los Angeles River, but about other, similar sorts of associations made by Anglo Los Angeles. "Remembering a River" is about "new channels," not so much of loving, but of the river itself, about its startling transformation from nineteenth-century stream to twentieth-century flood control device. Amanda Mathews Chase thought and wrote about Los Angeles Mexicans and a kind of curious ethnic affinity with the river. In doing so, she revealed ethnocentric patterns of belief that characterized Mexicans as primitive, close to nature. This in turn led to a perception that Chase turned into metaphor, of Mexicans having particular and proximate knowledge of the Los Angeles River. It would seem as if she was not alone in her thinking.[7] But that is getting slightly ahead of the Los Angeles River story. To understand dimensions of ethnicity and water, we have to start well before 1906, before Amanda Mathews Chase, before any "hieroglyphics of love."

THE RIVER AT THE CITY'S HEART

Were it not for the Los Angeles River, the city that shares its name would not be where it is today. Were it not for the Los Angeles River, Los Angeles would not *be* at all. The Los Angeles River has always been at the heart of whichever human community is in the basin: Gabrielino village, Spanish outpost, Mexican pueblo, American city. The river has been asked to play many roles. It has supplied the residents of the city and basin with water to drink and spread amidst their grapes, oranges, and other crops. It has been an instrument by which people could locate themselves on the landscape. It has been a critical dividing line, not only between east and west, north and south, but between races, classes, neighborhoods. As this chapter will explore in some depth, the river has also been a place where ideas and beliefs about the past, present, and future of Los Angeles have been raised and contested.

> Here where the river gently winds through the girdle of hills, lies a soil so saturated with the past that however far back the mind roams one can never detach it from its human background. . . . It is always there, quiet and unobtrusive, like a great artery running through the human body.[8]

Pulled from the pages of Henry Miller's *Tropic of Cancer*, this requiem describes the soil around every river as much as it does that of the novelist's beloved Seine. Believe it or not, it also conjures up the Los Angeles River. Rivers are saturated with the past. They can *tell* stories as much as they can *be* characters in stories if listened to and studied carefully enough. What is especially significant is that rivers can reveal as much about cultural transitions and cultural conflicts as about economic, landscape, or political change. The puny Los Angeles River, so unlike the noble Seine, is also a river in which human memory mingles with water. It is a river all about memory, a place where nature and culture surely flow together.

Ask Southern California residents today about the Los Angeles River, and the response may well be quizzical. "What Los Angeles River?" As a river, the Los Angeles River is an inside joke, an urban legend. It is something that supposedly once *was* but rarely *is*, something that can be dismissed with cynical humor (or, as in the case of a recent ad for Nike outdoor climbing gear that made use of an image of the river as an entirely dry industrial site, attached to hip, wry commercialism).[9]

There are good reasons for jokes. The river really isn't much of a river anymore, and it hasn't been so for a long time. It still has water, it still has flora and fauna, it can still drown the unfortunate or careless, the drunk, the young, or the unwary.[10] But instead of a river, the Los Angeles River is now a gray channel, concrete-lined at both sides and bottom, a sad ghost that, wrote Lawrence Clark Powell, "no one would dignify with the name river."[11] The Los Angeles River is today more flood control instrument than river, victim of a century-long "fluvial lobotomy."[12] The Los Angeles River is a mechanized, cold river, held firmly in place by concrete and engineering logic.

This channel river is of course a human invention. Socially constructed and physically engineered, it is, however, no less historically significant for supposedly no longer *being* a river than it was *as* a river many years ago. A once-river can be important. As seeming proof of its non-river status, local politicians, usually City Council members or county supervisors anxious to make the papers, rise up every once in a while with an argument that the river, precisely because it isn't a river, really ought to be a freeway. That would solve the Los Angeles basin's overcrowded roadway problem, they say. After all, city bus drivers do practice in it.[13]

Just over two hundred years ago, there was the river without Spanish or English name. With headwaters twelve miles northwest of present-day downtown Los Angeles, the Los Angeles River is historically a lovely, if

Figure 17. The river that was: The Los Angeles River, late nineteenth century. Courtesy of the Huntington Library, San Marino, California.

small, river. Alternately above and below ground until just north of Cahuenga Pass, where it pops up above ground, the river gathers strength and direction as it meanders southeast. Near where Glendale, once Riverdale, is today, the river turns to the south and runs east of present-day Dodger Stadium through Elysian Gap. Just below where Elysian Park is today, the river once made a graceful, lazy S-curve before straightening out in its final stretch to the Pacific Ocean. The river's entire course is about fifty miles. Once, almost before human memory records, it flowed far west of its current concrete bed, which now takes it through one of the city's most glaring deindustrialized shells out back of Union Station.

Juan Crespi, the diarist of the late eighteenth-century Portolá expedition, made certain to note the river's delights. In the late summer of 1769, walking to a point somewhere near where the Pasadena Freeway approaches downtown today, Crespi and party stumbled onto the little river. "We set out from the valley in the morning and followed the same plain in a westerly direction," he wrote. "After traveling about a league and a half through a pass between low hills, we encountered a very spacious valley, well grown with cottonwoods and alders, among which ran a beautiful river from the

Figure 18. The Los Angeles River flowing next to the Elysian Hills, late nineteenth century. Courtesy of the Huntington Library, San Marino, California.

north-northwest, and then, doubling the point of a steep hill, it went on afterwards to the south. . . . We halted not very far from river, which we named Porciuncula. . . . This plain where the river runs is very extensive. It has good land for planting all kinds of grain and seeds, and is the most suitable site of all that we have seen for a mission, for it has all the requisites for a large settlement."

Such an idyll had attracted others well before the colonists, people who doubtless had a name for the beautiful little river. As Crespi and party reached the river's banks, "about eight heathen from a good village came to visit us; they live in this delightful place among the trees on the river."[14] The encounter proved peaceful. Gifts were exchanged, and the Indians blew smoke in the faces of the Spaniards, a gesture of friendliness. Crespi's diary indicates that the land surrounding the river was rich and fertile, and he was careful to note several times that grains and other produce would grow in abundance with but a little concerted labor.

A decade later, acting on information like that supplied by Juan Crespi, the Spanish governor of the Californias, Felipe de Neve, decided to build a pueblo on the Porciuncula. This was in part to establish a beachhead southern settlement to support nearby San Gabriel Mission (Mission San Fernando would be established not long after the 1781 founding of Los Angeles). The region promised agricultural and, as important, livestock potential, for as de Neve noted to his superiors, the river had "much water easy to take on either bank and beautiful lands in which it all could be made use of."[15]

Made use of it was. The tiny pueblo, adopting a longer version of the river's name and sacred commemoration, came into being. The river, of course, was a crucial component of the city's growth and early prosperity. Though not navigable, it proved a mostly reliable and convenient water source. Untapped by many wells, the river ran far fuller than it does today. Wandering Frenchman Auguste Bernard Duhaut-Cilly noted in the late 1820s that the tiny pueblo of Los Angeles, then comprised of eighty-two houses, had been built along the banks of a river "which does not run dry in summer."[16] It flooded now and again, or "boomed" as people remembered, but the landscape and the common sense of the people helped mitigate the inherent dangers of wintertime floods. Settlers generally built, if they moved away from the central plaza at all, on slightly higher ground flanking the river. Anglo arrivals would wonder, in later years, why the region's Indians and Mexicans did not live on the rich land at the river's edge. They would find out when floods came.

The area that would become Boyle Heights, just east of the river, became a bit more crowded with adobes after the floods of the 1820s. But topography and vegetation helped to blunt flood impacts. The water had to fight its way through thick brush and trees in the marshy flatlands or *la cienaga*. In those days, the river rarely made it all the way to the Pacific. It petered out somewhere west and south of the little pueblo in the countless tule marshes and ponds of the grizzly bear's terrain.

Where the river did run, near the plaza and to the north, it occupied a vital role in village life and folkways. Women took washing to water's edge and, using large flat stones, beat and rubbed clothes clean. Families chose traditional locations against the riverbank reserved for their use, and it was frowned upon to encroach. Children swam in the river as it flowed not far from the plaza. It was here, in the river or its irrigation canal tributary, the *zanja madre*, that residents observed the annual "Bath of the Virgins" (*El Bano del las Virjines*) ceremony to honor San Juan. Some Anglos, by folk tradition at least, thought little of the ceremony except as an opportunity to tease the adolescent girls who, dressed in white, took part in ritual bathing.[17] The centrality of the river for emergent Anglo culture and economy was better represented in Abel Stearns's mill, built in the 1840s to grind local grain by river power.[18] Sometime shortly thereafter, a waterwheel was built in the dammed-up river waters not far from Stearns's mill; the wheel buckets dumped water into the tributary *zanja* so that irrigation could take place at some distance from the river itself.[19]

In those days everyone noticed the river. It was a prominent feature of the landscape and, unlike today, it occupied a critical place in the region's cartography as a virtual compass helping to define direction on the basin landscape. Reading early Los Angeles descriptions, one is struck by the repetitive presence of two critical directional landmarks, both long since deemphasized in the modern city: the plaza—long ago the city center—and the river. One went out from, or into, the plaza, and one went across, up, or down the river.[20]

Buildings, homes, plots of land were on this side of the river or that. People lived on the east side or the west side. Travelers went up the river toward the San Fernando Valley or down the river toward the ocean. For late nineteenth-century residents in the village proper, the Poor House loomed just across the river, as did the City Orphanage. Here, too, on the banks of the river, occurred one of the most important battles of the Mexican War period, as Kit Carson and his ragtag body of soldiers defeated Mexican troops in the January 1847 "Battle of the Mesa." The school for Mexican kids was upriver, and the children trudged to it by following or, depending on the season, walking in the riverbed.

The Los Angeles River was the sole source of city water, either the river itself or one of its tributary *zanjas* dug out by Indian or Mexican labor. Women made daily visits to the river to fill clay *ollas*. A man with a heavy water jug resting in a wheeled cart or suspended from the handles sold river water on the streets and doorsteps of the growing village.

Everyone noticed the river. Coming overland in the Gold Rush years, Vincent Hoover made careful diary entries in his tiny leather-bound books. Entering Los Angeles along the same route taken by Portolá seventy years earlier, Hoover wrote: "Los Angeles is Situated on the river of that name and contains about 1500 inhabitants. The town is built of adobe houses and irregularly laid out. There are quite a number of American residents nearly all of which are married to Spanish women."[21]

James Clarke also knew this river, and he made sure to orient himself in reference to it in letters to family members. In an 1854 letter to his brother, Clarke explained his whereabouts by drawing a word-picture of mountains, valleys, and waterway grids. "Our valley is from 30 to 40 miles long opening to the Pacific between two high bluffs or mountain spurs fifteen miles apart on the very beach, and running back so as to make the valley from 25 to 30 miles wide which is watered by the two rivers of Los Angeles and San Gabriel and by these rivers the valley is irrigated[,] ditches or *zanjas* conducting the water all through the vineyards and fields."[22]

By mid-century, the government of the United States had glanced upon the Los Angeles River basin with a gaze more covetous, and more powerful, than that of any individual American settler. Even in the earliest years of California statehood, federal agents and actors knew that a river basin meant more than water, more than agricultural promise. Valley floors—level and straight—could provide the setting for a more ambitious wish for the region, the railroad. Engineer and surveyor Albert Campbell noted the possibilities of the region in a report of 1853–1854, part of the much larger federal survey of possible transcontinental rail routes: "From El Monte, passing a few hills, we enter the valley of Los Angeles. The stream upon which it is situated is about fifty yards wide and two feet deep. There were numerous acequias irrigating vineyards, orange and olive groves, peach orchards, gardens, and corn fields."

The little town of five thousand inhabitants "had the sombre cast of a Spanish pueblo, relieved, as it were, by innovations of American comforts," Campbell noted. But already, a portent of the future, there "was the bustle and activity of a business place. Many new houses were in process of construction. Everywhere was indicated a thriving population and a land of intrinsic wealth."[23]

Making the river a critical part of the landscape made sense in the early days of the little village's history. Local knowledge, based on lived experience in the Los Angeles basin, incorporated the river into the rhythms of everyday life. Indeed, the river was omnipresent. Los Angeles needed no more water than the river could provide, and it was an especially prominent landscape feature along with other local markers such as the Pacific Ocean or the San Gabriel Mountains.[24]

As late as the mid-1850s, even legal descriptions of property reveal a localized culture dependent on time-honored tradition, tradition clearly, if wishfully, expecting the river as a constant. Property boundaries often utilized the river as a fixed feature of the landscape, as in this description from the pages of the *Los Angeles Star* of a small lot not far from the plaza: "One lot of land situate in the eastern part of the city of Los Angeles, facing on a road that runs in front of the lands of Manuel Coronel, and on to the river of Los Angeles, bounded on the north-east by the land of Francisco Ruiz. . . ."[25]

The legal grid of the village itself included the following directional sequence: "fifty yards up the Los Angeles River from the city dam, then a line drawn east 200 yards, thence south to the lands known as Felis Gallardo's, then southwest (following the garden of John Temple) to the streets of William Wolfskill, south to the lands of Don Coronel, northwest to the road of San Pedro, which will exit at the garden of Antonio Lugo, thence following that direction to the corner at Eighth and Principal streets, on to block 30, all said to include the hill of Ft. Moore, both city cemeteries, the spring of the college, the foot of the mountain at the dam, and the bank of the Los Angeles River." The four square leagues thus entailed were to remain, supposedly, the city's definition in perpetuity. These boundaries were themselves dependent on the perpetuity and stability of the Los Angeles River.[26]

While these were no doubt legible methods of marking property and boundary, rivers are hardly reliable as fixed entities. They move irregularly. Or they stop moving altogether. The Los Angeles River has been no exception. Henrique Abila, testifying in a land claim dispute in 1869, commented on just this tendency. The disputed lands, marked off on an old hand-drawn map, or *diseño*, through reference to rock or tree landmarks, could still be discerned. But the river had fallen down on the job: "the springs have diminished in size, shortened in or disappeared altogether, attributable to the change of course of the river Los Angeles."[27]

The "change of course of the river Los Angeles" is of great importance in the history of the region. For if rivers can have moods, can be temperamental, then the Los Angeles River has proved the moodiest of all rivers in Southern California: one year overflowing in seeming fury, the next becoming desperately dry. Periodic flooding of the major rivers of the Los Angeles basin (the Los Angeles, the San Gabriel, and the Santa Ana) once meant little in terms of damage or danger. Topography, sparse settlements, and native experience with local rivers all combined to allay flooding problems of dire seriousness.

Those patterns began to change as the basin changed. Floods and rains and droughts have long been part of the climatological features of this part of Southern California. Boosters used to boast that Anglo agricultural prowess would eliminate drought (as in "rain follows the plow" assurances), and engineers used to argue that they could eliminate floods. Seldom are such claims heard today. A table of Los Angeles River flooding throughout the nineteenth century reads, if not like clockwork, at least like inevitability. One authority has argued that, square mile for square mile, the Los Angeles basin is the most susceptible region of the nation as far as dangerous floods are concerned.[28] As early Los Angeles basin resident Sarah Bixby, whose pioneering uncle tried to coax the Los Angeles River into a defined bed, noted, the Los Angeles River was really two rivers: one in summer and fall, another in winter and spring.[29] Tourists wanted to call the region's rivers "streams bottom side up," but that description would be found wanting every other February or so.

A great flood will occur in the Los Angeles area once every one hundred years. Or so statistical probability suggests. A large flood will occur six times more frequently. Moderate floods will strike once every ten years or so. In 1815 and again in 1822 and 1825, rains and floods proved so severe as to alter fundamentally the location of the Los Angeles River on the landscape. Where it once flowed out toward the marshy flatlands surrounding Ballona Creek, and thence indirectly to the ocean, it now answered to a new geography. Picked up by ferocious floods, the river moved from along Alameda Street in front of where Union Station now stands to an angled course heading more directly south. Waters inundated the plaza, and Indian wickiups from the nearby village floated away.[30] Undaunted by the possibilities that the river might someday return to its old channels, some village residents blithely erected buildings and roads in one of the former beds. The nighttime 1825 flood came with such a terrifying roar that people dashed from their homes and ran into what hills they could find nearby. After this great flood, residents later remembered, the only thing that could be seen standing above the new downtown Los Angeles lake created by the floodwaters was a lone, giant sycamore tree. Don Jose del Carmen Lugo, scion of the ranching Lugo family, remembered years later that the river near his family's house had become "a sea of water . . . running with great violence, making enormous waves." The 1825 flood scarred the landscape so much that its paths could still be seen nearly fifty years later.[31]

Later floods moved the river less but did more damage to human habits and habitats. Eulalia Perez, a Mexican woman who would later be celebrated by astonished Anglos as the oldest inhabitant of the Los Angeles basin—some claimed that she was well into her thirteenth decade by the 1880s—remembered the floods of the winter of 1833. Rising rivers in the basin became impassable, she recalled, and for weeks people on one side of the river were prevented from crossing over to friends and family on the other.[32] Years later, the winters of 1859–1860 and 1861–1862 brought heavy flooding (the latter saw rain of nearly thirty days straight), so much so that street corners in the village overflowed and became impassable. First came water, then came the mud. One resident recalled looking out a window in

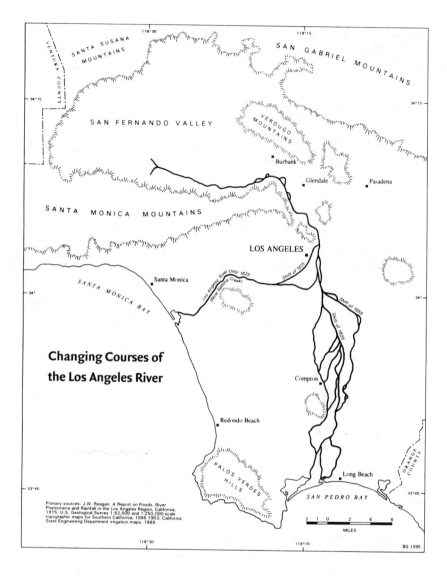

Map 2. Los Angeles River, stream flow over time. Courtesy of Blake Gumprecht.

downtown Los Angeles and thinking that the streets, caked in a thick, greenish mud, were laid in glass. The 1861–1862 floods—"the Noachian deluge," a later engineer called them—created a lake stretching from Ballona to the Laguna ranch (now taken up by the city of Commerce) that covered nearly twelve miles. "It seems incredible . . . to those who have seen year after year the expanse of sand which we call a river," a prominent city resident remembered years later, "but on this Christmas day it was a torrent." One holiday affair on the west side of the river was in danger of failure until a "Sonorean" named Jesus was impressed into duty, swimming across the swollen river to the east side to claim party provisions. Even then, Anglo opinion, it seemed, was that Mexicans *knew* the river, and they didn't hesitate to put them to the test, death-defying though it may have been.[33]

In 1867–1868, the Los Angeles River again changed course, moving boldly into Louis Willhardt's grapes in the flatlands and wiping out the orchards of neighbor Thomas Jefferson White. Residents cut down some of White's trees in a hurried attempt to turn the river away from the Whites' brick house. It worked, but houses did float that year, ripped from flimsy foundations by waters cresting three and four feet on Alameda Street. The little city dam laid against the river near the plaza washed away, and citizens were forced to return to the old method of water delivery by cart and *olla*.

Floods returned in the mid-1870s. By the 1880s, it had become commonplace to hear warnings about building homes against the river's banks or, even, in the river itself, as a few people stubbornly persisted in doing. Yet there were Angelenos who paid little heed.[34] Wrote Alfred Moore, in a burst of fateful hubris and poor memory in 1882, "I have lived on the Aliso tract, the most central part, for the past eight years, and never saw a flood yet." This same confident man congratulated one woman for her "pluck" in building a home within a few feet of the river. He also gave a good word to a Mrs. Bigelow on buying, building, and improving her properties amidst the orange groves on First Street, awfully near the river. "We need not," Moore concluded, "feel at all alarmed about a flood."[35]

Fate enjoyed the temptation. The winters of 1884 and 1886 brought floods as damaging as residents could remember. The river flooded with an "ungovernable fury." The *Los Angeles Times* devoted a special extra ("2:45 O'Clock P.M.") edition to the floods of February 1884, with a sort of sonnet running down the entire left side of the front page.

The Flood. Los Angeles River Leaps its Banks, Sending Down a Mad Current of Water, Sweeping Away Bridges and Houses, Deluging the Lower Portion of the City, Destroying Human Life and Property, And Rendering One Hundred Families Homeless. . . . [36]

Whole vineyards washed away in the flatlands, where the river stretched to nine hundred feet wide. Horses drowned as unwise owners tried to ford

Figure 19. The Los Angeles River in flood, 1880s. Courtesy of the Huntington Library, San Marino, California.

buggies across watery streets. "The river is utterly uncontrollable," warned the Los Angeles *Express*.[37] Milkman George Stoltz drowned in the river's tributary stream, the Arroyo Seco, which ran from Pasadena toward downtown Los Angeles. J. J. Phillips, who ran a laundry establishment at the river's banks, watched helplessly as first his business and then his house dipped into the torrent and floated away. Dr. J. P. Widney's house on Sansevain Street, recently built at a cost of $2,000, fell victim to the rushing water. Most of the newly homeless were poor. Some of their houses had been built in the riverbed itself. Concepción Parra lost her house and all its furniture. Perdona Coma, one of those whose house was unaccountably in the riverbed itself, lost (miraculously enough) only her bed. The extended Diaz and Zernal families, tied together by marriage, were not so fortunate. They watched their houses and everything inside of them wash away.

Men labored to stem the tide of the river by hastily stacking sandbags at the junction of the river and First Street. Alfred Moore, who had with such confidence insisted two years earlier that Angelenos need not fear any floods, lost his Aliso tract house and all his possessions. So did his son and his son-in-law. Mrs. Bigelow's cottages facing First Street had to be evacuated, and the trees in her orange grove swayed under the pressure of the floodwaters.

A forty-year-old adobe, once a part of the Ramirez rancho but now on the estate of land baron Matthew Keller, melted and drizzled into the

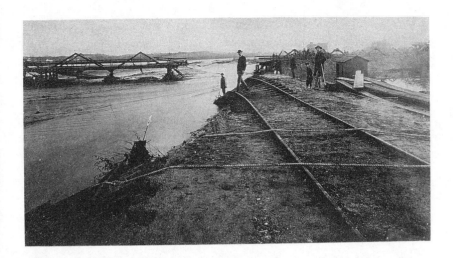

Figure 20. Flood damage in the 1880s. Courtesy of the Huntington Library, San Marino, California.

floodwaters. The East Los Angeles bridge, full of as many as two hundred curious onlookers, shuddered and then fell into the churning river below. No one knew if all had jumped clear. Water covered the valley stretching from Boyle Heights to the plaza, where it stayed for weeks. The ground was so wet, locals said, that it would "bog a saddle blanket." Receding floodwaters left all manner of debris and silt scattered across the landscape, amidst the battered orchards and orange groves below Alameda Street.

When the floodwaters finally receded, public debate over how to "conduct the Los Angeles River through our city when it gets on a bender" accelerated. Plans to reinforce the riverbank with a series of levees went forward. Downtown streets were graded and scraped clean; workers and horses then pushed and pulled the piles of dirt and debris up against the riverbank. Some thought that the effort could be carried further, with the construction of willow brush-nets. "While there is but little water in the river it can be done," wrote one citizen to the *Los Angeles Times* in December 1885, "as no one knows but it may be a dreadful river again before the ides of March come around."[38]

The dreaded floods did come. Within weeks of the dire warning, and well before the Ides, the rising river produced familiar scenes of havoc. Downtown Los Angeles slipped beneath the waters, as did railroad and trolley tracks, hills, trees, and people. The river looked to one observer like a "boiling yellow lake." Lawman Martin Aguirre became a hero by wading into the rushing waters to save two men trapped in a streetcar teetering on a broken bridge. He then spent the whole day of January 19 going back into the river over and over again to rescue a grand total of nineteen people trapped one way or another in the raging waters.[39]

In 1889, floods carried stones of twenty-five pounds and more into the streets of downtown Los Angeles; boulders weighing as much as *twenty tons* began answering gravity's call in the San Gabriel Mountains. Rainfall from high up in the foothills raced in minutes to the valley floor. Dogs in the city pound drowned in their cages. Bridges snapped and floated downstream. Wood from high in the San Gabriels and Santa Monicas came down with the floodwaters, choking farmlands but providing easy-to-gather fuel for months and months. In the aftermath, various property loss cases went to court. In one important decision, Judge Matthew Allen ruled that Los Angeles River floods resulted from the whims of the Almighty, not the capriciousness of any locals or their planning decisions.[40]

Farmers never knew what to expect from periodic flooding. On the plus side, any good-sized flood promised a pay-off in driftwood and fertilizer. Receding floodwaters always left behind tons and tons of alluvial silt, so rich in nutrients that crop production and land values increased overnight. But floods too strong could destroy a lifetime's work. One local resident remembered one season's heavy floods because he had never seen so many unusual things in the river: whole stacks of hay, entire fields of pumpkins, chicken houses, plows, horses, pigs, and cattle, houses, and barns.[41]

Yet despite these problems, new arrivals, encouraged by booster rhetoric, happily figured the Los Angeles River—or a placid version of that river— into visions of the future. Because of its reliability as a water source, the river promised to help Americans embrace what was once a foreign land. They could use the river to claim the region. For the river basin was, one self-congratulatory pamphlet gloated, "peculiarly adapted for farming operations by the Anglo-Saxon race."[42] Boom period maps inevitably characterize the river as a large and peaceful, centralized feature of the landscape, always beautiful, full, and graceful. A representative lithographic depiction of the river from the volatile 1880s shows it as a lovely ribbon of white across and through the center of the city. "The Los Angeles River has been more fully utilized than any other," a booster pamphlet declared in 1876, "and yet there is still plenty for all."[43]

The river proved immensely useful, not merely as a source of water. For one thing, the riverbed had a seemingly endless supply of gravel, and gravel could be hauled out for construction use or for dumping into city streets

Map 3. Bird's-eye view of Los Angeles. Note the peaceful ribbon of the Los Angeles River in the background.

to combat knee-deep wintertime mud. Then too, the river, like any river, made a terrific conduit for carrying things away even during nonflood seasons. People took advantage of this, and they saw the Los Angeles River as an ideal sewer. Early Los Angeles sewers emptied straight into the river and adjacent dry beds amidst the abandoned vineyards of earlier times near Winston and Los Angeles Streets. If rains and the river cooperated, the refuse was carried downstream beyond offense (the city would not build an ocean outfall until 1893–1894). As late as the late 1880s, citizens suggested that the best sewer plans for the expanding city must consider utilizing the convenient, almost intestinal, Los Angeles River. "The river runs directly through the city from end to end, much as the Thames runs through London, or the Seine through Paris, the Spree through Berlin, the Danube through Vienna, the Tiber through Rome, and as the Euphrates ran through Babylon," offered the writer "Cosmopolitan" in a letter to the *Los Angeles Times*. As such, the river was "the natural and proper outlet for the sewage of Los Angeles city." Downstream residents ought to have little complaint with what the river brought their way, nor could they expect the city to build "a new river of brick" in order to control the river's outflow.[44]

Locals used the river as a convenient trash dump (the city dump itself was at river's edge), tossing in not only the daily refuse of the living, but the bodies of countless dead horses and dogs, picked up off the streets and thrown unceremoniously into the riverbed to await decomposition and enough current to travel downstream. An 1887 stable fire, for instance, killed eighty horses. All were dumped, "to putrify and breed typhoid fever," in the riverbed.[45] The local *zanjas* had protective laws that supposedly kept people from washing or throwing refuse in them, or from slaughtering cattle and pigs in or near them. The river offered the obvious and convenient alternative. "The carcasses of all dead animals," reported the U.S. Census for 1880, "are taken to the river-bed south of the city and there buried in the sand." Garbage, ashes, street sweepings, manufacturing wastes: all were likewise dumped into the riverbed.[46] More prosaic activities continued as well, events that observers inevitably filtered through cultural lenses. An 1890s visitor to the city, for instance, appreciated the aesthetics that poverty, more than likely ethnic poverty, presented. As he noted, "mid-stream, in the Los Angeles river, I saw women washing clothes by beating and wringing them; a picturesque scene."[47]

But such romanticizing required a distanced view. The closer one got to the river, the less picturesque its denizens and their actions became in the eyes of observers. Before long, the river became known as a place of bad smells and bad people, a place where, Anglos expected and insisted, crooks, Mexicans, Indians, and Chinese congregated. Sonoratown, "Nigger Alley," and the first Chinatown were all not far from water's edge. Long before Mulholland Drive became known as a place to drop off murder victims, the Los Angeles River and its *zanjas* seem to have been favored locales.[48] Prostitutes loitered down near the river; boys smoked cigarettes and gambled at water's edge. Worried citizens wondered what else could be going on in the deep underbrush at the river's banks. During the infamous siege of Chinatown in the 1870s, the first Chinese man to be lynched by the crowd had been plucked from the river's bank, where he had tried to hide unsuccessfully amongst the thick willows.[49] In the 1880s, a group of fifteen to twenty teenaged and younger boys and girls passed the time down at the river and its bridges, apparently "playing hoodlum" in those same willows, much to the consternation of adults.[50]

As Los Angeles grew, particularly in the boom years after transcontinental railroad connection, the river began to occupy a more important, if increasingly troubling, role in city planning. Uncomfortable with the ways in which the river attracted garbage and "the dangerous classes," city officials began to tie the river more and more to nascent city beautiful efforts, efforts that would find full flower, at least in the imagination, in the new century. In the late 1880s, with the increase in regional rail service, the city and the railroad companies began to construct more bridges and viaducts that spanned the river from various downtown streets. The increase in river vistas further encouraged the city to clean the river up. By 1890, the viaduct on First Street, over which the local cable railway ran, became a favored Sunday promenade for strollers wandering into the city from Boyle Heights or vice versa.

Yet the river continued to be a problem every wet winter. It spilled over its flimsy bank, water rushed through the streets of downtown, and storm sewers and drains backed up. "I thought we would be taken off our feet by the mad rush of water down the gutters and streets," a nervous tourist wrote near century's end of his experiences on a February morning.[51]

Locked in a tempestuous battle over where to put, or even build, a union railroad station, some planners suggested that the riverbed might make a possible, though expensive (not to mention dangerous!) location.[52] More important, the river had become a critical dividing line for a new feature on the urban landscape: industry. By the early years of the twentieth century, the "river beautiful" competed with the "river industrial." Once the orange groves and vineyards of earlier years began to fade away, the river lowlands began to look better and better for nascent Los Angeles industries and, as it had for years, railroad corporations. In the various industrial zoning ordinances adopted from 1908 forward (the first of their kind in the nation), the Los Angeles River helped to delineate industrial sites from nonindustrial sites. Where the river had once been key to describing the boundaries of the city itself, it now helped to break the city up into industrial parcels. For instance, city ordinance 17135 declared that "Industrial District No. 1" would include the following perimeter sequences: "northwesterly along the center line of Buena Vista street to its intersection with the center line of the official bed of the Los Angeles River; thence southerly along the center line of the official bed of the Los Angeles River as defined by Ordinance No. 6035. . . ."[53] In short, the river had a newer cartographic role to play once the twentieth century arrived, one which helped further divide Los Angeles into specific ethnic and class spaces.[54] "I went to the River Station for an hour," social reformer G. Bromley Oxnam wrote in his diary in 1913, "and crossed over into the dirt and grime of Mexican Los Angeles."[55]

With the arrival of the new century, various city officials and reformers throughout the Los Angeles basin grew increasingly concerned about the large numbers of Mexican laborers who had begun to live in *colonias* on riverbed lands. Pushed to these cheap lands by patterns of land use, segregation, and poverty, Mexicans eked out lives "hidden," as one official put it in 1918, "out of sight in the brush."[56]

Zoning ordinances reveal one way in which the city elites thought of and utilized the river. But the grandest plans for the river emerged less out of engineering or zoning imperatives than from aesthetic and reform positions. In his classic book *The Better City*, reformer Dana Bartlett wrote of the river's ability to define the new—the better—city: "Think of what value to the city this river might yet become if placed under a special commission empowered to carry out a definite plan for its reclamation from base uses." Bartlett, who had founded the city's first settlement house, was nothing if not progressively wishful. The river could be adorned by many bridges ("each a work of art"), parallel to steam and electric rail lines, and further reclaimed to make a parklike esplanade for autos and pedestrians. Adjacent factories and warehouses would be "hidden behind a wealth of climbing vines and roses." The riverbed, once cleaned of its rubbish and properly graded, could even become "an extensive playground for the children of the congested districts." Or for at least "nine months of the year," lest those happy children get swept away by winter floods. At right angles to the riverbed (rigid adherence to geometry equaled order, as well as the control of nature) extensive piers would support three "civic centers" with lyceum halls, club rooms, athletic facilities, all with "steps leading down to the riverbed playground."[57]

The addition of nearly a dozen bridges for railroads and pedestrians and, eventually, automobiles, did not do much in terms of making the river beautiful. Taming and beautifying the Los Angeles River would require more concerted effort than building bridges. The future beckoned, and Los Angeles might get there by paying close attention to the river.

THE UGLY SHALL BE MADE BEAUTIFUL,
THE CROOKED STRAIGHT

The river along its entire length can be made into a line of beauty.
REV. DANA BARTLETT, *The Better City,* 1907

Time was, a concrete river was a beautiful thing. Lining a river with miles and miles of cool grayness was heralded as the ultimate in city beautiful rationalization, the apex of twentieth-century urban design's triumph over nature's messy whim. Consider Joseph Mesmer, a turn-of-the-century shoe, real estate, and brick magnate, owner of the palatial Linda Vista estate and orchard overlooking the Los Angeles River, president of two powerful city development organizations, and chairman of the municipal committee empowered to fill the river with cement. A contemporary periodical left little doubt as to the civic dividends such a project would return:

> This work . . . will be the crowning achievement of [Mesmer's] life. No other work could be projected that will have such beneficial results and mean so much to the city of Los Angeles. The transforming of the most unsightly sight of the city into a beautiful parking [*sic*], lakes and esplanades. See the impression the visitor will get upon his arrival in the city when he beholds this picture of artistic picturesqueness and beauty, also being a park six miles long in the center of the city. Consider the pleasure that will be afforded to thousands of our own people where they can enjoy their outing and recreation in walking over beautiful laid serpentine walks amidst shady trees, beautiful shrubs and flowers, while others enjoy the pleasures of boating, sailing and swimming in the six lakes of 3000 feet long averaging in depth from two to fifteen feet.

Concrete was key to this plan, a plan designed far more with beautification and aesthetics in mind than flood control. Lest anyone doubt the all-inclusive nature of the plan, this booster publication spelled out the construction details: "The river bed and sides are to be lined solidly with concrete. The parapet sidewalks above the surface level are to be 3½ feet high and of artistic design, on the top of which there will be placed at every 30 feet apart a beautiful electrically lighted gondolier, lighting the park at night as light as in the day time."[58]

This ambitious scheme, ca. 1910, planted an important seed. And it helps us better understand the irony of Los Angeles' appeal to natural living epitomized so aptly by the popular Chamber of Commerce slogan (also ca. 1910): "Los Angeles—Nature's Workshop."[59] But before Mesmer's vision could be made real, certain things had to happen within the realms of nature, memory, and culture. The first was easy: winter rains. In February 1913, heavy rainfall inundated downtown; one local confided to his diary that "many funny incidents happened on the wet streets, [or,] I should say, rivers."[60]

A year later, more rain fell. In late January and again in mid-February 1914, the Los Angeles basin got pounded by winter rains. The January rains soaked the ground, which lost all absorptive capability. In February came the deluge. On the night of the 18th alone, an inch and a half of rain

Figure 21. Los Angeles River, north from the Seventh Street Bridge, February 19, 1914. Courtesy of the Huntington Library, San Marino, California.

Figure 22. Salt Lake Railroad at Macy Street and the Los Angeles River, February 20, 1914. Courtesy of the Huntington Library, San Marino, California.

Figure 23. Postal worker and intrepid regional photographer Charles Puck adrift following 1916 floods. Courtesy of the Huntington Library, San Marino, California.

fell on the city. In just three days, nearly twenty inches of rain fell in the San Gabriel Mountains. The mountains could only absorb so much of the deluge; the rest ran downhill as floodwater. Damage was severe; later estimates put the cost to the basin at well over $10 million.[61]

Just as it had done in the past, the water came down, first from the skies and then from the mountains. But the basin had changed. Roofs and roads had replaced open land. Water collected only long enough to gather more strength and more vertical slope. In downtown Los Angeles, the Los Angeles River flooded at a discharge rate normally used to describe the Colorado River. The river dumped four million cubic yards of silt into the harbors at Long Beach and San Pedro. Los Angeles went without outside communication for a week. Rail traffic got knocked out, and telegraph messages to San Bernardino were sent via Chicago. Damage estimates reached into the tens of millions of dollars. Many people died. Property washed away. And when the rains returned two years later, they left in their wake flood control bonds and a wishful piece of legislation, the Los Angeles County Flood Control Act, voted in by a worried, frustrated, water-logged citizenry.

And what of memory? The people of Los Angeles, then as now, deal less day to day with geologic or climactic time than with human time. And human time has many a memory blind spot. Like the ever-confident Alfred Moore, who in the 1880s declared floods a thing of the past, people simply chose not to remember that the Los Angeles River posed a significant hazard. Instead, it was far too easy to continue to market Los Angeles as the world's capital of sunshine and perfect weather. And all that "menaced" land that lay at the river's edge, all those bowl-shaped spreading grounds atop aquifers next to the mountains, proved too easy a target for real estate sale and development. As the past century has shown, a flood will take advantage of developed land to wreak havoc all the more. The Los Angeles growth machine of the early 1900s had virtually begged nature to provide a terrible flood. By 1910, there were nearly a half a million people in the city who had never seen the damage a flood could do to the basin. There were probably an equal number who did not (or chose not to) remember.[62]

But it is within the realm of memory, and the larger realm of culture, that we find an interesting and revealing variable in the flood control and concrete equation. Obsessed with the Los Angeles future, elites paused to take the past seriously, if only for brief moments stolen from a morning or afternoon here and there. Joseph Mesmer's plans for his river committee, borrowing heavily from city beautiful prophet Charles Mulford Robinson's ideas, focused almost exclusively upon Los Angeles as *the* American city of the future. But that new river in that new city could not become reality without some attention paid to the ancient river, the real river. Planning to beautify a river through concrete is one thing. Actually doing so, particularly with a river as volatile as the Los Angeles River, required a different mindset, one that ironically contemplated, say, 1820 and 1850 as much as it did 1920 or 1950. Because to do Mesmer's "work of a lifetime" justice (or to do it at all), the river had first to be known. It had to be remembered before it could be corralled.

THE FLOODS OF MEMORY

"It was commonly understood and talked of in the early days by old Mexican people that the Los Angeles river flowed out through the southwest part of the city by Ballona and into the Santa Monica Bay until the flood of 1825."

"Mr. Cate has heard the Mexicans talk of the Los Angeles river having flowed into Ballona in early days, and he thinks it is entirely possible, even today, for the water to go over that way."
Flood Control Interviews, William Workman and D. M. Cate.

In his majestic 1985 book *Rivers of Empire*, environmental historian Donald Worster argued that historians could learn a great deal about the modern West by strolling along the gray, artificial banks of any number of irrigation canals which criss-cross America's arid regions. Such locales—which prompted Worster's insightful "reflections in a ditch"—offered both study and illustration of "ecological and social regimentation." Living things shunned concrete canals because, as Worster points out, a riparian ecosystem has been replaced by the sterility of efficient civil engineering. What is more, the "hydraulic society" responsible for making straight channels out of temperamental streams induces and supports a regimented social order, which is itself "increasingly a coercive, monolithic, and hierarchical system, ruled by a power elite based on the ownership of capital and expertise."[63] The modern canal becomes in this reading, then, both symbol and engine, both cause and effect, of a rigid social structure predicated upon gain, growth, and mastery of nature. Such, then, are modern rivers of empire.

Yet social coercion and ecological manipulation are but two of any empire's programs. Imperial designs rarely suffer from any lack of ways or reasons to gain, swipe, or shore up power, and the American Southwest is no exception. In other words, concrete canals may tell other stories in addition to bald environmental destruction and coercive imposition of economic order. Concrete might also tell us about ethnic clashes in the West, about how Anglo visions of the future might have necessitated the manipulation of Latino understandings of the past. Concrete might convince us that infrastructural designs and schemes are inherently cultural (a notion Worster would clearly support), and that the much-maligned, laughable Los Angeles River is itself, ironically enough, if not a great river of empire, then at least a river of great empire.

From his office in downtown Los Angeles, civil engineer J. W. Reagan chaired a committee ("Committee of Menaced and Flooded Areas") and oversaw an extraordinary history project. Agents were sent into the field (the field being the entire Los Angeles basin) to interview people, particularly those who made up the "dwindling remnant of the early pioneers of this County," about rivers.[64] Blandly titled "Research Los Angeles County Flood Control 1914–1915," the dozens and dozens of interviews weave together an amazingly rich fabric of Southern California social history. We learn a great deal about the growth of the Southland, the decline of regional farming, folkways, and, of course, an immense amount about rivers: where and when they flowed, what damage they did, what should, could, and would be done about them.

But we also learn something more. Because it turns out that those interviewed were not necessarily ordinary people chosen entirely at random by the field workers. There is clearly a presumption on the part of the committee that age and ethnicity matter. Alongside the community leaders, the powerful capitalists and planners (Joseph Mesmer, for instance, is interviewed at length[65]), the Anglo pioneers, and the powerful farmers, are elderly Mexicans. This cannot be an accident. It is as if instructions to interviewers included the charge to "find the oldest Mexicans you can."[66]

It is clear that the surveys were designed (if only accidentally) to validate the past in an explicitly utilitarian, and yet oddly thrilling, sort of way. The volume, the engineers proudly stated, had been "written in the language of the pioneers themselves."[67] In other words, these engineers at work in Reagan and the U.S. Engineer's office on Figueroa Street began to map the courses of the basin's rivers by deliberately establishing a cartography of memory. Knowing everything there is to know about rivers requires different sets of knowledge and information. The engineers, J. W. Reagan most prominent among them, knew hydraulics; they knew all about the acre footage of river flow; they knew groundwater equations and aquifer storage capacities. But what they did not know was history, particularly the "pre-history" of Mexican Los Angeles (to say nothing of the Native American history and memory of and in the region). And there were precious few places to turn in 1914 to fill any gaps. Aside from the boosters extolling the sweetness of the mission period or the slow pace of "what was," Los Angeles had few repositories of local historical knowledge. Even the region's Historical Society had urged Angelenos not to spend too much time pondering the Mexican or Spanish period of the basin. As the organization's president had put the matter, with poignant finality, "a score or two of names, a few crumbling adobes, and all is told."[68] Newspapers were unreliable; mission records were unattainable. The United States Weather Bureau, the repository of scientific knowledge about Los Angeles floods, had a data bank that went back only thirty-seven years into the region's past. Knowing about the floods of 1878–1879 might have been useful, but a memory bank that thin could not much help engineers understand rainfall and hydrologic patterns on or in the landscape.[69] What they needed to know could be stated, certainly much more simply than the engineers themselves put it: "If the year of maximum floods can be identified, it is possible from the information which exists as to other floods, to arrive by synthetic process at a rational approximate of maximum discharge quantities."[70] In other words, how big were the floods of memory? Where could engineer Reagan's interviewers turn?[71]

The answer must have been obvious. They turned, in part, to the river itself. William McEuen, who had just finished his M.A. thesis at the University of Southern California with Emory Bogardus, had declared that most of the Mexicans in Los Angeles could be found "within a mile of the Los Angeles River." So the river was itself a vector of ethnicity, in that the interviewers probably used it as a guide to finding Mexicans. But ethnicity was but one guide; it had to be supplemented by age. The interviewers' work provided a meeting ground between past and future, between what Los Angeles was and what Los Angeles would be. Their questions clearly reflected a respect for memory and for age and for a period of local history that, already by 1914, must have seemed ancient. But in order to catch the rivers where they would most likely be, in order to cement them in once and for all, engineers had to know their histories. The engineers had to know what river flowed where, when, and with how much force. They had to know how to, if only in a rudimentary fashion, create a hierarchy of floods, particularly since it was suggested that 1914 was *not* as big as floods could, or did, get in the basin.[72] Was the great 1889 flood the proverbial hundred-year flood? Should it provide the critical benchmark for hydrologic planning? Or was it 1825? 1815? "To state that knowledge of the greatest volumes of water carried by the various streams is fundamental to flood and conservation studies is to state an axiom," is how one prominent engineer put it. Even as the *Los Angeles Times* declared "Science to Reshape County's Waterways," engineers recognized the necessity of other tools. Or, put in another way, geology could reveal a great deal, but so could an eighty-year-old Mexican woman.[73]

The interviewers asked their subjects about rivers. They were, in effect, looking to find private Mexican memory to go with the very public memories that events like La Fiesta had already shaped in Los Angeles. Now their effort was truly aimed at shaping the basin's physical environment itself, and they needed historical help. They worked from a series of questions. Did their subjects know about the basin's rivers? Did they remember them? What did floods do and, more important, where did floods go? And what they got in return was a wealth of information, often contradictory, always interesting. They learned about regional topography, that before massive settlement the expanse of land stretching west from Los Angeles to the Pacific had been grizzly bear country overgrown with willows, elders, cottonwoods. They learned about vast vineyards all along the banks of the Los Angeles River. People told them about overland travel, about the arrival of the railroad in Los Angeles, about the soldiers stationed over by the ocean during the Civil War.

Judge Ygnacio Sepulveda granted an interview in his downtown office and was interrogated "as to the floods of his time." He agreed that his lineage ran deep in local history, but that the truly knowledgeable members of his family, those who could map a century of floods, were dead. The judge did point out something that other Mexicans said again and again: the Los Angeles River had not always flowed where it did in the twentieth century. It moved in the early 1800s, not once but twice, and had once found the Pacific by going out through what was now Exposition Park.[74]

Jose Ruiz, sixty-eight, recalled a time when there were but four or five ranchers between Los Angeles and San Pedro. "In the early days," Ruiz remembered, "the old people used to say that the Los Angeles river flowed out through the southwest of Los Angeles and into the Ballona." His father told him that he once saw the valley from Boyle Heights to the plaza one solid sheet of water. In those days, though, given the lack of development, "no one thought much of the floods . . . they would only cover the ground and not wash to amount to anything."[75]

After admitting that old maps were terribly difficult to locate, Surveyor S. B. Reeve insisted that "memory maps" were the only way to proceed. "It would not be too much trouble," he said, "to get a few of the old timers together and make up a map of the old flooded district, and make plans whereby the river could be readily controlled."[76]

Joe Bernal, who remembered swimming in the river when it ran down Alameda Street, talked of an old aunt who told him about the river's history. "Yes," he recalled she said, "the Los Angeles river at one time had its channel near the plaza, passed at what is now 2nd and Alameda Sts., then to near 6th and Los Angeles Sts. then in a southwesterly direction towards the Ballona for a long distance, then swung southeasterly and skirted the edge of the hills at Dominguez."[77] Mr. Bernal also remembered visiting the home of the Lugo family and asking Mr. Lugo about the Los Angeles River; he was told much the same story, that the river once flowed elsewhere and that one could know the route simply by looking closely at basin soils: where there was sand there had once been a river.

"Years ago," William Crain remembered, "when I was a young man, I used to talk to the old people, both Americans and Mexicans. They interested me more than the young people. The Mexicans have told me many times, and it is a sort of legend among them, that in the early days the Los Angeles river ran out through the southwestern part of the city, and emptied into the Ballona Bay. It is entirely feasible physically, and what has been may come again." F. Z. Vejar, eighty-four and a Los Angeles native, ratified this oft-told story and told many others as well, apparently. But these others were dismissed: "Mr. Vejar has many stories of the early days, during the Mexican rule and later that of the U.S., but they in no way bear upon the subject."[78]

Mr. J. Frank Burns spoke of being employed by the Santa Fe Railroad to find out about floods in regards to certain legal cases. He said that he had interviewed Pio Pico at ninety-three and another man who was 137 years old. Both had insisted that the river changed course radically in 1825.[79]

Mrs. Lopez had been born in Los Angeles in 1831. She had moved to the San Fernando Valley at twenty, on her wedding trip, and had stayed ever since. Speaking in Spanish translated by her daughter, Mrs. Lopez recalled the big floods of 1858–1859. She remembered the date very well, she said, because she had to travel to Los Angeles to attend a christening, and she was able to look the information up in her family Bible. She had been trapped for two weeks in Los Angeles at that time and, upon returning to the valley, noticed that many adobe homes had simply melted away in the rains and floods.[80]

Jesse Hunter remembered the big floods of the 1860s. He also recalled asking his father, long ago sometime around mid-century, why "the Mexicans always built their houses on the ridges and hills and carried water up to them instead of building down by the water, and his father said he didn't know, but after 1861–62 he knew why they built on the high ground."[81]

Mr. J. R. Ramirez, interviewed at home on North Broadway, told of growing up in Los Angeles in the 1840s. His grandfather's grandfather had come to the area in 1786 and made the first wine and brandy in the basin. His grandfather, an Avila, had made adobe bricks in a kiln down near the river and had grown grapes where the Southern Pacific railyards stood. He had little faith in the utility of flood control efforts. "When Mr. Ramirez was told that we were looking for data to enable the engineers to perfect their plans to control the river, he emphatically said it could not be done. Then he showed where the water had been in 1825, and said that there was not money enough to control such floods. Those floods will come again, he said, and no one can keep them from it."[82]

What Reagan's engineers were after was evidence of the river's wanderings and its excesses, a way to map reminiscence. They did just this: under J. W. Reagan's supervision, a map of Los Angeles basin rivers was drawn which suggested cyclical patterns of flooding of greater and lesser extent since the nineteenth century. This is not to suggest that the engineers placed inordinate faith in comprehensive Mexican, or any, memory. On the contrary, Reagan made sure to point out that it was "quite possible that there may have been other floods which were not recalled. It would be an exceptional memory which could recall every serious flood."[83]

But exceptional memory was not the critical point. Simple, individual memories of flooding and destructiveness were all that mattered. They could be aggregated. In the report drawn up following the oral history-taking, the Los Angeles County Supervisors introduced the important findings by suggesting that both physical and mental (i.e., "memorable") evidence dictated "that equally great and even greater and more disastrous inundations will occur in the future."[84]

The engineers also wanted proof that the river could be corralled and held. For it is in the wake of all this interviewing that plans were developed that eventually led to the concretization of the Los Angeles River. What planners and engineers in part wanted to do was protect the new Los Angeles Harbor at San Pedro from the deleterious effects of river-borne silt. If they could move the river and send it into Alamitos Bay near Long Beach, the new harbor—pride and joy of both engineering and commerce—would be the beneficiary of modern flood control.

One way to interpret the interviewers' search for information is as mere intelligence gathering from the past. But another way of looking at things reaches for a broader interpretation than what might have gone on in any given sitting room between an interviewer and an interviewee some ninety years ago. Awareness, even validation, of the past was predicated upon asking about it. Interviewers quizzed their informants. When were you born? Can you talk about growing up here? Do you remember the Los Angeles River? Where did it flow? When did it flood? How big were those floods? Do you have any maps?

This sensitivity to the past had a purpose, one aimed directly at the future and, more explicitly, the city of the future. These engineers did appreciate the regional Mexican past. They did ask about it, and they did write it down. But viewed through a fairly skeptical lens regarding ethnic perceptions and the rise of Los Angeles, such validation can be seen as taking up but a cultural instant, worth only the time it took for Mexican memory to be put to work as science in the quest for the Anglo city of the future. These unusual interview documents, as saturated with the past as Porciuncula itself, nonetheless had within them ultimate designs on the future. While these reminiscences are indeed oral histories, it is important to keep in mind that the oral historians approached their work as engineers first: the history they gathered was meant to be put to work, to make a bridge between memory and the future. That future—in the city of the future—required that the river go away or at least go where it was *supposed* to go. Similar behavior was required of the basin's Mexicans as well. In the end, the river of memory and Mexican memories of the river linked ethnicity and water far more intimately than any novelist's metaphor could possibly accomplish. And unlike most metaphorical wordplay, these associations came complete with hard-edged realities, such as further ethnic segregation, isolation, and destitution down at river's edge.

All of this was part and parcel of those processes of cultural and ethnic transference explored years ago by Carey McWilliams in *Southern California Country*. As McWilliams notes, study of "the local annals" reveals "at least the outlines of the process by which, through a kind of occupational erosion, the Hispanos steadily declined in influence and power." For McWilliams, the transitions are explicitly work-related: Mexican vaqueros become sheepshearers following the demise of the cattle business; sheepshearers in turn become farm laborers; those farm laborers in turn become street vendors and peddlers. Pushing Mexicans aside allowed them to become that "picturesque element" for a short period of time until, by the end of the century, "visitors had ceased to note the presence of Mexicans."[85] It is that erasure—or at least retreat from, or at least whitewashing—of the region's culture, politics, and political economy, which provides us with a different lens through which to examine the life and death of the Los Angeles River. Because what is so striking about the flood control interviews of 1914 is the mere presence of Mexican voices and Mexican people, brought back and made real by the infrastructural demands of "the better city" of the future. Anglo Americans had interviewed elderly Mexicans before in California history—Hubert Howe Bancroft's early oral histories stand out in this regard. But this was different. Antiquarianism had been replaced by utilitarianism. In the former case, the words and stories themselves were the object. In the latter case of the young hydrologists talking to octogenarians, the personal histories were but means to an engineered end.

Carey McWilliams notes that the swamping of Mexican life and culture took place with a "truly awful swiftness." But in the case of the concretization of the river into an Anglo icon, things would move slowly. The surveys doubtless helped create a certain body of historical knowledge, but massive flood control measures did not begin immediately. The receding waters of 1914 and 1916 floods left behind the bond acts that were to provide the financial and engineering wherewithal to channel and move rivers, build dams, and protect harbors.[86] The work proved far less manageable than had once been thought; more concrete would be needed.[87] Despite (or because of) help from the Army Corps of Engineers, things moved slowly. Yes, the Los Angeles River would be cemented in place. But it would take much more time and much more money than anyone in early twentieth-century Los Angeles could have imagined.

The introduction of tens of thousands of automobiles (Los Angeles had, by the late 1920s, the highest per capita car ownership of any American city) helped further to cement the river's future. As early as 1924, the city and county Traffic Commission had designed a "Major Traffic Street Plan," adopted by the voters, which called for a "river truck freeway" to connect the San Fernando Valley with the harbor district. Such a visionary plan would also go a long way toward rationalizing the river; by the twenties, the Los Angeles River had been virtually personified as a mischievous troublemaker. "Was there ever anywhere a river more subject to 'ups and downs'?" the *Los Angeles Times* wondered. "It [will] never stay put. At one time it flowed along Los Angeles street and then it deliberately moved to Alameda street."[88] The time was fast approaching for more concerted action against such willfulness.

By the mid-1930s, Joseph Mesmer's dream of a concrete river—the utilitarian river if not the river beautiful—had new allies in the form of federal flood control funds and a more aggressive Army Corps of Engineers. By this time, too, flood control as a civic problem had become an unquestioned given on the part of city engineers and politicians: Los Angeles had floods, Los Angeles had temperamental rivers, therefore Los Angeles must undertake drastic flood control measures.[89] Just as the rains of 1914 had brought about concerted action and regional "re-memories" of flood dangers, so too with the devastating floods of the Depression years. What is more, the federal government proved more than willing to step in with both money and labor.

New Year's Day, 1934, was among the worst, when the Los Angeles River communities of Burbank, Montrose, and Glendale got hit by a massive and deadly flood. Poor migrants from the southern plains had set up tent and temporary communities in the bed of the river and nearby tributary streams. It was "the natural thing," according to Woody Guthrie, that Okies would congregate in river and creek bottoms. But on "that fatal New Year's Night," Woody sang in his mournful dirge about the flood, "a cloudburst hit the mountains, it swept away our homes. A hundred souls was taken, a million hearts was grievin'." "This world will long remember," Guthrie sang, those folks "that crossed the golden river in that fatal New Year's flood."[90]

The world has not long remembered those victims, nor the "wild Los Angeles River" that flooded. But "immediate memory" did prompt the flood control engineers of Los Angeles to step up their actions following the devastation. By 1937, the Army Corps had $70 million to spend in Los Angeles on flood control work. Momentum and money increased in the aftermath of the deadly 1938 flood, which killed close to a hundred people across Los Angeles County.[91]

Planners were quick, as they often were, to combine flood control plans with beautification projects if they could get away with it under the watchful eyes of the Corps. As one report of the era put it, with specific reference to the Los Angeles River, "large areas of proposed park lands in the rivers and drainage channels will have double value to the public because they will serve both park and drainage purposes." In other words, the objectives were mutually reinforcing: channel the rivers and develop them into narrow urban greenbelts. The major recreational planning document of the period, brought out just as the Depression hammered Southern California, recommended the construction of nearly one hundred regional "parkways," many of which were multiple designs bringing together flood control plans, freeway developments, and urban green space. The document pointed out that much of the residential areas lying up against the river were "of low valuations and poor developments."[92]

Despite some real concern on the part of certain city and county officials about the wisdom of turning the Army Corps of Engineers loose willy-nilly in the rivers of the Los Angeles basin, the city did nonetheless plunge into the paving project.[93] At one point, the channel projects were to include "the world's highest dam" nestled cozily above Azusa in the San Gabriels, but that particular endeavor was shelved when it ran into bad public relations, potentially unstable geology, and an embarrassing kickback scandal which sent a county supervisor to state prison after $80,000 mysteriously showed up in his pocket.[94] The Corps had some early problems with the Los Angeles River: their first attempt at concretization washed away in March rains. But

Figures 24–26. 1930s channelization of the Los Angeles River. Courtesy of the Huntington Library, San Marino, California.

the die had long ago been cast, and the Los Angeles River, and its cousins the San Gabriel and Rio Hondo, were paved over in about twenty years of labor (though the work is ongoing), with the help of a virtual ocean of thick concrete. Los Angeles basin flood control today represents the most ambitious, expensive, and concrete-intensive such project west of the Mississippi. The Los Angeles River, Army Corps engineers say, is "the river we built."[95]

Is a built river dead, by definition? Of course not, despite indications within technical and legal literature that others believe it is.[96] And few who believe so are shy about suggesting foul play. The following is from a sharp-eyed WPA observer in the mid-1930s. Notice how it reads like the obituary of a loyal civil servant:

> [The] Los Angeles River has been pictured in recent years by local wits as a stream whose bed must be sprinkled regularly to keep down the dust. Despite all merry quips coined at its expense, the fact remains that, save for a few scattering wells, the Los Angeles River, for a period of 133 years, served as sole water source for this community. From the day the pueblo

was founded in 1781, the river continued faithfully to serve the town until the increasing needs of a growing city exceeded its limited supply.[97]

Throughout the past century, city officials and planners have celebrated the control of nature as exemplified by their rationalization of the river. Sometimes they have been right, sometimes the river has surprised them. If anything, the Los Angeles River is a stubborn stream. In the winter of 1907, assistant Los Angeles city engineer E. A. Tuttle wrote to his boss and boasted that recent flood control measures had, for the first time in history, made it possible for the city to weather the rains of winter without fear of the Los Angeles River. He was wrong, to be sure, but the mere fact that Tuttle believed it illustrates how the city was firmly engaged in remaking the river and turning it to other than traditional uses.[98]

Engineer Tuttle has been echoed ever since, most particularly by the truck river freeway enthusiasts of the twenties and again during the Second World War. In early 1941, city planning documents argued that the river would be a good defense industry ally in that trucks could be used to transport war materiel in the riverbed (planners apparently got the idea by watching construction trucks in the riverbed, busy supplying concrete for the channels). Of course, planners noted, the river did have water two months out of the year, but this was being taken care of by the "great concrete channel."[99] By 1943, the regional planning commission, in the pages of its "Summary Report on Feasibility of Los Angeles River Freeway," had determined that truck traffic in the riverbed itself was not practical. "This conclusion was based on the fact that the channel was designed for one purpose only[:] to carry the maximum runoff that occurs during periodic floods."[100] But they still thought they could construct wings on either side of the riverbed to carry traffic. In that way, though the river itself might be now unreliable, the channel would still *flow*. A new river had been, if not created, at least envisioned, one no longer filled with water but with cars and trucks. Planners could hardly rein in their enthusiasm.[101]

The newly industrialized river—what writer D. J. Waldie has called "the river the Anglo city misplaced"—helped create more rigid pockets of Mexican housing and neighborhoods.[102] For in addition to acting as a marker for industrial development, as in zoning legislation, the Los Angeles River simultaneously "zones" ethnicity and class. It has of course been that way for years, even long ago when the river's moods made its banks risky and thus cheaper land. But the process accelerated once the river was assigned industrial chores. In the late 1930s, for instance, right in the heart of the public works assault on the river, University of Southern California student Charles Withers went looking for Mexicans in Los Angeles, as his peers had been doing for decades. Like a watery magnet, the river drew him to his subjects. He went first east of the plaza, "following the general line of the river and of the railroad tracks. This was perhaps the poorest district, and the most frequently studied in the past twenty years by those interested in the Mexican and his problems. It had a distinctly Mexican flavor, with shops, theaters, recreational facilities, and so forth, of a typically Mexican turn. In this district were those localities known as the 'Plaza,' 'Dogtown,' and the 'Flats' of the packing house district. This last spread across to the other side of the river in some places. . . . The houses were ancient, ramshackle, and crowded."[103] It was as if a sharp quarantine began in the lowland flats running along Macy Street, falling down toward the river itself, a critical dividing line that exists even today.

⊷ ▰✛▰ ⊶

Maybe it is easy to pick on the Los Angeles River because it has always been puny and never all that reliable. It looks like a creek next to other rivers of the American West. But it clearly once was something that it is not anymore, and the transition from what once was to what is now cannot be divorced from political, cultural, or social currents. At least two certainties are apparent. The first is that the river's most critical transition (from river to flood control channel) is tied to a regional disassociation with a distinct ethnic past. The river displayed a disturbing propensity to flood, and such floods were all too obvious reminders of an unruly nature in a place that demanded—and claimed—control over nature in the name of the urban future. A different future beckoned to the planners and builders of Los Angeles, if and only if the river could be corralled, contained, and controlled. That process, precisely because it was predicated on knowing regional history as a tool by which to embrace the regional future, revealed attitudes and behaviors about ethnicity and race.

The second sure thing is that the concrete did not come down from the mountains all by itself. A concrete river used to be a beautiful thing, a place where exuberant Angelenos would be able to stroll placidly amidst the visionary city that they had created, the city of the future, the city that had beautified itself by perfecting Nature. But concrete rivers are not beautiful today. The enduring irony of the Los Angeles River is that those exuberant future-obsessed Anglos do not inhabit the river's spaces. It is the immigrant and homeless, mostly Latino, people living in a depressing deindustrialized corridor who drink the water, swim and wash in it, and even farm its banks and belly.[104]

But of course ethnic boundaries could be and most assuredly are drawn with other markers in addition to environmental features like topography and a river. In this, Los Angeles is no different than any other American city. One of these markers was, and is, certainly labor, as we will investigate in chapter 4's discussion of the making of modern Los Angeles on the backs of several generations of Mexican laborers working at the biggest brickyard in the world.

FOUR

The Color of Brickwork Is Brown

As Walter let the soil fall from his hand, he knew that here he and his brother would build a brickyard. Walter contemplated the immensity of the place, the unlimited possibilities, the millions of bricks they could produce and the hundreds, thousands of men who would work for him. Here they will be happy, he thought as he grabbed another handful of red earth. Hundreds of people fell from his hand.

ALEJANDRO MORALES, *The Brick People*[1]

I have left the best of my life and my strength here, sprinkling with the sweat of my brow the fields and the factories of these gringos, who only know how to make one sweat and don't even pay attention to one when they see that one is old.

SIMONS BRICK COMPANY EMPLOYEE JUAN BERZUNZOLO

Always, Walter Simons has interested himself in the individual concerns of his workmen and although it has been more or less of an onerous task he has been well repaid for keeping in close touch with his employees.

SAMUEL CLOVER, *Saturday Night*, December 19, 1925

To the Mexican Los Angeles owes much. The drudgery of county and city has been his. He has handled the pick and the shovel, he has been the harvester. Upon his labor the prosperity of Southern California in large part rests. The charm and the fascination that distinguishes Los Angeles among American cities is largely his. Gardens and homes, streets and parks show the influence of Latin-American culture. The city is greatly in his debt.

KARL DE SCHWEINITZ,
"Social Work with Families in Los Angeles," 1927[2]

The paved Los Angeles River—the river industrial—created an entirely new environmental feature on the landscape of the city so proudly referred to as "nature's workshop." As we have seen in chapter 3, engineers and urban planners cemented a new river into existence guided, in part, by building on the seventy- and eighty-year-old memories of aged Mexicans. Reminiscence, explicitly ethnic reminiscence, became a critical accompaniment to stark hydrologic data gathered by servants of science. The irony, that a rural Mexican past held information important to the race toward an urban, self-consciously Anglo Saxon future, seems not to have occurred to the engineers-turned-oral-historians, the politicians, or community leaders. This should not be surprising. Irony had nothing to do with the desire to make the river the key to city beautiful campaigns heralding the city of the future.

Regardless of any such insight, however, there can be little doubt that the paving of the Los Angeles River, especially once the ambitions about making the river into a scenic playground evaporated, helped to demarcate further ethnic boundaries on the urban landscape. Proximity to the river had long been one marker of Mexican Los Angeles, just as the river itself had bounded (and continues to do so to this day) neighborhoods separate from the commercial districts of downtown. Concrete and fencing drove the point home. The riverbed itself, for at least much of the year, had also been claimed as Mexican space, home to poor communities or *colonias* forged from scrap wood or abandoned rail boxcars. With tons of cement, however, came a much more glaring, literally concrete reminder about Mexican spaces and places. It was as if the river itself was synonymous with Mexican life in Los Angeles, an immobile vector which, much as Pacific Electric and Los Angeles Railway tracks had done for decades, segregated downtown Los Angeles into rigid class and ethnic compartments.

But so, too, did work, as always, as everywhere in America.

——— ❈ ———

There is no easy job in a brickyard. Digging hard clay from the ground, pulverizing it, adding water, shaping bricks from the mixture, firing them into solid, heavy rectangular blocks, stacking these into endless pile after pile after pile—it is all backbreaking labor. A brickyard is a swarm of labor. Men going here and there, pushing and pulling wheelbarrows, carts, and dollies, moving earth and clay and brick. Each day is long. The work goes on even after dark, the brickyard awash in the eerie shadows made by gas-fired flames. Of course, work stops when it rains. Rain makes the yard

Figure 27. Mexican workers, Simons brickyard, early twentieth century. Courtesy of the Huntington Library, San Marino, California.

sloppy, slippery, and messy. The kilns that fire the damp clay into rock-hard bricks can't do their work. But it does not rain much in Southern California, not outside of the few wet winter months. Brickyard work goes on and on, day after day, brick after brick after millions of bricks. And when that busy brickyard is located in one of the fastest growing metropolitan areas of the nation, indeed of the world, the maxim rings all the more true: there is no easy job in a brickyard.

There's another brickyard truism, at least in Southern California during the period under study in this book. The color of brickwork is brown.

By the early twentieth century, the San Gabriel Mission, that vaunted site of Los Angeles nativity, had become an icon of the tourist experience. Visitors tramped there by the thousands year in and year out. People could see into the past from Mission San Gabriel, or so they told themselves or read in their colorful guidebooks. The past beckoned, it called these tourists from the pealing of the mission bells or the vistas seen from atop the mission's famed outdoor stone staircase. That past, they learned, was a simpler time. The people, they learned, were a simpler people. It was a pretty past, a romantic time and place. It must have felt good to think about this romantic past, particularly if you could almost see it.

By 1912, along came someone to put that past on the stage. Mission tourists could not only wander the quaint spaces of Catholic history, they could see it all enacted in John Steven McGroarty's hugely successful *Mission Play.* "As you muse and ponder, it all seems a dream," wrote one woman of her time at the mission.[3]

But it was actually all careful make-believe, not a dream. Because if a tourist with a little less imagination and a little more present-mindedness stood at the top of what one local newspaper had once called that "queer outside staircase," he or she might have seen something different from the dreamscape of the pastoral past. The present loomed out there, a present with very different conceptions of Mexicans and missions than the post-cards and curios on sale for a nickel or so at Mission San Gabriel.[4]

Standing at the top of that stairway and looking west, what did a viewer see in 1900? In 1915? In 1928? A metropolis rose from the Los Angeles basin, a city on the make. Smokestacks belched industrial smoke, synonymous with progress. High rises pushed five, then six, then fifteen stories into the sky. If one turned to look due south, or very nearly so, just a few miles up and over the neighboring Montebello Hills there lay a commercial operation that had everything to do with the ways in which Anglos in Los Angeles thought about Mexicans. But it was not the wishful manipulations of history that made this world. It was instead the dust and smoke and clatter of the industrial present and future of Los Angeles that dictated the story lines of this tale. Here, however, the equations were perhaps a bit more straightforward than in the stage directions, characters, and plot of John McGroarty's treacly melodrama. Here racial logic offered an easy Los Angeles triptych. More Mexicans meant more workers. More workers meant more bricks. More bricks meant more money.

That is how the Simons brothers figured it. Owners of a huge brick company that operated plants all over the basin, from Pasadena west to Santa Monica, with the biggest of all in Montebello, the Simons brothers (and millions of their bricks) played a profound role in the industrial, residential, and commercial expansion of Los Angeles. They rode the growth wave from the fabled boom period of the 1880s across the divide of the century, through the slowdowns of the Depression and the Long Beach earthquake of 1933, which damaged the brick industry, into the Second World War, limping all the way to the 1950s. This chapter is about Simons brick, about Simons brickyard workers, and about attitudes toward those workers and others like them.

*An interesting chapter might be written upon the history and decay of
the old adobe structures, many of which were prominent land marks in
the city ten years ago, but have now disappeared.*

EDWIN BAXTER, "Leaves from the Last Decade," 1893[5]

Our story must open well before the Simons family migrated to Los
Angeles in the 1880s, alongside those tens of thousands of other midwest-
erners wishing to jump-start their futures. To understand brick in Los
Angeles, we need first to understand adobe, and the ways newcomers to Los
Angeles saw transitions between building materials as synonymous and
simultaneous with transitions in racial realities. We have to start with an
assumption prevalent in Los Angeles, as in other places, in the middle of
the nineteenth century. Brick meant progress. Using brick as a building
material meant pushing the past away while beckoning the future. Brick
also meant Anglo America, which itself could be a stand-in, another
metaphor, for progress, albeit often slow progress. Of the 1850s, for instance,
acerbic writer Morrow Mayo once noted that "a brick building was started,
but before it was well under way six Mexicans were lynched, the preacher
left town, and the project petered out, leaving the Catholics as the sole survivors." Brick was at least a step in the right direction, although Mayo seems
here to poke fun at Anglo assumptions that building blocks alone could
coax the arrival of "civilization," even if the building in question was a
church.[6]

Adobe, on the other hand, that ubiquitous building material of water,
clay, and straw or weeds, stood for the past, a dark-skinned past at that, even
a different epoch. "Los Angeles in the Adobe Age" was the title historian
J. M. Guinn used for his 1898 discussion of the pre-American city, a none-
too-subtle linking of time and mud.[7] Historian Michael Gonzalez points
out that Anglo visitors to early Los Angeles "equated cracked adobe with
benighted citizens."[8] Never mind that adobe made for the ideal construction material in the Southwest. Never mind that it kept buildings cool in
the summer, never mind that it was relatively easy to work with and inex-
pensive. Never mind that adobe itself stood for home itself, as in "the Avila
Adobe," the "Andres Pico Adobe," or the "Lugo Adobe."

Maybe that was the point after all, at least at some deep cultural level.
Adobe meant home, but California was less and less a home to Mexicans

Figure 28. Making adobe, early twentieth-century Los Angeles. Courtesy of the Huntington Library, San Marino, California.

as the nineteenth century drew to a close. Rarely could even the elite of the group count on being called "Californian" any more, as that signifier moved on over to describe Anglos, regardless of status. Those former *Californios* found that theirs was an existence increasingly consigned to the past. As a young Los Angeles photographer and amateur ethnographer noted in the mid-1880s, "most of the Mexicans live in the old adobe houses which are so rapidly disappearing."[9] Henry Workman Keller meant the houses were falling away, but he could just as easily have meant the people: the linkage was a common one. Adobe meant backwardness to American arrivals; adobe was Catholic, adobe was the missions, adobe was the unusable past. Its quaint revival qualities, especially when accompanied by red tiled roofs and stout timber beams, would not be appreciated by Anglo arrivistes for another generation or more.[10] Tourist John Lauderdale, traveling through Southern California at the very end of the nineteenth century, noted a connection between architectural and human history. Visiting a friend near an old rancho, Lauderdale saw an adobe home where an "old Mexican" had once lived. The structure was now used only for storage. "There are so many instances of this kind," Lauderdale wrote, where those that came before had "to give away to the stronger white man." Adobe could symbolize those supposedly immutable transitions.[11]

Brick, on the other hand, meant progress as against dirty, ugly, unprogressive adobe. Brick stood for the Anglo future. Brick was stolid, solid, and firm. Brick—at least fired brick—could be counted on to be of standard size, regularized and identical brick after brick after brick. Brick *was* a metaphor, there's no mistaking it in the historical record, but it was much more than that. Brick built modern Los Angeles, that Los Angeles before the major earthquakes of the twentieth century consigned brick to its own past. Brick took up where adobe left off or, more accurately, where adobe was left off, exactly at the moment of racial turnover, exactly at the moment California became American. Brick replaced adobe just as it had to, in the equations of the era, so that Los Angeles could become the much-boosted, much-boasted Anglo city of the western American future.[12]

We turn to the story of a place called Simons. It opens in the earliest years of the twentieth century. In 1905 or thereabouts, before death and a bitter family schism split their fraternal partnership, brothers Joseph, Elmer, and Walter Simons embarked on an expansion of their Simons Brick Company. Bricks, brickwork, and progress, growth and ethnic transformation: all intertwined in the web of social relations that was the Simons Brick Company. These plans of the brothers Simons, and their outcome, tell us a great deal about elite Anglo attitudes toward Mexican labor in the City of Angels during the first half of the last century.

On a one-hundred-acre tract in Montebello, about seven miles southeast of downtown Los Angeles and a couple of miles into Los Angeles County, right against the Atchison, Topeka & Santa Fe's tracks, the Simons Brick Company planned an expansion of its brick-making operations. This expansion was to include company housing for the Mexican labor force of about a hundred and fifty men and their families. The Simons brothers simply began to build barrack-like housing adjacent to the deep pit where workers mined the reddish clay good for molding into bricks. By the late spring of 1907, the newly christened Mexican village of Simons, almost within sight of the first and ancient location of the 1771 San Gabriel Mission (as well as the newer mission of 1775), had become a fully engaged brick-making company town, turning out as many as 160,000 bricks a day.

The brick business boomed. The Simons brothers also needed to traffic in workers to keep the operation humming along. They made certain that the region's itinerant Mexican railroad workers and agricultural laborers knew of the availability of jobs at Simons. Through kin networks and local employment agencies, word about brickyard work spread. But the brothers Simons had a more fundamental plan in mind as well. Almost as soon as they had put up the neat row of cheap company houses, they started the Simons Company baby bonus. Every baby born to a brickyard family entered the world with a shiny new $5 gold piece courtesy of the company. So successful was the infant industry that by 1907 the Simons brothers had grown uncertain of the cost-benefit ratio of the innovative program. They contemplated cutting the baby bounty in half, since already sixteen "five dollar babies" had been born to the wives of brick workers, including a set of twins born to Manuel Garcia and his wife. In any event, as the *Los Angeles Times* approvingly reported, the "baby prize fund" was but "one of many striking features of the development of this new town of Simons."[13] Industrial paternalism had taken on a whole new meaning in the brickyards of burgeoning Los Angeles, and the sequential and chronological logic of the baby bonus is simple to discern. Have a baby, earn $5, make that baby a lifelong worker in a company town brickyard.

As the brick baby bonus program abundantly shows, *El Pueblo de Simons* was a company town, one of an extremely few in Southern California.[14] Mexican railroad workers lived in numerous regional rail company *colonias* scattered throughout the Southland, and many of these had a company town look and feel to them. But Simons was different, an industrial village that put home right up against work, all beneath the authoritative gaze of a company and a patriarch with the same name. Segregated by ethnicity and geography, Simons would eventually grow to number more than three thousand brickyard workers and their families. It would exist for nearly half a century. It was, in many ways, an archetypical company town, albeit thousands of miles away from the textile mill villages of the American South, hunkered down in a clay pit hole below the Montebello Hills east of downtown Los Angeles. The Simons Company, Simons brick, and Simons workers built a fair amount of modern Los Angeles. Through fifty years of almost impossibly hard work, the Mexican laborers of the brickyard shaped, dried, cooked, and stacked millions and millions of common bricks. These bricks left the yard bound for construction sites in the expanding commercial, residential, and educational avenues of greater Los Angeles. When they were finished with each day's long work, the workers walked from one end of the brickyard to another, from the clay pits or the drying racks or the gigantic piles of stacked bricks to their small village of company houses.[15]

As the historian Margaret Crawford has written, American company towns, despite their variety, have been characterized by a fundamental pairing of linked landscapes. "On one side is the industrial landscape, shaped by the processes that engendered it; on the other, the model town, a concrete demonstration of a social or physical ideology." The brickyard town at Simons, California, was no different. It exhibited this fundamental, yet symbiotic, division. It was a modern industrial venture tied to a mushrooming metropolis, and it was as well what the *Los Angeles Times* admiringly called "a model industrial town."[16]

Telling the story of Simons requires that both landscapes be understood. It might, in fact, be useful to talk of two places called "Simons Brick Company Yard No. 3," the one being a place where Mexicans lived and worked, the other being what outsiders thought about when they thought about "this new town" and its "many striking features." The first Simons was a place shaped by the physical demands placed upon hundreds of low-skilled laborers. The second Simons was a place that existed more as the product of regional social attitudes, cultural idioms, and history.

THE BRICK MAN'S BURDEN

It made sense for the brick-making brothers to put the new town of Simons where they did. Critical components were already in place or on site: good and plentiful clay deposits, a convenient railroad connection, cheap land, and a labor force of unskilled, cheap, Mexican workers. In 1905, before the Simons Company erected worker housing on site, a priest visiting the little village of Montebello noted not only the region's beauty, but also that the village was "all Mexican," populated by what he romantically called the "sons of Montezuma."[17] For the Simons brothers, then, it was but a short step from a village of Mexicans who worked in their brickyard to a brickyard village of their Mexican workers. The place had the clay, and it had the men who could dig it from the earth. Company housing merely closed the industrial circle.

Then, too, the Simons brothers had experience in brick making and labor management that they learned from their father. Family patriarch Reuben Simons came from Leicester, England, right in the grimy middle of the industrial revolution. He immigrated to the United States and, after a brief stop in Hamburg, Iowa, he and his family joined the midwestern army marching west to Southern California in the late 1880s.[18] He immediately went into the brick business. Business proved lucrative and brisk.

By 1905, Reuben Simons and sons Joe, Walter, and Elmer (the latter would die in 1913, not long after the expansion of the Montebello plant) had been making bricks in the Los Angeles basin for nearly twenty years, at operations not only in Montebello but in downtown Los Angeles and near the Arroyo Seco in Pasadena as well. In Pasadena, especially, the Simons family had been in the right place at the right time. That city's steady growth and big, sturdy houses, plus a few grand tourist hotels, proved a boon to the local brick and construction trades from the mid-1880s forward. By the close of the century, the Pasadena operation turned out some forty-five thousand bricks a day at a twenty-acre plant just adjacent to the streetcar line. Mexican workers went into deep pits to excavate clay, and mules hauled the heavy loads out from the hole.[19] The company built small cottages for the fifty or so Mexican workers in its employ (and a honeymoon cottage for a Simons daughter) within sight of the Oak Knoll mansions, some of Simons brick, which wealthy Chicagoans and others had begun to build as refuges from eastern winters.[20]

Simons brick could be found in some of the important commercial buildings of downtown Los Angeles business blocks and in the foundations of the region's best tourist hotels, the Carleton and Raymond among them. When downtown San Francisco fell and burned in the earthquake and fire of 1906, Simons filled the first orders for Southern California brick used in Bay Area reconstruction.[21] The Montebello plant was "Simons Brick Company Yard No. 3," and within a few years, it became one of the biggest brickyards not only in the Los Angeles basin but also in the entire American West. Especially in the 1920s, when building permits in Los Angeles ran over $100,000,000 a year, brick played a critical role in metropolitan expansion both "up" and "out." Prior to the twin disasters of the Great Depression and the Long Beach earthquake, Simons Brick Company Yard No. 3 was said to be the world's largest manufacturer of common brick.[22]

It is important to note the interplay of culture with commerce in the success of the Simons Brick Company. The firm profited precisely from the creation and maintenance of that "Spanish Fantasy Past" that we have examined in earlier chapters. Mission revival aesthetics created demand for not only the company's standard brick, but also the decorative "padre brick" and "Simons Spanish Roof Tile." The Simons Company had a hand in the National Association of Brick Manufacturers' publication "Homes of the Spanish Type," that listed a number of California models constructed of brick, often in faux-adobe style. Homebuilders who chose the "San Jacinto" model, for instance, could expect "a genuine whiff of the atmosphere of Southern California where three centuries ago the adventurous Spanish Padres were laying the foundation for an architecture which is just now happily coming into its own."[23]

Nowadays prized for their quality, distinctiveness, and connection to the regional past, the Simons bricks of the 1910s and 1920s inevitably helped push mission revivalism forward. And there were an awful lot of bricks by which to build ostensible links to the mythic past. But that part of the myth's social ramification, which tended to create tangible dichotomies between the "Spanish past" and the "Mexican present" helped the Simons brothers as well. Mexican laborers, not Spanish, not mythic, not part and parcel of some quaint regional consciousness embraced by the Anglo elite, invariably and inevitably occupied the bottom rung of the wage and social ladder, looking for precisely the sorts of jobs that the brick industry provided. Bricks might have been part of the Anglo perception of the Spanish Fantasy Past, but brickwork certainly was not. There isn't much romantic about a brickyard. In fact, it probably took a fair amount of societal cognitive dissonance to distance the worker from the product in this regard (that is, if anyone buying Simons bricks ever thought about Simons workers at all). But low wage rates, harsh living conditions, and the mere presence of the company town in the first place seem testimony enough that such dissonance did exist. Such were the complicated intersections between ethnic discrimination, labor value, and elite cultural proclivities in the growing metropolis.

Los Angeles has a reputation as a city blind to its own history, and in the case of Simons Brick Yard No. 3, the stereotype holds. Very little remains to remind passersby of the once vibrant community that existed at Simons through the first half of the twentieth century. The houses have long ago fallen or been torn down and burned, the clay pit filled in. Few remember the place or the people, and it is more likely that a Simons brick would elicit comment today than a Simons brickyard worker. But time was that the place was famous, less for the people who lived and worked there than for the sheer volume of bricks that regularly left the brickyard in stacks of thousands and thousands at a time. Even today, brick company officials in the Los Angeles region recall, "a Simons brick was a good brick." From their distinctive product, with every sixth brick stamped S I M O N S in the damp clay, to their equally distinctive company town labor practices, Simons and the Simons Brick Company—even the bricks themselves—were major Southern California social and industrial institutions.

Figure 29. The Simons Brick Company's Yard No. 3 in Montebello. Worker houses are in the background, bricks stacked into kilns are in the center, and drying racks are in the foreground. Courtesy of the Huntington Library, San Marino, California.

As testimony to the regional renown and curiosity of its Yard No. 3, the Simons Company printed early twentieth-century color postcards that proudly displayed the brickyard (transported across the county/city line by caption to "Los Angeles, Cal."). The unusual postcards, which mimic the fashionable mission postcards of the day, came complete with text, describing the "industrial town of Simons" which "consists of more than 450 people, housing accommodations, restaurant, general merchandise store, post-office, school house, amusement hall, water works, electric plant, etc." Turning out thirty rail cars of brick a day, ca. 1907, the yard owed its success to "efficient labor used in all departments, the superior quality of clay and the fact that the most modern equipment is used."

The *Los Angeles Times* discovered Simons in the summer of 1907. By then, the brick company had succeeded in amalgamating a little town with a big industrial enterprise, in establishing those connections between the two landscapes which Margaret Crawford points out as fundamental to company towns. The newspaper approved. Laid out in neat right angles to the railroad track, the village's few streets had been graded and landscaped with small trees. Flowers sprouted alongside the slightly sunken rail bed, and little mission-style porticos graced the Simons rail stop. Fifty workers' homes swung out neatly and tightly packed behind the company offices. Just a few hundred yards away, millions of freshly made bricks stood stacked in gigantic rectangular piles or kilns, where they would be cooked by flames of natural gas. Each massive kiln (there were already twelve in place in 1907) held an estimated 600,000–800,000 bricks, looking like so many Assyrian temples neatly placed in the southern San Gabriel Valley.[24]

Walter Simons would later say that he built Simons in part so that brickyard workers could live "their way of life, away from towns."[25] Putting town and industry together had been an experiment, but one that had paid off with great success, the *Times* crowed. Simons was nothing short of "a model industrial town," where "problems that have puzzled sociologists for years are being worked out in a gratifying manner." Lest readers wonder what those puzzling problems were, the delighted anti-union *Times* spelled them out: "It is a town without any labor troubles, for the workmen are so content that walking delegates cannot reach them in an effort to create strife. Rents are low, there is no poverty nor want, there are no saloons, there are no bad debts, there is a home with a little garden spot for every one who wants it, with an abundance of land to till for garden purposes, and plenty of good water."[26]

The language here seems lifted from the booster literature urging Anglo working-class and bourgeoisie settlement in greater Los Angeles. What is striking is that this is supposedly the description of an industrial paradise for Mexican laborers. They too, the *Times* reporter suggests, could, through the good offices of their industrial patron, share in the California Dream. Shepherded by the kindly paternalism of their employer, landlord, and majordomo, Mexican workers might experience some of that California so gracefully extolled in the newspaper's words and images.

Despite the *Times* assertion about contented nonunion laborers, it is likely that the Industrial Workers of the World (IWW) tried to get into the brickyard to organize the workers at some point in the pre-Depression days, but that history now seems lost. Some people with Simons memories speak of failed organizing attempts as early as 1919, perhaps by the IWW, which, given the period's repressive antiradical climate, would indeed have been a challenge.[27]

In any event, everything about the experiment looked promising to the chief anti-labor newspaper of the American West. The Simons brothers had successfully reached out to the hinterlands of Los Angeles, just over the county line in the flatlands east of the Los Angeles River. Here they had proven themselves "in the van of manufacturers who are turning to industrial tracts near Los Angeles as the best places for conducting their enterprises." The area's fresh air, good and clean water, and freedom from the big city's attractions and diversions made the experiment all the more laudable. The sheer isolation of the village (it was, after all, "down the hole" as well as out in the countryside) offered the Simons brothers a virtual guarantee of paternalistic social control.

Workers were supposedly so pleased with their lot, so happily obedient, that "one never hears a whistle blow or bell ring out there!" Indeed, "life seems to agree with the inhabitants," who "like working at home [and] seem to enjoy their task" within constant sight of their small houses. It is almost as if these workers had been magically transported back in time, back to the era of romance and supposed ubiquitous happiness in early California. The community's women, the *Times* continued, were especially happy with the state of affairs in the brickyard. For one thing, they enjoyed having credit at "the one store of the town" in order to buy groceries, shoes, and dry goods. The store had been created, an admiring journalist later wrote, out of full consideration of "Mexican preferences . . . stocked and operated by persons thoroughly conversant with the national tastes of the Mexican."[28] The women also appreciated that the men of Simons had only a relatively short distance to walk once the workday was complete; company policy and size made it impossible for the men to cross paths with any city vices by which to diminish their paychecks. They'd also be unlikely to run across any labor organizers. The workday ended, the workers trudged home.

The *Times* story of 1907 makes Simons into a virtual mission, twentieth-century style. In many ways, the perception of the place seemed to conjure up, at least for the anonymous *Times* reporter who visited that day, mission-like images so popular during the period. In this case, though, the Indians of old, supposedly so cared for by the Franciscan padres, had become Mexican industrial laborers, now kept in place by the contingencies of a restricted labor market and attractions offered by paternalistic employers. It was as if the dependent wards of one century had simply changed places with those of another. Benevolent guardianship had been likewise transferred from church to capitalist. Like those early Californians, native or Mexican alike, these people, too, were happy. Dissonance is a dark cloth through which little light can shine.[29]

Even the sight of Simons children playing in the streets, the poorest of them barefoot and in loose-fitting clothes of white muslin, evoked praise from the admiring *Times* reporter. A half dozen old burros, no longer strong enough to pull heavy loads of brick in the yard, wandered among the children. A little two-wheeled cart hitched to one or more of the burros rolled the children around, offering the reporter a laudable representative scene by which to compare Simons to millionaires' row. "Take that two-wheeled cart with a tiny pickaninny driving and the box filled with varied sizes of black, brown and white children, with others trailing behind on burros, and there isn't a happier lot, even on Chester Place."[30]

There's no mistaking that the Simons yard and accompanying houses had a vague mission look and feel to them. A sense of community self-containment and authoritative embrace of workers existed at Simons as it had in the various missions of a hundred years previous. The brickyard even boasted a central·plaza. Company offices, red-tiled in vogue mission revival style, greeted visitors to the yard. A church was soon to be built, as well as a school. Already by 1907, a company cafeteria had been established, where a woman by the name of "Queen Ann" Creel, who had apparently been a Red Cross nurse under Clara Barton, cooked meals for the seventy-five bachelors among the labor force.

Workers' houses, which rented for three and four dollars a month, sat closely next to one another, about fifteen feet apart.[31] Houses were so close to one another that, as a visitor later recalled, "I don't think you could have gotten a Model T between them."[32] Built of rough-hewn lumber, the houses stood in worked-out clay deposits. Houses had no foundations: moisture seeped upwards and invaded in the winter. The houses had no electricity, gas, or plumbing; electricity did not arrive in some until the 1930s. Newspapers covered the interior walls of many (all the houses were single-wall construction) as makeshift wallpaper. Outhouses stood out back. Outside spigots drew water from the company's on-site well or water tank. Brickyard workers stacked pairs of bricks side by side beneath the spigot to support large pots and burned fires to heat water for bathing and cleaning. Oil heaters—which occasionally exploded—or heavy wood stoves inside the homes doubled for cooking and heating. Valley lumber companies occasionally dropped scrap lumber in the yard, which Simons families scavenged for fuel.

Cows, pigs, chickens, ducks, and goats wandered around the front and backyards of those with enough money to afford livestock. Some kept rabbit pens. Roads were unpaved. Between the feet of grazing animals grew gardens of chiles, pumpkins, squash, sweet potatoes, even sugar cane, tended mostly by the community's women. Some brickyard workers worked double shifts, growing quantities of crops for sale as well as holding down brickyard jobs.[33] Peddlers came around regularly; there was "el gallino," the chicken man, and Francisco Romo, the "watermelon man." Other vendors sold meat, since the company store mostly stocked dry and canned goods. A woman called "the Jewess," or "La Judia," sold used clothing, and others wandered in selling vegetables or trinkets. Most sold to the workers on credit. Simons women cooked throughout the day. One resident remembers that his mother made tortillas "three times a day, seven days a week."[34]

Machine foreman Genaro "Henry" Prado, a Simons fixture for decades, wore a gun on his hip, a star on his chest, and he carried handcuffs. "Don Genaro" acted as a kind of unofficial sheriff in the brickyard, every now and then getting help from watchman Thomas Armer or the Los Angeles County Sheriff's Department if he needed it for one reason or another. Prado and his family had started out living alongside the rest of the Simons employees in the *hoya*, but before long he had been given a company house among the *casas de arriba*, on the level ground above the clay pit. The Prado house had running water, indoor plumbing, and a telephone. "Don Genaro" also had, at least for some time, one of the few cars in all of Simons. While it is tempting to interpret a Mexican foreman at Simons in much the same light as an African American driver on an antebellum plantation, there simply is too little information upon which competently to assess Prado's role or attitude.

For nearly thirty years, Walter Malone oversaw day-to-day operations at Simons. Malone had arrived in Southern California shortly after military service in the Spanish-American War, where he had been in combat in the Philippines. For a brief time, he drove a six-horse tally-ho rig for local land baron E. J. "Lucky" Baldwin, shuttling tourists and visitors from Los Angeles to the Baldwin estate in the San Gabriel Valley, which had its own version of a Southland company town.[35] Malone began working for the Simons brothers first as a muleskinner, probably around 1902. From there, he moved up the Simons ladder. When the big Montebello brickyard expanded, Malone became general superintendent of all Simons yards. This included the Santa Monica yard, off Pico Boulevard, which specialized in making roofing tile; the old Pasadena yard; the main Simons yard; and an adjacent one, "the Montebello yard," over on Mines Boulevard, which had a smaller operation specializing in wire-cut brick. Company headquarters were at Eighth and Boyle in downtown Los Angeles, which also had a yard specializing in roofing tile. The company kept a ranch near Calexico in the Imperial Valley, where they grazed livestock and grew feed for their mules. Malone's son remembers that his father had been told by Simons workers that he would never last as yard superintendent: the workers had run dozens of previous superintendents out, they would do the same with him. Malone apparently responded that the time spent as a sergeant in the U.S. Army in the Philippines had taught him a thing or two. In any event, he stayed until his death in 1933.

Walter Malone had a much higher profile in the yard than any other official for the company, more so, even than any of the Simons brothers themselves, who were not often seen. General Superintendent Malone appeared in the yard each morning at seven, ever-present cigar chomped between his teeth. Workers quickly figured out a Malone habit: if the cigar was unlit, he was in a good mood. If it was lit, Malone was in a foul temper, and workers crossed him at the peril of their jobs, if only temporarily.[36] But by all accounts, Malone was well thought of by the yard workers, as were his sons Jack and Walter Jr.[37] Henry Prado named his son after Malone (Walter Leon Prado would later be killed in combat at the end of the World War II). The Malone family home, still standing solidly in a middle-class neighborhood of Montebello, is built entirely of Simons brick.

MIGRATION, MUD, AND MUSCLE

The coming of the Mexican Revolution, coupled with the city's rocketing growth, proved of benefit to the Simons brothers. More immigrant workers began to arrive in the yard, especially from the Mexican states of Jalisco, Michoacán, and Guanajuato. Guanajuato apparently supplied the majority of Mexican-born workers, who may have not known what sort of labor awaited them in the United States. "We wear ourselves out twice as fast [here] as there," were the words of one immigrant from the medium-sized agricultural town of Penjamo, Guanajuato, which was a common hometown for many Simons workers.[38] Former yard laborers remembered that they could board a train in southern Mexico, cross the border at El Paso, grab a western-bound transcontinental, and get off the train almost in the brickyard itself. Simons did have a spur, off the Santa Fe line, but this was a freight carrier for stacks of dried brick. People generally would disembark at various stops nearby and walk to the brickyard to take up work.[39] As novelist Alejandro Morales reconstructed the migration of one family:

> The signs were not what we were accustomed to so we asked, but no one could help us because we asked for "Simones" and here they know the place as "Simons." We walked and walked until we found a man who told us that we were far from our destination. He told us to go to a movie house nearby and talk with a man who knew how to get to Simons. We found that man and my father asked him for Simons. And the man thought for a moment.
> "Oh yes," he said. "I believe I know where. I'm not sure but I think it's in that direction. Follow the tracks, the railroad tracks in that direction. Follow them and where you see the houses from where you stand on the tracks, that will be Laguna Road. When you are there, walk on and look to the right. The houses are painted white." [40]

For their part, the Simons brothers encouraged chain migration, just as they encouraged families to have children through their baby bonus payouts of gold coins. They not only urged brick workers to contact relatives in Mexico about the availability of Simons work, they also encouraged Mexican laborers to write their families and the Mexican government pleading for Mexico to stay out of the First World War. The tensions over the publication of the infamous Zimmermann telegram, which suggested a partnership between Germany and Mexico to reclaim the Southwest, obviously worried men like the Simons brothers on more than one level. Besides its frightening suggestion about bringing the world war very close to home, the threat of Mexican involvement in the war created the specter of a laborless brickyard. No Mexicans meant no bricks and no money. More Mexicans meant more bricks and more money, and the Simons brothers knew a boom building period when they saw one.[41]

Tensions south of the border apparently had some ramifications in the brickyard. A public health officer, sent to survey the brickyard during the Second World War, reported that, at the height of the Revolution in the early 1910s, "some of the Simons Brick Yard employees took Mexican politics very seriously." At one point, a fight broke out in the yard, a "miniature war," the health officer called it. As many as eight men were killed in the ensuing knife- and gunplay. No other accounts of this event can be found. It is true that tensions existed between workers at Simons. The

Revolution provoked hostilities and fights, as did disputes between native-born and Mexican-born workers.[42]

If nothing else, arrivals at Simons Brick Company Yard No. 3 could expect to work hard. As Walter Malone Jr., the son of the Simons yard superintendent from the early years of the twentieth century reminds us, "there is no easy job in a brickyard." In the words of Ismael Vargas, whose father came to the United States in 1906 and worked on western railroads until landing at Simons, where he spent the rest of his life as a laborer, the workers in the yard were simply "beasts of burden" and "peons." To foreman Henry Prado's daughter, Simons workers were treated "like slaves." And to Simons worker Juan Berzunzolo, years and years of brickyard work exhausted both body and spirit: "I have left the best of my life and my strength here," he told an interviewer in the 1920s.[43] Perhaps a contemporary student investigation, Ruth Ewald's master's thesis of 1922, put the equation best. There were, she said, a number of "old-fashioned" capitalists in Los Angeles "who considered foreign labor in the same class with the horse."[44]

Carlos Almazan remembered going to an employment office in Los Angeles sometime in the 1920s and being told that there was work at "Simons, Laguna," the latter term referring either to the once-great rancho of the region or the local lake (later called Sleepy Lagoon). He went. "They paid me $4.00 for working eight hours, but what eight hours! I was left almost dead, especially the first day."[45]

Most of the brickyard work took place in the spring, summer, and fall. Wintertime rains, if only occasional in Southern California, made it difficult to dig clay and make bricks. Consequently, the Simons plant had to produce as many bricks as possible in a relatively short "season." Laborers generally worked a nine-to-twelve hour shift, depending on their actual duties. Most, like those who worked in one of the brick-making machines, began their day early, around 3:00 a.m., with a walk from home to brickyard. Around 7:30 in the morning, they broke for food brought out to them by their wives and children. By the early afternoon, with the sun at its hottest, most shifts were complete. One Los Angeles-area brickyard worker, Bonificio Ortega, who probably worked at Simons, recalled that he came home from the yard too tired to try to learn English.[46] Wages worked out to about 20 cents an hour or less in the early years of the century. Juan Berzunzolo worked for $1.50 a day in 1913. A Simons foreman estimated that subsistence expenditures, for a family, ranged from $5 to $7 a week. Despite the *Los Angeles Times* declaration of 1907 that Simons was a place "without poverty or want," it is hard to ignore the mathematics of destitution. Simons brick workers and their families epitomized the working, Mexican poor of industrial Los Angeles.[47]

Some of the work, like that done by the men in the brick-making machines and by the setters, who placed bricks in the kilns, was piecework. Brick loaders got paid by the hour. By the late 1930s, brick burners made something like $6 a day for a twelve-hour shift; Walter Malone Jr. remembers working an hour-long delivery and unloading shift, taking bricks to a construction site at UCLA, for which he picked up a 37 cent paycheck. His cousin remembers Depression-era work in the Simons hay field at 18 cents an hour. In the late 1930s, a thousand Simons bricks sold for $12, up only $2 a thousand from the early 1920s. Delivery added $2.50 to each thousand. Workers transferred their pay into household staples: a sack of beans, pork chops, corn meal, cheese, bread, sugar, and salt. In the 1930s, Malone remembers, bodybuilders and college students from the coastal beach communities began showing up at the brickyard looking for work. They never lasted long.

The Simons brothers took advantage of the availability of electricity and steam early on. At the time of the congratulatory *Los Angeles Times* story of 1907, some machinery was already powered by electricity, though the lines did not extend to the workers' homes. The company ran electrical current to the mills that ground and mixed the brick clay, to conveyors, and to a small railcar that ran alongside the yard's one hundred mules to bring the clay to the mixers. Steam shovels dug clay from the pit, which sat some fifteen to twenty feet below street level.

Most of the work still had to be done with animal or human brawn. Edison company electricity never completely replaced mules in the brickyard. Mules, at least in the 1920s and 1930s, were the responsibility of Manuel Barber, who also kept the dusty brickyard sprayed with water. He would harness the mules early in the morning, between 3:00 and 4:00 a.m., and make sure that their shoes were in good shape. Blacksmith Carlos Arnold, whom Walter Malone Jr. remembers as "strong as an ox" and "able to do anything," helped with the shoeing of the 1,600-pound mules. Arnold also made the molds that stamped the distinctive signature S I M O N S on every sixth brick out of a brick-making machine. Around November 1 each year, with wintertime rains approaching, the mules would be de-shod and herded up into the Montebello Hills or taken out east to the Imperial Valley, where they'd be pastured till early spring. Brickyard work slowed in the late fall and winter; the yard made do selling what brick it already had on hand. Old-time Simons workers recall the smell of winter around the yard; smudge pot smoke from neighboring citrus groves filled the air. Workers would look for other work in and around Montebello or at one of the few year-round brick or tile companies nearby. Some would leave Simons, in search of whatever agricultural or other work they might be able to find near or far. One worker recalled picking lemons in the late 1930s, and the oddity of seeing Anglos picking alongside him. After speaking with them, he learned that they were from Oklahoma, refugees from the Dust Bowl.[48]

Brick making at Simons was divided among various arduous tasks. Anthropologist Manuel Gamio, working in the 1920s on studies of Mexicans in the United States, listed a dozen different classifications for brickyard labor in California. These included *cortadores, dampeadores, metedores de moldes, areneros, paleteros, templadores, arriadores, cargadores, asentadores, pichadores, arregladores,* and *apiladores.*[49] The clay had to be dug from the ground, then mixed with water, before being formed into bricks. Bricks would be made in one of more than a dozen brick-making machines that ran all day. New wet bricks would be hauled to open-sided drying A-framed racks, where they would sit for a week or more. By the 1930s, a simple electric cable system was in operation at Simons that would carry small pallets of bricks—six per pallet—to the drying racks. Pallets of bricks would dry two abreast in the racks, which stood somewhere around six or seven feet high. Bricks had to be watched in the racks lest they dry too fast; gunny sacking would be hung over the edges of the racks if the weather got too warm (which, in the southern San Gabriel Valley, happened often in the summers). Young Simons kids and teenagers, boys and girls alike, earned a penny a brick turning the drying bricks, or sometimes 32 cents per fifty-yard row. After drying, racked bricks would be stacked into "setter carts" by two men, called *cargadores*. Each cart held around five or six hundred bricks.

Mules or small gas-powered rail cars ("dinkies" or *dinkas*) dragged setter carts to "kiln seats," open, graded spaces near the racks. Here the bricks would be stacked by "setters" into the gigantic rectangular piles called kilns. Four men would begin to stack the bricks, most of them on edge, until they could no longer reach to the top. The crew would then split, with two men climbing atop the kiln. Those on ground level pitched bricks, two at a time, to those on top. Kilns were built adjacent to a three-inch main line of natural gas. Dozens of small openings at the base of each kiln, called arches, were then fitted with smaller, vertical gas lines branching off the main line. The gas jets shot into the inside of the kiln in a blaze of heat and flame. Peepholes above each arch allowed the "burner," who was always on duty when a kiln was fired, to peer into the inside of the kiln from a healthy three- or four-foot distance to see if all was operating smoothly. "Burners" occasionally miscalculated or were the victims of cantankerous gas jets. Workers coated the outside layer of bricks with adobe mud to seal off openings between individual bricks. The gas lines were ignited, and the bricks would cook for seven days and nights. Those on the bottom of the kiln might get over-cooked and brittle; those on the top might not get cooked enough. "The lighter the color, the weaker the brick," Walter Malone remembered.[50] If the kiln got too hot, the bricks might melt together. Sometimes this was done on purpose: the hacked-apart, sharp-edged shards of "clinker brick" would be used for decorative masonry along sidewalks, as edging, or for fishponds. The grounds of 1910-era craftsman-style homes, including some of the best known, utilized such clinker brick with abandon. Even today, a walk around the Greene and Greene craftsman neighborhoods of Pasadena reveals sidewalks, chimneys, driveways, and walls which are full of Simons brick, clinker or otherwise.

After firing for a week, the kiln would have to cool for several days, some-times as many as five. The kiln might even be sprayed with water to cool it. Then the adobe-coated bricks, called casing brick, would be hacked off. Sometimes the kiln would be filled with gas that the burner would deliber-ately not ignite. Once the gas reached the top of the kiln, a spontaneous and loud combustion would take place: this was called "smoking" the bricks, which made them a different color from those cooked more conventionally.

Stacking wet or cooked bricks required strong arms and backs. A wet Simons brick weighed six pounds, a cooked brick weighed about four and a half pounds. When unstacking, workers would toss bricks off the top of the kiln one or two at a time until the height of the kiln had come down to about ten or twelve feet. Then they would grab four bricks at a time, pressing them together as they picked them up, and throw them down to be placed in the waiting truck. Throwing four bricks at once from the top of a kiln, which could be twenty or more feet off the ground, was simply too dangerous to the men below. A bad catch could break a jaw or a nose or do worse damage. Those catching the brick would do so by carefully positioning the heel of their hand to blunt the force of the tossed bricks; the other hand would then quickly be positioned to sandwich the bricks together. Loaders and throwers swapped position every other load. Workers pitching bricks from the bottom of a kiln to men in the bed of a truck did so from their knees. Walter Malone Jr. still remembers with amazement the day his brother, whom the brickyard workers affectionately referred to as "El Loco," went down to the brickyard to load bricks. Jack Malone's crew consisted of himself in the bed of a truck and three old, arthritic Mexican men in their seventies. These men proceeded to throw four thousand bricks to Jack Malone in eighteen minutes. "There was an art to anything everyone did in the brickyard," remembers Walter Malone Jr. He also remembers the forearm and chest strength of brickyard workers. "You didn't mess with those guys too much."[51]

Brickyard work may have required a certain kind of muscular grace, but it was also dangerous labor. Crushed fingers and toes, smashed hands: these were part of everyday life in the yard. Ismael Vargas remembers the day that a clay grinder malfunctioned; a worker tending to it got his shirt caught in the conveyor belt carrying clay to the grinder and had his arm torn off.[52]

From the brickyard, Simons bricks went by truck or rail to construction sites around the Los Angeles basin or further away. Most went to the freight yard at First Street and the Los Angeles River. Simons trucks had Anglo (and Teamster) drivers; the ethnic border operated at the limits of the yard, with Mexicans filling the truck beds and white men driving the bricks to wherever they were headed.[53]

The Simons brothers knew how to make a company town, and they knew more about industrial paternalism than simply to greet each new baby with a gold coin. Simons executive H. B. Howarth described the company town in the early 1920s, noting that Simons was at that point one of the largest, if not the largest, brick plant in the nation. "The settlement is entirely Mexican," he said, "and has its own church and padre. There is a county school with four teachers, a government post office; a company store and a contented employes' [sic] list of nearly four hundred men, which is to be increased to five hundred. . . ."[54] From the workers' houses to the workers' recreation, the imprint of the company was upon everything, even down to the "marital relations court" that Walter Malone held on occasional Mondays to adjudicate disputes among workers and their wives. Company scrip or company credit bought groceries, shoes, and dry goods in the company store. Company invoices delivered monthly rental statements for company houses. A company hall held boxing matches and showed films. Ernestina Macias remembers seeing *Wings* and *The Bridge of San Luis Rey* when they first came out; bilingual moviegoers would whisper translations to family members as they sat together in the darkened hall.

Only occasionally would Simons residents travel to downtown Los Angeles by bus or streetcar, to cinema and grand showhouses like the Million Dollar Theater. "Ernie" Macias remembers going to the San Gabriel Mission to see *The Mission Play* many times.

As if taking their cue from the mill owners and company town overlords of the South, the Simons brothers started a company semi-professional baseball team in the 1910s. Workers wore their company uniforms—white pants, white shoes, a green jersey with a red brick logo, inscribed in yellow "Simons"—all across the Southwest as the Simons team took on all comers and apparently beat most of them. Company officials even okayed the recruitment of several ringers, including Meusel brothers "Irish" (Emil) and Bob, who worked brickyard jobs only for the length of the baseball season. Legend has it that games could become so contested that Simons bricks would occasionally be wielded as projectiles or weapons.[55]

Handball courts were not far from the Simons ball field; brickyard teams often played against other teams made up of Mexicans from different small barrios or industrial companies. There was a dancehall on Simons property as well. Workers congregated there or at one of several nearby dancehalls on weekends. Some attended, or participated in, bicycling races on the grounds of the American Legion stadium, which also held boxing matches. Some well-known regional boxers, including Jesus "Wild Man" Macias and Manual Martinez (who fought as Bert Colima II) either worked in the brickyard or came from families that did.

In another echo of the South, Simons also boasted numerous company bands. At first these were casual gatherings of workers. But in 1924, the company started a more official band made up of a handful of yard workers that performed in the Rose Parade in Pasadena. The group also played to acclaim at the tourist hotels of Pasadena. Within a few years, the band grew into a forty-two-piece orchestra, complete with the importation of a bandleader brought all the way from the National Band of Mexico City.

Workers living in Simons disobeyed company rules at the peril of their employment. Thomas Armer, a former deputy sheriff from Gila Bend (and Walter Malone's brother-in-law) helped to keep the peace and acted as night watchman. Liquor was forbidden; not only did the company store not carry it, it was against company rules to bring it in from the outside, though some workers apparently smuggled it into their little houses and others made their own white mule whiskey. The liquor ban, the admiring *Los Angeles Times* editorialized, was "especially appreciated by the wives of the Mexicans."[56] By the 1930s, the rules had been relaxed enough so that workers congregated after their shifts in one of the several Simons houses that sold store-bought or homebrewed wine and beer. George Armer recalls that this was "not allowed but not disallowed either."[57]

In keeping with the modern mission arrangement of the brickyard, the Simons brothers made sure to make religious arrangements for their workforce. In cooperation with the local Benedictine brothers, they established a Catholic church at Simons not long after the plant began operation. The Benedictines, whose religious charges up to that point had been mostly the region's Basques, began to minister to the Mexicans of Simons. By the end of 1912, the Benedictine order finished building the new Our Lady of Mount Carmel chapel. Land grant heiress Arcadia de Baker, who had married into an elite Anglo town-building dynasty (Robert Baker had helped found Santa Monica), donated the land for it. Within a year, aided by yard superintendent Walter Malone (who was, wrote one Benedictine years later, "ever solicitous for the spiritual welfare of the little settlement"), the chapel counted 280 parishioners.[58] Mount Carmel, or *Monte Carmelo* as the residents of Simons referred to it, would long be a central reference point in the lives of the brickyard community members, especially under the tutelage of longtime church leaders Raphael Defives and Charles Espelete. "Father Charles" is still remembered for his festive church bazaars.

Mount Carmel, like many other such "Mexican chapels," was the segregated counterpart to the larger Catholic church not far away. That hardly diminished its importance to the Simons barrio. Here, forty or fifty feet off the Santa Fe's tracks, the workers of Simons worshiped (men in the left pews, women in the right). Babies were baptized, most of them healthy, some of them "graven infirmitatem," some of them *post mortem*. Simons kids went to Thursday catechism classes at Mount Carmel after school; there they received confirmation and later got married. Almost all of the Simons workers and their families, including Superintendent Walter Malone, were Catholic. Residents remember that missing mass was frowned upon, both by neighbors and by the company. The handful of Mexican Protestants in the yard, derisively called "los aleluyas" by Simons kids, clustered together in one corner of the community.

The Mount Carmel chapel had its counterpart in the Simons school. By 1914, the Vail School (locally referred to as "the Mexican School") had opened up just across the street from the yard. Built to educate the children of brickyard workers, who earlier had to be carted by wagon to the Montebello School, the school still stands today, one of the few remaining structures from bygone days. Simons kids rarely went to the Greenwood

School in Montebello; they stayed at the Vail School. Even when they reached junior high, and were supposedly integrated, the Mexican students all had the same homeroom; some of the eighth graders could be as old as seventeen or eighteen. One student remembers that his teacher simply sat at his desk and read a book all day. "He didn't care." The junior high school principal threatened to send all the Mexican kids "back to Vail" unless they quietly accepted their second-class status in the school.[59] "The only time we heard English was when the teachers spoke the language," another former student remembered.[60] Another remembered a student having his name changed by a teacher from Jesus to Joe; the former name, the teacher said, "reminds me too much of our Lord."[61]

As a result of such discrimination (and the fact that apparently many of them were sick a good deal of the time) most of the Simons kids remained illiterate or semi-literate at best. Not until military service in World War II did most of them learn to read and write in either English or Spanish with any fluency.[62] At the end of the day, Ismael Vargas remembers, "the Anglo kids went one way, the Mexicans the other."[63]

Such discrimination outside the confines of the brickyard was hardly limited to schools. A health worker surveying the brickyard in the World War II years learned that "Montebello City authorities are not desirous of having the public playground and swimming pool operated by them used by the Simons residents."[64] Ismael Vargas remembers Simons workers and their families heading to the Vogue Theater in Montebello to see films on Sunday afternoons. At the entrance, the Anglo families paid and went one way into the theater, Mexicans the other, just as at the end of a school day. Even in the larger social world of Montebello and the southern San Gabriel Valley, the region's Anglos, Mexicans, and Japanese inhabited different worlds. They didn't socialize, they didn't interact, and they didn't share much except by accidents of time and space. Of course much of this was by majority design. Racially restrictive policies and practices occupied center stage in Montebello's city planning through the prewar era, as they did nearly everywhere else in greater Los Angeles. "It is the practice of the [Realty] Board to watch carefully to see that undesirable races are kept out of the older sections of town," wrote a prominent Montebello realtor in the mid-1920s. "Controlling race conditions and enforcing race restrictions" stood at the top of the board's goals.[65]

Not that many in Simons felt that they could push against the system. "We were afraid to go to a restaurant," remembers one Simons resident, "because we didn't know if we would be served." Not knowing was almost worse than knowing. Either way, there was little sense in pushing the boundary.

But people did come to the brickyard. A woman named Verona Spellmire, along with ten other women she recruited, began to visit the brickyard every week for a while, starting in 1919. Ms. Spellmire went to Simons to lead the workers in Catholic religious instruction, and she later branched out from the brickyard to wider missionary work among the Mexican and Mexican American populations of greater Los Angeles.[66] Social workers and society people wandered the three and a half miles east from downtown Los Angeles to see what Simons (they also called it "Simons Town") looked like. Walter Malone remembers seeing rich young Anglo women come out to the yard in their Buicks and Cadillacs, usually accompanied by a reporter from one of the local papers. These women came to the yard to see a slice of industrial life or a Mexican barrio, or to get a taste of social work. Once the reporter had gotten his story, or the photographer his shot, the women would quickly leave.

A MAN WITH A BIG HEART

Walter Simons presided over the brickyard operations with the racial paternalism of a company town baron, a position and attitude that brought him professional and social accolades. A respected and undoubtedly well-off industrialist (the brickyard became more or less his after a mysterious 1915 family feud split the brothers), Simons served several terms as president of the Los Angeles Builders Exchange as well as the California Common Brick Manufacturers' Association and Los Angeles Brick Exchange. In February 1924, he hosted the Common Brick Manufacturers' Association of America at the Biltmore Hotel (itself built of a million bricks), the first time that any large industrial body had come to the Los Angeles for its annual convention.

At the opening of the meeting (after the Simons band had serenaded the brick men at the train station), Walter Simons welcomed the conventioneers to Los Angeles. Expressing his joy at hosting "my fellow-craftsmen," he spoke loftily of the brick industry and its role in the buildup of Southern California. The mayor of Los Angeles, George Cryer, had spoken to the brick men as well, and he had boosted Los Angeles in typical terms of climate, growth, and culture. Walter Simons attached the brick industry to those sentiments. "We want to put in a program here to help along with the great movement of rendering this city a more fireproof proposition," he told his colleagues. And that meant brick, brick, and more brick.[67]

While in Los Angeles, convention attendees toured the film studios of Thomas Ince, wandered the seacoast at Venice and Santa Monica, and gaped at the homes of movie stars. Special excursions included a visit to the oil derricks ("thick as trees in a forest") in Santa Fe Springs, basin brick plants, and the Los Angeles harbor complex in San Pedro and Long Beach. Conventioneers drove the streets of Pasadena where millionaires lived. On one evening, they went to a special screening ("brick night") of *The Ten Commandments* at Graumann's Egyptian Theater in Hollywood. The brick men found the movie "one of the most powerful arguments for safe buildings that ever has been presented on stage or screen."[68]

The brick people took in all the requisite sights of 1920s Los Angeles: the remarkable oil fields, the "typical" homes of the wealthy, and the ostentatious displays of Hollywood. But they also saw the "fantasy past" mingled with the Los Angeles present. They went to the San Gabriel Mission and then immediately to the *Mission Play*, and they went as well out to the Mission Inn in Riverside and "Ramona's Marriage Place" in San Diego. Convention attendees also spent time at Simons, touring the plant, getting their photographs taken with children of the brickyard workers, listening again to the Simons "Mexican band," watching boxing matches between Simons employees, and even taking in a film (a brick construction movie called *The Great Idea*) in the company hall.

If we juxtapose the conventioneers' time at, especially, John Steven McGroarty's melodramatic *Mission Play* and Walter Simons's Yard No. 3, it seems as if the brick manufacturers availed themselves of the opportunity to make bookends of their industrial tourism. On the one hand, they could see Mexicans frozen in space at Simons, and on the other hand they could see them frozen in time at the *Mission Play*.

Some of the brick men from the East criticized shoddy home construction in Los Angeles, citing film sets as the apparent model for the work. "The eastern men here . . . ," remarked a local official, "are in love with the city, with its residential possibilities and with what has been accomplished. Their only criticism is of so much flimsy home building." One would imagine that the homes of Simons Yard No. 3 workers might as well have been used as the example of cheap housing.[69] Architects, including the noted Southern California architect Reginald Johnson, came before the group to point out that mission and Spanish revival buildings might best be produced with brick.

Figure 30. The Simons company band. Courtesy of the Huntington Library, San Marino, California.

No better representation of the regional regard for Walter Simons among his racial and class peers can be found than that which appeared in a long story devoted to Simons in the pages of *Saturday Night*, one of the more prominent of the elite Anglo social weeklies in the pre–World War II era. The profile, one of a series in the magazine's "California Men of Constructive Ability" stories of the mid-1920s, appeared at Christmastime, 1925. The timing was not coincidental. Walter Robey Simons, who had once prepped for the Baptist ministry, received the praise due a saint. Samuel T. Clover, the magazine's London-born president and editor, wrote the profile himself, and he wrapped Walter Simons in effusive praise.

Simons was more than an industrialist; he was a humanist, a man with a big heart, a man with abiding and deep love for his employees. And Clover sought to demonstrate such by remarking about Simons's regard for Mexican children. For he was, at Christmastime at least, Santa Claus, sort of. He did not actually pass out gifts to the Mexican children and Mexican mothers who gathered in the main plaza of the town: "one of the trusted Mexicans, long time in the company's service enacts that role." But Walter Simons did oversee the action, accompanied by his wife and a number of their wealthy friends. Gleeful Mexican children accepted their gifts of "dolls, toys, mufflers, frocks, shoes, hats and caps and other sensible presents while their mothers rejoiced in the receipt of material for new dresses, shawls, shoes and household necessities." Clover could hardly contain his enthusiasm, gushing in much the same way as the reporter from the *Los Angeles Times* decades earlier. "To see those merry-faced brown-skinned youngsters carrying off their treasures . . . is to get a new light on the melting pot of America."

Not all was such sweetness. Clover's very next sentence casts an ominous pall on Simons, darkens that "new light." "Not a few among the children were born in the town of Simons," he observes, "and will be citizens of the republic if they live." It is hard to know, these eighty years later, what exactly Sam T. Clover meant when he wrote those words. Likely he had in mind a couple of features of Mexican life in Los Angeles: first, there is the strained association of American birth- and citizenship rights, apparent in Clover's assumption that the Mexican American children will somehow grow and mature into citizenship, unlike Anglo children, presumably, who were citizens already at five or ten years of age. In the words of historian Mark Reisler, Anglos generally perceived Mexicans as "always the laborer, never the citizen." At the very least, every one of the $5 gold piece babies had been born American, though Clover seems not to have embraced that fact. Then there's the ominous "if they live" clause. What could it mean? Likely it had something to do with public perceptions of Mexican morbidity, and it is true that Mexican mortality statistics spiked higher than Anglo in this period in Los Angeles history, especially as far as children were concerned. According to one 1920 report, the "Mexican babe's chance to live is just one-third that of the average babe born in Los Angeles."[70]

In any event, the macabre statement hardly slowed Clover down. He praised Walter Simons for building the school where "teachers impart English and American ways" to the several hundred children. He singled out the vocational instruction for special comment; older children worked at a "model cottage," where they made furniture for the houses of Simons families. Their work was nothing short of "ingenious," in that they fashioned functional pieces out of dry goods boxes, shoeboxes, and rough scrap lumber. "There are natty little bureaus, covered with chintz, neat benches, kitchen tables, a lounge, bedsteads, a cradle, chests of drawers and a score or more of miscellaneous articles for the home, calculated to lighten the housework and afford comfort to all."

But this was not all purely function over form. On the contrary: "As an object lesson to the Mexican tenants, this model display is invaluable. It

Figure 31. Ernestina Macias (center, left) on the lap of Walter Simons, 1920s. Author's collection.

suggests to untrained minds what is possible to do with material many regard as only fit for kindling wood, thus subtly inculcating the virtues of thrift and economy." With this statement, Clover again makes use of a powerful regional metaphor. Whereas he opened his article with a discussion of Walter Simons amidst the happy Mexican children (i.e., the father among the workers), he moves here to remind his readers that Mexican stock itself might be regionally viewed by Anglos as "only fit for kindling wood," but such a view did not take into account such careful sculpting and forming as that practiced by the prudent and beneficent Southern California industrialist cut from Simons cloth.

In fact, Clover's article is all about building and forming and shaping, about making bricks, putting up buildings, and creating "happy and contented" people out of the more than 3,000 residents of Simons. Here, not far from the San Gabriel Mission, Walter Simons became Southern California's twentieth-century version of Father Junipero Serra, except of course that Native American neophytes had been replaced by Mexicans, just as they had throughout the region and regional economy from the mid-1850s forward. And the latter-day father to his workers sat in the back of his large convertible, waving to the brickyard workers as he drove past the yard every now and then.[71]

The mission parallels are striking, really, and in them we may find some possible answers to the question: why start a company town in Southern California? Examples were, of course, around. The railroad *colonias*, for instance, did put work and home together, sometimes literally, in the form of boxcar homes provided for Mexican workers. But a company town like Simons was rare, especially given its early roots, ca. 1906. Could the Simons brothers have imagined a mission metaphor for the place, as, I think, Clover suggests?

There's no doubt that self-contained Simons (the gates into the company housing tract were locked at night, to keep workers in or peddlers out, or both) existed as a place where Mexican laborers could be closely attended to, gradually brought forward toward "civilization."[72] This meant, at least by the first decade of the twentieth century, less about Catholicism and general religious devotion than attempts at nationalism and Americanization. Cleanliness swapped places with Godliness, at least in the minds of Walter Simons and the public health care doctor and nurses who made regular visits to the brickyard clinic housed in "Simons House No. 1." The World War I–era influenza epidemic carried off many Simons residents. Ernestina Macias remembers her childhood impressions of many a Simons "night party," which were in reality Catholic wakes held in the home of the deceased. By the early 1920s, public health authorities had established a health center in Simons, which was added to in a few years by a "prenatal conference" in the brickyard to address neonatal and infant care, one of six in Los Angeles County. The need for such a clinic was clear: according to one survey, Mexican infant mortality in Los Angeles County in the years 1916–1927 ranged from death in nearly one in three births to a low of one in ten.[73]

Simons workers bought Liberty bonds and war stamps at a furious pace during the First World War; Clover reckoned that, per capita, the Simons Brick Yard had purchased more than any other industrial plant in America. The plant was, he assured Los Angeles, "the envy of all eastern business men" who visited it.

Part of that envy, Clover suggests, came from the perception of worker contentment at Simons. The wage system, "equitable, mutually-agreeable," created worker loyalty. It is almost as if Clover juxtaposed the mission metaphor with a Mission Play metaphor to describe the brickyard as a place of peace, ease, and Mexican repose. Here, as the workers trudged back from their shifts in the afternoon, "one may hear guitars strumming lazily in the evenings, see colorful, and not infrequent, fiestas, and in other directions discover that in addition to efficiency at the plant there is idealism in the community."

"Never has the wise patron-employer sought to compel his workmen to conform to his views, rather than their own, in the way of living conditions." It was a calculated operation, carefully constructed "step by step," or so Sam T. Clover believed, "to allow free rein to the employees in all matters outside of actual business affairs." Such planning even extended to house construction (supposedly), in that undefined "Mexican preferences" were taken into account, and "as stores were opened Mr. Simons had them stocked and operated by persons thoroughly conversant with the national tastes of the Mexican."

But Clover's assumption that only in the workplace did Simons scrutinize workers falls apart after his own description of careful planning in the yard: "Today the theaters, schools, churchs [sic], restaurants, billiard halls, and all other improvements are operated by Mexicans, or by Americans [note that such national categorization negates even the possibility of Mexican Americans] peculiarly sensitive to the likes dislikes, inhibitions and prejudices of their Latin-American neighbors."

How else to make the labor force "happy and contented"? "In this wise way, Mr. Simons has tried to solve the problem of satisfying labor believing that, if he succeeded, production costs would be correspondingly satisfactory." Apparently, the modern mission worked. Walter Simons had "amply justified his hopes and proved the wisdom of his course." Certainly that was true in some terms. Walter Simons and his wife were able to turn the daily 600,000 Simons bricks into enough disposable income to live in a Hancock Park estate, maintain a vacation home in Balboa ("Walt-Mari"), and travel to South America, London, Paris, the Mediterranean, and the Nile. Walter Simons belonged to the elite social clubs of the Los Angeles basin: the Jonathan Club, the Bel-Air Country Club, the Los Angeles Athletic Club, the Newport Harbor Yacht Club (a vacation home stood next door), among others. By the mid-1920s, with its operation now spread over 350 acres, Simons Brick Company Yard No. 3 was being touted as the world's largest common brick manufacturing plant. More Mexicans, more bricks, and more money: out of such equations was modern Los Angeles built. The parent Simons Brick Company was, in this era, one of the six largest employers of Mexican labor in greater Los Angeles. Not surprisingly, another of the six was also a brick company.[74]

As countless community studies, particularly of mill and textile towns, have shown, company paternalism inevitably helped to solder the bonds of community, if only by making sure that employees lived and worked cheek by jowl. As if to make the parallel all the more striking, one former Simons resident, remembering his World War II training that took him for the first time to the Deep South, said simply, "Simons was Appalachia." The workers and their families living in Simons, "our little island surrounded by 'them,'" spoke Spanish. He recalled that one mark of distinction between Simons residents and those who lived in any of the small Mexican barrios of Montebello was language. Simons people spoke Spanish. Always.[75] Walter Malone, who knew some Spanish, nonetheless counted on brickyard timekeeper and postmaster Gil Romo to translate for him when necessary.

To Ismael Vargas, who was a young boy of El Pueblo de Simons in the early 1930s, "the whole world was Mexican." He remembers that he even suspected that "God was Mexican," so tight-knit was the Simons community. Children were brought up according to Mexican custom, and a father's authority in the home was rarely questioned. Those who had come to Simons directly from Mexico rarely took out citizenship or naturalization papers. They preferred instead, in the words of one former resident, to "milk a cow both ways." That is, they maintained lives both "here" and "there," in an apt instance of the maintenance of at least some agency within the paternal setting that Simons enforced. As one Simons worker reported, he had "always been with one foot in the stirrup."[76] At holiday time, especially on Mexican Independence Day, September 16, the workers held big celebrations, often organized by the "Comision Honorifica" specially established to put on Mexican fetes. Residents decorated their houses; a platform would be put together in the plaza, speeches made, queens crowned; music and dancing followed a parade through the yard.

As the area outside the yard, in Montebello and the southern San Gabriel Valley in general, began to grow, the earlier, simple ways of addressing each Simons house by number (as Simons no.1, no. 2, no. 3, etc.) gave way to naming houses by street addresses.[77] The company town displayed a mix of national and nostalgic regard in its street names: there were, not surprisingly, Jalisco Street and Guanajuato Street, but there were also Plymouth Street, Ford Street, Date Street, Railroad Street, and Southworth Street. Bachelor employees lived in the Simons boarding house or some of the small "bachelor shacks."

Some former Simons employees and their descendants have characterized the arrangement of the brickyard as a Southern California version of the Mexican hacienda, complete with a peon labor force and a racial hierarchy of overseers and owners. That may have some validity, but it is also clear that Simons was an up-to-date industrial manufacturing center, modernized by electricity, Plymouth gasoline locomotives, trucks, and the nearby railroad tracks. The several hundred acres of the Simons Brick Company was itself a little industrial Los Angeles, both indicative of, and critical to, the growth of the city in the early decades of the twentieth century.[78] During the 1920s, especially, when local brick production increased exponentially, the Simons Brick Yard hummed with the combined effort of brute labor and industrial innovation, an arrangement the company (like many industrial concerns of the era) was quick to defend. For instance, when challenged by the city of Los Angeles over a piece of their industrial property, the Simons Company responded with claims about the industrial future of Los Angeles. The city wanted to turn back time, Simons attorney Richard Culver claimed, "to turn this municipality into a flower garden and kill all legitimate manufacturing enterprises." Industry, Simons, and the future of Los Angeles went together hand in hand, the attorney claimed, for the good of the city, for the good of the region, and for the good of the workers who made brick after brick after millions of bricks.[79]

Of course, Simons did mean something to the workers who lived there, raised families there, and died there, and it is important for us to try and reconstitute some of that meaning if we can. But it is also important to recall that outside Simons, beyond *el puerton*, the plant stood for something entirely different. Outside, Simons had virtually no Mexican meaning at all (except for those who once worked there, might again work there, or who had family there). Of course these alternative, "outside" meanings (Simons as modern industrial plant, Simons as part of the east side's development, etc.) were critically bound up in the reality of Simons as a place of backbreaking Mexican labor, but the life and times of those "down the hole" never occasioned much comment. On the contrary, it is as if the bricks emerged from the clay pits already shaped, cooked, fabricated. Even the ads the company placed in trade and construction journals rarely showed the Mexican workers in the yard, choosing instead to focus on company trucks or the Plymouth "dinkies."[80]

I think that this other vision of Simons was part and parcel of the industrial growth of the city and, especially, the region east of the Los Angeles River; it was an industrial vision, at once inextricably tied to—and ignorant of—Mexican labor. Whereas the praise heaped upon Simons, and Walter Simons in particular, emanating from society publications and patrons, made sure to mention ethnic noblesse oblige and the perceived progressive care of Mexican workers at the brickyard, this newer appreciation had very little room for praise of paternalism.

We should briefly explore this industrial gaze that envisioned Simons not as a company town but solely as a company. By the mid-1920s, Simons Yard No. 3, which had once stood alone in the flatland hinterlands east of downtown Los Angeles, now existed at the center of an ambitious development scheme. The J. B. Ransom real estate development company, plotting an innovative melding of residential and industrial development, sang the praises of "Montebello Park," Montebello, and Simons itself in its promotional vehicles. East side industrial decentralization (which in many respects the Simons brothers pioneered) had become the wave of the future, the Ransom Company crowed. Not only did the city of Los Angeles demand industrial growth, the region offered unparalleled benefits in both actual and social climate, away from the "congested district" of downtown Los Angeles. Workers worked longer and better in the Southland's unending sunshine. What is more, there was "almost complete freedom from labor agitation," in part because "a plentiful supply of lower grades of labor is available from Mexico." Industrialists of the era deliberately and proudly structured discriminatory wage rates for laborers, slicing off 10–20 percent for Mexican workers, so that such availability would be seen as money in the coffers of area industrialists. For instance, a period Los Angeles Chamber of Commerce report on regional industrial development bluntly spelled out unskilled wage rates: 50–60 cents an hour for "American" laborers, 45–50 cents for "Mexican" workers. "We have a Mexican population . . . in excess of 50,000 people," the Chamber told the world, "and these people make excellent workers, the men as common laborers in different crafts, and the women make splendid workers in textile plants."[81]

The key arena for new industry was a rectangle of "wonderful territory lying east of the river." Approximately twelve square miles made up this district, bounded by Whittier Boulevard, Santa Fe Avenue, Slauson Avenue, and the Rio Hondo River. The Ransom organization had purchased several hundred acres of residential land in Montebello that it was now advertising for development into industrial workers' housing. The parcel bumped up against the "immense clay products plant of the Simons Brick Com-

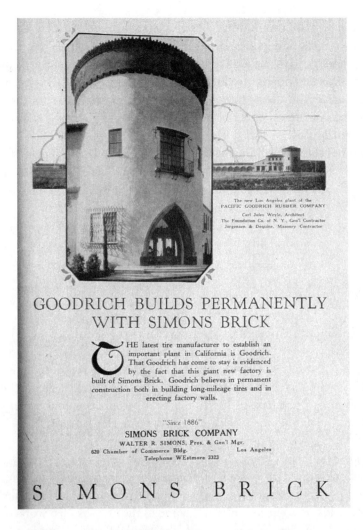

Figure 32. Building industrial Los Angeles together. Author's
collection.

pany." So proud was Ransom of the proximity of such mighty industrial
power that a photograph of the Simons yard, "the largest single unit brick
plant in the world," graced the public relations pamphlet.

Equally exciting was the development of Montebello, the "city of
flowers." Ransom pointed out that the community had embraced all the
best aspects of modern city planning: schools were contemplated, parks
begun; in short, "Montebello is amply equipped with all the civic features

of an up-to-date community." "As workers pour into the East Side factories, they must find homes for themselves and their families; and they will create a tremendous volume of business for stores, banks, theaters, professional men and others. To the homeseeker, therefore, who wants an ideal homesite, and to the investor who is looking for property with the likelihood of maximum increase in value, we unhesitatingly recommend Montebello Park."[82]

Montebello took off in part because Simons had been so successful and could be pointed to as evidence of the region's industrial promise (provided the company town was not brought into the equation). But as the one community began to grow and expand, the brickyard faltered. Late 1920s price wars between competing brick manufacturers, greater use of masonry block building materials, and the 1933 Long Beach earthquake all combined to hurt the brick business in Southern California, as did, of course, the arrival of the Great Depression. Tougher post–Long Beach building codes hurt the brick trade perhaps the most. As Los Angeles County planner William Fox remembered, the new codes (subsequently amended) did not sit well with Walter Simons. "The new code outlawed all brick construction," Fox told an interviewer, "and Mr. Simons of the Simons Brick Company—great big fat guy, practically the head of the Los Angeles Chamber of Commerce—just blasted me and the department and the board and everyone else. . . . The Simons Brick Company was out near Montebello, where it had the pits, and it did all the brick work in Los Angeles County. Now it was obsolete."[83]

Yard watchman Thomas Armer's son remembers that by the early 1930s, the "brickyard went to pot," with the fall-off in regional building construction. Workers did what work they could find: some cut and baled hay in the fields adjacent to the yard.[84] Some of the Simons men worked periodically, a day here and there, with the Works Progress Administration; such work in the "outside" opened their eyes to a wider world. One worker recalled that WPA or Civilian Conservation Corps work during the Depression offered Simons residents a chance to "see how the other half lived."[85]

The Simons Company still got important contracts, especially in the late 1930s, in part because Walter Simons patented an innovative type of brick, called a groutlock brick, which was reinforced with steel and concrete. With no small amount of hubris, Walter Simons declared his innovation "earthquake-proof."[86] The company's contracts included Royce Hall at UCLA, a massive, faux-mission-style Goodrich plant, part of Disney Studios, a Uniroyal plant in Commerce, and some of the early public housing projects,

Figure 33. Trucks ready to haul at Simons Brick Yard No. 3. Author's collection.

such as Aliso Village and Ramona Gardens in East Los Angeles, and Rio de Pueblo in Long Beach (originally designed to house World War II troops). Simons brick also graced the walkways surrounding the new Mission Playhouse in San Gabriel, where 1920s Angelenos and tourists went to see California history staged as a tearful romance. The Ramona Gardens project apparently kept the yard busy for a year, making and then hauling over a million bricks to the construction site.

General Superintendent Walter Malone died shortly after the 1933 Long Beach earthquake. The Simons yard closed for a day in honor of his memory. Yard workers wished to shoulder Malone's casket and carry it miles and miles from Simons to Calvary Cemetery in East Los Angeles, but his widow would not permit it. The workers did cover the gravesite with fresh-cut flowers in tribute to Malone's memory.

During the Depression, when the Simons store no longer operated, workers in the brickyard opened their own cooperative store, asking $5 dues from each brickyard family. Other stores catered to Simons residents as well. Constancio Macias, whose son became the well-known boxer "Wildman Macias," ran a store near "the hole," where he hung the flags of the United States and Mexico (American-born and Mexican-born Simons workers did not always get along, and appeals to both nationalities were both culturally and commercially sophisticated on Macias's part). The Immigration Service occasionally wandered into Simons, stepping up their visits in the repatriation era. But as one worker recalled, the overlap between racial stereotype and assumptions about nationality worked in the favor of some workers: "if you were light," Jess Garcia says, "you were o.k."[87]

Sometime in the late 1930s or early 1940s, brickyard workers apparently organized a wildcat strike, either in the hopes of gaining union recognition or in defiance of their union officials. In any event, many have suggested that the action simply resulted in wholesale firings of brickyard workers.[88]

Despite some big late-1930s contracts, the end of the 1930s and the

Depression did not mean that Simons roared back into action. On the contrary, the yard gradually fell into disarray. A survey done in 1940 listed nearly 800 residents of Simons, with children outnumbering adults by 150 people. Of all these people, only 60 were counted as U.S. citizens. The community's 182 houses had a total of four flush toilets. No bathtubs could be found. Health inspector U. Troiano found 90 percent of the houses unfit for human habitation. Rats scurried to and fro, reawakening fears of disease transmission. The Simons dump sat in uncomfortably close proximity to workers' houses.[89]

Within a year, health inspectors issued a stern warning to the Simons Company to put the brickyard housing in order within thirty days. Wartime conditions intervened, apparently, and the order was neither complied with nor enforced. By the mid-1940s, the yard had emptied out. Feeble attempts to find oil below the clay deposits amounted to nothing, and there wasn't enough work in the wartime economy to employ more than a skeletal crew of thirteen workers. Many of the brickyard workers had already been drafted.[90]

SIMONS ERASED

By the early 1950s, bricks and company towns were no longer so critical to the industrial equation of Southern California growth. Walter Simons, frail and in poor health, passed day-to-day control of the brickyard to his wife. The yard limped along, facing increasing competition not only from other products, such as masonry block, but from different kinds of brick (especially wire-cut). What is more, the small houses of Simons, which the company did little to keep up, had long ago begun to show their years. In May 1952, the Los Angeles County Health Department stepped in and issued an order that declared the Simons housing substandard. Most had not been improved for fifty years. A spokesman for the company told the Los Angeles Times that the houses were "just 1 × 10 frame buildings, temporary houses, really, although 50 to 60 years is not very temporary." By early August, the last remaining families, some 167, had moved out of "the hole." Some found work at nearby brick manufacturers like Vitrafax Brick in Vernon. The local fire department used the homes, many of which had already been knocked down, for fire-fighting practice.[91]

Within six months, about 250 acres of the former Simons brickyard and town of Simons had been sold for $2.5 million. One of the buyers was W. I. Hollingsworth who, less than twenty years earlier, had been one of the principals of the Mission Play Association, the consortium that had gained control of the play when John Steven McGroarty faltered. Simons land was actually valuable, not so much for the clay deposits still there in the pit, but because of the peculiarities of railroad law; the pit lay within the railroad's short-haul circle regarding freight pricing. The Bethlehem Steel Corporation eventually used the yard as a slag pit; its cranes and giant trucks filled in pits that had been dug out by generations of Simons workers. "Patron employer" Walter Simons died in November 1954, felled by a stroke and old age. His obituary observed that he had shown "great concern for the welfare of his employees," and that his death occasioned many a prayer "from numerous inconspicuous little homes in all parts of Los Angeles County." The brick magnate's estate added up to just over $2 million. Mrs. Simons, acting in her late husband's behalf, gave $3,000 to each of twenty-six loyal Simons employees, and an additional $3,000 to nineteen employees who had been with the brick company for twenty-five years or more. Henry Prado, by now an old man, was one of the workers who received the $6,000 bonus; he had been with the company since 1899. "It's the most wonderful news I ever had," foreman Lupe Martinez, who had started out at Simons in 1908, told a reporter. Martinez, then sixty, stated that he would use the money he received to buy war bonds, "for the day when I won't be able to work any more." Judge Necomb Condee, who reluctantly approved the distribution of money, shook his head and said such generosity was the "best answer to communism I've ever seen."[92]

A Spanish-language folk song, or *corrido*, from the early decades of the twentieth century includes a stanza in which immigrant Mexicans, traveling a working circuit across the great Southwest, arrive "at Laguna, without any hope."[93] That this is a reference to the hard work and low pay of unskilled labor seems likely, but I suspect that it also may be a specific reference to brickyard labor at "Simons, Laguna."

The Simons Brick Company Yard No. 3 was a place of great importance to the growth of Los Angeles in the first half of the century. The company literally helped to build the city: its hotels, its universities, its homes, and its businesses. Yet ninety years after the construction of the brickyard company housing, Ismael "Mayo" Vargas recalls Simons as a place where human potential was never allowed to flower. Workers at the brickyard worked entire lives trying to get hold of something approximating the California

Figure 34. Growing up in Yard No. 3: The young Walter Malone Jr.
Author's collection.

Dream. But the odds were against them down there in the hole. One needs
to bear in mind the line from the 1925 story about Simons, which suggested
that citizenship might await those poor Mexican kids playing in the streets
of "el pueblo de Simons," if they live.

The macabre statement suggests another enduring irony of Simons.
Because in a sense the reporter was right: a better world, a changed world,
awaited the workers of Simons if they lived. But the trial they had to pass
through was not so much living through a life of company town hard, segregated work; that alone would not and could not change the world. No,
their world would change if they could live through the trial of the Second

World War, something the magazine reporter could not possibly have anticipated. For it was that conflagration which forever changed the world of people who grew up at Simons and left it for military service and, in many cases, combat in the Pacific and the theaters of Europe. If they lived through this, and many, like Walter Leon Prado and Ismael Vargas's brother, did not, they would return to a world less willing to accept the obvious divisions of race and class enforced by a place such a Simons. But they had to risk their lives to see that world change.

Today, more than a half-century later, Simons people still gather, though today it is as often at rosaries or funerals as anything else. "We lived in extreme poverty, yes," remembers Ismael Vargas. "But to us it was Camelot. Simons was home."[94]

Simons brick is now a local curiosity in Southern California, somewhat hard to find and prized by people who know anything about it for their gardens and walkways. One fairly sizable collection of Simons brick can be found in Pasadena, just south of the major intersection of Lake and California Avenues, in the courtyard of a coffee place and bagel bakery. It is a popular place on Sunday mornings. People gather with their Sunday papers, their dogs, and their babies, sitting in the sun, chatting, passing the time, and sipping coffee. At their feet, Simons bricks, with that distinctive S I M O N S embossing on the odd one here and there, merit hardly any notice.

Simons, the brick, is barely remembered. Simons, the place and its workers, is wholly forgotten.

FIVE

Ethnic Quarantine

Anglo Saxon civilization must climax in the generations to come. . . .
The Los Angeles of Tomorrow will be the center of this climax.

CLARENCE MATSON, "The Los Angeles of Tomorrow,"
in *Southern California Business*, November 1924

Where else do you find the living conditions excelling those of
Los Angeles?

REALTOR BERNARD ROSENTHAL, 1923[1]

"What is it, anyway? Diphtheria? Typhoid? Scarlet fever?"
"*Quien Sabe?* How should I know? All I know is they're dying."
Victoria heard anguished sounds of a man coming from the parlor
couch. She watched his final death agony. The man, his body bloated
and black, took one last gurgling breath, shuddered and died.
"The plague," whispered Victoria.
"We are all dead."

MONICA HIGHLAND, *Lotus Land*[2]

In this chapter, we again visit the districts around the Los Angeles River in
the early decades of the twentieth century, not all that far from Simons
Brick Yard No. 3. But our focus is less upon the dividing line of the river
(past and present, east and west, Mexican and non-Mexican) and less upon
labor. Rather, we turn to a different kind of boundary forcibly placed
between Mexicans and non-Mexicans in Los Angeles. We address here a
form of segregation prompted or reinforced by more biological boundaries.
For just as taming an unruly river could produce tools by which to estab-

lish ethnic grids of place and memory, and just as laboring jobs could hold people fast to preconceived ideas about ethnicity and ethnic traits, so too could disease. For when nature in the form of disease rendered people unruly and dangerous, even an entire ethnic subset of the Los Angeles population, the response from organized authority in Los Angeles was swift and heavy-handed. Not only would that disease have to be corralled and controlled, so too would people.

As discussed in the introductory chapter, booster marketing of Los Angeles rested in large part upon repetition of simple images and symbols. Neatly tended gardens, attractive boulevards, and large, lovely homes: all came to represent apparently common sights of the "sunny Southland." Without doubt, the Southern California climate occupied a special and iconic place in the booster lexicon, creed, and programs. Characterized especially by warmth and dryness, the region's weather proved a powerful tourist lure. Boosters needed little convincing that sunshine merited a central place in their sophisticated selling of a city in the "semi-tropics," whatever those were. This reliance can easily be discerned in myriad references to sunshine and healthful aridity in promotional vehicles such as *Land of Sunshine* or the Southern Pacific Railroad's *Sunset*.[3] A wider embrace of nature's bounty and good health was exhibited by the hugely successful public relations firm known as the Los Angeles Chamber of Commerce, which adopted the catch phrase "Los Angeles—Nature's Workshop" as one of its slogans.[4]

Inherent in this campaign that sold a new commodity—Los Angeles itself—was a particular method, that of incessant reference to typicality and the typical. Image-making and, as important, image-remembering relied on sameness, on repetition, and on typicality, and this theme exists as backdrop to countless campaigns aimed at advertising Los Angeles from the railroad era of the 1870s and 1880s through the coming of the Great Depression. The marketing was hardly as complex as it was merely redundant, what with the lithographic and other reproductions of the same photos of the same neighborhoods, the same gardens, the ever-present palm trees, typical bungalows, typical street scenes, the typical warm winter day, typical semi-tropic vegetation, typical orange groves, with equally typical snow-capped peaks in the background, even "typical women." Postcards—nothing more than mass-produced and mass-distributed images of typicality—blanketed the nation with stock pictures of Los Angeles life and Los Angeles landscapes.

A Typical California Residence.

Figure 35. A "typical" postcard view of early twentieth-century Southern California for the wealthy tourist and potential settler. Courtesy of the Huntington Library, San Marino, California. All photos from the Bancroft Library in this chapter are the work of the plague abatement authorities.

What may seem like caricature today was critical repetition then, the construction of important and identifiable regional idioms explicitly designed to encourage capitalization, tourism, and settlement by creating scenes of the good life in Southern California. The idea was simply to represent, over and over again, the supposedly representative.[5] But is there more to the story?

The image in Figure 35 purports to describe both specific homes and a specific place (Los Angeles), sometime around the turn of the century. The image also describes order and neatness, every detail arranged to produce an aesthetic sum. It claims to represent "the typical." *Los Angeles is like this*, the image claims. *It looks like this, it feels like this, it is this*. These are Los Angeles homes, little different from other Los Angeles homes.

No better examples of this advertising reflex can be found than in the various publications and ephemeral productions of the Chamber of Commerce in the first two or three decades of the twentieth century. "Facts About Industrial Los Angeles—Nature's Workshop," put out by the Chamber's Industrial Department in the mid-1920s, aptly illustrates the power

Typical interior of Mexican home.

Figure 36. The photographic representation of supposedly "typical" ethnic traits, early twentieth-century Los Angeles. Courtesy of the Huntington Library, San Marino, California.

and the appeal of the typical. Glossy pages and clear black-and-white photographs invite the reader, the investor, the tourist, and the settler into a world of redundant images, scenes, spaces, and places—all rendered calm and serene in stark neatness and order. Here we find the city's "typical skyline," its "typical textile plants," the "typical workingmen's homes" of typically contented workers. Displayed proudly here are the "typical views of clay products and glass plants" and the oddly juxtaposed "oil and oranges— a typical refinery."[6]

The image in Figure 36 is also from the mid-1920s, also from Los Angeles. But it is disorderly—not neat, not beautiful. Yet the claim is that such views are also somehow "typical," apparently trustworthy representations of what Mexican Los Angeles looks like, what Mexican Los Angeles is like. Our concern in this chapter is to examine that assumption and the darker dimensions of the booster project enshrining typicality. Behind careful repetition of ostensibly benign representation of the typical this and the typical that lay deeper and uglier assertions, less about gardens, trees, or bungalows than about people, especially people of color.[7]

A bubonic plague epidemic, like that which struck Los Angeles in the fall of 1924, is a decidedly atypical event. But the municipal response to this public health crisis, refracted through a prism of stereotype, revealed anew the civic tendency to render Mexican lives, culture, and behavior as somehow typical, universal, and thus unquestionably understood. This story of plague and the people it attacked is also a story about terrifying disease and family tragedy.

On October 2, 1924, Dr. Giles Porter of the City Health Department answered a call at the small home of Jesus Lajun at 700 Clara Street, not far from the Los Angeles River. A day laborer for the Los Angeles Railway, Mr. Lajun was clearly ill, but Porter suspected nothing remarkable about the flu-like symptoms or Lajun's swollen and tender groin. Like her father, Francisca Concha Lajun, aged fifteen, seemed to be suffering from a bad case of the flu. She complained of a headache and a sore throat, and she had a fever. Francisca did not get any better the next day. A neighbor, Luciana Samarano, dropped by to help care for her. On the 4th, now desperately ill, Francisca was taken to the hospital, but she died on the way there. Cause of death was listed as "double pneumonia."

Weeks passed. Meantime, infection careened unseen through neighborhoods, homes, and bodies. Toward the end of October, physician George Stevens called Los Angeles General Hospital (the county facility) to report his suspicion that some highly contagious disease was whipping through the neighborhood where the Lajun family lived. He and another doctor, Elmer Anderson, had recently seen patients over there, all of whom complained of similar symptoms: chest pains, backache, fever. Stevens requested that a quarantine ward be set up to receive patients.

On October 29, an ambulance accompanied by Dr. Emil Bogen, resident physician of General Hospital, sped over to the same poor and predominantly Mexican district. There Bogen and the attendants found a group of people clustered around the front porch of a little house. In the house's only room, an old Mexican woman lay crying on a large bed. Her cries were regularly broken by a hacking cough. A Mexican man of about thirty lay on a couch against the wall. He did not cry, but he was clearly "restless and feverish." Several other people were in the room, and one agreed to translate discussion. Bogen found out that the man had gotten sick the day before, that he had a pain down his spine, and that he was running a dangerously high fever of 104 degrees. He had red spots on his chest. The old

Figure 37. 742 Clara Street, Los Angeles, epicenter of the 1924 plague outbreak. Courtesy of the Bancroft Library, University of California, Berkeley.

woman had been coughing for two full days. She spat up blood. The ambulance took these two people to the General Hospital.[8]

At another house nearby, a man, his wife, and their young daughter complained of the same aches and pains. They, too, exhibited disturbing symptoms, and they appeared extremely anxious. A cloud covered their corneas, and their faces had a sickly blue tinge. Four boys, all brothers, were desperately sick at yet a third house. Bogen learned that their mother and father had already died of what was thought to be pneumonia. Still others were sick nearby, the interpreter said. Authorities took the boys to the hospital.

The little clapboard house at 742 Clara Street, where the boys had gotten sick, would become the death house.[9] Before it was all over it must have seemed as if evil possessed this house, which, in a way, it did. In addition to the boys, others at 742 Clara complained of lingering sickness. Physicians took cultures from two of the sick adults, and they inoculated a guinea pig with the cell samples. The animal soon died, as did the two people. Worried health investigators at General Hospital began piecing together information about those who had already died, including the parents of the sick and now-orphaned brothers. Original diagnoses of the sick people, running the gamut from meningitis, influenza, pneumonia, and typhus, began to be reconsidered.

"Lucena [it seems likely that her name was actually Luciana] Samarano, age 39, female, Mexican, 742 Clara Street," is how the medical inspection began that described the boys' mother. She had fallen ill in the middle of October, shortly after she began to care for her teenaged neighbor Francisca Lajun, and she died within five days at the tiny house where she, her family, and a handful of roomers lived. Six months pregnant, Luciana delivered a stillborn infant shortly before dying on October 19.[10] Doctors first ascribed her death to heart disease. Family members held a wake at the Clara Street house that was attended by many family members and friends. Burial followed at the Municipal Cemetery.

Luciana's husband Guadalupe got sick a few days after his wife died. So did Jessie Flores, a family friend and next-door neighbor who had nursed Luciana Samarano during her illness. Guadalupe went downhill very fast. A Spanish priest, Father Medrano Brualla from Our Lady, Queen of the Angels Church in the nearby plaza, had been summoned. The situation looked hopeless, but it was decided to send Jessie and Guadalupe to the hospital anyway. Father Brualla administered last rites on that day, October 26. Jessie Flores and Guadalupe Samarano died (of "lobar pneumonia"). So did Father Brualla.[11]

Unsuspecting health officials released Guadalupe Samarano's body to remaining family members so that they might hold services at 742 Clara Street, just as they had held them for his wife. Horace Gutiérrez, Luciana's young cousin, got sick next, and it was his illness and rapid death that confirmed the presence of an epidemic. As Horace lay dying in the hospital, Dr. George Maner, the hospital pathologist, happened to engage in a conversation with several of the younger physicians who expressed confusion over the symptoms of several critically ill patients, Gutiérrez and Guadalupe Samarano's brother Victor among them. At first facetiously, Dr. Maner suggested that perhaps the patients were suffering from plague and not meningitis, as many suspected. Maner had just finished reading about plague in Manchuria. But when he found evidence of just that beneath his microscope after performing an autopsy on Horace's body, the physician no longer joked. He sought the advice of a colleague, who, upon seeing the distinctive, unmistakable microscopic representation of *bacillus pestis*, supposedly exclaimed, "Beautiful but damned."[12] An ancient disease, the Black Death, had arrived in the city of the future.

The four Samarano brothers tried to fight off the sickness. Ten-year-old Roberto had become ill the same day as his mother's cousin. At the hospital, Roberto was hooked up to an intravenous drip of Mercurochrome. Like Horace Gutiérrez, he died on October 30, his body "practically riddled with plague infection."[13] Soon all the boys were deathly ill. Gilberto died next, then Victor. Little Raul hung on. Horace Gutiérrez's sixteen-year-old brother Arthur died. Fred Ortega, a boarder at 742 Clara Street, died. Joe Bagnola, another boarder, died. Alfredo Burnett, Luciana Samarano's son from an earlier marriage, was admitted to the hospital at the end of October along with all the others, exhibiting "weakness, fever, irritability, and stupor." He died on November 11.

Many more people would sicken and die, especially those who harbored the plague infection in their chests, from where it could easily migrate, person to person. People who had visited 742 Clara Street to help with chores got sick and died. Luciana Samarano's sixty-three-year-old mother, who lived at 342 Carmelita Street, developed a cough, then a fever, and died in a matter of days. Samarano relatives who lived next door at 741 Clara Street died. Guadalupe Valenzuela, fifty-two years old, from Marianna Street in Belvedere Gardens, just across the city line into Los Angeles County, could not fight off the disease. Neither did her son, Jesus, nor her daughter, Maria. Jesus and Maria were cousins of Guadalupe Samarano. At least one of them had been to pay respects at Luciana Samarano's funeral in the middle of October. Jesus died first, at home, on Halloween. Health officials learned from Maria that relatives were expected from New Mexico. Guards rushed to meet them on the train station platform and prevent them from coming to the house.[14]

Throughout the first week of November, now a month after the first victim died, the body count rose. Fear and rumor spread through the neighborhood. The Jimenez brothers lived at 742 Clara Street, but when everyone in the house started getting sick and dying, they quickly moved to nearby 730 Date Street. But they did not move quickly enough. One day after moving, Mike Jimenez got sick. Then Jose fell ill with fever, aches, and pains. Both brothers died within days. At the end of their lives, they turned a dark color because they could no longer oxygenate their blood (hence the "black death"). A Los Angeles novelist describes the chaos as people sickened and died in one house:

> She watched, her hand at her throat, as one man tore desperately at his shirt collar, and then pitched forward, his face in his soup. Another man looked at her in horror, sure perhaps that he'd been poisoned, stood up, overturning his chair, and ran upstairs. He howled as he ran. The man who had collapsed into his bowl straightened convulsively, his poor tortured body bent back onto a crescent shape, and fell heavily under the table.[15]

Figure 38. 741 Clara Street, with siding removed to trap rats. Courtesy of the Bancroft Library, University of California, Berkeley.

Eulogio Peralta, twenty-two, from Bauchet Street, died. A credit slip found among his effects from the Fox Outfitting Company, where he worked downtown, showed Peralta's address as 742 Clara Street. Like the Jimenez brothers, Eulogio Peralta had tried to outwit and outrun the plague by moving away when people started becoming sick and dying. Like the Jimenez brothers' move, it was too little, too late, and the plague caught him and killed him.[16]

Thomas Vera, a young man who lived in a shack out back of 712½ Clara Street with three other adults and two children, died. He had been a friend of the Jimenez brothers, Mike and Jose, and he spent a lot of time with them. Emmett McLauthlin also died. With his brother Frank, Emmett ran an ambulance service out of his home on Hope Street. He had helped move Guadalupe Samarano from 742 Clara Street to the county hospital at the end of October.

Thirty-two-year-old Mary Costello almost died. The pneumonic ward's attending nurse when Guadalupe Samarano and Jessie Flores had been admitted to the county hospital in late October, she complained of headache, backache, chills, and pains in her chest. Exhibiting "marked general malaise," Costello was hospitalized in an isolation ward at the end of the month. By Halloween she was spitting up blood. Doctors hooked her, and

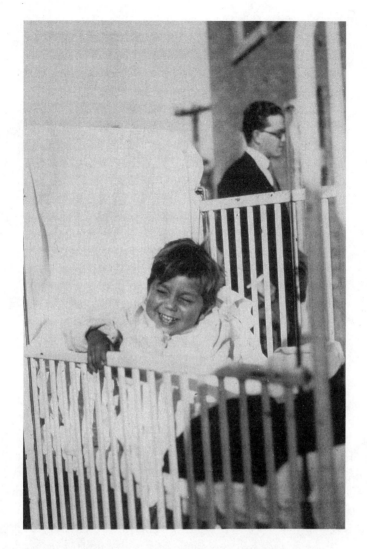

Figure 39. Plague survivor Raul Samarano. Courtesy of the
Huntington Library, San Marino, California.

nine other plague sufferers, up to an intravenous injection of a Mercurochrome solution. This "desperate measure" did not kill nurse Costello. On
the contrary, physicians noted an improvement in her condition. After a
week, she was slightly better. By month's end, still exhibiting the symptoms
and characteristic weariness of a bout with pneumonic plague, Mary

Costello had seemingly beaten the disease. Raul Samarano also fought off the pneumonia consistent with this strain of plague bacillus. He was the only member of his family to escape death.[17]

The 1924 plague outbreak in Los Angeles was the last major outbreak of the disease in the United States. Nearly forty people died, most all of them connected by networks of kin or neighborhood. Dr. Emil Bogen later described the epidemiological chain, or vector, originating from Luciana Samarano: "During the following two weeks, her mother, sister, uncle, nurse, and the nurse's sister, and her four sons, and her husband, his mother, brother, five cousins, six boarders, four friends, his priest, nurse and ambulance driver and a neighbor all developed similar symptoms, and only the nurse and one son survived." Ninety percent of those killed by the disease were of Mexican descent.[18]

VECTORS OF ETHNICITY

The situation calls for drastic action.

DR. WALTER DICKIE to the President
of the Los Angeles Chamber of Commerce, November 15, 1924[19]

Plague is a mysterious, especially frightening disease. Its arrival in Los Angeles in the mid-1920s, in a poor neighborhood within sight of downtown, elicited a powerful response from the city's worried leaders. It took them by complete surprise; plague was not the sort of thing expected in the proud city of tomorrow. Any suggestions or even predictions that plague might pop up in Los Angeles, and there were actually a few, would have been ignored or unnoticed by the city's powerful and prominent.[20] To say the least, the plague startled Los Angeles. In an era and city rife with Americanization programs, many of which were explicitly concerned with purity and hygiene, plague represented the height of uncleanliness. Its presence demanded desperate cleansing measures.[21] The intravenous injections of Mercurochrome that nurse Mary Costello and others endured, for instance, were thought to be a way of sterilizing the body's infected organs and blood.

A similar activity took place in particular Los Angeles neighborhoods, where authorities attempted cleansings as well, often with agents no less fierce than Mercurochrome. Not unlike patients in an isolation ward at the county hospital, these neighborhoods underwent physical isolation, quarantined by force and heavy rope. Ironically enough, many had already been virtually quarantined by the restrictions imposed upon populations socially and politically ostracized by ethnicity and class. Plague presented another method by which to enforce isolation of Mexican neighborhoods and Mexican people. In ordering and describing this work, city authorities let ethnocentric blame creep into their reasoning and their documents, not to mention assertions of white supremacy over and above supposed Mexican typicality. To follow the city's response to the plague, we must turn our view to facets medical, political, and military.

Dr. Walter Dickie, Los Angeles resident, secretary of the California Board of Health, and the man who would take charge of medical affairs surrounding the outbreak, apparently first read about the epidemic in his morning newspaper at the end of October or beginning of November. The as yet unnamed disease had taken nine lives and seemed to be a kind of especially virulent pneumonia. Dickie immediately wired an official of the city health department, inquiring as to the cause of death of Luciana Samarano. The reply read simply: "Death L.S. caused by Bacillus pestis."[22]

Word began to spread now, in both official circles and the infected neighborhood. Benjamin Brown, a surgeon attached to the United States Public Health Service, wired the U.S. surgeon general of the gravity of the situation in early November, his telegram encoded for secrecy. "Eighteen cases ekkil [pneumonic plague]. Three suspects. Ten begos [deaths]. Ethos [situation bad]. Recommend federal aid." The surgeon general responded by dispatching a senior surgeon to Los Angeles to monitor the situation and make regular reports.[23]

Acting on the basis of their own diagnosis, the city health department ordered a quarantine of the "Mexican district," a downtown section of small homes and industrial sites around Macy Street and near the river. The quarantine began at midnight on the October 31. Patrol of the roped-off area, housing an estimated 1,800 to 2,500 people, was left to the Los Angeles Police Department and guards employed by the health department. With rope supplied by the Los Angeles Fire Department, authorities blocked off the Macy Street neighborhood. In and out traffic was forbidden. Guards were placed at both the front and back of any home known to house or have housed a plague victim. Authorities urged residents to clean their homes inside and out. Public health physicians told people to wear thick clothing at all times. Everyday activities ceased, and "gatherings of all nature" were prohibited. Children were to stay home from school and keep away from movie houses. Pacific Electric trolley conductors, running their cars down Macy Street, shouted to riders that no one was to get on or off the cars at any of the regular stops.[24]

Los Angeles city government also responded. Mayor George Cryer called an emergency meeting for Monday afternoon, November 3. Present were medical personnel representing federal, state, and local agencies, as well as others less versed in the particulars of infectious disease transmission or prevention: various "members of the Board of Directors of the Chamber of Commerce, the local publishers, and the business and financial interests of the city." These civic and commercial leaders understood that the plague outbreak might make the city a victim as well. The hastily convened committee of experts, which constituted nothing less than the ruling oligarchy of the city, would meet more than once during the scary weeks of the epidemic's virulent phase.[25]

All medical and preventive work in connection with the epidemic was placed under the direction of Walter Dickie of the Board of Health. He suggested that the city adopt or continue various emergency procedures. All cases of possible plague were to be sent to the county hospital, and a laboratory was to be set up immediately; "all undertakers [were] instructed not to embalm any bodies of Mexicans or others dying suddenly or of undetermined causes until the bodies [could] be examined by a representative of the State or City Health Department"; and rodent trappings would begin immediately in order to establish the boundaries of the epidemic.[26]

The quarantine continued and grew to include other neighborhoods. Rumors spread that a hundred, two hundred, Mexicans were dead and dying. Between residents and the police powers stepped the Los Angeles County Charities, trying to ensure "cubicle isolation" of homes. Nurses told parents to prepare a mixture of hot water, salt, and limejuice for their children to gargle with several times a day. Charities staff made a card index of every member of every home, and they delivered packages of food and bottles of milk to each house.[27] Catholic Charities sent a priest into the field, alongside a Spanish-speaking social worker. Physicians and nurses began daily house-to-house tours, hailing occupants, who by public health standards of the day were called "inmates," from streets and sidewalks to determine if anyone within had fallen sick. People caught outside their homes or neighborhoods had to sleep in the Baptist Mission church at the corner of Bauchet and Avila Streets, because the authorities would not let them pass through the ropes.

The quarantine, which lasted two weeks, would eventually stretch to include five urban districts. There can be little doubt, given the way in which these neighborhoods were described, by language and by perimeter, that officials perceived an overlap between ethnicity and disease: as Walter

Figure 40. The Baptist Mission church, plague abatement headquarters. Courtesy of the Huntington Library, San Marino, California.

Dickie put it to the Chamber of Commerce on November 6, "We hope that the city and the Chamber will insist that all of that area where Mexicans live is put in sanitary condition and undoubtedly there is a great deal of that area that ought to be condemned and destroyed." The aim was to ensure that large and small congregations of Mexican people got snared within the net. The quarantine comprised the Macy Street District, largest of the five and site of the Clara Street address; the South Hill Street District, which included "one large apartment house, occupied by Mexicans"; the Marengo Street District, "including several isolated Mexican homes"; the Pomeroy Street District, with "two isolated Mexican homes"; and the Belvedere Gardens District, just outside city boundaries, where an unknown, though considerable number of Mexicans lived. Macy Street and Belvedere had verifiable cases of plague; the others had only verified cases of ethnicity. In other words, Mexicans lived there.[28]

Records from Belvedere Gardens describe the perimeter established by Carmelita Street, Brooklyn Avenue, a ravine just off Marianna Street, and Grandview Street. Like the city's efforts, the county quarantine was highly militarized, the imposition of order upon the chaos of an epidemic. Health authorities later boasted that the epidemic ended so quickly precisely because the county's eventual four hundred quarantine guards and support personnel "were placed on a military basis and the organization was perfected." Some quarantine guards, most of whom were paid $5 a day (except those working in closest proximity to the plague contagion, who were paid more), had been soldiers in the First World War. Some even had wartime quarantine experience.[29]

Although they were dealing with an emergency situation, county officials gave the quarantine careful thought. The plans reveal ethnic as well as epidemiological attitudes. The Belvedere operation was placed in the hands of the county health chief, J. L. Pomeroy, a man with significant quarantine experience who believed that special guard details were "the only effective method of quarantining Mexicans." Because Pomeroy worried that Belvedere residents might disrupt quarantine procedures, he and his men "worked quietly" throughout the day of November 1 "so as not to unduly alarm the Mexicans." Pomeroy wondered about "a general stampede" and admitted that "we feared [the Mexicans] would scatter." The quarantine was established in the neighborhood with stealth. "We waited until midnight so as to give them all a chance to get in. . . . then the quarantine was absolute."[30]

Guards, sworn in and issued badges, took up field patrol on one of three eight-hour shifts. Shifts had captains as well as quartermasters, guards "walked post," and surplus military and armory equipment provided the materiel of guard camps. Guards complained of run-of-the-mill soldiers' ailments. One burned himself when a coffee pot blew its top. Another rushed to get a dose of "lockjaw preventive serum" when he stepped on a nail.

Guards did more than prevent the daily comings and goings of people in the neighborhood. Despite general orders that listed rule number one as "No Shooting," they spent a good deal of time killing stray cats and dogs, a handful of chickens, a donkey or two, even a goat.[31] They also damaged or destroyed a considerable amount of property within the militarized perimeter. Mrs. Pasquale Moreno, for instance, had her sewing machine requisitioned by quarantine guards, who broke it. Firewood, at least in the early days of the quarantine, proved scarce, and quarantine guards, trying to stay warm under chilly November skies, looted the neighborhood. Mr. L. S. Camacho, who lived on Brooklyn Avenue, later sought damages from health authorities for the destruction of a house he owned on San Pablo Court. There quarantine guards in search of combustibles ripped off plaster boards and an entire door, and stole a stepladder, all of which they promptly burned. Neighbors swore that they had seen the guards attack the little house. In a later investigation of the claim, the county health department's special agent agreed that "half of the rear of the house was torn out by the guards." Mr. Camacho was granted his compensation request of $15. Officials also saw to it that Mrs. Moreno's sewing machine got the repairs it needed.[32]

We do not know what came of Benigno Guerrero's claim for damages in the amount of $60 for the Mexican food destroyed at his business, the name of which he translated as "Quality Tamales Home" in Belvedere. But we do know that he wrote a letter to health officer Pomeroy.

My dear Dr. Pomeroy,

Enclosed you will find the bill of food that I have being forced to destroy. That food was my only capital to keep my business going and I am sorry not to possess your language to impress you with the idea, than such small amount of money was the only means to provied [*sic*] food for my family, wife and four children; 8, 6, 3 and 1½ years old. Bring your attention to that situation, my dear Dr. Pomeroy and you will grant than the bill be payed.

Sincerely very truly yours,

B. Guerrero.[33]

Most of the property destruction was by plague-fighting design, and not the result of individual action by quarantine guards. The overall plan, borrowed from San Francisco's program of plague eradication earlier in the century, was a combination of slash-and-burn destruction and a campaign to lift structures well off the ground with blocks so that cats and dogs, those lucky enough to escape execution as strays, could run under the buildings hunting rats. In the words of Walter Dickie, "The quickest and cheapest [method], the one we are adopting, is to take everything off the ground in the blocks infected and raise it 18 in. above the ground and take the siding off all sides of the house except the front so dogs and cats can go under, so when you get through, you can see all under."

Accordingly, various sanitary details in both the city and county ripped the siding from homes, especially at the foundation level, buried garbage, and burned spare lumber, old furniture, clothing and bedding, even entire shacks. Workers sprayed houses and other buildings with petroleum or sulfur, and they scattered lime and rat poison everywhere. Some squads utilized hydrocyanic gas, a cyanide mixture. Others rigged hoses to truck exhaust pipes and pumped carbon monoxide into buildings. By the end of 1924, quarantine guards had performed well over ten thousand plague "abatements" of greater and lesser destruction. The men, it was later

Figure 41. Plague abatement wrecking crew. Courtesy of the Bancroft Library, University of California, Berkeley.

reported, "had to destroy a large part of Los Angeles." Photographs suggest that this was not an exaggerated comment.[34]

The destruction of these homes and shacks without compensation was likewise part of the overall plan. In conversations with the City Council and Board of Directors of the Los Angeles Chamber of Commerce, which had quickly established its own health and sanitation committee, Dickie advised that the structures to be "cleansed" first be declared nuisances. This meant that no compensation would be paid to property owners, no provisions made to house the homeless. "I wouldn't advise any compensation at all," said Dickie. Council members wondered aloud about the legality of such a move, but once assured by Dickie that "no compensation" was the way to go, they assented and agreed that it would be simple to have these structures declared public nuisances. Nor were destroyed houses or buildings replaced. An official report less than a year after the plague outbreak stated that over a thousand shacks and old houses, "housing Mexican wage earners mostly," had been destroyed and that, all told, roughly 2,500 buildings had been yanked down, burned, or carried away as scrap. It is clear from the photographic evidence of this early example of urban renewal—renewal as urban clearcutting—that the destruction was widespread and ferocious.

Figure 42. Mexican shack in rear of tortilla factory, 612 N. Alameda. Courtesy of the Bancroft Library, University of California, Berkeley.

Figure 43. Looking west on E. 6th Street from Imperial. Courtesy of the Bancroft Library, University of California, Berkeley.

Figures 44–45. Wrecking crew at work, back of 2039 E. 7th Street. Courtesy of the Bancroft Library, University of California, Berkeley.

That little, or nothing, was done to replace the thousands of structures destroyed in the quarantined districts was made clear in the follow-up report of the city health department. The Bureau of Housing and Sanitation bluntly declared that "no new construction has been undertaken to house the people thus dispossessed, [and] they have been scattered to other parts of the city and county, many of them into other houses or quarters that are unfit for home habitation, a menace to the city at large and a barrier to the progress of the life and character of the persons living in them."[35]

It is not hard to imagine that the plague offered the city the opportunity to remake the landscape, to smooth it out along easily defined lines of race and ethnicity. This was, after all, a Southern California experiment with ethnic cleansing in several senses of that grim phrase. Fire, sledgehammers, and sanitary detail commanders did their work with brutal efficiency.[36]

Not only did buildings have to be destroyed. Rats had to be killed, thousands and thousands and thousands of them. The Chamber of Commerce appointed a committee to explore, in conjunction with the City Council and medical personnel, ways to raise the money needed to kill plague-carrying rats and squirrels. The City Council eventually granted the extraordinary sum of $250,000 for November 1924 through July 1925, and twice that for the next twelve months, to be used primarily in rodent eradication programs. An entirely new city department arose to wrestle with the rat problem. Like some sort of latter-day Hudson's Bay Company, the department hired hunters and trappers, and it placed $1 bounties on dead rats and ground squirrels. When it became clear that the bounty would not ensure enough dead rats, officials opted to pay rat killers a salary of $130 a month. The staccato "pop pop" of small-caliber weapons could be heard throughout city and county day and night, and rodent poison appeared everywhere. Workers spread the poison, a thick syrup containing phosphorous or arsenic, on little squares of bread and cast them about entire neighborhoods, both quarantined and not. Its resemblance to molasses apparently caused rat killers some concern that the poison atop "dainty poison croutons" would find its way into the mouths of children (later, the officials of the federal Public Health Service would discontinue the practice for just this reason). Once the city began killing rats, people in the infected neighborhoods, who had been kept in the dark about what was killing them, knew that the epidemic had a name: plague.[37]

Plague preventive work took on the appearance of a desperate fire-fighting operation as the city tried to extinguish both *bacillus pestis* and the urban rat. Squads worked their way and spray through entire neighborhoods in lock-step formation, attacking rats, structures, and unfortunate stray animals house by house, block by block.[38] This militarized sweep was not entirely limited to ethnic neighborhoods. "It is important to remember," a report noted, "that the danger from infected rats exists . . . even in residence districts occupied by native Americans [i.e., native-born whites],

Figure 46. This shack near downtown Los Angeles was essentially given a racial identity by the plague abatement authorities, who captioned this image "Negro shack in business section, near 2039 E. 7th Street." Courtesy of the Bancroft Library, University of California, Berkeley.

Figure 47. Plague abatement as erasure: The obliteration of the "Negro shack" on E. 7th Street. Courtesy of the Bancroft Library, University of California, Berkeley.

Figure 48. Plague eradication destruction in the Utah Street district east of the Los Angeles River. Courtesy of the Bancroft Library, University of California, Berkeley.

and these must be dealt with as definitely as the foreign districts." Be that as it may (apparently inhabitants of "foreign districts" could not, by definition, be "native Americans"), rat eradication work tended toward particular intersections of ethnicity and poverty. The program would work best "especially in the foreign quarter . . . in the Mexican, Russian, Chinese and Japanese quarters by the destruction of all structures not worth rat proofing."[39] Photographic evidence of the campaign suggests that this was done with alacrity and comprehensive thoroughness.

The carcasses of countless rats stacked up at an emergency laboratory established in the Baptist Mission at Bauchet and Avila, where people rendered homeless by the quarantine sought shelter. Later moved to a more permanent location on Eighth Street, the lab (the "ratatorium") acted as headquarters for the ferocious rat-killing, counting, and testing operation. The sheer exuberance of the rat-proofing work came in for praise, while the destructiveness of the effort was neatly sidestepped. The *Arizona Republican*, for instance, while admitting to have "jibed" Angelenos "for their self-assertiveness," thought the rat-proofing work worthy of praise and emulation. No other city in America was "so guarded" as Los Angeles, and the rat killing was the city's "greatest exhibition of readiness and efficiency."[40]

Back at the county hospital, health care workers tried to ward off the

Figures 49–50. Just southeast of downtown Los Angeles, between Alameda Street and the Los Angeles River, the industrial town of Vernon had a number of impoverished Mexican communities. Plague abatement authorities burned this Vernon *colonia* to the ground in the fall of 1924. Courtesy of the Bancroft Library, University of California, Berkeley.

chance of infection. Anyone suspected of either having plague or coming into contact with a plague victim had been immediately shuttled from the quarantined neighborhoods to the county hospital. There, in isolation at the recently completed contagious disease building, hospital personnel labeled them with red tickets to distinguish them from other patients. Physicians unaccustomed to wearing gloves during autopsy procedures took up the habit. Hospital workers wore gowns, rubber gloves, caps, and gauze masks. When that protection was deemed insufficient, they started wearing face masks made from pillowcases, eye holes cut out and covered over with clear celluloid. Physicians later noted that "procuring and working in these masks was a matter of considerable exertion, and also of considerable comment and divertissement."[41]

Plague victims awaiting almost certain death in the quarantine ward underwent all sorts of treatment. Doctors stimulated them with caffeine, digitalis, adrenalin, and pituitrin. Morphine, codeine, quinine, and atropine depressed them. They were rubbed, vaccinated, and injected with alcohol, "Murphy drip," calcium lactate, leucotropin, and extract of leucocytes. Anti-plague serum, which did exist in 1924, arrived only in time for use in one case. Emil Bogen mentioned that some had suggested use of the bacteriophage for plague, which had been "popularized by Sinclair Lewis in his recent novel *Arrowsmith*."[42]

THE PERILS OF BAD PUBLICITY

The thing that interests us and probably you more than this list of fatalities is what is the cause of this outbreak.

DR. WALTER DICKIE before the Board of Directors,
Los Angeles Chamber of Commerce, November 6, 1924[43]

By the middle of November, although occasional plague deaths would continue into the new year, public health officials believed the epidemic over.[44] Declaring the outbreak officially ceased, the *Herald Examiner* wrote that the "pneumonic plague . . . is no more. It came suddenly, struggled feebly, and passed away after a remarkably short life."[45] By Thanksgiving, the Chamber of Commerce had received a signed statement from Dickie that the plague was over, a document that the organization deemed "just the thing to be good publicity."[46] Dickie even went out of his way to thank local business and newspaper leaders for the role they played in keeping word about the plague mum. Damage control, already underway by then, accelerated. The Chamber's Publicity Committee put forth a number of plans for combating unfavorable reports about Los Angeles. The *Los Angeles Realtor* in its December 1924 issue ran a feature by Chamber president William Lacy. Entitled "The Truth about Los Angeles," the article urged readers not to believe all that they had heard about the city's recent problems. Hysterical talk about "a slight drought," a power shortage, a foot and mouth epidemic, and "a slight epidemic of pneumonic plague" ought not deter people from visiting or investing in Los Angeles. It was a credit to the people of the city, Lacy continued, that concerted and cooperative work stamped out "the few cases of pneumonic plague."[47]

Commercial figures such as Lacy found themselves in a propaganda war with the East, mostly of their own making. For years, as eastern papers and publications pointed out, Los Angeles boosters crowed about the unique symbols of Southern California living. Sunshine, fat oranges, equally fat babies, pretty little bungalows, palm trees: boosters bombarded eastern cities and eastern folk with these ever-so-familiar images. But now, as Los Angeles found itself in a public relations tight spot, competitors and critics seized the opportunity to point out booster hubris in the City of Angels. Even typicality had its limits, if not its opponents. Advertising the city of the future as it battled a medieval epidemic proved a challenge.

In a hard-hitting piece for the *Nation*, the former editor of the Los Angeles *Daily News,* William Boardman Knox, took the Chamber of Commerce to task for keeping the plague epidemic, as well as other health problems, under journalistic wraps. According to Knox, the plague and resulting quarantine provoked a mass exodus from the city as well as an economic collapse: "land values dropped 50 percent; bankruptcy courts were flooded with yesterday's millionaires; bank clearings were cut in half." In other words, Knox intimated, "don't believe all you hear (or *see*) about Los Angeles." The typical might, after all, be but self-serving artifice, less than what met the eye. "What are a few broken children, probably of people who don't count anyway," he wrote of a recent polio outbreak, "compared to the welfare and prosperity of a great metropolis?"[48]

The city's commercial elite attempted to combat the rash of unfavorable publicity. At stake was the continued viability of the campaign to establish the yardstick of typical Los Angeles places, diversions, and scenes. Worse, winter tourism from the East to the West was threatened. But Chamber of Commerce stalwarts were, if anything, masters at spin. Even before the plague epidemic had become known at all, the organization had pledged to redouble its efforts at selling Los Angeles after being chastised by one of its leaders for not doing enough. "I think the Chamber is in the most dangerous moment in its career," Paul Hoffman told his fellow Chamber directors exactly one day before public health officials learned of the epidemic. "We have got to impress the people of Los Angeles with the fact that we are going on to bigger things—If we go on as we have been doing, I don't think that is enough."[49]

Action apparently became all the more imperative in the wake of the epidemic. The Chamber's Publicity Committee, as Knox intimated in his *Nation* essay, was not about to let unfavorable news get in the way of advertising Los Angeles. And they had certainly kept bad news about the city's health record quiet before. Earlier in 1924, the Chamber had wrestled with news about a smallpox outbreak. Chamber directors exchanged fears about what widespread knowledge of smallpox would mean. "It would be a black eye we couldn't get over for years," said one. Another added that "it is my personal feeling to suppress publicity."[50] An outbreak of bubonic plague only cemented the Chamber's position. All through November Chamber directors reiterated the desperate need to counteract eastern news of trouble in the Southland, even to the point of agreeing to print up special postcards (what else?) that every Chamber member could then rush east—a booster shot if ever there was one.

The local press stood by ready and willing to help. George Young, manager of the *Examiner*, eased the minds of the Chamber's Board of Directors when he assured them, with specific reference to the plague, that editors all along the Hearst chain "would print nothing we didn't think was in the interest of the city." Indeed, one resident of Los Angeles, who would grow up to be a local physician, remembers the plague as "a big hush up." Even his father, who owned a suitcase factory on Los Angeles Street, within walking distance of the Macy Street quarantine, knew little, if anything, of the outbreak. It was as if knowledge of the epidemic had been consigned to a "need to know" hierarchy of individuals and institutions.[51]

The Spanish language paper *El Heraldo de Mexico*, which generally supported the plague suppression efforts, referred to "the hermetic silence in which authorities have locked themselves." News of the plague dominated *El Heraldo*'s headlines for days and days in November.[52] Not so with the English-language papers, which tended to downplay the path of the disease and the eradication efforts. *Examiner* editor Young, backed up by Harry Chandler of the *Los Angeles Times*, even thought that a virtue could be made of "the close squeeze we just had." Once the rat eradication program did its work, "we could then advertise Los Angeles as the ratless port."[53]

Faced with a medieval problem like Black Death in their "Los Angeles of Tomorrow," nervous boosters from the Chamber sought out health officials for briefings throughout the month, even after the various quarantines had been lifted. For instance, at a Saturday meeting on November 15, Walter Dickie spoke at length about the plague in front of directors of the Chamber of Commerce and the Los Angeles City Council.

Standing before a map of greater Los Angeles, Dickie pointed out that the black pins jabbed into it were "pneumonic plague cases." His few yellow pins represented bubonic cases. Though they certainly knew it, Dickie nonetheless pointed out to the assembled civic leaders that the epidemic, and the rats that helped spread it, were "not only a health problem but an economic problem." In this, Dickie made explicit reference to the port of Los Angeles. "I realize that the dream of Los Angeles and the dream of officials and the Chamber of Commerce is the harbor. Your dream will never come true as long as plague exists in Los Angeles and as long as there is any question of doubt in reference to the harbor." Unless the harbor received a clean bill of health, as soon as possible, Dickie warned, "half of the commerce of your harbor will quickly vanish." "No disease known," Dickie stated ominously, "has such an effect upon the business world as the plague." Chamber leaders and councilmen must have blanched.[54]

Desperate times did indeed call for desperate measures, Dickie warned. Even if the determination of plague foci or origins of each case looked to be complete, no one could be sure about much of anything, at the harbor or anywhere else. The proximity of the Macy Street quarter to downtown Los Angeles and important industrial sites made the problem all the more acute. Dickie did not want any rats from the Mexican quarter chased into downtown. "You are not a great way off from [the] Baker building," he pointed out, obviously gesturing to his map and the heart of the city's commercial district.

Just as Dickie did not want Mexican rats coming downtown, Anglo Angelenos did not relish the thought of Mexican people from the plague districts or other districts coming into downtown, as they did every single day for work or shopping. Mexican cafe, restaurant, and hotel workers who lived in the Macy Street district lost their downtown jobs. Others who did not live in plague districts but who were nonetheless Mexican, and therefore somehow dangerous, did so as well. Management at the Biltmore Hotel, for instance, fired its entire Mexican labor force of 150 when they arrived at work, regardless of the home addresses of these men and women, and notwithstanding the obvious fact that had they lived in a plague district the quarantine would have kept them from reporting to work in the first place. The action provoked outrage and threatened to become a proverbial international incident. A delegation of Mexican government officials and journalists met with the Chamber of Commerce to protest the action. They spoke with Clarence Matson, whose 1924 prophecy about the city's Anglo Saxon future (printed precisely at the moment the epidemic broke out) opens this chapter. The Chamber pledged to look into the matter.[55]

Dr. Dickie wanted more laboratory support, more manpower for rat killing and rat proofing, and more medical teams for autopsy work. The latter request was "so that all Mexicans that die and all suspicious deaths that come into the Bureau of Vital Statistics shall be examined." The association of disease with ethnicity could not have been made more grimly explicit: "If it is not a general rule to autopsy *all* Mexicans that die of acute illness and are suspicious, many foci are going to be overlooked." In other words, this plague outbreak had become (indeed had been since the beginning) peculiarly Mexicanized. The epidemic was, according to a public health official, "confined to the Mexican quarter in the northeasterly section of the city."[56]

Dickie oversaw the placing of thousands of rat traps and would need thousands more. But he admitted that the Macy Street district—where 90 percent of the plague victims had encountered the disease—had not received as much attention, for instance, as the harbor. In a remarkable admission and plea for help, Dickie implored his audience of elite Anglo businessmen: "I wish you gentlemen would go down to the Macy St. district. We haven't done anything because it is a question whether that area is worth the money you will have to put on it to clean it up and after you clean it, whether it will pay the property owner to put it into shape for human habitation. That is something [that] should be considered by the city."[57]

Dr. Dickie did not mean that *nothing* had been done in the Macy Street quarter. After all, the houses and structures there had been attacked by the sanitary squads who sprayed, burned, knocked down, and lifted up. But he did mean to ask the Council and Chamber whether or not they would see to it that the area be, essentially, razed and rebuilt. "All has to be gutted out and destroyed and go back to the original structures and each original structure must have the ground area all exposed so that there can be no place for harboring rats."[58] Those assembled assured the physician that they well understood his warnings. "We are thoroughly alive to the situation," they said, and they would support clean-up efforts even if they cost a half million dollars.

Dickie ended his comments before the assemblage by arguing that the city must do more about the housing conditions of "the foreign population." "There is no reason why these Mexicans shouldn't be housed in sanitary quarters in the environment they are used to living in," he pointed out. Conditions such as those that existed threatened the ability of industrial Los Angeles—and Los Angeles industrialists—to turn the resident Mexican population into "an asset to this city." The city risked epidemics of smallpox, plague, and typhus of far greater proportion than the current crisis. Dickie chastised the city's elite for their shortcomings in noblesse oblige. "As long as you have the foreign population, Mexicans, Russians, and various nationalities, you have to take care of them." City/county boundaries did not make any difference. Elites may not have wanted to think about the population of nonwhite workers, but those very people had become both indispensable and, at least for the moment, troubling. "You have an opportunity now, seeing that you have this condition here, of cleaning that section from one end to the other. . . . you should have decent housing for these Mexicans. . . . It has never been done." Nor would it be. Like other such plans for renewal in these districts of Los Angeles (recall the Rev. Dana Bartlett's vision of the Los Angeles River as urban park), Dickie's suggestions would go unheeded. Far easier and cheaper was urban renewal, 1920s-style: knock them down.

Over in Belvedere Gardens the situation was just as bad as, if not worse than, that within city limits. Chamber members expressed concerns about a public school on the east side, over toward Belvedere, which one referred to as "the largest Mexican school in the world." The river—"your river bed," Dickie called it—was at the center of a huge rat infestation across city and county lines. "I haven't seen anything in my life to equal it," Dickie said, whereupon Councilman Boyle Workman piped up that houses in Belvedere Gardens were "built out of piano boxes."[59] If anything, the plague offered a crash course in the economics of poverty and ethnicity to an important slice of Los Angeles elites.

Destruction would have to take place before construction, an activity that the city and county officials pursued with enthusiasm, despite later findings that this was not necessarily the best plague-fighting tactic.[60] Furthermore, the publicity problem occupied a great deal of time, and this seemed to take precedence over any committed plans for renewal. Even health officials got into the act. In his report describing the city's health care response to the plague, City Health Commissioner George Parrish listed each plague victim and his or her address, hoping in some way to combat what he called "the grossly exaggerated reports published in the Eastern newspapers, with the evident intention of stopping the ceaseless migration of tourists to this wonderful city."[61]

Officials also engaged in a congratulatory discussion of their own in explaining why this had been but a "slight epidemic."[62] For one thing, it seemed as if the plague had limited foci, with at least ten cases, including most of those in the county, traced directly to 742 Clara Street. The alacrity with which Angelenos began killing rats also proved fortunate. And lastly, officials thought that they had been lucky in another respect, again couched in terms of supposed ethnic typicality. "The Mexican," read one contemporary report, "unlike the Oriental, does not attempt to hide his sick or dead. Being a Catholic people, they always, when ill, call the Priest, and generally are prompt in securing medical aid." Officials saw this Catholic practice in marked distinction to the Chinese response to the deadly plague outbreak in San Francisco's Chinatown a generation earlier. What they did not reflect upon was the irony of their position, in that they relied upon certain supposed Mexican traits (i.e., Catholic practice) to help them abate the outbreak at the very same time they expected many of those self-same essential ethnic traits—reduced to simple Mexicanness—to be so susceptible to disease and disease transfer.[63]

TYPICAL RATS, TYPICAL MEXICANS

Revelation of cultural practices such as Catholic wakes and burials, and, more important, revelation of the tendency of the dominant culture to stereotype such practice as typical of Mexican ethnicity, encourage us to read the reaction to the plague epidemic of 1924 as part of the typifying project that city elites furthered during the period. Knowing how those inside the various quarantines felt or acted in the face of organized, even militarized, public health or police authority is a difficult task. Outside of official pleas for reparations, there is little information or documentation in quarantine or political records. It is equally—if not more—difficult to know what the epidemic and fear of disease meant to these thousands of people caught behind the quarantine ropes, though we can safely assume that they were terrified.[64]

In an analysis of the plague couched within a broader social and cultural context, we may see Anglo authority's reaction to it as an important part of a veritable public relations campaign to validate the booster paradigm of typical Los Angeles. Conventional reduction of things, events, landscape features, and individuals to archetypical representation both created and reinforced cultural tendencies toward ethnic stereotype.[65] For instance, in attempting to determine how certain plague victims encountered the disease, officials relied upon reflexive assumptions about Mexican behavior and Mexican attitudes. How did teenaged Francisca Lajun, who lived down the street from 742 Clara Street, contract the plague that quickly killed her? The answer was unclear, but ethnic stereotype supposedly could explain some part of the mystery. As such, Mexican-ness, or simply being Mexican, created an environment that could foster disease.[66] In the Board of Health's opinion: "That evidence could not be obtained to connect these two cases [Francisca Lajun and anyone at 742 Clara Street] may be explained by the reluctance of the Mexican to impart information, especially when he does not fully comprehend the reason. If the tendency of the Mexican to visit relatives and friends during their illness is recalled, the explosive nature of this outbreak, limited to friends and relatives, is partly explained."[67]

Similarly, Chamber of Commerce leaders declared before health personnel that they knew about the living conditions of Mexicans, or at least enough to understand the transmission of the disease, even though it is clear that most had never been into the Macy Street Mexican quarter before. By their reckoning, this knowledge alone could rightly be substituted for epidemiological expertise. Experience as capitalists and paternalists, and even as tourists, provided the necessary skills and reference points. Describing a Mexican vector would not be hard for these people to do, and they would assume themselves to be right in so doing.

"I am not only familiar with the housing conditions of our [sic] Mexicans," William Lacy said, "but familiar with the Mexican peon's way of living in Mexico." There, fifteen years previous, Lacy had witnessed an outbreak of plague on the West Coast in which, he said, the "Mexican population died like fleas." The only recourse had been to "blast practically half the city down and drive the people into the country in order to clean up the city." Los Angeles had better not repeat that history. On the contrary, the aim was to keep the population quarantined in place. "As we are bound to have that population," Lacy said, "we must assume the responsibility of providing them a place to live peaceably." He seemed not to realize the odd juxtaposition of peaceableness with health, as if the plague had made the docile Mexicans of Los Angeles unruly.[68]

But of course that was true. The plague had rendered Mexicans unusually unruly, dangerous in the eyes of many whites, not only because they had the disease but also, I suspect, because the disease was seen to be peculiarly Mexican, as if nonwhiteness itself had some of the same connotations as disease. Perhaps Anglo anxiety in this chicken-and-egg manner helps explain the even more interesting language of some of William Lacy's colleagues. D. F. McGarry closed one discussion by pointing out that the city's Mexican population could not easily be dislodged from the poor districts. "In many instances they are there because of cheap rent contiguous to their work. They cannot afford to live in quarters that would be acceptable to us or as should be for the ordinary citizens."

The assumption that Mexicans were somehow not "ordinary" is interesting enough itself, as if they naturally existed in some special category reserved for them as *Mexicans*. But McGarry followed this remark with a fascinating slip, by referring to "this particular plan of eradicating them from those districts, which is highly proper and wise." Rat killing and potential solutions to a Mexican problem merged, with eradication as the verb, if not action, of choice. Perhaps it was just too difficult for the Chamber of Commerce member to think about where to put *them* should the quarantines, be they social, economic, or medical, ever be lifted? For his part, Dickie agreed with McGarry, pointing out that "your [*sic*] Mexicans should not be permitted to live next [to] certain industries like food packing establishments and slaughter houses"—even though it was those very Mexicans who were doing the work in these industries.[69]

There is little doubt that the cross-over of words and concepts between rats and Mexicans occurred. Recall Dr. Pomeroy's fear that the Mexican population in Belvedere "would scatter" or "stampede" if they knew of the plague or of quarantine plans. Even the militarized response to the plague— best expressed by the quarantine and sanitary details—had as its purpose a goal of aggressive cleanliness aimed at both rats and Mexicans. Just as Mercurochrome was thought to be a cleanser for the plague's internal manifestations, so too with petroleum spray and chloride of lime aimed at the lives of those within the confluence of poverty and Mexican ethnicity, effectively quarantined well before the epidemic hit. The metaphors, at least, had been around awhile, and their use wasn't limited to city officials. Even housing reformer John Kienle of the University of Southern California, part of the corps of young progressives under the wing of sociologist Emory Bogardus, slid words around in troubling ways. In his important 1912 thesis, "Housing Conditions among the Mexican Population of Los Angeles," Kienle wrote that he "inspected" local barrios "in order to show the spread of the Mexicans."[70]

This is not to suggest that, given the epidemiological history of the 1924 plague outbreak, the specifics of such associations had no validity whatsoever. Certain links of sociability, ethnicity, neighborhood, and kin obviously contributed to the patterns of plague vectors. Tracing these made sense in public health practice, and the physicians and other health care personnel acted quickly in stamping out the epidemic and saving lives, Mexican and others. Yet the irony of an extraordinary event like an outbreak of the Black Death is that it offers us a glimpse into the everyday life of the past, if only because of the large fissures the uncommon event opens into that society's rhythms. In this case, it is in the generality of elite Anglo comment and point of view, the instinctive, reflexive reach to such phrases and social categories as "the Mexican" that we recognize the broader implications, the broader assumptions of ethnic and racial typicality, epidemiology and disease. The most obvious expressions of Anglo categorization in this regard were also the simplest and most graphic. Illustrations that accompanied the contemporary public health document describing the plague outbreak explicitly labeled such environments as the "typical interior of [a] Mexican home" and a "typical back yard." It is as if the photographer—in this case probably a public health official—merely wandered over from his Chamber of Commerce assignment of shooting "typical factories" or "typical palm trees" to take pictures of "typical Mexicans" (although the absence of people is interesting; they were likely either dead by then or behind quarantine perimeters). So-called typical images of Mexican lives and homes, homes far removed from the stock bungalow images, no doubt served to relieve a fair amount of anxiety in the health or civic community. Reaction to such images might accomplish two related tasks. First, if the plague indeed rendered Mexicans something other than peaceable, those photographs that repositioned them into typical spaces and places might serve to render them less unruly in the minds of elite Anglos. Second, typical images of degradation and filth could seemingly help solder the perceived connections between plague transmission and Mexican ethnicity. Any of these photographs would inevitably co-mingle disease with poverty, poverty with Mexican ethnicity, Mexican ethnicity with disease. It was, after all, typical.[71]

Descriptions of the districts, really nothing more than extended captions to the images, confirmed patterns of seeing and believing. Quarantined neighborhoods, bulging under an "ever increasing Mexican population," exhibited the "*usual number* of over-crowded rooming houses and temporary shacks on the back lots." Even the cumulative collection of typical Mexicans could create a homogeneous group. "The unobstructed and uncontrolled immigration from Mexico tends yearly to increase *this class* of inhabitants."[72]

The practice of assigning ethnic Mexicans to rigid social, cultural, and occupational containers, boxes even more rigid than those created by street or district boundaries, encouraged Anglos to look at Mexicans in particular ways. Plague in 1924 offered a kind of proof of the theorem. If the dominant view tended toward an image of all ethnic Mexicans as a class of equally degraded, poverty-stricken laborers living in rat-infested congregations, what could offer greater affirmation than a nasty outbreak of pneumonic plague that killed mostly Mexicans? Even these many years later, it isn't difficult to discern the outlines of ugly circular logic.

The 1924 plague epidemic in Los Angeles killed people in a few distinct neighborhoods, it killed people who came into contact with one another, and the dead were nearly all ethnic Mexicans. These were not mutually exclusive categories. But nor were they part of an essentialist triangle, where the one category (place, culture, ethnicity) naturally led to the other. Yet an examination of the reaction to the plague reveals a tendency on the part of the dominant culture to view and to explain the plague epidemic along such lines, lines of familiarity and lines of typicality.[73]

Such a response could do little to break down conventional understandings of ethnic life and culture in Los Angeles. On the contrary, contemporary language certainly helped reinforce ideas about the typical Mexican and restricted laborer space in the industrial economy, and not just in Los Angeles. This was a Californian practice, a southwestern practice. By early 1926, for instance, a zoology professor at the University of California had no qualms whatsoever about linking plague and Mexican ethnicity. Blaming "the Mexicans, with their various diseases . . . their tendencies to huddle together," Professor Samuel Holmes fairly insisted that the plague outbreak was the product of essential ethnic traits. Mexicans would, he declared, "increase our mortality, increase our infant mortality, be the means of spreading various epidemics throughout our population, and in general, deteriorating the physical welfare of the people. I do not believe there is any doubt about that."[74]

Having embarked upon a booster city-building journey that demanded iconic images and symbols, Anglo Los Angeles produced an ambitious glossary of typical images and places, a project that, alongside obvious socioeconomic stratification, effectively snared ethnic Mexicans and held them fast. Just as Anglos in Los Angeles felt certain that they understood

Infant Mortality Rates by Race and Ethnicity
Los Angeles County, 1925 and 1926

	1925	*1926*	*1925 + 1926*
White	5.5%[a]	4.5%	5%
	(2,592 births,[b]	(2,839 births,	
	144 deaths)	119 deaths)	
Japanese	6%	4%	5%
	(383 births,	(256 births,	
	23 deaths)	11 deaths)	
Mexican	15.8%	12%	14%
	(1,283 births,	(1,340 births,	
	203 deaths)	167 deaths)	
Black	15.3%	26.6%	21%
	(13 births,	(15 births,	
	2 deaths)	4 deaths)	

a. Expressed percentage is total annual (reported) deaths of infants less than one year old over total annual (reported) births by race/ethnicity.

b. Raw numbers from *Annual Report of Health Department, Los Angeles County* (Los Angeles: Los Angeles County Health Department, 1926).

NOTE: Undercount of both births and deaths is highly likely and almost assured, especially for nonwhites. For instance, the African American figures (13 births in 1925; 15 in 1926), as expressed against total African American population in Los Angeles County for the period, appear much too low and may help account for the spike in African American infant mortality in 1926 (reported figures are four infant deaths in 1926 expressed against 15 births). The raw data from the period nonetheless indicate a striking difference in infant mortality among whites and those of Japanese descent as opposed to African American and ethnic Mexican Angelenos.

the bungalow and the palm tree, so too did they self-consciously assert that they understood this Mexican, frozen in time and quarantined in space. In the very year that American immigration restrictions drew lines across which certain Europeans could not move, a West Coast epidemic portrayed a Los Angeles desperate to restrict Mexicans—if not by immigration law, then by other means. The 1924 Los Angeles plague outbreak was certainly—tragically—about vectors of disease. But it was just as certainly and every bit as tragically about vectors of ethnicity. City leaders effectively worked to eliminate the former, but they did little, even when they had the chance, to think more broadly and more humanely about the latter.

SIX

The Drama
of Los Angeles History

The story of Junipero Serra and the Missions for dramatic purposes
has been lying around since 1833, at least, for anybody to grab. But
no one grabbed it until I did so in 1912. Now it is mine.

JOHN S. MCGROARTY to Charles F. Lummis, 1916

The plays could be made most touching and instructive at the
same time, without connecting the Fathers in an *unholy* way with
everlasting, silly femininity, as some would-be poets have done with
no foundation in fact, but merely as a manifestation of their own
unclean dreams. Godspeed to your work in that line.

FR. ZEPHYRIN ENGLEHARDT to John S. McGroarty, 1910

Both as Business and Art, it is intolerable to have in your beautiful
pageant some of the frightful anachronisms now there. The Babbitts
don't realize them; but every once in a great while some one will go
to see the Mission Play who will know that Father Serra didn't teach
the California Indians to weave dam [*sic*] bad Navajo blankets!"

CHARLES F. LUMMIS to John S. McGroarty, 1926

In the spring of 1912, the ocean liner *Titanic* clipped an iceberg in the
Atlantic Ocean and sank. Newspapers across the nation and the world covered the *Titanic* story with tabloid zeal. Who lived? Who died? Who was
brave, and who was cowardly? Who was to blame? What were the last
moments aboard the doomed ship like for those on the brink of icy eternity?

It all made for compelling reading, as the papers featured story after story about the tragedy. Papers in Los Angeles proved no exception to the aggressive coverage of the event. After all, the tragedy had all the right elements, foremost among them the premature assurances that the *Titanic* was not supposed to, and in fact could not, sink. The fateful iceberg collision offered high drama. Passengers on the ship included members of the American aristocracy: Guggenheims, Astors, Denver's "Unsinkable" Molly Brown (initial reports mistakenly placed her among the casualties; she lived, hence the sobriquet). Well-known Los Angeles poet John Steven McGroarty did his level best to memorialize the dead.

They were soldiers and sailors and masters,
Of the Arts and the gentle graces:
Shrine them, O God! In Thy memory,
As they died, with smiling faces[1]

Were it not for the *Titanic* disaster, it is likely that Los Angeles newspapers would have devoted more space to a local event of greater importance to poet McGroarty than his *Titanic* eulogy. As it was, this Los Angeles happening still merited significant coverage even with the ocean liner's disastrous descent to the bottom of the sea. The story is there, bouncing from the news and editorial pages back and forth to society and entertainment reports. In between stories of the *Titanic*'s fate peeked a regular set of articles about the coming of an important event to Los Angeles, the debut of a play written by none other than John McGroarty.

Advance fanfare suggested the opening of McGroarty's *Mission Play* was no ordinary premiere. Out on a limb, the *Times* called it "the most unusual dramatic event in the history of the Southwest."[2] Adding that "profound public interest has been aroused" in the opening night performance, the newspaper predicted a long and healthy run before packed houses. On the evening of April 29, 1912, the show had its anticipated debut. It was, one theater critic noted, "a pageant-drama unprecedented in the annals of this country."[3] Acted out on a stage said to be the largest west of Chicago, on the grounds of the San Gabriel Mission, with a cast of well over a hundred, *The Mission Play* entered the hearts and minds of Southern Californians for the first time. It was by all accounts a virtuoso performance. The audience shouted and cheered. People laughed and wept. They even hauled the elated playwright into the glare of the footlights for an ovation, not at the conclusion of the drama, but at the end of only the second of three acts.

When the play did end, the audience shrieked and shouted all over again. The playwright, weeping, stood before them and accepted their praise.

Over the course of the next generation, the drama would evolve from an evening's festive entertainment to a regional institution, and it would grow to become the single most successful American theatrical performance of the age. It is this institutional role of *The Mission Play* that occupies our attention in this final chapter.[4]

An extraordinary event like the plague epidemic of 1924 disrupted, as we have seen, prevailing notions of Mexican "peaceableness," and Los Angeles responded to this threat with destructive vigor. Yet other regional idioms already existed that operated as bulwarks to keep ethnic boundaries solid and intact. *The Mission Play* was one such feature of Southern California culture, and, unlike the plague abatement work of only a year or so, it did its work over the course of decades.

HISTORY IN THE ACTIVE VOICE

Without even knowing it, the *Los Angeles Times* predicted much of *The Mission Play*'s later impact by simply pointing out that the drama's script "has been taken almost literally from the history of California."[5] Before long, that qualifying "almost" would be excised from public perceptions of the play. The ever so slight distinction between drama and history would be erased, and regional culture would canonize the play as Southern California history itself, come back to life exactly where all assumed it had begun, under the stars at the San Gabriel Mission, that ancient engine of civilization. Within two months of the spring 1912 opening, the play's first important critic, Willard Huntington Wright, stated simply that watching *The Mission Play* was like watching history itself.[6] In other words, the play allowed viewers to travel back in time.

There can be no doubt that the play had its historian, or at least a kind of amanuensis, in John Steven McGroarty. A reporter for the *Los Angeles Times*, staunch Irish Catholic, and sentimental poet, McGroarty had finished a history of California—*California: Its History and Romance*—at the close of the first decade of the twentieth century. He may have in fact begun writing *The Mission Play* at the same time that he was finishing the California history volume, but regional lore has told the story differently. According to later versions of *Mission Play* genesis, McGroarty finished his state history, then cast about for something else to do. Along came Frank Miller of the Mission Inn in Riverside, a red-roofed Spanish revival hostelry of international fame, with an idea. Someone, Miller felt, should write the history of California as the drama it so obviously was, as an epic production that could be tossed into the widening stream of the region's tourist trade. Miller had been to Oberammergau and seen the Passion Play in 1910. Surely Southern California's dramatic past deserved similar enshrinement? But who could do it?

Wealthy and well connected, Miller sought advice. Ivy League scholars were suggested, including Henry Van Dyke of the literature department at Princeton. But Miller either did not like the options or failed to entice any members of the academic elite to come west long enough to write the epic. Stanford University president David Starr Jordan, as famous a Californian as there was in 1910, suggested a different path. Believing that "a Western man is an Eastern man who has had some additional experiences," Jordan recommended that Miller find himself a writer born, or reborn, in California.[7] Why not get John Steven McGroarty to do it? After all, McGroarty had been writing Californiana for the *Times*, he knew the region, he could put words together. Miller knew McGroarty. He had already overlooked him for one reason or another. But David Starr Jordan had made a convincing argument. A deal was struck. McGroarty got time off from the newspaper from his boss, the mercurial Harrison Gray Otis, another friend of Miller's, and the poet/newspaperman/now-playwright traveled east from Los Angeles to a writing desk at the Mission Inn.[8]

Expectations, his own and Frank Miller's, dictated that McGroarty write a blockbuster. Such expectations apparently did not induce writer's block: McGroarty supposedly finished the project in just eight weeks.[9] Subject matter for the drama could hardly have caused him worry. By 1910, Southern California lay drenched in the glare of the Spanish Fantasy Past, prefixing things right and left with "mission," and working diligently to create monuments to a faded, though glorious antiquity, by propping up and painting the crumbling missions.[10]

While writing, McGroarty paused long enough here and there to seek advice. He wrote plaintively to the Rev. Zephyrin Englehardt, author of *The Missions and Missionaries of California*. Had he portrayed things right? "I am finishing the manuscript of a production which is to be known as 'The Mission Play,'" McGroarty wrote proudly. "It will be brought out in December, and I trust to make it worthy of the great theme it portrays." McGroarty had already shown the manuscript drama to the archbishop, "our beloved Bishop Conaty," who had expressed pleasure in it. Could Fr. Englehardt make time to look at it if the playwright traveled to Santa

Barbara to meet with him? "I know that you are working hard," McGroarty apologized, but "for the sake of the cause and for the sake of truth and history and the love I, as well as yourself, bear the sons of St. Francis, I trust you may find it possible to grant my request."[11]

Fr. Englehardt quickly wrote back, saying that he would be pleased to assist McGroarty "get out 'The Mission Play' historically accurate." He hinted at some competition between McGroarty and another writer and added prophetically that the drama "ought to take with the people here." Clearly the project intrigued the cleric, and he saw it as a way to popularize the legacy of Fr. Serra and the mission system. "I can furnish but the dry skeleton of history, because I must cling to the bare truth; but it would be like putting on flesh and skin by acting it all on the stage. This would be a supplement of priceless value." Not that the project came without challenges. Fr. Englehardt insisted that McGroarty not render the Franciscans "in an *unholy* way with everlasting silly femininity."[12]

A year passed, during which time McGroarty tried out an early version of *The Mission Play* before an audience in San Diego. By early September 1911, the playwright sent a completed draft to Englehardt in hopes that the priest would "tell me if it contains anything objectionable."[13] McGroarty took seriously Englehardt's views, but it is equally clear that the playwright wished to make certain that the play's dramatic impact not be diminished. A letter from McGroarty in answer to some of Englehardt's criticisms is especially telling. "Nearly every change you point out," McGroarty admits, "I must, somehow, make, but there are one or two things I would love to retain—especially the Spanish dancers from Monterey in the second act. You know, the Play must *catch* the public—our separated brethren as well as our Catholic people."

McGroarty wanted it both ways. He admitted to Englehardt that "of course I never meant to take chances on [*The Mission Play*]," yet he wished to hold onto whatever spark the thing might have in terms of attracting a broad audience. This ambition shattered his friendship with Englehardt, who clearly felt taken advantage of by the playwright.[14] Another friend, the irrepressible man of letters Charles Fletcher Lummis, the single most important publicist of the state's mission past, recognized the perils of McGroarty's relentless ambition. "In my 53 years, I have never even found so Irresponsible a Cuss as you," Lummis chastised McGroarty in a letter about the playwright's work. "Now you've got to learn—not for my sake but for yours—not to go crazy when an idea hits you. That's the time to get sane. You've got to learn to keep your Word, to be Responsible, to have some Balance. Else you'll wind up a Total Failure. Your Mission Play, [and] everything else, will crumble unless you learn the Common Law. Wake Up!"[15]

Despite the harsh words of friends and critics, McGroarty did what others before him had not succeeded in doing. He captured the historical narrative and the pageantry of La Fiesta de Los Angeles and corralled it all onto the pages of a theatrical script. He then set up a ticket office. It worked. *The Mission Play* made John McGroarty famous, if not rich, and it helped to launch him on a career as Southern California's representative man, in symbol and, eventually, in the halls of the United States Congress as well.

THE MAN AND THE PLAY

John Steven McGroarty came from hardscrabble Pennsylvania coal country. He had been born in 1862, into a big Irish family.[16] As a young man, McGroarty took a great interest in temperance, remembering years later that, while still a teenager, he marched at the head of a temperance parade of ten thousand coal miners.[17] He tried teaching, then moved on to journalism. Then he went into law, as a justice of the peace, and was admitted to the Pennsylvania bar near the end of the nineteenth century. Shortly after marrying Ida Lubrecht of Wilkes-Barre, McGroarty grew restless, left the East for the excitement and opportunities offered by the West, and relocated to Butte, Montana. There he worked as a legal adviser to Marcus Daly, the Butte copper king who made millions from the Anaconda Mine. McGroarty and his wife also operated a boarding house, and McGroarty may have managed the Anaconda Water Company. Following Daly's death, and on the lookout for the main chance, McGroarty traveled the Southwest, invested in Mexican mines, and even went to Mexico alone near century's end to oversee his investment. The venture, like so many others made by countless Americans during the period, failed. From Mexico, McGroarty traveled next to Seattle, where a telephone venture also failed.

Business losses, perhaps even broken health: the McGroartys joined the march to Los Angeles. He started as an itinerant bookseller, then found work under Harrison Gray Otis at the *Times*, where he moved up the ranks and became an editorial writer. He also edited a journal in which he had a stake, *West Coast Magazine*. In between editorial duties, McGroarty published sentimental and undistinguished, albeit successful, poetry about his adopted state. He was, as Kevin Starr nicely phrases it, of "the lo! hark! school."[18] *Just California* (1903) and *Wander Songs* (1908) helped establish him as a recog-

Figure 51. John Steven McGroarty. Courtesy of the Regional
History Center, University of Southern California.

nized regional writer. McGroarty also developed an eye for spotting literary
talent. In the same year in which *The Mission Play* appeared, he sponsored
publication of Robinson Jeffers's first book, *Flagons and Apples*.

McGroarty's editorial tenure with *West Coast Magazine* no doubt helped
prepare him to write *The Mission Play*. The journal published all manner
of sentimental and romantic Californiana; it was in many ways a smaller
clone of Charles Fletcher Lummis's *Out West*, minus Lummis's quirky bril-
liance. Lummis would in fact write briefly for McGroarty, bringing his
"Lion's Den" column over from *Out West* into *West Coast*. Amidst the
fiction and local interest stories, the magazine took a small role in trying to
explain or comment on social and political issues. It published such pieces,

titled in the popular pseudoscientific argot of the day, as "Problem of the Emigrant," and of course "The Mexican Problem."[19]

Grafton Publishing brought the journal out, and they also published McGroarty's *California: Its History and Romance*. By the early 1910s, the magazine operated as an advertising vehicle for John Steven McGroarty. The front and back covers, the photogravures, the articles, reviews, and editorials often related to one McGroarty story or another: his history book, his book on the El Camino Real, the much-anticipated *Mission Play*, McGroarty's verse. Even as McGroarty labored over his script, regional anticipation grew almost palpable, as if the Los Angeles basin's population engaged in a collective holding of breath: *The Mission Play* is coming!

Writing *The Mission Play* was, of course, only the first step toward making theatrical history. Even though Frank Miller had backed away from the play before its debut, for reasons that are unclear, McGroarty had the support and the experience to make his play into a public relations event, an experience. In this he rested upon the example of such phenomena as Helen Hunt Jackson's novel *Ramona* and La Fiesta de Los Angeles, both of which had connected profoundly with a narrow regional perception of the past. But it would be inaccurate to call *The Mission Play* a mere imitation of previous theatrical or literary productions. McGroarty organized The Mission Play Association, which borrowed money and issued stock in the venture.[20] Then, acting as producer and director, he worked to raise additional money, build a playhouse, and put on the play.

The Mission Play as cultural phenomenon broke new ground even as McGroarty and others, literally, broke ground. Having received the okay from Bishop Thomas J. Conaty, McGroarty went ahead with his plans to build his playhouse and a miniature replica of the El Camino Real, the famed "King's Road" upon which the state's missions had been built. At the groundbreaking ceremonies for the Mission Playhouse, built just adjacent to the San Gabriel Mission on the full-sized El Camino Real, McGroarty and Miller made sure to add spectacle to construction ritual. Those present to turn earth included the Catholic bishop, the president of the Native Sons of the Golden West, a representative of the Los Angeles Chamber of Commerce (foreshadowing that organization's later involvement with the play), and two Franciscan friars, returned now to California to mark the commemorative celebration of their good works and their goodness. Wielding hoes and giant hatchets, of all things, and tools supposedly used in the founding of the San Gabriel Mission, the men stabbed at the earth.

A band played the Spanish National Hymn before a large crowd of smiling onlookers.[21]

The playhouse, with its thin facade of mission architecture and roofline, looked every inch like a motion picture backlot. The building (one reviewer called it a sort of "monastic refectory") apparently shook when the nearby trains roared past; actors held their lines until the noise faded. But it did its job. As many as fifteen hundred people could see *The Mission Play* within its confines. McGroarty and staff added one additional enticing feature that made the Mission Play experience into the first California history theme park. In a short walkway alongside an outside wall of the Playhouse—the Mission Walk—the state's twenty-one missions, each rendered in careful miniature, sat in geographical sequence. The mini missions were a brilliant interactive innovation, a triumph of cultural tourism, and they rarely escaped comment. Playgoers could see the play, make a short pilgrimage on the tiny El Camino Real to look at all the missions, and thus experience the past, even, as they often reported, see it before their eyes.[22]

Creating anticipation for *The Mission Play* around such staged events as the groundbreaking and Mission Walk helped prime the pump of regional excitement. McGroarty also chose his actors carefully. It is important to remember that many of the play's personnel, not only at the outset but for years afterwards, included some of the best, or certainly the best-known talent the American theater could offer. For director, McGroarty picked Henry Kabierske, well known in theatrical circles and also head of the famed Philadelphia Historical Pageant. The combination of McGroarty and Kabierske particularly thrilled critics. "With such a patrician patriarchate of Illuminati, could the Mission Play be anything but the unqualified success it is?" asked one.[23] Shakespearean veteran Benjamin Horning played the role of Junipero Serra, founder of the California mission system. For the lead female role, McGroarty chose an actress already steeped in romantic readings of Southern California history. Eleanor Calhoun, who had recently, through marriage to a Serbian prince, become the much longer-named Princess Lazarovich-Hrebelianovich, came from fairly humble settings in California's Central Valley. Her father, Ezekiel Ewing Calhoun, had been a judge in the country town of Visalia. Her mother had written "Scenes of Early California Life," as well as what her daughter later called "other biological writings." Her sister Virginia had written and acted in a stage version of Helen Hunt Jackson's world-famous *Ramona*, the source from which most fantasy blessings of Southern California flow.[24] Years earlier, Eleanor had been William Randolph Hearst's girlfriend. Now, as Princess Lazarovich-Hrebelianovich, she apparently helped underwrite the show with her new wealth (and received a hefty salary for her acting).[25] Accompanying the star talent were locals: members of various Spanish and Mexican families, as well as what the *Los Angeles Times* called "a company of genuine Indian supernumeraries."[26]

Again it all worked, it all came together. Or at least it was a good start. The opening show witnessed the attendance of local notables, clergy, and members of the society set, launching the play on its long career. There were a few problems. The flimsy playhouse threatened to topple like a house of cards. Newfangled automobiles cluttered the site, and exhaust from their engines proved a vexing and unanticipated problem. But playgoers loved the drama, cheering themselves hoarse when Benjamin Horning as Fr. Serra declared that he would fight to maintain the missions against all obstacles.

McGroarty expected that the first year's production might last a week. The play instead did a run of ten weeks, 127 consecutive shows, thus shattering the American theater record. Within a year, it had become a Southern California phenomenon, neatly hooked into, and thus expanding, the mission fantasies of the region. Railroads incorporated *The Mission Play* into their advertisements, both locally and across the nation. Playwright and play became almost synonymous: McGroarty kept a tiny office at the Playhouse and received mail addressed simply "John McGroarty, The Mission Play, San Gabriel."

Critics fell over themselves in praise of the play and its author. "It is a sermon in action presented with historical fidelity," read one representative *Mission Play* advertisement. It was, the Catholic journal *Tidings* proclaimed, "an historical pageant and sermon in action." Professor Richard Burton of the University of Minnesota, author of *How to See a Play*, declared that the entire history of California could now be seen in an afternoon.[27] McGroarty bathed in the bright light of renown. He was "a Celt and a Californian, a poet and a journalist, a man of sincere faith and fertile fancy, unspoiled by literary fads, and fashions, capable of feeling the beauty and pathos of the mission-story, and willing to tell it on the stage so simply that a child could see its meaning."[28] In their early appraisals of *The Mission Play* and its success, a number of critics found it necessary to point out that what made the play so remarkable was that it took seriously the regional background of Southern California. It enshrined and thus rendered immutable a set of historical conceptions and arranged them into a single narrative.

The play was both a discovery and celebration of regional heritage, one that its audiences—largely white and Protestant—could nonetheless claim as their own. Writing in the pages of *West Coast*, critic Willard Huntington Wright pointed out that conventional American historical pageants along the lines of the Passion Play were a virtual impossibility. "We have no historical background distinctly our own. Our racial beginnings are too near to us to have become invested, as yet, with the atmosphere of romance."[29]

Whatever Wright's precise meaning, it is clear that he believed that Southern California's racial environment had indeed reached that level of maturation to become invested with the "atmosphere of romance." The arrival of McGroarty ("a documentary historian," wrote Wright) and *The Mission Play* on the local scene seemed to Wright (and other critics) the long-awaited solution to an American historical problem. How could history serve romance, how could romance serve history? Because Wright—not to mention McGroarty—accepted the notion that California history and California romance *were the same thing*, *The Mission Play* solved the problem. The story of race, the story of ethnicity, the story of California: all could be played out on stage in San Gabriel in perfect adherence to truth. The past had its share of poignancy, yes, but it was the poignancy of sacrifice, faithful devotion, or self-abnegation. The play's appeal lay precisely in the willingness of its audience to suspend disbelief, to mis-remember everything about the dark ground of the region's even recent past.

McGroarty's supposed scholarly fidelity paid off; it would be difficult to uncover anything but unqualified praise for the drama. A typical published response: "The Mission Play is nobly conceived, splendidly executed, a prose-poem for beautiful diction, a living page of stirring history, a glowing picture of days gone by, a potent sermon of faith and hope and self-abnegation."[30]

The play could even do more, seemingly. When a San Francisco journal accused Southern California of neglecting the needs of its local Mexican population, *The Tidings* fired back that, on the contrary, Los Angeles Catholics were "shouldering the white man's burden . . . so stoutly." Part of this had to do with the fact that the downtown Plaza Church "is almost exclusively given to the Mexicans," as *Tidings* wrote. As well, the town of San Gabriel, an "almost . . . wholly Mexican settlement," featured a great deal of Catholic relief work among the Mexican population. Though the defensive writer did not come right out and say it, the implication was clear; in San Gabriel, *The Mission Play* did the work of the church among the Mexican population.[31]

Figure 52. Act 1 of *The Mission Play*: Return of Portolá from Monterey. Author's collection.

Writer Mary Austin loved *The Mission Play* and saw in it religious labor as well. In a letter to McGroarty in the winter of 1913, she echoed the sermon metaphor, saying that he had dealt with religion with "courage and delicacy." "I wish to congratulate you on the way in which the religious spirit, which was the mainspring of the Mission Enterprise, was felt all through the play and yet never obtruded."[32] Energetic social reformer Bromley Oxnam, already a force in Los Angeles housing reform in his early twenties, felt much the same. "I saw the Mission Play," Oxnam wrote in his diary. "The play is good, very good. . . . I had learned to love Junipero Serra and his faithful fathers thru the pages of history." But seeing history staged offered greater uplift and example. "I have learned what sacrifice means and truly these men were inspired with a gospel of service. . . . may I serve as truly as they served." Another viewer put it more succinctly. *The Mission Play*, he wrote the playwright, made people want to go to mass.[33]

So what was *The Mission Play*? In simplest terms, the play was a three-act drama, impressively staged if not acted. Several hundred people made up the acting company. Costumes, most made by Ida Lubrecht McGroarty, the playwright's wife, were bright and designed, at least in part, for historical accuracy. An intermission between Acts 1 and 2 offered playgoers the chance to stroll the tiny El Camino Real and look at the mini missions, or to sit and listen to period music provided by the company's Mexican band.

The university professor who declared that one could see the entirety of California history in a San Gabriel afternoon actually had a point. *The Mission Play* shrink-wrapped history into palatable sections, easily enough linked by quaint notions of progress. Every bit an invention of tradition, *The Mission Play* primly avoided the bloody ground of the state's past. A prelude offered a fitting metaphor to the play's historical point of view. Ghostly figures pantomime scenes from the "misty past," standing behind a scrim curtain. In this case, though, the curtain was more of culture than fabric, as the play proceeded on to its melodramatic narrative of "the three great epochs" of California history. First, the state's coastal natives ("Savages" in the script), lurking off stage—history's and the playhouse's—sense the approach of their "White Conquerors." *Ave Maria* plays as background music. A Spanish soldier enters, looks about imperiously, and exits. Bells peal in the distance. A Franciscan enters: "Spirit of the everlasting Faith of the Cross of Christ." He assumes a prayerful attitude, then extends his hands to the audience in benediction. He exits, and Act 1 commences.

The play opens in 1769, "when California began." Set on the Pacific's edge at Pt. Loma, south of Los Angeles, Act 1 featured a sleepy Franciscan and several lazy Spanish soldiers bemoaning their fate, fearful of the natives. Gaspar de Portolá, head of the expedition, is out looking for Monterey Bay. The soldiers epitomize the waning days of Spanish imperial greatness. They don't like California much, nor do they have any energy to make anything of the place. The pious Junipero Serra dominates the scene, as McGroarty showers him with selfless goodness. The state's natives do not appreciate the founder of the mission system, or his project, in the manner they should. Serra and his assistants wish to baptize a native child; with that act, they will believe that their efforts have found favor in God's sight and that the mission necklace can be strung north from San Diego. "God grant that we shall now really begin the evangelization of California," Serra prays, gazing aloft, crucifix at his breast.

Unlike Serra, de Portolá feels no kindness toward the state's natives. "California is filled with Indians," he tells the padre. "But they are nearly all like these wretched natives in San Diego." The conquistador wishes to depart, to return to Mexico. Serra forbids this with an exhortation (audiences loved it): "We shall NOT abandon California." With the arrival of local Indians at the camp, bringing a child for baptism, all appears saved. Serra prepares to anoint the child with holy water, naming him Ubaldo for a

Spanish captain lost at sea. At this moment, the assembled Indians, confused and apparently frightened by Serra's baptismal gestures, rush from the stage in alarm, taking the child with them. The tumult stuns Serra. He blames himself—"O mea culpa! Mea culpa!" The mission experiment fails as a ship appears to take Serra and company back to Mexico. Curtain.

Act 2, fifteen years later, celebrates the flowering of the mission system. It did not die on the San Diego coast after all. The Spanish found Monterey Bay, near where Serra founded Mission San Carlos to further the Christianizing work among the natives. The effort has paid off: even young Ubaldo, the object of the first act's baptism fiasco, has grown up Christian, devoted to Serra as much as he is to the church. Amidst flowers and music, Christianity flourishes in California. No longer are the Indians savages, no longer are they "so stupid, so dirty, so hopeless" as they were fifteen years previous.

Serra is now an old man. Yet he refuses to cut back on his work; he sleeps on a bare board, he goes without food, he walks from mission to mission. He plans mission strategies with his underlings, he hears progress reports about the number of Indians brought to the faith. He hears a fellow Franciscan boast about the utility and beauty of Mission San Luis Obispo's red-tiled roof—"now used in all parts of California."

The crux of Act 2 is Serra's accomplishment; near death, he reflects back on his work in California as a tribute both to God and to the native people of California. "To be remembered in California—Oh, God grant that I shall not be forgotten in this dear and lovely land," he cries.

In opposition to Serra, whom McGroarty renders part George Washington, part Jesus Christ, is the evil Spanish Commandante, head of the province's military installations. He rides to Mission San Carlos in search of a bride, a young woman of Indian and Spanish parentage. Serra forbids the soldier from fulfilling his mission, claiming that because she has at least a drop of Indian blood, Anita is under the authority of the mission fathers. Serra offers that the Commandante may marry the Indian girl provided she give her uncoerced consent. The Commandante balks, arguing that it is beneath him to marry a half-breed. Serra then quickly performs a marriage between Anita and the Indian Pablo, to whom she is engaged. The enraged Commandante threatens anew to take the girl, whereupon Serra upbraids him ferociously. Serra and the other Franciscans run the Commandante off. In celebration, the young Indians of the mission, shouting "La Fiesta! La Fiesta!" dance a dozen numbers. Serra, a silhouette at prayer, offers a blessing to a young Indian. Curtain.

Act 3 makes a large temporal jump. It is now 1844. Serra is long dead. The

Figure 53. Act 2 of *The Mission Play*: Fiesta scene. Author's collection.

act opens amidst mission ruins at San Juan Capistrano. Ubaldo is now an old man, the caretaker of the broken, dilapidated mission. Anita, the former object of the Spaniard's lust, is an old woman (no longer, it would appear, half-Spanish), a basket maker. Ubaldo sleeps, dreaming of the glories of the mission past. The entire act is a mission requiem. The secularization of the missions by the Mexican government has caused them to collapse, both as institutions and buildings. The central character of the final act is Señora Josepha Yorba, a member of an elite *Californio* family who, like Ubaldo, mourns the destruction of the once-grand missions. Señora Yorba and Ubaldo reminiscence and mourn the loss of the romantic past, and they both wonder what the presence of so many "Americanos" means to the missions and California.

The scene darkens as Señora Yorba begins to talk of Monterey, site of Serra's triumph in Act 2. "There is nothing there now but—memory." As the evening grows later, Indians who live nearby are seen coming into the mission property carrying a burden. Ubaldo, under orders not to allow Indians access to the secularized missions, panics. Señora Yorba intercedes and allows the Indians to enter. They carry the body of a dead Franciscan friar. The padre has starved to death in this time of drought and want. As they prepare him for burial in sanctified ground, Señora Yorba discovers the gold chalice of the mission hidden in the Franciscan's robes. That the

Figure 54. Progress as linear tableau: A *Mission Play* advertisement from the early twentieth century. Courtesy of the Huntington Library, San Marino, California.

Indians have meant to bury it with the friar (and not steal it) astonishes her, and she exclaims to God that His "dusky neophytes" have "kept the faith."

At the finale, Señora Yorba cries that "the dream is done . . . gone to return no more. The dear and lovely dream that was so bright and fair." What lives is the Cross and the Faith. The missions have gone, but God's Mission remains. As the play closes, Ubaldo stretches out his arms and cries, "O Cross of Christ!" Curtain.[34]

Buoyed by his first year's success, McGroarty doubled the play's run in 1913 to twenty weeks. Kabierske was by now gone. Benjamin Horning took over directing duties in addition to his portrayal of Junipero Serra. Gone, too, was the Princess. The female lead was assumed by Lucretia del Valle, daughter of Reginaldo F. del Valle, scion of a *Californio* land grant family and, not incidentally, vice president of the Mission Play Association. In her role as Josepha Yorba, Lucretia del Valle added artifactual accuracy to the role. It was widely reported that she wore family heirlooms as part of her costume: her *mantilla*, other clothing, her jewelry. She reportedly played the role nearly a thousand nights. "Chief Sheet Lightning," said to be a Sac and Fox Indian, was described as "the Mission Play cicerone."[35]

McGroarty, who later claimed to be as much as $100,000 in debt on opening night (which seems a wild exaggeration), doubtless sensed that the play might be a moneymaker of serious proportion. He was, after all, the same man on the lookout for the main chance that he had been wandering across the mining regions of the Rocky Mountain West. He had dabbled in Los Angeles real estate (who hadn't?), and *West Coast Magazine* had given him space to write such pieces as "The Value of Property and Sentiment in the Real Estate Business."[36] Now he had hit upon mining history, and it seemed to be working. Clearly the play could bring in money. Gross receipts for 1913, for the first ten weeks of the show, amounted to over $35,000.[37] Yet McGroarty made pains to claim poverty as well as motives more exalted than the pursuit of lucre. In a long letter to Archbishop Thomas Conaty, who rented McGroarty space at the mission, the playwright threw himself on the mercy of the church. If the archbishop couldn't reduce the play's rent ($5,000 a year), it would prove the play's "undoing as a factor for the propagation of religion and the uplift of the drama. I trust you will feel, as I do, that the American stage as at present conducted is a menace to the morals and religion, and that such Plays as the Mission Play are the best weapons for battling this menace." The playwright knew melodrama.[38]

The Mission Playhouse began hawking autograph copies of McGroarty's history of California at shows, and McGroarty hatched an idea to take the romance on the road. During the 1914 season, the Mission Players went to San Francisco and San Diego. In 1915, out-of-state tourists going to those two cities for their respective Pan-Pacific Expositions probably made plans to see *The Mission Play* when in Los Angeles.

The traveling *Mission Play* must have made at least some money, because by 1916 McGroarty could pen harsh words about protecting his show against perceived threats from others wanting to make history pay. Charles Fletcher Lummis, an on-again, off-again friend of McGroarty's, had notified the playwright of plans to make a motion picture of the life of Fr. Junipero Serra. Portions of the proceeds were to go to Lummis's cherished Landmark's Club, an energetic effort to restore dilapidated missions. Would McGroarty support the effort? McGroarty left little doubt as to his position. "The story of Junipero Serra and the Missions for dramatic purposes has been lying around since 1833, at least, for anybody to grab. But no one grabbed it until I did so in 1912. Now it is mine and I purpose [*sic*] to have and to hold it against all comers, with all the law there is to back me. And, there is plenty of law of that kind."[39]

Maybe it was time to take *The Mission Play* outside California, McGroarty reasoned, perhaps thinking that he could evade those wishing to capitalize on his drama and, in the process, make money from curious easterners. What he learned was that the play's popularity with tourists visiting California did not translate into popularity with non-Californians. The trip, which included stops in Reno, Salt Lake City, St. Louis, Kansas City, Omaha, and Chicago, failed miserably. Lucretia del Valle supposedly tried to salvage the show by turning her entire salary over to the play. A historical pageant about

California meant apparently little to non-Californians, at least not as long as they were not in California doing those things tourists wanted and were expected to do. "The poet's dream has gone to smash!" wrote the *Los Angeles Times*, adding that while "California may fascinate its tourists with its mission heritage," the romance "cannot be exported." One critic in Kansas City went so far as to question the play's historical measure, blasting McGroarty as a simple booster and "hysterical Californian, dyed-in-the-wool. The Mission Play suffers a good deal by being saddled with the cult of the professional Californian," the critic surmised. "By itself Mr. McGroarty's play picturing the rise and fall of a vivid religious life in California, is quite interesting to anyone who has a sense of values in the theater, who likes pageantry, and who can make out the difference between the shrewdly artful and professional drama and the drama which is artfully simple. . . . It is the missions the play speaks of, just as fundamentally its chief charm is its atmosphere rather than its historical or religious qualities."[40]

Kansas City's shrewd critic suggested, at least between the lines, that *The Mission Play* was not the great rendering of California history that California critics seemed all too ready to believe and champion. What's more, the critic's antagonism to the California boosterish qualities hinted that the play might not attract Kansans in Kansas, Chicagoans in Chicago, or Missourians in Missouri. If they were in California, tourists doing the Southern California tourist circuit, *The Mission Play* might be an obvious attraction, because the audience—knowing what it wanted of California's past—could play the role of Greek chorus. But maybe things were different elsewhere?

Apparently so. Broke, stranded in Chicago, and down $40,000, the embarrassed Mission Players hitched a ride back to Southern California with the Southern Pacific Railroad. The humiliation of the trip bothered McGroarty for years, and it supposedly brought on a nervous collapse for Ida Lubrecht McGroarty. History could sell, but only if it was packaged and offered with some discretion; maybe it would do best if the play stayed closer to home.

The disastrous 1916 tour hurt the play's finances badly. Once back home, the play and McGroarty tried to regain footing, although McGroarty's business abilities were clearly not his strong suit. He did, however, make the shrewd move of hiring E. K. Hoak, a talented and well-known figure in Southern California tourist hotel management (his son would later be the chief designer of Union Station), to take over some of the organization of the production. Tyrone Power Sr. joined the troupe, as did his wife, Patia, cast as the new female lead. McGroarty also worked hard to replace George Osburn, Junipero Serra in the previous season, who died just prior to the fateful road trip east. He approached Frederic Warde, another famous Shakespearean actor, about the possibility of taking on the role. Warde read the play and loved it. In his memoirs, he wrote that he had never before "read a manuscript that made such a deep impression upon me as this simple, unconventional, dramatic composition. The character is so completely sympathetic and full of dramatic possibilities there is little credit due for my success, but I will confess that I felt particularly gratified when John McGroarty publicly announced that when he was writing the play I was in his mind for the part."[41]

Warde proved, apparently, a good choice, if not a coup, among the play's fans. George Searle of the Los Angeles Soldiers' Home, for instance, wrote that Warde could "feel proud in that he has [compelled] the Native Californian the Mexican and myself to believe in [the] reincarnation of Fray Junipero Serra."[42]

THE MISSION PLAY AND THE 1920S

I count the day I spent at the Mission Play as one of the happiest days of my life.

THOMAS R. MARSHALL, vice president of the United States[43]

Those old days mark the Golden Age of California. In that wonderful time, everybody was happy, well fed and content. Nobody was poor. Nobody was rich. It was an age of easy toil, of prayer and sun and peace and laughter.

JOHN S. MCGROARTY, 1921[44]

Despite the abysmal failure of the 1916 road trip, *The Mission Play* made it through the decade and into the 1920s. McGroarty tightened up the play's contractual powers with actors, and he moved the drama along the path toward becoming an institution. Part of that process, at least as McGroarty figured it, was to make certain that history and drama be performed "in a correct and painstaking manner," as he put it in an actor's contract. Already by 1916, McGroarty seems to have realized that the drama's appeal lay in its ability to portray history, and he knew as well that that ability rested upon the fragile foundations of theatrical performance. As such (and as with La Fiesta's staging years earlier) great care and attention to detail extended to "strict regard" of makeup and "the proper dressing of the characters assigned."[45]

Playgoers continued to make the journey from the big city to "the little Spanish town," or, as McGroarty later referred to it, with euphemistic care, "a sleepy old adobe pueblo."[46] Once there, they could park their automobiles in the Mission Garage ("official parking for the Mission Play") at the corner of Mission Drive and Ramona Avenue. On their way into the theater, the audience members might stop to look at "Ramona's Home" (a real house for a fictional character, designed to lure fans of Helen Hunt Jackson's melodramatic novel) and the old grapevine of Mission San Gabriel ("Mother of all the Grapevines in California"). Playgoers continued to pay their $1, $1.50, or $2 per seat; they continued to walk the miniature El Camino Real before and between acts; and they continued to weep and cheer and applaud. They stopped for trinkets at the Mission Curio Shop, and they drank tea at the Ramona Tea Shop. And when they got back to the workaday world, the world of the twentieth century, they wrote John Steven McGroarty and told him what a fine thing he had done in writing *The Mission Play*.

Not all the fan mail came as a result of *The Mission Play*. McGroarty continued to write for the *Los Angeles Times*, and he had, by the early 1920s, become a well-known public figure in Los Angeles. He spoke often at public events, school commencements, and banquets. He had cards printed that advertised a visit from McGroarty and the Mission Play Artists for various events, "with or without costume." He turned down offers to write historical dramas for Texas (about, not surprisingly, remembering the Alamo), Florida, and the Pacific Northwest. His books continued to sell. But it was *The Mission Play* that had made him a public figure, and almost any printed reference to him included the phrase "author of the Mission Play." More than any of his other projects or books, the play earned for McGroarty a reputation as a man who knew Mexican life and culture precisely because he had staged it. Walter Malone, the general superintendent of the Simons Brick Company nearby in Montebello, admitted as much in a letter he wrote to McGroarty—tellingly in Spanish—in the mid-1920s. Play and playwright clearly went hand in hand in the public consciousness, and thus it would be until McGroarty's death in 1944.[47]

McGroarty's public utterances, not unlike his columns for the *Los Angeles Times*, tended toward platitudes and simple morality tales. "Some day California will be a place where there are no criminals," he told the no doubt delighted, if surprised, dinner guests at a Pomona banquet. "All the

Figure 55. *Mission Play* window advertisement, ca. 1920. Courtesy of the Huntington Library, San Marino, California.

natural beauties and wonders of this state tend to take the evil and little-ness out of human nature." In regional journalism and public circles, John Steven McGroarty seems every bit the kindly, naive precursor to longtime *Los Angeles Times* fixture Jack Smith.[48]

Letters McGroarty received, carefully preserved in the pages of his "Happy Book" scrapbooks, reveal an adoring public. Countless missives refer to him as "Conductor," a nickname picked up from his Sunday news-paper column. Others salute him as Dear Brother, Brother John, St. John, even, as one lengthy salutation put it, "the Mental and Spiritual Stabilizer of California." It is clear that letterwriters loved McGroarty (his importance in their lives is a bit unsettling), and they loved *The Mission Play* as well.[49] Not only did they write in explicitly religious terms to McGroarty—"the play was better for my soul than a thousand sermons . . . altogether sublime and uplifting," wrote one—they also described their experience again and again not as seeing or attending *The Mission Play*, but as witnessing it. It was as if (and playgoers weren't shy about relaying this to McGroarty) the past and the present changed places, and those lucky enough to be in the Playhouse could—in what seems to be a religious admission—witness the transition. Harry Peterson, director of the Stanford Museum, an early fan of the play, thought that it was "one of the greatest missionaries for arousing that sentiment for early and historic things. . . . it stands out as clearly to me to-day as it did the evening I witnessed it." Even an out-of-towner like W. E. B. Du Bois, the famed African American writer, historian, and civil rights advocate, felt moved to write McGroarty, thanking him especially "for the beautiful experience of witnessing your Mission Play. I shall not soon forget it."[50]

The profoundly provincial cast of McGroarty's admiring letters helps us to recall something that usually is neglected in writings about *The Mission Play*. In addition to its obvious appeal to tourists, *The Mission Play* was a very local institution as well, and people in Los Angeles responded (and "witnessed") it over and over again, schoolchildren and adults alike. "I enjoyed it very much," orphaned schoolgirl Maisie Marjenhoff neatly wrote in 1922, "and I will never forget it as long as I live."

Nor did teachers miss the chance to praise the playwright for his pedagogical work. The play offered lessons to (and not just about) Latinos as well, apparently. "These Mexican boys and girls have profited," Principal C. A. Pugsley of the John C. Frémont School in Pasadena wrote to McGroarty, "by the new impressions they have formed of the ability and skill of their own countrymen. They are glad as a race they have figured in the history of a country sufficiently well to deserve such recognition as the Mission Play gives." The ironies swirling around such a discussion are almost too many to keep up with: Mexican children at a school honoring a Bear Flag soldier of fortune learning from a melodramatic rendering of the good old days of California that they "have figured" in the history of California "sufficiently well to deserve such recognition as the Mission Play gives."[51]

Good press and fan mail rolled in through the early-to-mid-1920s (along with two honorary doctorates), even as *The Mission Play* lost steam and, apparently, money.[52] Devoted fans wrote poems, sent drawings, and told McGroarty how wonderful he was. *The Mission Play*, one enraptured letter writer exclaimed, "is not a play to me, not an imitation, a makebelieve, it was real. It was the thing itself."[53] Masons wrote McGroarty telling him that they loved the play, and that they could see where he had slyly incorporated Masonic rituals and secrets into it. A. N. Palmer, of the Palmer Method of Penmanship, wrote a beautifully scripted letter to McGroarty congratulating him on the play, which he admitted to seeing at least once a year on his annual Pasadena vacation.[54] Catholics and Protestants alike praised McGroarty for holding up "the great spiritual ideals that we know must prevail if a community spirit of the highest type is to be developed."[55]

Not everyone believed that the play merited such praise. Charles Fletcher Lummis, whose own friendship with the playwright went back and forth, had reservations about *The Mission Play*. As he wrote to McGroarty, "Both as Business and Art, it is intolerable to have in your beautiful pageant some of the frightful anachronisms now there. The Babbitts don't realize them; but every once in a great while some one will go to see the Mission Play who will know that Father Serra didn't teach the California Indians to weave dam [*sic*] bad Navajo blankets!"[56]

But Lummis, for all his booster blather, had long been a stickler for accuracy, particularly regarding his beloved Southwest, and few could be counted upon to be as critical. Such snipes about the play's accuracy were rare (even though Lummis was undoubtedly right about the looseness with detail). Ella Rebard, a Los Angeles resident spending time in Mexico City, thought that she had discovered a kindred spirit in the playwright. She wrote McGroarty a fan letter in March 1922, at about the same time that the playwright boasted of the show's 1810th performance. Rebard praised all McGroarty's writings. She, like he, recognized "the countless virtues" of the Mexican people: "their loyal friendships, kindness of heart, patience and fortitude in the petty ills of life deserve high appreciation and encomiums." Rebard had gone to Mexico, she said, "to study the traits of the people, and . . . shall endeavor to convince the world in general that the *virtues* of the Mexican far exceed his faults."[57]

A number of the letters in McGroarty's Happy Book volumes came from African Americans, many of whom, like W. E. B. Du Bois, wrote in the early 1920s to thank the playwright for his work. McGroarty was actually a well-known friend to the black community of Los Angeles: his columns in the *Los Angeles Times* were marked by a refreshing sense of racial egalitarianism, and the city's African Americans took time to express their gratitude. "I have not forgotten that when the Negro has needed a friend to speak out for him in those days when the Negroes of the south were looking toward to west for relief, that it was your pen, that rift of dark clouds of public sentiment through the columns of the times in our favor."[58] The playwright even apparently arranged a special excursion to the Mission Playhouse in the mid-1920s for African Americans, a night that seems to have been a business failure for the organization.

(McGroarty's egalitarian racial attitudes extended only so far. In a 1925 speech that revealed a curious understanding of California history, as well as real racial animus, McGroarty told the Kiwanis club of Highland Park that if it had not been for Father Serra and the Franciscans, "the state would have been taken over by the Mongolians who were migrating here." One wonders just which "Mongolians" were migrating to California at the end of the eighteenth century.)[59]

Amado Chávez, former mayor of Santa Fe, saw *The Mission Play* in the spring of 1923 while on a Los Angeles vacation. Upon his return home, he wrote McGroarty to thank him "for the noble work you have done in writing that magnificent play. You are fair, impartial and just." Chávez told McGroarty at some length about the Fiesta in Santa Fe ("that promises to become famous"). And while the commissioner of Indian Affairs had recently prohibited Indians from taking part in the Santa Fe Fiesta's many dances (Chávez was certain that McGroarty had read of this decision "with indignation"), Chávez was convinced that the Fiesta was something McGroarty should see and hoped that he would visit Santa Fe.[60]

McGroarty also worked to create a larger dramatic context for *The Mission Play* by making it part of a California history dramatic trilogy. He wrote and produced *La Golodrina*, about Mexican California, and he added *El Dorado*, about the Gold Rush era. But none of McGroarty's dramatic writings (he wrote non-California dramas as well) came close to approaching *The Mission Play*'s popularity. Despite the paradox offered by the play's apparent inability to make a lot of money, it did become famous and it did become something of a regional institution. It clearly outgrew, in terms of regional regard, the little "Spanish town" of San Gabriel. By the early 1920s, the play had become part of the cultural fabric of the growing metropolis. In his folksy newspaper columns, McGroarty often made a point of disparaging Los Angeles as "roaring town." But his *Mission Play,* by the 1920s at least, had become an important institution in just that place (and in the cultural construction of that place).

The vice president of Southern California Edison Company gave words to this institutionalization in a 1923 speech. "In the course of a day's work I come very closely into personal contact with many of the men who are very justly considered the builders of the Southwest. These men give due credit to our wonderful climate, to our port, and to many other of the assets of the Southwest which are making it one of the world's great centers of population, and creating corresponding prosperity for all of us. The point I wish to make is the intangible asset which has its most concrete expression in *The Mission Play*." The speech concluded with a glowing tribute to the playwright that seemed to grant him the creator's role for the entire mission revival phenomenon. "Ride with me some day through the cities and towns of California," R. H. Ballard continued, "and you will see the reflex of the Mission Play wherever you go. To whom is the Southwest indebted for its individuality which has become world famed?"[61]

Other expressions of the play's incorporation into the urban frame included advertisements. "Time has left the sandal-footed padre and sturdy pioneer who followed him only a memory," a *Mission Play* program ad for the California Bank declared awkwardly in 1923, "but has builded for him in these large cities now thriving on our western shores everlasting monuments to their zeal and courage." McGroarty had staged the story of "barbarism to civilization in California," the bank copy continued, and Californians could take an active role in that latter stage by banking with California Bank.[62]

Yet despite widespread fame, despite the attendance counts that claimed all was fabulously successful in San Gabriel, *The Mission Play* began to sputter sometime around the early-to-mid-1920s. There are probably many reasons for the decline. Despite his often obvious wishes to get rich, McGroarty seems not to have had much business sense. Plans for a new, much-needed, playhouse, designed by famed architect Arthur Benton, moved very slowly due to financial problems and poor decision-making that muddled the finances of a building program with day-to-day production costs. A cornerstone for the new playhouse had been laid in early 1923, but construction stalled. Also, McGroarty's new home in the hills of Tujunga, north of Los Angeles, burned to the ground during the night of the party celebrating its completion, which no doubt affected the playwright's ability to mind *The Mission Play* store. What's more, as a veteran *Mission Play* staff member pointed out, the play was, by the 1920s certainly, up against "modern Movie Theaters" and "downtown Motion Picture palaces." *Mission Play* staff were forced to make stop-gap repairs to the playhouse, the costumes, and the props. By 1924, the play stumbled into the season $11,000 in debt.[63]

By 1925, the enterprise was in deep trouble. McGroarty began to look around for help. One direction he turned was to well-off and well-connected friends. One such friend, T. C. Peck, an executive with the Union Pacific rail system in Los Angeles, took the matter up with none other than the membership of the Los Angeles Chamber of Commerce.[64] No doubt recognizing the public relations benefits of the play, which staged the Spanish Fantasy Past so explicitly, stalwart leaders within the Chamber took notice of the play's plight and made ambitious rescue plans. The idea itself is fascinating: the most successful public relations body in the history of Southern California, recognizing the financial and cultural potential within a simplistic theatrical production, reaches out and grabs that vehicle. In the language of one of the documents produced by the Chamber in 1926, the organization "manifested immediate interest in this crisis of affairs of the Mission Play."[65] In quick order, *The Mission Play* went from being an institution to being institutionalized. By early 1926, the Chamber of Commerce, in a letter to business affiliations across the region, declared that it was "cooperating with other interested parties in the effort to rehabilitate this 'PLAY,' that has so much of historical and romantic value to the Southland as to be an asset to us all."[66] How did all this come about?

The Chamber of Commerce, upon hearing of the plight of *The Mission Play* and its parent association, did what it could do best. It appointed a committee ("The Mission Play Committee of the Los Angeles Chamber of Commerce") to study the problem, chaired by wealthy businessman W. I. Hollingsworth. Not unlike similar Chamber committees that analyzed various local industries and capital opportunities, the Mission Play Committee made a comprehensive study; though this time the subject of the scrutiny was a pageant/drama. The committee determined several critical things. One, *The Mission Play* was a profitable, or potentially profitable, investment opportunity, with a potential return of $20,000 a year. Two, the play could be handled on a profitable basis for a season of twenty weeks. And three, the play had become so important to the region and the region's sense of self, that the desire for its continuation was "universal."

Recognizing that time was of the essence, the Mission Play Committee acted quickly. It did so in full recognition that *The Mission Play* represented a serious business proposition, one that had already sucked in significant capital. The sheer amount of money tied to *The Mission Play* in one way or another is stunning. The Mission Play Committee noted that $190,000 had been spent in attempts to get a new playhouse built; the committee expected that another quarter of a million dollars would be necessary before the play could be housed in a new, multipurpose, playhouse. When finally completed in the early part of 1927, the playhouse was said to have cost three quarters of a million dollars.

The Chamber of Commerce could not, by the provisions of that organization's charter, produce the play. But it could own it. In fact, it already did. The Chamber held "an option of the entire assets of the Mission Play

Association—real estate, production rights and physical equipment." The next step was easy and, to the business leaders in the Chamber of Commerce, old hat. They would form a corporation. But this corporation, for all intents and purposes, would not sell land or manufactured goods. This corporation would sell tickets to history.

Incorporation papers of the new Mission Playhouse Corporation (alternatively called the Mission Play Corporation) began by noting the play's important role as a regional cultural and historic institution. The play had long been "the point of contact between our people,—together with countless thousands of visitors,—and the beginning of the history of California." That special role, that contact, could be subdivided. Further documentation stated that "the Mission Playhouse Corporation has been organized within the Mission Play Committee," complete with a stock offering of 4,000 shares at $100 a share. All aims could be expressed in a simple motto: "To make the Mission Play safe and preserve it for future generations."

Three-fourths of the stock in the new corporation was to be preferred stock, and the remaining one thousand shares were to be common stock that was not to be sold. The preferred stock would pay stockholders a 7 percent annual dividend from the net profits of the corporation before any additional dividends were to be distributed on the common stock. Holders of the preferred stock could retire or redeem their investment at any time within five years. Upon the retirement of the preferred stock, the common stock was to be allocated to a nonprofit corporation that had two purposes: to perpetuate *The Mission Play* and to perpetuate "the old Southern California landmarks," or at least those not devoted to religious services.[67]

For his part, McGroarty tried to drum up interest in the new corporation rising from the ashes of his once-proud Mission Play Association. In an appeal to railroad and land magnate Henry E. Huntington, McGroarty suggested that Huntington would likely "know all about the struggle" to keep *The Mission Play* alive. After all, McGroarty reminded him of a walk the two men had taken through the grape vine grounds adjacent to the San Gabriel Mission years earlier, when they had discussed the play and its financial future. "I remember," McGroarty wrote, "that you showed me a pair of shoes that you had half-soled because you could not afford to buy a new pair." Be that as it may (and despite the fact that Henry E. Huntington had not been poor at any time during his adult life), McGroarty knew that Huntington in the mid-1920s was one of the nation's richest men. Could he, "out of your love for California," help *The Mission Play* and make it "safe for all generations to come?"[68]

Huntington did not leap into action, but he must have offered some encouragement. Within a few weeks, McGroarty appeared again at his San Marino doorstep, in the form of a letter and a blank stock subscription. "We can't truly say we love California unless we take care of the Mission Play," the playwright pleaded. And of course all was not philanthropic altruism: "the beauty of it is that we are making a good 7% investment at the same time that we are performing a patriotic duty. . . . Please do this, dear Mr. Huntington. Do it for me, for the Mission Play, for California."[69]

Huntington was not the only businessman to receive such encouragement. Wealthy insurance company executive George I. Cochran, who played a role in the Chamber of Commerce takeover of the play, also thought about kicking in some money. In a letter to W. I. Hollingsworth, president of the Mission Playhouse Corporation, Cochran described his faith in the play, as both a financial and historical treasure. His purchase of preferred stock, Cochran wrote, "is not a subscription but a loan. I claim some business sense, and I firmly believe that in time all money subscribed will be repaid in full, both interest and principal." In short, Cochran believed in the resurrected play. "This enterprise seems to me to have real business merit, and will not only return one's money but result in establishing an institution which will add to the attractions of Southern California and furnish an endowment to perpetuate both the Playhouse and the old landmarks of our State."[70]

Pleading could pay off, and history could pay! A significant cross section of the elite Anglo businessmen of Southern California reached for their checkbooks. Preferred stockholders bought in: Henry E. Huntington and E. L. Doheny put in for $10,000 apiece, the Retail Merchants Association pledged $6,000. Harry Chandler of the *Los Angeles Times* opted in for $5,000, as did George Cochran of the Pacific Mutual Life Insurance Corporation and land baron Samuel Rindge. The same amount was pledged by W. I. Hollingsworth (he had made his money in real estate and ship building), banker Henry M. Robinson, the Title Insurance Corporation, and transportation mogul Eli Clark. Frank Miller, who started the whole operation years earlier at his Mission Inn, put up $3,000. Old-time settler and Los Angeles chronicler Jackson Graves put up $2,500, as did Pacific Electric executive D. W. Pontius and electric power millionaire A. C. Balch. Impresario L. E. Behymer came aboard with a $100 investment in the play's future.[71] A holding company on Wilshire Boulevard, the William E. Hampton Company, that had been involved with the faltering play for several years (and actually owned a portion of the play's equipment), acted as a kind of liaison from the Chamber to *The Mission Play* dramatic staff and other personnel.

Did these men support *The Mission Play* because it could make them money, or did they do so because they loved its romance? We cannot fully know, but it does not make any difference. The point is that the institutionalized *Mission Play* represented an important cultural feature of the region. The Spanish Fantasy Past had been cleverly staged and, now, in a process nearly as clever, it had been commodified as a joint stock scheme. The play had become, at least for some of these investors, not just historical theater, but history itself. It was, Hollingsworth boasted, "the very foundation and history of California and one cannot gather, from months of reading and study, so much education in the early history of California as can be secured from one witnessing of the play."[72] Hollingsworth praised the play, and he himself received praise for saving it. The Los Angeles Chamber of Commerce *Bulletin*, customarily the venue for reporting dry stories about the local economy, gushed: "His splendid work in placing the Mission Playhouse Corporation on a substantial financial footing and securing the construction of a magnificent new Playhouse as a permanent home of the Mission Play, is worthy of the highest commendation."[73]

Amidst the oil mania of the mid-1920s, amidst the scandals offered by Julian Petroleum (in which Hollingsworth was implicated) and other fiascos, the newly constituted Mission Play stands out as a stark example of how the Southern California past, carefully massaged and constructed, was part and parcel of the orderly maturation of the city. But the effort was a bit like trying to do cultural taxidermy: *The Mission Play* had had a good run, and it had been important. But could it be institutionalized and remain alive?

To superintend and manage their new venture, the businessmen hired (at one dollar a year) probably the only person in Southern California who had the kind of experience and reputation necessary for the play's resurrection. Lyndon Ellsworth Behymer, impresario *extraordinaire*, had been involved with Los Angeles show business since the late nineteenth century, when he had helped produce La Fiesta de Los Angeles. Known throughout the nation and well respected for both his promotional skills and his prodigious energies, L. E. Behymer would attempt to resuscitate history. Behymer ("the tireless Behymer," Lummis called him) believed that he alone could pull *The Mission Play* back together, less because of his theatrical experience than owing to his public relations and publicity skills. In other words, Behymer wished to take the play in a different direction than McGroarty seemed willing or able to do. "We consider the Mission Play one of the greatest assets of So. California, not only from a cultural viewpoint," he wrote in January 1926, "but from a purely advertising viewpoint."

This was a new Mission Play, or it was the recognition that *The Mission Play*'s importance lay less in great drama than in its inimitable ability to attract people to its simple morality tales, its so effectively told, uncompli- cated stories of the past. Specific actors, very important to McGroarty's con- ception of the play, meant little to Behymer. The play had transcended mere drama, if, indeed it had even been mere drama. "There has been no pag- eant in American history," Behymer confidently continued, "that means more to the ear, the eye, the religion or the history of this country than that produced by the Mission Play. The Eastern public looks for it, expects it. It is the only advertising medium that I know of that an Eastern paper or magazine will mention because they have nothing of that character amid their own surroundings. . . . they have no Missions or no Mission Play and are always glad to speak of this remarkably distinctive asset."

That enthusiastic assessment apparently spoke volumes to the Chamber of Commerce leaders. Within a few weeks, Behymer wrote that "I am working under the instructions of people who have perfect faith in my abil- ity as a showman."[74]

John Steven McGroarty stayed with the play, in a kind of emeritus role, working with the actors and getting paid $500 a month for his services. His wife, too, remained, working to revamp the costumes for the winter open- ing of the 1926 run. But things had clearly changed; McGroarty was in the way (as was his brother-in-law, who had been with the play since 1912), and had been informed that he had to step aside. The play belonged to the com- pany now, and, in a way, so did John Steven McGroarty. Behymer declared that he did "not feel it is necessary for me to report anything to Mr. McGroarty." There's little doubt that *The Mission Play*'s inventor resented the treatment. Behymer's staff reported that McGroarty consistently missed speaking engagements, luncheons, and even radio addresses—"he always had an excuse." Perhaps his old friend Reginald del Valle tried to urge McGroarty to retire gracefully; he wrote McGroarty in the spring that the play had itself become a landmark, "a living monument to you," and that it was now under the "protection of the State and shall serve as a heritage to those who shall follow us in the life of our state."[75]

Yet despite its vaunted backers, and their equally vaunted expectations, the play did not do so well in its first rejuvenated season. For one thing, not much maintenance had taken place in the many years since the 1912 premiere. Behymer had come on board very late (perhaps only a week to ten days before the start of the season). And maybe the play had become dated? Even the irrepressible Behymer did not expect much from the 1926 season. "It is going to be very hard to reach the general public," he wrote to his boss. "The clubs I have visited so far are enthusiastic but it takes time to penetrate the consciousness of the public and overcome previous engagements made before this proposition was presented to them."[76] When the play opened under the organizational aegis of Behymer on February 7, right in the middle of a very wet winter, the receipts for the evening amounted to just over a thousand dollars. The totals for the rest of the week fell off from there, sometimes sharply. The evening show on the 10th brought in only $223, and the nighttime performance three days later only $200. In a letter to his Mission Playhouse Corporation bosses, Behymer complained that *The Mission Play* had become an empty shell, almost unable to generate any publicity of its own: "No pictures, no publicity, nothing but what we managed to create."[77]

Impresario that he was, Behymer felt that the play could not longer be expected to draw an audience simply by word-of-mouth or because tourists would expect to see it. On the contrary, he wanted to mount an ever-aggressive publicity campaign to push the play. And for the most part, the Los Angeles Chamber of Commerce, confident that "Bee" knew what he was doing, backed him with funds. The organization sent out mailers to all associated Chambers of Commerce, three hundred in all, asking them to make *The Mission Play* known to their members and constituents. But the appeals were also enthusiastically local. *The Mission Play* could, Behymer fervently believed, still speak to Angelenos. He oversaw the posting of 3,000 posters in Los Angeles, the distribution of 28,000 circulars, 1,000 window cards, and special advertising placards placed at apartment houses by someone who drove around the city. Behymer wrote hundreds of letters from the "Mission Play Association" to all manner of local groups and associations: the Civitan Club, the Optimist's Club, the Democratic Club. To each he urged Mission Play loyalty, hoping that they would support "this splendid advertising medium, this historic institution."[78] Behymer or his few assistants, who made up the entire "Department of Publicity and Excursions," also visited thirty-eight clubs, ten department stores, two universities, and eight "manufacturing establishments." Behymer worked hard, and he expected the same of his underlings. "It isn't talk I want," he wrote to one who was not meeting his expectations, "but results." "We are only getting started," he assured his bosses.[79]

His representatives tried to visit all the major organizations, conferences, meetings, and conventions in the area. They stopped in at the annual Iowa picnics of midwestern migrants in Lincoln Park in east Los Angeles (where, astonishingly enough, as many as 100,000 Iowans might gather together to celebrate their roots). They made their pitch to the National Association of Harpists. They took the idea to the Southern California Retail Hardware Association, the National Horse Show Committee, and the Pickwick Stage Company. To the Tile and Mantle Contractors Association of America, about to come to a Los Angeles meeting, Behymer made an especially fervent appeal. Your members, he wrote to the president and local host, will have no doubt heard of "the wonderful epic of California, this pageant of 100 years down the road of yesterday." Behymer definitely knew his business: "The Mission Play of San Gabriel is the Oberammergau play of America, only more so—because it not only tells the story of the early Padres and the building of the Missions, but in its great fiesta scene it portrays the folksongs, the dances, the music, the avocations, the religion of the early days when California was merely a province of Mexico and a legacy of Spain." In short, "the book 'Ramona,' was only a reflection of the glories of the period which the play exemplified. . . . The Mission Play is just as much an American institution as the Grand Canyon, the Yosemite Valley, the Niagara Falls or the capitol at Washington."[80]

To other groups, Behymer made the simple pitch that The Mission Play was history come alive and made accessible to all. "The greatest authority on California, its early history, its Missions and its customs is the Mission Play," he informed one convention official.[81] In keeping with the play's historical appeal, Behymer's publicity assistants often went in "Spanish" costume to their advertising assignments and made sure to distribute their flyers, circulars, even sets of color Mission Play postcards which McGroarty had pioneered.[82] Advertising boards, thirty in all, publicized The Mission Play on sidewalks and walls throughout Los Angeles and Hollywood. Behymer even employed an "Official Lecturer," R. Hayes Hamilton, who, armed with a dozen Mission Play lantern slides, gave nightly lectures at the expensive tourist hotels in Pasadena, Los Angeles, even San Diego. Hamilton also showed a Mission Play motion picture at tourist hotels, and he gave a history lecture, "California under Four Flags," designed to increase interest in the drama. Behymer advertised the play in eastern papers, and he worked closely with travel bureaus, Ask Mr. Foster and Ames Brothers particularly. He even convinced Ames Brothers to work The Mission Play into their "See America First" system of western tourism.

Displays and artifacts helped advertise the play. Through the graces of John McGroarty, Behymer supplied one advertising firm with "priceless relics of great historical value," which were proudly displayed in the windows of downtown Los Angeles banks. The Owl Drug Store proved a good friend of the play, turning some window display cases over to the publicity department as well as advertising the play at the well-attended "Owl Drug Company Fashion Show."

Behymer also used the radio to advertise the season. For instance, in a letter to the management of Anthony Radio in Los Angeles, Behymer asked that the six o'clock announcer read a prepared statement, both for the benefit of "the tourists and our home people." The radio station apparently obliged Behymer free of charge, seeing the service as a kind of professional courtesy extended from one advertising medium to another, and aired the announcement:

> The Mission Play, the epic of 100 years of history of the origin and building of the Missions, the life of Junipero Serra, with its beautiful and allegorical first part, the picturesque, exciting and interesting fiesta scene in the second act, and its tribute to the early history of California in the third act, may be seen every afternoon (excepting Monday) at the Mission Play House, San Gabriel, at 2:30, and at 8:30 the evenings of Wednesday and Saturday of each week. There is no other opportunity of hearing the songs of yesterday, or seeing the attractive dances and typical scenes of early California.[83]

In keeping with the play's pedagogical character, Behymer sent a letter to *every* public school in Southern California, announcing the coming of the rejuvenated *Mission Play*. He even invited former Mexican president Obregon, who sent his regrets. Undaunted, Behymer counted on an eventual head of state visit to San Gabriel that would provide priceless publicity and photograph opportunities.[84]

It was, Behymer later remembered, "tough sledding." The rain didn't help matters, nor did regional outbreaks of both influenza and smallpox, which prompted physicians to warn against large public gatherings. Weekly receipts in 1926 never rose much over $5,000. And the transitions inevitably left John Steven McGroarty a bit "out of the loop." Behymer even wrote to the playwright to assure him that he was still a critical part of the drama, at the very least in spirit. "We are aware of your deep interest in the work, in every word, song and note, the same as we are aware of the necessity of making this a permanent institution. It matters not whose fault it is that it has failed in the past; it is up to us to build it up artistically and in a business-like way so there will be no failure in the future."[85]

Expressions of loyalty aside, however, it is clear that McGroarty had become something of a liability. *Mission Play* personnel complained to Behymer that McGroarty had lost either interest or energy or both. He seemed uncomfortable with the business and production transitions inherent in the Chamber of Commerce take-over, and he was petulant about promotional affairs. One staffer complained to Behymer that McGroarty had behaved poorly at a performance designed specifically to advertise Ford automobiles. Apparently the Ford Motor Company had agreed to fill the hall for *The Mission Play* performance. When they did not do so, McGroarty decided against driving a new Ford onto the stage at the close of the play, as had been agreed. Staffers also resented McGroarty's racial egalitarianism. Sometime around "Ford night," he staged a special performance of *The Mission Play* to which he invited an African American audience. Attendance was not what he expected, apparently, and some *Mission Play* staffers never forgave him for it.[86]

By March 1926, the publicity blitzkrieg seems to have begun to pay dividends, at least local ones, even though Behymer still feared that the play might yet fall completely "into the hands of speculators." Of course, *The Mission Play* had already fallen into the hands of speculators, but to Behymer they were the right kind of speculators.[87] Audiences grew, if only slightly. Many of the tickets belonged, as ever, to schoolchildren and locals. The tourist crowd in *Mission Play* seats was, Behymer figured, lower than it had been for decades. It was not that he needed the tourist trade to account for so many tickets. Rather, tourist dollars were like dominos standing next to one another. Get a few moving, and they'd be an economic boost to the whole community. "Without [tourists] it is difficult to proceed—not that their patronage amounts to so much, but the money they spend enables other people to patronize entertainments."

It is tempting to wonder if tourists and locals saw the play for different reasons or saw the play differently. Might tourists have seen *The Mission Play* because it was on their list of things to do in the exotic, semi-tropic paradise? And might locals have chosen to see it again and again for its pedagogical meanings, both about time and about race and ethnicity? That the play could teach history—in fact was supposed to be a history lesson— remained an important perception. "When one realizes that over two and a half million people have witnessed the play," Behymer wrote in the mid-

1920s, "it gives an impression of what people from the East and Middle West have obtained regarding the founding of the Missions." Surely that was just as true, even more so, for the residents of Los Angeles who bought *Mission Play* tickets over and over again.[88]

The special bookings of 1926 reveal just how many locals Behymer and Co. enticed to see the play or to see it again. Chambers of Commerce from all over the Los Angeles basin sent delegations to *The Mission Play* as did, curiously enough, department stores. Bullocks Department Store sent a party of over three hundred people. Robinsons added more than a hundred, and the May Department Store brought nearly five hundred people to the show.

Many who saw the play were schoolchildren and their teachers, coming both together and separately. Children came from all over the Los Angeles basin and outside of it. They came from nearby Montebello, from San Dimas, and David Starr Jordan High School in Watts; from Rosemead, Santa Monica, Yorba Linda, John Muir Junior High in Pasadena. The March bookings included three to four hundred children from Alhambra grade schools, several hundred Rotarians, employees from banks and department stores, a bloc of Southern California Edison tickets, the Los Angeles City Teachers Club, and the Chambers of Commerce from Pasadena and Long Beach, as well as the students of the Lincoln Park School, Alhambra High, Rose Hill Grammar School, and Jefferson High, many of whom had either decided or been required to "attend in Spanish costume." The Los Angeles City Teachers Club brought 190 teachers to the play. A delegation of Los Angeles County employees came in a bloc of 213.[89]

The publicity effort, which Behymer placed above all other tasks of producing the play, exhausted everyone. "It took hundreds of visits to clubs and schools, many talks over the radio, and a thousand and one things to try and put the Play back where it belonged, with an unresponsive public, because many Los Angeles people had seen it and there were no new patrons coming in," Behymer remembered. The mere fact that he had been able to make a run, albeit with a rusty or indifferent cast, for as long as fifteen weeks: that was the success. Nearly seventeen thousand people came to *The Mission Play* in 1926, at just over a thousand per week. Each person brought in between $3 and $4 a week to the corporation. The season lost money, about $5,000, but it was "a success because it was only a question of saving [*The Mission Play*] for the future." Losing only several thousand dollars "was almost a miracle."[90]

Behymer had his hands in every Mission Play pie. He traveled all over

Los Angeles County trying to drum up interest. He wrote press releases. He oversaw advertising copy. He worked with scenery and costume design, and he supported the hiring of an actress who could sing "Spanish songs in a Spanish way." With his publicity machine up and running, he turned his attentions to the corporate ownership of the play, urging Hollingsworth to add a prominent Catholic. Perhaps prominent attorney Joseph Scott would be interested, or even oilman E. L. Doheny? The organization could use a rabbi or two as well, Behymer suggested, maybe a Baptist, even "a good hustler for finances like Harry Haldeman." School district people should be included as well, he insisted, knowing perhaps better than anyone else that it was the schools' endless supply of students that might make or break the play. The backers of the play should also try to get people from the community, he urged, as many as 150, to act as an informal advisory or steering committee. Behymer wanted to increase *Mission Play* publicity, and he knew that he had to involve the larger community as much as possible.[91]

The efforts to continue, create, and further public interest in *The Mission Play* often pointed to the play's past success as indication of its institutional status. It is impossible to verify the attendance numbers, but the claims were astounding. In July 1926, Behymer claimed that *The Mission Play* had been performed 2,600 times, though not in consecutive sequence. This, he said, made the play the most successful in America, by far, and meant that it had been "witnessed" by two and a half million people. Behymer then engaged in some showman's hyperbole. Of those two and a half million people, he claimed, "25% of them have written letters of approval."[92] Six hundred thousand letters are a lot of letters.

Behymer's public relations activity lay atop a foundation of money problems. Attempts to raise funds, like a Biltmore Hotel luncheon in May 1926, worked to some degree. At the beginning of the summer of 1926, the corporation desperately needed more. Architect Arthur Benton's playhouse, with seating for 2,500 and designed to look like one of the state's twenty-one missions, stood uncompleted, an expensive facade of mere potential. The corporation had extended itself through the stock offerings to local big shots, and it needed capital, and a lot of it, to remain solvent and on the up and up. W. I. Hollingsworth, who through the mid-1920s rose to become the single most important business figure associated with the play, leaned hard on Behymer to help raise both consciousness and money.[93] The corporation needed approximately $100,000 in the last two weeks of June, almost double what it had raised so far. Hollingsworth remained confident that he could lean on his board for some of it, but he expected Behymer to, in addition to his production duties, bring in *Mission Play* support from wealthy patrons willing to put up $5,000. "I am sure you will do [your part]," he wrote.[94]

Behymer responded with a mixture of self-importance and enthusiasm. He quickly fired back a letter which pointed out that he had taken on his responsibilities as *Mission Play* manager without salary (he was apparently paid $1 a year), simply because he felt he could make a go of it. He believed that the revitalized *Mission Play* "would pay dividends continuously thereafter that would be satisfactory to each investor who might become a stockholder in the enterprise." Everyone should support the play, he wrote, adding that he thought the stock subscriptions were but loans. The rejuvenated play would not only be able to buy back the stock, it would make money, become a permanent institution, and deliver cash to the landmarks restoration projects. It simply remained for the Chamber of Commerce to, in Behymer's words, keep *The Mission Play* out of the "hands of selfish commercial interests." In other words, the civic-minded capitalism and joint stock operation of the Mission Play Corporation was the right approach to keeping history alive, Behymer believed. There is no indication from the record just what he may have been referring to with his comments about "selfish commercial interests," but it is interesting to speculate that perhaps the motion picture industry may have tried to grab hold of the project, the corporation, the script, or the acting company itself.

Fund-raising moved far more slowly than the Board of Directors either expected or wanted. By August 1926, *The Mission Play* was dying. Hollingsworth even expected that the Board would have to give up. Behymer offered an interesting idea: *The Mission Play* could be historically and thematically merged with another play so as to save on labor and overhead costs and, along the way, create a bookend historical drama. He wanted to merge *The Mission Play* with *Hiawatha*, staging them on alternate nights. And why not? The *Mission Play*'s Indians, he observed, could do double duty, first as Native Californians, next as Indians of the East Coast and woodlands. That way, the seamless narrative of western expansion could be neatly portrayed; the duo dramas "would unite the early life of the Eastern part of our country with the early life of the Far West."[95] There is no indication that the playhouse staged such a pairing, nor any indication how the Indian actors felt about the "an Indian is an Indian" casting.

· Funding woes continued. Hollingsworth sent Behymer blank subscription forms which asked potential stock purchasers "Do you care to save the Play for California?" Behymer wrote to Harry Chandler in November and asked to have the money that he had personally advanced the play returned. And he asked to be put on a salary. He had not lost his enthusiasm for the play; on the contrary, he believed that the 1927 season would be a good one. The people of Los Angeles had supported it in 1926, they would even be more supportive in 1927, he believed. The addition of a new playhouse (if the money could be raised), new costumes, new actors, new scenery: all boded well.[96]

More than any of the others associated with the play, and certainly more than the businessmen who sat atop the company, Behymer knew what hills he had in front of him. The play was undercapitalized (hundreds of thousands of dollars went into the playhouse alone). The public was saturated; and Los Angeles entertainment possibilities were probably as diverse as those of any city in the world. The play had to change with the times. As Behymer wrote to McGroarty in early 1927, "A large percentage of Los Angeles people have seen the Play several times and would go again if advised new features had been added." Behymer added that McGroarty had "given me no credit for anything I did for the Mission Play last year. . . . Some day you will find out just how much grinding labor it took to put the Mission Play over."[97]

The 1927 season opened with Behymer again on the road, visiting clubs, trying to make clear, as he put it, "the duty of the Southern California public as to patronizing it." He wished to also emphasize the play's own civic responsiveness: profits would be going to the restoration project devoted to the state's landmarks.

Somehow the corporation raised enough money to build the immense new playhouse. Erected not far from the now dilapidated old structure that McGroarty had put up in 1912, the new playhouse, finished not by Arthur Benton but by the firm of Dodd and Richards, was a three-times-bigger copy of the Mission San Antonio de Padua (though it was of brick and steel, finished in faux adobe). The building's interior boasted Indian designs on the ceiling, Spanish textile banners, and a gold-encrusted Indian's head hanging over the stage. At the roofline above the stage, a proudly engraved one-word sign revealed that the playhouse had been constructed by the most up-to-date standards: A S B E S T O S. An Aeolian Pipe Organ graced the interior, the gift of department store magnate Arthur Letts, land and development baron Harold Janss, and "other patriotic Californians."

The playhouse officially opened at a gala, $100-a-ticket showing of *The Mission Play* on March 5, 1927, thereby beating the opening of the new City

Hall of Los Angeles by a year. The event thrilled Behymer, and it also thrilled McGroarty, who basked in accolades and praise in between his introductions of W. I. Hollingsworth and Henry E. Huntington.[98] The evening had become famous even before it was staged, advertised to prospective donors as a night "which will go down in the history of California as being a representative gathering of the people who do things."[99] To Behymer, the event was "dignified, beautiful, educational and even religious." In short, it was a "real humdinger." He admitted that he couldn't "remember when so many of the real people of the Southland assembled under the same roof." Seeing that those in attendance apparently left behind $60,000 in donations to furnish the new building, Behymer's real people were also the "really wealthy people" of 1927.[100]

THE END OF THE RUN

Oh Conductor!
I've seen it again! The Mission Play!
For sixteen years I've been seeing it, every once in a while, and I hope to
go right on.

ENNA M. HAMPTON to John Steven McGroarty, ca. May 1927[101]

McGroarty's fans tied the opening of the new playhouse and the rejuvenation of *The Mission Play* directly to their favorite author. And they told him about it. Harry Ogilivie said that he thought of the play as a necessary escape from the busy and harried world of the modern technological city. An anonymous fan agreed, linking one theatrical history lesson with another: "the Mission Play is our Fiesta." This letterwriter wrote a long, unsigned missive to the playwright following the gala opening of the new playhouse. What a night it had been! Playgoers strolled amidst the Mexican band led by "Jose." "It made us happy to see that the Mexicans of your little Spanish town gathered in the courtyard to pay homage to you," the enraptured fan continued. "We rejoiced to see the little children with flashing dark eyes, black hair, and olive skins merrily talking in their native tongue to the Spanish Entertainers." Walking among the performers, "we almost forgot we were living in nineteen twenty seven." But one of the padres had neglected to take off his horn rims, and the twentieth century returned in a flash, though not for everyone. According to one student of the play, San Gabriel's Mexican population, especially the children (who "enact the minor roles year after year") "live their parts. It is all real to them."[102] These people lived in the past anyway, prevailing presumptions insisted, why not let them act it?

The play almost induced a kind of cultural amnesia as well: "The American women looked beautiful in their colorful Spanish shawls with glistening fringe. We almost forgot that they could speak English." But the real world again returned, and righted itself. White was white, nonwhite was nonwhite. "We gave our checks to an olive skinned usherette who smilingly exchanged them for a gay program."

The new playhouse did not ease tensions or problems immediately. By the spring of 1927, with personal debts rising, Behymer had grown deeply frustrated with the businessmen who owned the play. Back in December, he had been at least temporarily placated by Harry Chandler, who assured him that he would be treated fairly and with respect, if only because the Mission Play Corporation was made up entirely of "fair-minded, public spirited men who believe in fair play and even handed justice."[103] The goodwill did not last, and Behymer grew increasingly angry. He had put up some of his own money to try to get the play off the ground when he had come aboard. This loan had remained unpaid, and Behymer blamed Mission Playhouse Corporation head W. I. Hollingsworth. Through the months of the 1927 season, Behymer tried to get his money back. He asked Hollingsworth to pay him $500 a week until the debt was repaid. He wrote several times to Harry Chandler ("You know very well, Mr. Chandler, your promise"). Complaining in one letter to Chandler that he could no longer "continue to hold the bag," Behymer admitted that he had lost all patience with being told over and over again that Hollingsworth was out of town. Instead of a reply, Behymer received a note from Norman Chandler, Harry Chandler's son, informing him that his father happened now to be out of town![104]

The corporation tried at one point to repay Behymer by giving him free tickets to *The Mission Play* (which he could then presumably sell), but he angrily rebuffed them. Charging, in a June letter to D. W. Pontius, that he had been treated "in a most contemptible way by your friend Hollingsworth and the Board of the Mission Play," Behymer demanded action and repayment of his $3,374.47. He had been working long and hard, he wrote, "to put the Play over in the minds of the public and before the clubs," and it had devolved into a thankless task. "I recognize the ability of Mr. Hollingsworth and all of you boys in putting over this magnificent temple of the drama," Behymer admitted. But he added that were it not for him, "the Mission Play would be dead today." He had continued to work "when the rest of you were slipping or attending to your own affairs. . . . Even McGroarty was down and out and his play practically gone when I took hold of it, and I tried to keep it alive and before the public long enough for the interest to be again aroused, and the Playhouse built." Behymer closed this appeal by reminding Pontius that the play had accomplished a great deal in its lifetime; it would "go down the ages as indicative of the early life of California." Such nobility could be matched by the Board's willingness to pay their debts, he said.[105]

For their part, the Board of Directors proved willing both to wait Behymer out as well as take him on if necessary. Pontius responded to Behymer's angry letter by informing him that he had agreed, when he took on the play, not to incur any expenses that could be passed on to the Board of Directors. Directors Pontius, Chandler, and, presumably, Hollingsworth looked to Behymer's $3,000 loan as precisely that kind of expense, and they therefore felt no obligation to pay it. It was nice of Behymer to support the play in such a way, the letter implied, but his decision had no bearing upon the Board's obligations.[106]

Despite a new playhouse, the late 1920s were hard on *The Mission Play*. Even so, McGroarty continued to receive fan mail along the same lines as that which had been coming to him for years. "No one could see your play without having a greater reverence and feeling for our wonderful state," Roy Cloud wrote him in 1928. Cloud had been the "Grand Historian" of the Native Sons of the Golden West and was now the executive secretary of the California Teachers' Association. "I want to personally thank you for giving to the world such an unusually fine portrayal." Lt. Commander H. G. Gatlin of the United States Navy went Cloud two steps further. He wrote McGroarty that the Mission Play "is more than mere history—it is dynamic and electric."[107]

Such support notwithstanding, *The Mission Play* had run out of steam. Attempts were made to draw people for other reasons. People could tour the mini-mission display even when the play was not in season, for instance, and thus spend "a delightful and instructive hour." Or they might wish to browse in the newly redesigned shop and curio store. "Native Mission Indians," at work in the Indian craft store, "will add the final touch of early California atmosphere" and would themselves be on display along with "some of the choicest of the old mission relics."[108]

In 1930, *The Mission Play* eked out an existence, putting on its 3000th performance in February of that year. As the Depression deepened, things looked bad, even though residual if weary respect for the play as a second-ary school curricular adjunct lingered.[109] Some members of the Chamber of Commerce consortium attempted to revive the worn-out drama. George Cochran and Hollingsworth seemed particularly interested in trying to make another go of it. *The Mission Play* may have exhausted its utility by 1935, but tattered costumes and equally tattered plot didn't deter the business elites from trying to lift the limp play up. In the early spring of 1936, Behymer reported to Harry Chandler that E. K. Hoak had come round trying to talk up *The Mission Play*. Hoak thought that the production could be thematically linked with the region's less-famous, less-renowned *Pilgrimage Play*. And if the themes didn't quite link up, at least there could be a scheduling synchronicity in terms of utilizing the cavernous Mission Playhouse (which is today the San Gabriel Civic Auditorium). *The Mission Play* could be held in wintertime and the *Pilgrimage Play* could be held in summer: seats could stay filled. "I know the Mutual Life Insurance people are very anxious to see the Mission Play start again next January," Behymer wrote Chandler. While McGroarty (who was by then in his mid-seventies) might object, Behymer felt certain that "he would see the light and fall into line."

Besides, Behymer surmised, the journalist-turned-playwright-turned-politician was simply "too immersed in politics to raise much of a row." In the early 1930s, McGroarty had surprised his party, his opponent, the *Los Angeles Times*, and probably even himself by being elected to the United States House of Representatives. He served a term. His legislative moment came with his introduction of the quirky Townsend Old Age Pension Plan, which he energetically championed, on the floor of the House.[110]

The play refused to die, despite ironically being consigned to a hazy past itself. "It used to be popular in the old days," remarked the secretary of the Chamber of Commerce in 1936, hardly a decade removed from the play's descent.[111] Within a few years, newspapers in Los Angeles urged their readers to "Honor a Man, See a Play, Memorialize an Epic." The revitalization had to be held at the Pasadena Civic Auditorium; the Mission Playhouse had become a Spanish-language movie theater, with its dressing rooms broken up into apartments. The revival lasted but nine shows.[112] As late as 1945, Behymer, now a very old man, noted in a letter to a friend that people were still trying to revitalize *The Mission Play*. He recalled the lean years when the new playhouse had been stalled, when he and others "were acting as wet nurses" to the play. They patched the roof of the dilapidated old playhouse, paid Mrs. McGroarty to refurbish the old costumes she had sewn long before. "It was tough sledding, even if no snow around."[113]

Attempts to bring back *The Mission Play* went on through the 1940s and into the 1950s, and it is interesting to note that the publicity images and programs increasingly sexualize the Latina lead into a younger and more erotic figure.[114] Even today, there are attempts to bring the play back. But it seems unlikely to happen. Like *Ramona*, *The Mission Play* has outlived its usefulness as parable and history lesson. On the one hand, it is quaint. On the other hand, when we realize the hold it once had upon the regional imagination and the region's historical sensibilities, the play is troubling.

We should not forget the power that the play once had. *The Mission Play* *was* California history in greater Los Angeles for twenty or more years. The lessons it taught, the representations it staged stuck with people. We should not forget those crowded evenings at the Playhouse and at the San Gabriel Mission where, for a dollar, one could witness, and one could imbibe John McGroarty's "hundred years of yesterdays."[115]

Whitewashed Adobe

A score or two of names, a few crumbling adobes, and all is told.

IRA MOORE, President of the Historical Society
of Southern California, 1887[1]

In California, we did not believe that history could bloody the land,
or even touch it.

JOAN DIDION, 1993[2]

In the city of Los Angeles, sometime in the 1870s, a man named Victor Hall
pasted a recipe in his scrapbook. Such an odd thing to do, offering the
future a concise, if mundane, set of instructions on "How to Whitewash."
The recipe goes like this:

How to Whitewash

Procure fresh-burnt lime, not that partially air-slacked. The large lumps
are best. The fine portions and small lumps will not make a wash that
will stick well. For this reason, lime that has been burned several months
is not as good as that just from the kiln. Put a pound or two into a vessel,
and pour on boiling water slowly, until it is all slacked, and is about as
thick as cream. Then add cold rainwater until it will flow well from the
brush. Stir often when using it. A few drops of bluing added will give it
a more lively color. One or two tablespoonfuls of clean salt, and one-
fourth pound of clean sugar to a gallon of the wash, will make it more
adhesive. If the walls have been whitewashed, let them be swept thoroughly, and if colored with smoke, wash them clean with soap suds. A
brush with long, thick hair, will hold fluid best, when applying it over

head. If a person has the wash of the right consistence, and a good brush, he can whitewash a large parlor without allowing a drop to fall. When it appears streaked after drying it is too thick, and needs diluting with cold water. Apply the wash back and forth in one direction, and then go cross-wise using a paint-brush at the corners, and a thin piece of board to keep the brush from the wood work, or the border of the paper. Coloring matter may be mingled with the wash, to give it any desired tint. To make a light peach blow color, mingle a small quantity of Venetian-red. For a sky-blue, add any kind of dry, blue paint, stirring it well while mixing. To make a wash of a light straw-color, mingle a few ounces of yellow ochre, or a chrome yellow. The coloring matter should be quite fine to prevent its settling to the bottom of the vessel.[3]

A half century later, proud Angelenos dedicated the city's tallest building, the new City Hall. Soaring above downtown, the 450-foot building symbolized the remarkable growth of the metropolis. "This monument symbolizes the soul of a struggling, fighting, building people, never knowing defeat and always climbing upward until today it may be said of them: This is their City. They have created it; they have transformed it from a sleepy Spanish-California pueblo to one of the mightiest communities of a continent."

That transformation—political, social, cultural, demographic, architectural—as well as the mere assumptions behind convictions of such transformation, relied upon whitewashing. Not necessarily the kind outlined in Victor Hall's carefully kept scrapbook, though that literal labor was an important part of turning the Los Angeles adobe past into something literally and figuratively whiter. At a much larger scale, cultural whitewashing of the Los Angeles past and the Los Angeles landscape had no set of easily followed instructions. But it worked nonetheless.

Certainly by the late 1920s, Americans had "leveled" Los Angeles, manipulating the Mexican past and the Mexican population in countless ways. We've seen how important facets of that leveling played themselves out in arenas of work, landscape and environment, cultural production, city building, and public health emergency. Other, equally apt, examples could be highlighted, including such seeming disparate topics as electoral politics and the removal of the Mexican presence in local political office, the Anglo fetishization of mission-style architecture, including the incorporation of southwestern succulent and cacti gardens, even the literal whitewashing of David Siquieros's angry Olvera Street mural *Tropical America* in the early years of the Great Depression.[4]

Writer Richard Rodriguez offers a longer timeline for this process, arguing that it took a century for "La Ciudad de Nuestra Señora la Reina de los Angeles de Porciuncula [to] become . . . L.A." But it didn't take that long. Los Angeles had whitewashed the Mexican past and the people in it well before the coming of the Second World War.

From the war forward, the direction of regional history regarding race and ethnicity changed in profound and lasting ways. The story of how whites and ethnic Mexicans interact looks terribly familiar through the lens of such wartime events as the Sleepy Lagoon murder trials and the Zoot Suit riots, almost as if the clock had been turned back one hundred years to the era of the Mexican War. But the return of Mexican American servicemen to Southern California following wartime duty changed the world. The history of Los Angeles, of Southern California, of California, the American West, and the entire nation changes, fundamentally, from the postwar period into and across the years of civil rights and Chicano activism, and the accelerated growth of the ethnic Mexican population, the Mexican American middle class, and the Mexican American electorate. Those are topics for other books to take up, and each has its own stories of struggle, setback, and triumph.

This book about the ways in which patterns of ethnic discrimination and dominance played themselves out in an earlier Los Angeles ends here, with a poignant, if romantic, coda. Photographer Edward Weston, looking back over the Los Angeles landscape and Los Angeles history in 1946, at precisely the moment that regional history changed so profoundly, observed that "the real-estate boys raped the southland [and] heavy industry killed it. The Mexicans would have done much better."[5]

Maybe Weston was right. But his hindsight supposes an impossible reversal of history. The hope is not in going back in time, but in going into the future with a greater understanding of the past and our profound connections to it. We now inhabit the "city of the future" that Los Angeles dreamers and city builders imagined long ago. Los Angeles was built upon, grew up with, and has been sustained by attitudes and behaviors that furthered the ethnic and racial conquest of the American Southwest. At the extreme, the Mexican War of 1846–1848 and its aftermath were but the most violent and concentrated example of that conquest. More subtle patterns of discrimination and appropriation reverberated through the metropolis as it grew to regional, national, then international prominence, and they have not gone away.

NOTES

INTRODUCTION: CITY OF THE FUTURE

1. Boyle Workman, *That City That Grew* (Los Angeles: Southland Publishing, 1935), p. 25.

2. Huntington quoted in William Friedricks, *Henry Huntington and the Creation of Southern California* (Columbus: Ohio State University Press, 1992), p. 1.

3. Sherley Hunter, *Why Los Angeles Will Become the World's Greatest City* (Los Angeles: H. J. Mallen, 1923), p. 29.

4. McGroarty quoted in *Los Angeles Times*, Annual Midwinter Number, January 1, 1920.

5. See, for instance, *Los Angeles Times*, November 11, 1918.

6. See J. E. Scott, *Los Angeles: The Old and the New* (Los Angeles: Western Insurance News Supplement, 1911).

7. John D. Fredericks, from remarks before the Board of Directors of the Los Angeles Chamber of Commerce, Los Angeles Chamber of Commerce, Board of Directors stenographic minutes, October 15, 1923; from the Regional History Center at the University of Southern California. Hereafter Chamber of Commerce, Board of Directors stenographic minutes.

8. See the published speeches and poems by contest entrants in *Los Angeles Realtor* 4 (November 1924).

9. Yeats quote from Leonard Pitt and Dale Pitt, *Los Angeles A to Z: An Encyclopedia of the City and County* (Berkeley and Los Angeles: University of California Press, 1997), p. 12. Carey McWilliams wrote that the Yeats remark refers instead to California in general, and was uttered as early as 1904 or as late as just

before the First World War. See Carey McWilliams, "Resourceful California," *Westways* (March 1980): 24–27, and McWilliams, "Eirinn Go West," *Westways* (March 1978): 65. Advertising booster quotes from Hunter, *Why Los Angeles Will Become the World's Greatest City*, p. 25.

10. Harry Chandler stationary from spring of 1922, copies in the Richard Henry Pratt collection, Beinecke Rare Book and Manuscript Library, Yale University.

11. Mike Davis, *City of Quartz* (London: Verso, 1990; paperback, Vintage, 1992). See also David Rieff, *Los Angeles: Capital of the Third World* (New York: Simon and Schuster, 1991), and Joel Garreau, *Edge City: Life on the New Frontier* (New York: Doubleday, 1991). Other books and studies matching the pattern include Paul Glover, *Los Angeles: A History of the Future* (Los Angeles: Eco-Home Network, 1989); Andrew Rolle, *Los Angeles: From Pueblo to City of the Future* (San Francisco: MTL, 1995); and *Los Angeles: City of the Future?* [audiovisual tape] (South Burlington, Vt.: The Annenberg/CPB Collection, 1992). Some studies are more thematic, e.g., *We Have Seen the Future: The Demise of Christianity in Los Angeles* (Glendale, Calif.: Barna Research Group, 1990).

12. For a similar argument along lines of Los Angeles development and suburbanization (e.g., Los Angeles as the model of the future), see Garreau, *Edge City*. Historian Greg Hise points out that the "edge city" phenomenon is not nearly so new (in Los Angeles or elsewhere) as Garreau suggests. See Hise, *Magnetic Los Angeles: Planning the Twentieth-Century Metropolis* (Baltimore: Johns Hopkins University Press, 1997), 12.

13. Clarence Matson, "The Los Angeles of Tomorrow," *Southern California Business* (November 1924).

14. From "Los Angeles," by William Akin, published in *Los Angeles Realtor* 4 (November 1924). The "white spot" designation was not in itself an explicit racial commentary; the reference has more to do with manufacturing and industrial conditions.

15. Mike Davis, *Ecology of Fear* (New York: Metropolitan Books, 1998). See also Davis, "Golden Ruins, Dark Raptures: The Literary Destruction of Los Angeles," presented before the Getty Research Institute, October 16, 1996.

16. Joseph P. Widney quoted in Frederic Jaher, *The Urban Establishment: Upper Strata in Boston, New York, Charleston, Chicago, and Los Angeles* (Urbana: University of Illinois Press, 1982), p. 629.

17. Bogardus, in particular, published a great deal on Mexican issues as well. See, for example, "The Mexican Immigrant," *Journal of Applied Sociology* 11 (1927): 470–488; "Mexican Immigration and Segregation," *American Journal of Sociology* 36 (July 1930): 74–80; and "Second Generation Mexicans," *Sociology and Social Research* 13 (January 1929): 276–283.

18. I utilize here David Gutiérrez's definition of "ethnic Mexican," drawn from his monograph *Walls and Mirrors* (Berkeley and Los Angeles: University of California Press, 1995), p. 218, n. 3. In some ways, Gamio was but building, albeit

for different purposes, on the oral historical tradition of California history pioneered and institutionalized by H. H. Bancroft. See Mario Gamio, *The Life Story of the Mexican Immigrant* (New York: Dover; reprint, 1971). Originally published in 1931, this collection of composite and specific oral interviews was a companion volume to the anthropologist's *Mexican Immigration to the United States* (Chicago: University of Chicago Press, 1930).

19. In other words, much of this work is largely about internal dimensions of Mexican community building and the processes inherent to, in George Sanchez's words, "becoming Mexican American." See, for instance, Albert Camarillo, *Chicanos in a Changing Society: From Mexican Pueblos to American Barrios in Santa Barbara and Southern California, 1848–1930* (Cambridge: Harvard University Press, 1979); Rodolfo Acuña, *Occupied America: The Chicano Struggle toward Liberation* (San Francisco: Canfield Press, 1972); Mario Barrera, *Race and Class in the Southwest: A Theory of Racial Inequality* (Notre Dame: University of Notre Dame Press, 1979); Ricardo Romo, *East Los Angeles* (Austin: University of Texas Press, 1983); Richard Griswold del Castillo, *The Los Angeles Barrio, 1850–1890* (Berkeley and Los Angeles: University of California Press, 1979); Leonard Pitt, *The Decline of the Californios* (Berkeley and Los Angeles: University of California Press, 1966); Antonio Ríos-Bustamante and Pedro Castillo, *An Illustrated History of Mexican Los Angeles, 1781–1985* (Los Angeles: University of California, Chicano Studies Research Center Publications, 1986); Francisco Balderrama, *In Defense of La Raza: The Los Angeles Mexican Consulate, and the Mexican Community, 1929 to 1936* (Tucson: University of Arizona Press, 1982); Pedro Castillo, "The Making of a Mexican Barrio: Los Angeles, 1890–1920," Ph.D. diss., University of California, Santa Barbara, 1979; Robin Scott, "The Mexican-American in the Los Angeles Area, 1920–1950: From Acquiescence to Activity," Ph.D. diss., University of Southern California, 1971; Edward Escobar, *Race, Police, and the Making of a Political Identity: Mexican Americans and the Los Angeles Police Department, 1900–1945* (Berkeley and Los Angeles: University of California Press, 1999); and Richard Griswold del Castillo, "Southern California Chicano History: Regional Origins and National Critique," *Atzlán* 19 (1988–1990): 109–124.

20. See, for instance, Gutiérrez, *Walls and Mirrors*; Tomás Almaguer, *Racial Fault Lines* (Berkeley and Los Angeles: University of California Press, 1994); Lisbeth Haas, *Conquests and Historical Identities in California* (Berkeley and Los Angeles: University of California Press, 1995); Douglas Monroy, *Thrown among Strangers* (Berkeley and Los Angeles: University of California Press, 1990); George Sanchez, *Becoming Mexican American* (New York: Oxford University Press, 1993); William McClung, *Landscapes of Desire: Anglo Mythologies of Los Angeles* (Berkeley and Los Angeles: University of California Press, 2000); Douglas Monroy, *Rebirth: Mexican Los Angeles from the Great Migration to the Great Depression* (Berkeley and Los Angeles: University of California Press, 1999); and Ernesto Chávez, *"¡Mi Raza Primero!" (My People First!): Nationalism, Identity, and Insur-*

gency in the Chicano Movement in Los Angeles, 1966–1978 (Berkeley and Los Angeles: University of California Press, 2002).

21. Alexander Saxton, *The Indispensable Enemy* (Berkeley and Los Angeles: University of California Press, 1971), p. 2.

22. The most thorough and thoughtful work on the cultural creation of the Spanish Fantasy Past since McWilliams is Phoebe Kropp's 1999 University of California, San Diego, Ph.D. dissertation "'All Our Yesterdays': The Spanish Fantasy Past and the Politics of Public Memory in Southern California, 1884–1939." See also Charles Montgomery, *The Spanish Redemption: Heritage, Power, and Loss on New Mexico's Upper Rio Grande* (Berkeley and Los Angeles: University of California Press, 2002), 97–104. Kevin Starr, *Inventing the Dream: California through the Progressive Era* (New York: Oxford University Press, 1985), is also very helpful, especially chap. 3, "Art and Life in the Turn-of-the-Century Southland." See also David Gutiérrez, "Significant to Whom? Mexican Americans and the History of the American West," *Western Historical Quarterly* 24 (November 1993): 519–539, and Monroy, *Rebirth*.

23. See Gutiérrez, *Walls and Mirrors*, pp. 21–22.

I. THE UNENDING MEXICAN WAR

1. Quoted in Thomas R. Hietala, "'This Splendid Juggernaut: Westward a Nation and Its People,'" in Sam W. Haynes and Christopher Morris, eds., *Manifest Destiny and Empire: American Antebellum Expansionism* (College Station: Texas A & M Press, 1997), p. 53.

2. Horace Bell, from undated clipping from the *Los Angeles Morning Republican* [ca. 1877–1878], Bell manuscripts, Bancroft Library, University of California, Berkeley.

3. Richard Henry Dana, *Two Years before the Mast: A Personal Narrative of Life at Sea* (New York: Harper, 1840), p. 137. Dana also referred to laziness as "the California fever." An insightful study of the racist characterization of Mexicans by whites in the nineteenth century is Arnoldo De León's *They Called Them Greasers: Anglo Attitudes toward Mexicans in Texas, 1821–1900* (Austin: University of Texas Press, 1983); see also Gutiérrez, *Walls and Mirrors*, chap. 1, and Reginald Horsman, *Race and Manifest Destiny: The Origins of American Racial Anglo-Saxonism* (Cambridge: Harvard University Press, 1981).

4. Senator John Fairfield of Maine quoted in Hietala, "'This Splendid Juggernaut,'" p. 53.

5. Horace Bell, *On the Old West Coast* (New York: Morrow, 1930), p. 38.

6. William Wallace diary, June, 1855, Beinecke Library. For more on the filibustering campaigns of the era, see Robert E. May, "Manifest Destiny's Filibusters," in Haynes and Morris, eds., *Manifest Destiny and Empire*, pp. 146–179; quoted at p. 163. As May writes (p. 155), "in 1851, other U.S. filibusters invaded

Mexico by sea from California. That year, California quartermaster general and former Mexican War officer Joseph Morehead boarded forty-five men on the bark *Josephine* out of San Diego and set sail for Mazatlán, apparently intending a subsequent invasion of Sonora." These efforts were followed in 1852 by a failed attempt on the part of forty Californians, in league with Ecuador's former president, to take over the government of that nation (their ship blew up and killed half of them). In 1855, the "Zerman expedition" headed south from San Francisco to Baja, probably intent on territorial expansion as well. Diarist William Wallace makes note of an 1855 excursion of "Sharp Shooters" led by a Colonel Wheat. John L. O'Sullivan, Manifest Destiny's phrasemaker, urged, as early as the spring of 1846, "the immediate acquisition of California." Hietala, " 'This Splendid Juggernaut,' " p. 51.

7. Benjamin Truman, *Semi-Tropical California: Its Climate, Healthfulness, Productiveness, and Scenery* (San Francisco: A. L. Bancroft, 1874), p. 26.

8. California vigilante quoted in Montgomery, *The Spanish Redemption*, p. 50.

9. See J. M. Guinn, "The Passing of the Old Pueblo," paper read in December 1901 and printed in Historical Society of Southern California, *Proceedings* 6 (1903–1904): 113–120. On the "All Mexico" campaign, see Gutiérrez, *Walls and Mirrors*, pp. 14–16; see also John D. Fuller, *The Movement for the Acquisition of All Mexico, 1846–1848* (Baltimore: Johns Hopkins University Press, 1936). Territorial, as opposed to demographic, acquisitiveness regarding Mexico is aptly captured in the words of another spokesman for Manifest Destiny's aggression, Senator Lewis Cass of Michigan. "We do not want the people of Mexico," Cass argued, "either as citizens or subjects. All we want is a portion of territory, which they nominally hold, generally uninhabited, or, where inhabited at all, sparsely so, and with a population, which would soon recede, or identify itself with ours" (quoted in Gutiérrez, *Walls and Mirrors*, p. 16). "Journalists and political leaders savaged the Mexicans during the war," writes historian Thomas Hietala, "attributing U.S. military successes to the corruption of the enemy's church and state, the cowardice of its soldiers, and the degeneracy of its people" (" 'This Splendid Juggernaut,' " p. 52). William H. Brewer, *Up and Down in California* (Berkeley and Los Angeles: University of California Press, 1966), p. 15. William Wallace described the arsenal kept by a nervous friend in the mid-1850s, "upon his person: a six shooter, a Bowie knife, a heavy sword cane, and two derringer pistols." For a brief survey of Gold Rush era anti-Mexican thought and deed, see Richard H. Peterson, "Anti-Mexican Nativism in California, 1848–1853: A Study of Cultural Conflict," *Southern California Quarterly* 62 (winter 1980): 309–327; see also Sister M. Colette Standart, "The Sonora Migration to California, 1848–1856: A Study in Prejudice," *Southern California Quarterly* 58 (fall 1976): 333–357.

10. Bell, *On the Old West Coast*, pp. 164–165. See also pp. 213–230 of Michael J. Gonzalez, "Searching for the Feathered Serpent: Exploring the Origins of Mex-

ican Culture in Los Angeles, 1830–1850," Ph.D. diss., University of California, Berkeley, 1993.

11. See Marjorie Tisdale Wolcott, ed., *Pioneer Notes from the Diaries of Judge Benjamin Hayes, 1849–1875* (Los Angeles: Privately printed, 1929), p. 107. Hayes diary entry is from November 24, 1854. See also William Wallace diary, clipping for August 23, 1857 (clipping from the *Alta California*, from "Our Los Angeles Correspondent").

12. Wallace diary, March entries, 1855.

13. Wallace diary, March and April 1855.

14. Wallace diary entry, September 16, 1857.

15. Wallace diary, July 21, 22, 1856. Of course, Anglo intermarriage had a role to play as well, with numerous Anglo arrivals in the basin marrying young Latin women. Los Angeles Anglo pioneer Henry Dwight Barrows, desperately in love with fourteen-year-old half-Mexican Juana Wolfskill (they would eventually marry), could apparently not even bring himself to mention her by name in his own diary, so embarrassed was he by the attraction. This is the recollection Caltech seismologist Kerry Sieh has of the affair, having perused H. D. Barrows's diaries when they were in the possession of a granddaughter. See also Michael Konig, "Henry Dwight Barrows: Builder of a Changing Los Angeles," M.A. thesis, University of San Diego, 1977. For more on the murder of Ruiz and resulting tensions, see Lawrence E. Guillow, "Pandemonium in the Plaza: The First Los Angeles Riot, July 22, 1856," *Southern California Quarterly* 77 (fall 1995): 183–197. For a recent analysis of the land transfers between *Californios* and Anglo arrivals see Karen Clay and Werner Troesken, "Ranchos and the Politics of Land Claims," in William Deverell and Greg Hise, eds., *Land of Sunshine: Towards an Environmental History of Los Angeles* (Pittsburgh: University of Pittsburgh Press), forthcoming.

16. The apt phrase is Leonard Pitt's, from *Decline of the Californios: A Social History of the Spanish-Speaking Californians, 1846–1900* (Berkeley and Los Angeles: University of California Press, 1966), title to chap. 9, "Race War in Los Angeles, 1850–1856." Pitt quotes at the end of the chapter the Anglo remark that the period saw a "war of the races."

17. Article IX of the Treaty of Guadalupe Hidalgo is straightforward. Mexicans residing in territory to be transferred to the United States "shall be incorporated into the Union of the United States, and admitted as soon as possible, according to the principles of the Federal Constitution, to the enjoyment of all the rights of citizens of the United States." Treaty text drawn from Richard Griswold del Castillo, *The Treaty of Guadalupe Hildalgo: A Legacy of Conflict* (Norman: University of Oklahoma Press, 1990), appendix I.

18. Gutiérrez, *Walls and Mirrors*, p. 18.

19. Wallace observed this during the campaign season in the fall of 1857. One early morning, men began to gather the "piebald classes" in a downtown corral.

By 8:00 a.m., they had seventy-five men ready to vote. The men were paraded "under guard" to vote. "This is the first time I ever saw men corralled at an election," Wallace wrote. "It certainly was not creditable." Wallace diary, September 7, 1857. Morrow Mayo discusses such practices in *Los Angeles* (New York: Knopf, 1932), p. 33. For a comparison with voting dynamics among whites and Mexicans in Texas, see Evan Anders, *Boss Rule in South Texas: The Progressive Era* (Austin: University of Texas Press, 1982).

20. "Homes for the defeated" is historian Merry Ovnick's apt phrase. See Merry Ovnick, *Los Angeles: The End of the Rainbow* (Los Angeles: Balcony Press, 1994), p. 59. See also, more generally, Kay J. Anderson, "The Idea of Chinatown: The Power of Place and Institutional Practice in the Making of a Racial Category," *Annals of the Association of American Geographers* 77 (December 1987): 580–598. Anderson notes that, in the case of various Pacific coast "Chinatowns" of the nineteenth century, there was no need for any corresponding designation of "Anglo town."

21. Similarly, the 1850s in Los Angeles can be seen as a local struggle over which ethnic group would triumph as the "Angelenos" of the second half of the century. For a discussion of this, see Gonzalez, "Searching for the Feathered Serpent," especially "Epitaph," pp. 212–230. For an 1850s discussion of the different categorical ethnicities, a good place to start is with the diaries of Judge Benjamin Hayes. See Wolcott, *Pioneer Notes from the Diaries of Judge Benjamin Hayes*, esp. chap. 3.

22. Wallace diary, September 16, 1857.

23. Socrates Hyacinth [Stephen Powers], *Afoot and Alone: A Walk from Sea to Sea* (Hartford, Conn.: Columbian Book Company, 1872), p. 284. This volume also has a superb description of Anglo/*Californio* intermarriage; see pp. 282–284. A recent scholarly analysis of intermarriage between *Californio* women and girls and Anglo arrivals is María Raquél Casas, "'In Consideration of His Being Married to a Daughter of the Land': Interethnic Marriages in Alta California, 1825–1875," Ph.D. diss., Yale University, 1999; for the latter, post–Mexican War period, see chap. 5.

24. Hayes quoted in Gonzalez, "Searching for the Feathered Serpent," pp. 211–212.

25. For a report of the events, see the *Los Angeles Star*, July 26, 1856. This is also excerpted in full in Robert G. Cleland, *Cattle on a Thousand Hills* (San Marino: Huntington Library, 1990), appendix III. Ozro Childs, who rode Paul Revere–like for help from the Mexican-hating "El Monte boys," would later open a nursery (and begin the nursery trade in the region) and get rich. He was, Victoria Padilla writes, one of the "first great citizens" of Los Angeles. His wife would be the first Queen of La Fiesta de Los Angeles in the mid-1890s. See Victoria Padilla, *Southern California Gardens: An Illustrated History* (Berkeley and Los Angeles: University of California Press, 1961), p. 141. William King notes suc-

cinctly of El Monte in the era that it was "a bastion of American culture and the center of considerable vigilante activity." King, "El Monte, An American Town in Southern California, 1851–1866," *Southern California Quarterly* 53 (1991): 317–332. The field of Southern California studies is in great need of more scholarship on El Monte and its residents in this period. A good starting point for more recent periods is Matt Garcia's chapter, "Memories of El Monte: Dance Halls and Youth Culture in Greater Los Angeles, 1950–1974," in *A World of Its Own: Race, Labor, and Citrus in the Making of Greater Los Angeles, 1900–1970* (Chapel Hill: University of North Carolina Press, 2001).

26. Wallace diary entries, late July and early August 1856.

27. A *New York Tribune* columnist described Crabb as an "ultra pro-slaveryist." A partial list of Crabb's followers can be found in "Execution of Colonel Crabb and Associates," p. 71, drawn from an article in the *New York Tribune* (ca. late May, 1857). Horace Bell writes that Crabb was from Tennessee and a schoolmate of fili- buster William Walker (*On the Old West Coast*, p. 321, n. 2). The other state sena- tor was William H. McCoun of San Joaquin. See Wolcott, *Pioneer Notes from the Diaries of Judge Benjamin Hayes*, p. 171. See also John Coleman Reid, *Reid's Tramp, or a Journal of the Incidents of Ten Months Travel Through Texas, New Mexico, Ari- zona, Sonora, and California* (Selma, Ala.: John Hardy, 1858). Reid notes the ironic fact that Crabb's Sonora expedition was first organized in Sonora, California.

28. Wolcott, *Pioneer Notes from the Diaries of Judge Benjamin Hayes*, p. 171. See also Robert H. Forbes, *Crabb's Filibustering Expedition into Sonora, 1857* (Tucson: Arizona Silhouettes, 1952), esp. pp. 2–6. Forbes had taken part in an early twen- tieth-century retracing of Crabb's expedition led by the Smithsonian Institution.

29. Horace Bell recalls that one local man who joined up had lost at love. John Hughes, the Irish owner of a Los Angeles bar and rooming house, fell in love with a Mexican woman in Los Angeles. She chose another, "and the disconso- late Hughes joined the Crabbe [*sic*] filibustering expedition to Sonora and was killed." From Horace Bell, undated article in the *Los Angeles Morning Republi- can* [ca. 1877–78]; in Horace Bell manuscript collection, Bancroft Library. Bell tells a slightly different version in *On the Old West Coast*, p. 151. See also Wallace diary entries, January through May 1857, and "The Execution of Colonel Crabb and Associates," *Message from the President of the United States* (February 16, 1858); House of Representatives, Executive Document 64 (35th Congress, 1st Session), especially John Forsyth to Secretary of State Lewis Cass, April 24, 1857; hereafter "Execution of Colonel Crabbe and Associates."

30. Wallace diary, tipped-in news clipping (Wallace was undoubtedly the author), "Interesting News from Los Angeles [likely the *Alta California*], Janu- ary 29, 1857." See also the helpful discussion in Ronald Woolsey, *Migrants West: Toward the Southern California Frontier* (Sebastopol, Calif.: Grizzly Bear Pub- lishing, 1996), esp. chaps. 6 and 7; see also Cleland, *Cattle on a Thousand Hills*, appendix III, pp. 250–263.

31. *Los Angeles Star*, February 7, 1857. This is also excerpted in Cleland, *Cattle on a Thousand Hills*, appendix III. "Cries for vengeance" quote from *Los Angeles Star*, January 31, 1857.

32. Quoted in Woolsey, *Migrants West*, p. 80.

33. From Bell, *Reminiscences*, p. 403; quoted in Woolsey, *Migrants West*, p. 81.

34. Wallace diary, January 31, 1857. Los Angeles pioneer Louis Mesmer recalled that the vigilance groups—"there were so many companys [*sic*]"—numbered more than 5 percent of the total population. See H. H. Bancroft Co., "Louis Mesmer Dictation," n.d., Bancroft Library. Even more astounding was the prediction that six hundred armed Mexicans were about to lay siege to Los Angeles. This dire forecast came from the pen (and the fevered imagination) of a very worried Judge William Dryden, a man convinced that the objective was "to destroy all Americans." See Gonzalez, "Searching for the Feathered Serpent," p. 216.

35. "Louis Mesmer Dictation." Horace Bell was later told that more than 150 were killed "to avenge the death of Sheriff Barton and his posse," which seems an exaggerated number. Bell relates a story that was told him by a friend about the indiscriminate murders following Barton's death. A Mexican man, with no ties whatsoever to the murder of Barton, had been killed at the San Gabriel Mission, then mutilated and beheaded after death. The ubiquitous William Jenkins was present at the atrocity, along with the martially named King brothers: Andrew Jackson King, Samuel Houston King, and Francis Marion King. See Bell, *On the Old West Coast*, pp. 100–110; *Los Angeles Star*, March 21 and 28, 1857; and King, "El Monte," p. 319. See also John Forster to John S. Griffin, January 30, 1857, Abel Stearns Papers, Huntington Library. Forster describes Andres Pico's movements, as well as those of "the force from the monte." Historian Edward Escobar is one of a very few scholars who have bothered to suggest trajectories connecting the violence of the 1850s to later periods in the twentieth century. In his study of the Los Angeles Police Department and Chicano activism, Escobar writes that the post-Barton bloodshed, "an orgy of lynchings," claimed more Southern California Mexican lives than the fighting during the Mexican War: Edward J. Escobar, "Chicano Protest and the Law: Law Enforcement Responses to Chicano Activism in Los Angeles, 1850-1936," Ph.D. diss., University of California, Riverside, 1983. See also Escobar, *Race, Police, and the Making of a Political Identity* (Berkeley and Los Angeles: University of California Press, 1999). For an overview of the social banditry of Mexican outlaws in the period, see Pedro Castillo and Albert Camarillo, eds., *Furia y Muerte: Los Bandidos Chicanos* (Los Angeles: Atzlán, 1973).

36. Barton's ghostly resentment of his killers is reminiscent of gambler Dave Brown's hanging in Los Angeles just prior to the Barton murder. Brown stabbed his friend Pinckney Clifford to death and was sentenced to die for the crime. A Mexican named Alvitre was also sentenced to be hanged for killing a white man

(and, as the sentencing judge put it, as an example for other Mexicans currently "betraying too many signs of hostility"). The latter man was hanged (a stay of execution arrived a week late) under Sheriff Barton's supervision, but Brown earned a reprieve from the California Supreme Court. As a consequence, a force of Mexicans led by Mayor Stephen Foster showed up at the Los Angeles jail, stormed it, and grabbed Brown, who protested being put to death "by a lot of greasers." According to Morrow Mayo, prospective hangman Juan Gonzales was thus pushed aside by a group of Americans who honored Brown's last wish but hanged him nonetheless. Foster resigned as Los Angeles mayor upon leading the vigilantes and was then quickly reelected. See Pitt, *The Decline of the Californios*, p. 161, and Bell, *Reminiscences of a Ranger, Or Early Times in Southern California* (Santa Barbara, Calif.: Wallace Hebberd, 1927), pp. 242–243; see also Wolcott, *Pioneer Notes from the Diaries of Judge Benjamin Hayes*, pp. 108–109 and Mayo, *Los Angeles*, pp. 48–49. Ronald Woolsey has placed lawman Barton's tenure at the center of Mexican-Anglo tensions during the 1850s. See Woolsey, *Migrants West*, chap. 6. For his part, Horace Bell interpreted Barton's murder very differently than did Wallace (or, for that matter, Barton himself). As opposed to a morality tale of good (white) versus evil (nonwhite), Bell believed that Barton had been murdered in part for assaulting his common-law Native American wife. Her brother, a man by the name of Andres Fontes, had witnessed Barton (whom Bell called "an uncouth, illiterate man") mistreat her. Barton then saw to it that Fontes was sent to San Quentin on a charge of horse stealing. Fontes swore revenge. Allied with Flores, Fontes made certain that Barton paid for his misdeeds. Such details never surface in contemporary accounts of the murder. Rather, tales of the death are invariably woven into a tragic story of civilization's battle against barbarism, no doubt a better fit for prevailing racial presuppositions. See Bell, *On the Old West Coast*, pp. 72–73; see also Gonzalez, "Searching for the Feathered Serpent," pp. 214–215.

37. See *Los Angeles Star*, February 21, 1857.

38. Henry A. Crabb to Señor Don José Maria Redondo, March 26, 1857, in "Execution of Colonel Crabb and Associates," p. 31. See also *Los Angeles Star*, February 14, 1857.

39. Ignacio Pesqueira to "Free Sonorians," March 30, 1857; "Execution of Colonel Crabb and Associates," pp. 32–33.

40. See Jose Maria Yanez to "General in Chief of the Forces of the Western States," April 10, 1857, "Execution of Colonel Crabb and Associates." One internal Mexican document claimed that the filibusters had gotten drunk, along with other Americans, at the Colorado River "and that amid their glee, they said that Sonora was theirs." If so, they were wrong. Mexican calls to arms utilized such phrases as "Arouse Soldiers of the Country!" and "Free Sonorians: To Arms All of You!"

41. Crabb was supposedly married to a Sonoran woman; see Pitt, *Decline of*

the Californios. See also "Execution of Colonel Crabb and Associates," especially Forsyth to Cass, April 24, 1857. It is interesting that Wallace has the news even before most Mexican, much less American, authorities; he knows of Crabb's demise in early March.

42. "California's brightest ornaments" phrase from John W. Park to John Forsyth, September 1, 1857, "Execution of Colonel Crabb and Associates," p. 62. United States officials, horrified at the summary execution of so many American citizens, made weak claims that Crabb and his men deserved to be taken as prisoners of war—a tacit agreement on their part that the U.S.-Mexican War did, at least in some isolated parts of Sonora, still exist. See, for instance, Lewis Cass to John B. Floyd, July 25, 1857, "Execution of Colonel Crabb and Associates," p. 49. Morrow Mayo writes that Mexican authorities sent Crabb's head back to Los Angeles, but he offers no evidence of this. See Mayo, *Los Angeles*, p. 49. See also "Statement from Juan A. Robinson," a dictation recorded for H. H. Bancroft; Bancroft Library.

43. Charles Edward Rand to [his parents], May 19, 1857; Beinecke Library. The *New York Tribune* said just as much: "The excitement throughout California consequent on the reception of this news has been intense, and a very general feeling of revenge seems to actuate the minds of the masses." See "Execution of Colonel Crabb and Associates," p. 70, for reprint of article (ca. May 20, 1857). See also "Crabb's party annihilated" (unnamed newspaper story, no author given), reprinted in "Execution of Colonel Crabb and Associates," pp. 72–75.

44. Benjamin Truman, among others, referred to Los Angeles as "Los Diablos" in the 1860s. See Gary Kurutz, *Benjamin C. Truman: California Booster and Bon Vivant* (San Francisco: Book Club of California, 1984), p. 32. Michael Gonzalez writes of the Rev. James Woods and his argument that 1850s Los Angeles "might be called the City of Demons," or, even more succinct "a perfect hell." Gonzalez, "Searching for the Feathered Serpent," p. 22. See also Guinn, "The Passing of the Old Pueblo," and Mayo, *Los Angeles,* p. 42. A brief catalog of crimes in early 1850s Los Angeles can be found in Cleland, *The Cattle on a Thousand Hills,* chap. 5.

45. Guinn, The Passing of the Old Pueblo," p. 119. For a grim, clinical catalog of Indian deaths decidedly not induced by divine visitation, see J. Kuhrts, "Reminiscences of a Pioneer," *Publications of the Historical Society of Southern California* 7 (1906–1908): 59–68.

46. See Gutiérrez, *Walls and Mirrors,* p. 21; Castillo, "Making of a Mexican Barrio," p. 73. Percentage statistics drawn from Richard Griswold del Castillo, "La Raza Hispano Americana: The Emergence of an Urban Culture among the Spanish Speaking of Los Angeles, 1850–1880" Ph.D. diss., University of California, Los Angeles, 1974, p. 66. Jackson Graves, a keen observer who penned an important chronicle of life in Los Angeles during the boom and after, suspected that half of the village population in 1875 was made up of "native Californians,"

a reference to Mexicans and not Indians. He also notes the demographic impact of smallpox outbreaks among Anglo and native populations alike. See Graves, *My Seventy Years in California* (Los Angeles: Times Mirror Press, 1927), pp. 96, 99. See also Arthur F. Cowan, *Early Mexican Labor Migration: A Frontier Sketch* (Westport, Conn.: Greenwood Press, 1979), esp. chap. 2. In his article discussing the 1856 killing of Ruiz by Jenkins, Guillow ("Pandemonium in the Plaza," at n. 25) quotes an American pioneer as suggesting that the Latin population of mid-1850s Los Angeles was four-fifths of the total population of 5,000. Census data of the 1850s (also quoted here) put the figure of Mexicans and *Californios* at about 70 percent of the total.

47. On city council language and representation, see, for example, J. Morgan Kousser, "Incumbent Protection and Anti-Hispanic Gerrymandering in the Los Angeles County Board of Supervisors," author's files; see also Kousser, *Colorblind Justice: Minority Voting Rights and the Undoing of the Second Reconstruction* (Chapel Hill: University of North Carolina Press, 1999), esp. chap. 2. See also *Yolanda Garza et al., [and] United States of America v. County of Los Angeles, California; Los Angeles Board of Supervisors, et al.*, United States District Court, Central District of California nos. CV 88–5143 Kn (Ex) and CV 88–5435 Kn (ex): "Findings of Fact and Conclusions of Law," filed June 4, 1990: 1–132. Mexicans disappear from municipal and regional governing bodies, and the minutes of some bodies stop being printed in Spanish, ca. 1875. As such, Anglo society pushes Mexicans into the past, renders them quaint, if disappointing, reminders of the Spanish historical presence and of little merit to contemporary Los Angeles, much less to the city of the future.

48. Truman, *Semi-Tropical California*, p. 27

49. Truman, *Semi-Tropical California*, p. 27.

50. Andrew James Copp, *Autobiography of Andrew James Copp* (Sierra Madre, Calif.: Sierra Madre Press, 1927), p. 46. Similarly, *Greater Los Angeles Illustrated* recalled the Los Angeles of the mid-nineteenth century as "untouched by any spirit of progress, culture or art . . . [witness to] the lethargic going to and fro of a somnolent collection of human beings unconscious of the beauties and glories of the encompassing woods and hills, and the exquisite penciling of landscape, sea and sky." From *Greater Los Angeles Illustrated* (Los Angeles: The Pictorial American, n.d. [ca. 1905]).

51. *Greater Los Angeles Illustrated.*

52. Michael Gonzalez briefly discusses the tendency of historians to echo the sleepy metaphor. See Gonzalez, "Searching for the Feathered Serpent," chap. 1.

53. Henry Holt, "A Foreign Tour at Home," *Putnam's* 4 (April–September 1908): 154–161. See also "Southern California Through the Camera," pamphlet published by the Los Angeles "All Year Club" in the 1920s.

54. See *Greater Los Angeles Illustrated* for the "old California" discussion. Tomás Almaguer has adeptly analyzed this expectation, particularly as regards

Native Americans in California; see Almaguer, *Racial Fault Lines: The Historical Origins of White Supremacy in California* (Berkeley and Los Angeles: University of California Press, 1994), esp. chap. 4. Regarding the disappearance of the region's Native Americans, especially the Gabrieliño, see William Mason's helpful essay, "Indian-Mexican Cultural Exchange in the Los Angeles Area, 1781–1834," *Atzlán* 15 (spring 1984): 123–144.

55. Sanchez, *Becoming Mexican American*, p. 71.

56. Guinn, "The Passing of the Old Pueblo," pp. 116, 120.

57. The early Historical Society had a single Latino officer, R. F. Del Valle. See inaugural address of J. J. Warner, January 7, 1884, and address of President Ira Moore, 1887, in *Publications of Historical Society of Southern California* 1 (1884–1891); Moore quoted at p. 12 of 1887 *Proceedings*. See also *An Illustrated History of Southern California* (Chicago: Lewis, 1890), p. 729. It should be noted that the Historical Society did make a call in the late 1880s for the County of Los Angeles to translate and preserve Spanish-language documents from the Mexican period. For a history of the society, see Jane Apostol, *The Historical Society of Southern California: A Centennial History, 1891–1991* (Los Angeles: Historical Society of Southern California, 1991).

58. Helen Hunt Jackson, *California and the Missions* (Boston: Little, Brown, 1919), pp. 177, 180. These are collected essays that originally appeared in the 1880s.

59. See inaugural and retirement addresses of E. W. Jones, *Publications of the Historical Society of Southern California* 1888–1889 (esp. p. 13) and 1890 (pp. 5–7).

60. See C. A. Higgins, *To California over the Santa Fe Trail* (Chicago: Passenger Department, Santa Fe Railroad, 1907), pp. 124, 127, 130.

61. *Greater Los Angeles Illustrated,* p. 74.

62. T. S. Kenderdine, *California revisited. 1858–1897* (Doylestown, Pa.: Doylestown Publishing, 1898), p. 172.

63. McWilliams, *Southern California Country,* p. 315.

64. McWilliams, *Southern California Country,* p. 317; it is ironic that McWilliams regenerates "the Mexican problem" in precisely the same year in which Higgins (*To California*) witnesses its/their decline. Mary Mooney, "Side-Lights on Old Los Angeles," paper read before the Historical Society of Southern California, December 12, 1900, and printed in Historical Society of Southern California, *Proceedings* 6 (1903–1904): 43–48. Graves quoted at page 137 of *My Seventy Years in California*. See also McWilliams, "The Mexican Problem," *Common Ground* 8 (spring 1948): 3–17. A concise discussion of Mexican labor in the period can be found in Gutiérrez, *Walls and Mirrors*, pp. 44–51.

65. Sometimes the former would arrive at the behest of the latter. See, for instance, Criminal Case 929 [1917], *United States v. Baltazar Aviles*, et al., National Archives, Laguna Niguel. This case involved *Los Angeles Times* publisher Harry Chandler and his alleged plot to smuggle guns and mercenaries south. As

Job Harriman commented in the *Western Comrade*, the plan was but the latest shot in the never-ending Mexican-American War. "Was not Harry Chandler, with his criminal associates, indicted by the United States grand jury for conspiring to incite war between the United States and Mexico?" Chandler and codefendants were acquitted of the charge of violation of the Neutrality Act.

66. Chamber members will, in fact, literally incorporate the term in the mid-1920s. See Chamber of Commerce, Board of Directors stenographic minutes, April 17, 1924.

67. McWilliams notes that other labels include "The Better Italy" and "The American Italy." He writes that the Los Angeles region was just what domestic tourists desired: "an Italy without Italians, an Italy in which they could feel at home, an Italy in which, perhaps, they might settle and live out their days in the sun." *Southern California Country*, pp. 96–97. One senses from the historical record a similar wish on the part of Anglo Angelenos or tourists for a Mexico without Mexicans.

68. See Commercial Federation of California, *Weekly Letter 25*, December 10, 1919; "origin and heritage" quote from Nelson Rhoades, "Los Angeles' Relation with Mexico and Latin-American Countries [and] Latin American Commerce," in *Davis Commercial Encyclopedia of the Pacific Southwest* (Berkeley: Ellis A. Davis, 1914); Chamber of Commerce, Board of Directors stenographic minutes, September 27, 1923. At this latter meeting, Director Weaver lapsed into the tried-and-true association of "Our Mexico" with "Our Mexican," in commenting on Mexican women: "I was sorry that I had four children and a wife." Another example of this kind of thinking and stance, one that mixes commercial and erotic attraction to Mexico and Mexicans, can be seen in F. M. Steadman's photographic essay, "Typical Mexico and Its Opportunities," *Camera Craft* (March 1901): 402–406. See also Chamber of Commerce, Board of Directors stenographic minutes, November 1, 1923, and January 24, 1924.

69. A representative example of the phraseology and the ideas that went with it from the 1920s is Glenn E. Hoover, "Our Mexican Immigrants," *Foreign Affairs* 8 (October 1929): 99–107. Standard works on ethnic stereotyping and patterns of racial exclusion in the Southwest include Gutiérrez, *Walls and Mirrors*; David J. Weber, ed., *Foreigners in Their Native Land: Historical Roots of the Mexican Americans* (Albuquerque: University of New Mexico Press, 1973); Mark Reisler, *By the Sweat of Their Brow: Mexican Immigrant Labor in the United States, 1900-1940* (Westport, Conn.: Greenwood Press, 1976); Neil Foley, *The White Scourge: Mexicans, Blacks, and Poor Whites in Texas Cotton Culture* (Berkeley and Los Angeles: University of California Press, 1997); David J. Weber, *Myth and the History of the Hispanic Southwest* (Albuquerque: University of New Mexico Press, 1988); Camarillo, *Chicanos in a Changing Society;* and De León, *They Called Them Greasers.*

70. See Harry Carr, *Los Angeles, City of Dreams* (New York: Grosset and

Dunlap, 1935), chap. 28. My thanks to the late Professor Clark Davis for pointing out this passage in Carr's book.

71. Louis Adamic, *The Truth about Los Angeles* (Girard, Kans.: Haldeman-Julius Publications, 1927), pp. 16–17.

72. See Carr, *Los Angeles*, p. 380. I suspect similar associations of eroticism and commerce with such advertisements as that in a 1910 Los Angeles newspaper headline which celebrated Sinaloa as "The Land of Virgin Wealth."

73. See Kropp, "'All Our Yesterdays.'" For a representative view, see also H. C. Dillon, "Mexican Rule in California, 1824–1848," read before the Badger Club of Los Angeles, March 3, 1909; copy in the Newberry Library, Chicago. Carr quote from William McClung, *Landscapes of Desire: Anglo Mythologies of Los Angeles* (Berkeley and Los Angeles: University of California Press, 2000), p. 72.

74. The phrase is George Sanchez's; see Sanchez, *Becoming Mexican American*, p. 70.

75. Robert N. McLean, *That Mexican!: As He Really Is, North and South of the Rio Grande* (New York: Fleming H. Revell, 1928), p. 7.

76. S. H. Bowman, "A Brief Study of Arrests of Mexicans," in August Vollmar, *Law Enforcement in Los Angeles; Los Angeles Police Department Annual Report, 1924* (New York: Arno Press, reprint, 1974), p. 134.

77. Characterizations here, and below, are drawn from John Kienle, "Housing Conditions among the Mexican Population of Los Angeles," M.A. thesis, University of Southern California, 1912, and William Wilson McEuen, "A Survey of the Mexicans in Los Angeles," M.A. thesis, University of Southern California, 1914. See also Castillo, "Making of a Mexican Barrio," pp. 89–100; Gladys Patric, *A Study of the Housing and Social Conditions in the Ann Street District of Los Angeles California* (Los Angeles: Los Angeles Society for the Study and Prevention of Tuberculosis, 1917); and Bessie Stoddart, "The Courts of Sonoratown," *Charities and the Commons* 13 (1905): 295–299. For a brief discussion of Mexican labor segmentation, see also Escobar, *Race, Police, and the Making of a Political Identity*, chaps. 2 and 3.

78. From Los Angeles Municipal Charities Commission, *Annual Report July 1, 1913–July 1, 1914* (Los Angeles: Municipal Charities Commission, 1914), p. 67. See also Interchurch World Movement of North America, *The Mexican in Los Angeles* (Los Angeles, 1920). "Indifference to physical hardships" quote comes from Anna Christine Lofstedt, "A Study of the Mexican Population in Pasadena, California," M.A. thesis, University of Southern California, 1922. The "almost any living quarters" statement is from Stuart R. Wood, "The Mexican in California," *Transactions of the Commonwealth Club of California* 21 (March 23, 1926): 7. During this period of increased migration from Mexico, estimates of unemployed or underemployed in the city ranged as high as 30,000. Historian Edward Escobar estimates that the Mexican population of Los Angeles grew from perhaps 5,000 in 1900 to as many as 50,000 by twenty years later. Even these

tremendously conservative figures suggest that the Mexican population was growing at a faster rate than the Anglo. One writer, a Methodist minister and home missionary in Los Angeles, suggested that there were 93,000 people of Mexican descent in Los Angeles in 1925, while another observer from the mid-1920s argued that as many as 65,000 Mexicans came to Los Angeles *every* year. See Edward Escobar, "Mexican Revolutionaries and the Los Angeles Police: Harassment of the Partido Liberal Mexicano, 1907–1910," *Atzlán* 17 (spring 1986): 1–46; Vernon M. McCombs, *From over the Border* (New York: Council of Women for Home Missions and Missionary Education Movement of the United States and Canada, 1925), p. 28; and Charles S. Johnson, "Los Angeles and Its Population," chap. 6 of Erle Fiske Young, "Family Case Work: A Manual for Social Case Workers in Los Angeles County California" (Los Angeles: Western Educational Service, 1927), typescript; see also Sanchez, *Becoming Mexican American*, pp. 70, 76, 90. Paul Taylor cited 27,000 Mexican school-age children in metropolitan Los Angeles in the late 1920s; see Taylor, "Mexican Labor in the United States; Racial School Statistics, California, 1927," *University of California Publications in Economics* 6 (November 27, 1929): 265.

79. For this listing and for the "drudgery" quotation above, see Karl De Schweinitz, "Social Work with Families in Los Angeles," chap. 4 of Young, "Family Case Work." In the words of early sociology student and social worker Elizabeth Fuller, who wrote an important thesis on Mexican housing in Los Angeles, "Los Angeles so far has considered the Mexican immigrant chiefly as an individual asset. He has been allowed to drift into the worst sections of the city and to be exploited by the landlords." Fuller, "The Mexican Housing Problem in Los Angeles," *Studies in Sociology* 5 (November 1920): 6.

80. See Alberto Rembao, "What Should Be Done for Jaun [*sic*] Garcia," *Pomona College Magazine* (1929): 145–148; Elizabeth Fuller, also has a fictional Garcia family in her work. Another contemporary description of housing conditions can be found in Dana Bartlett, *The Better City* (Los Angeles: Neuner, 1907), pp. 244–245 (Bartlett very nearly predicts the plague outbreak of 1924–1925, discussed below in chap. 5). For additional background on occupational distribution (or lack thereof), see Ricardo Romo, "Work and Restlessness: Occupational and Spatial Mobility among Mexicanos in Los Angeles, 1918–1928," *Pacific Historical Review* 46 (1977): 157–180. For more insight into the condition of early twentieth-century housing, see Municipal League of Los Angeles, *Bulletin*, February 16, 1925, which summarizes a number of earlier reports on Los Angeles housing. See also Dana Cuff, *The Provisional City: Los Angeles Stories of Architecture and Urbanism* (Cambridge: MIT Press, 2000), esp. chap. 21.

81. Fuller, "The Mexican Housing Problem," p. 1.

82. A perfect example of this tendency to criminalize ethnicity is the report of S. H. Bowman in the annual report of the Los Angeles Police Department for 1924. In his "Brief Study of Arrests of Mexicans," Bowman expressed the "rough

measure of the criminality of the Mexican Population" [*sic*] as the raw arrest figures over a twelve-month period. That the statistics reveal nothing about who is or isn't a Mexican, how many Mexicans existed in the general population, or how arrest records (and not conviction records) could reveal *anything* about a sub-group's criminality seems not to have entered his "research design" at all. Such was the reflexive racial characterizing of the era. Bowman assumed "a reasonable degree of justice" in the resolution of the cases. Arrests included those for bathing or camping in the Los Angeles River, keeping "late and unusual hours," passing handbills, slaughtering animals, throwing glass in the street, attempting suicide, keeping an unlicensed dog, and "wearing Masonic pin without rights." The photograph of young Mexican boys, taken near the Los Angeles plaza by an anonymous Anglo is from Photo Album 184, California State Library, Sacramento.

83. See, for instance, the California Commission of Immigration and Housing, *Report on an Experiment Made in Los Angeles in the Summer of 1917 for the Americanization of Foreign-born Women* (Sacramento: Commission of Immigration and Housing, 1917). Other English phrases utilized the paired hygiene and language approach common to Americanization: "I have a tub. I heat some water on the stove. I put warm water in the tub. I put my baby in the tub." Cuff, *The Provisional City*, reproduces period photographs made by the city Housing Commission in the first part of the twentieth century; see esp. chap. 21. Historian Gayle Gullett's book *Becoming Citizens: The Emergence and Development of the California Women's Movement, 1880–1911* (Champaign: University of Illinois Press, 2000) analyzes the ethnocentric Americanization practices among reform-minded Anglo women in Los Angeles; see esp. chap. 3, "The Politics of Altruism." Helpful, too, is Matt Garcia's *A World of Its Own*, esp. chap. 2, 'The Colonia Complex Revisited.' Garcia discusses a Southern California citrus-belt variant to Americanization's language/hygiene instruction in Los Angeles, as exemplified by the "I swat the fly" recitation. A 1920 Americanization manual urged educators working with Mexican populations in eastern Los Angeles County not to use irrelevant phrases such as "see the red hen crossing the street," but to instead use such phrases as "see the Mexican picking oranges." See Garcia, *A World of Its Own*, p. 68.

84. On the diversity of the population, ca. 1920s, see, for instance, Sanchez, *Becoming Mexican American*, pp. 90–91.

85. While the number seems an exaggeration, the archbishop of Los Angeles wrote in the late 1920s, "We have over two hundred thousand Mexicans in this City who are in an impoverished condition. . . . This problem . . . is becoming quite alarming." Archbishop John Joseph Cantwell [the note is actually from Cantwell's personal secretary] to Rev. Patrick Coughlan, January 20, 1927; similarly, Cantwell to Cardinal Sbarretti, November 14, 1927; both at Archival Center, Archdiocese of Los Angeles, Mission San Fernando. .

86. See G. Bromley Oxnam, *The Mexican in Los Angeles* (Los Angeles: Los

Angeles City Survey, 1920), p. 14. Arrest records of the Los Angeles Police Department for a twelve-month period in the early 1920s reveal that of those identified as "Mexican," 72 percent were classified as "laborers." This may not tell us much, but even this figure is low: others arrested are classed in laboring occupations. See Bowman, "Brief Study," p. 132. In the 1920s, the place-holding appellation is occasionally "Vincente," as an alternative to "Juan Garcia."

87. As a special gubernatorial investigatory committee put it in 1930, "there exists a prejudice against the Mexican which manifests itself in the common classification (though not by the census, which calls them Caucasian and white) as 'not white.'" From Governor C. C. Young's Mexican Fact-Finding Committee, *Mexicans in California* (Sacramento: State Printing Office, 1930), p. 176, quoted in Charles D. Withers, "Problems of Mexican Boys," M.A. thesis, University of Southern California, 1942, reprinted 1974 by R. and E. Associates (San Francisco, 1974), pp. 22–23. See also Gutiérrez, *Walls and Mirrors,* and Sanchez, *Becoming Mexican American.*

88. "Mexican" as a descriptor of both nationality and ethnicity in the nineteenth and first half of the twentieth century is tremendously common. For instance, social workers routinely assigned foreign status to all "Mexicans" in their survey work, regardless of nativity of the individuals undergoing scrutiny. In other words, it is important to remember the very recent vintage of such a phrase (and social category) as "Mexican American." See, for instance, Young, "Family Case Work," chap. 5.

89. See Los Angeles Chamber of Commerce *Bulletin*, January 24, 1927, p. 2. For an excellent discussion of the creation of this so-called Spanish Village, see Kropp, "'All Our Yesterdays,'" for a lengthy discussion of Olvera Street and its relationship to the Spanish Fantasy heritage; see also Kropp, "Citizens of the Past? Olvera Street and the Construction of Race and Memory in 1930s Los Angeles," *Radical History Review* (fall 2001): 35–60.

90. "Are we Americans big enough to recognize the inherent value to us and to our community of these groups and in cooperation with them to build a community which will truly represent the best aspects of all those races?" See the Los Angeles Chamber of Commerce *Bulletin*, June 22, 1936, p. 1. "China City" failed. What remains to be written is a longitudinal examination of the racial attitudes toward Chinese in Los Angeles; an excellent introduction to the patterns of discrimination aimed at the Chinese in the late nineteenth century is Michelle Armond, "Legal Dimensions of the Chinese Experience in Los Angeles, 1860–1880," senior honors thesis (history), California Institute of Technology, 2000. While "China City" can be seen as a relatively benign example of cultural appropriation, its relationship to the racist sentiments that produced the 1871 massacre ought to be examined. See also, more generally, Anderson, "The Idea of Chinatown." Even as late as 1924, an officer of the Los Angeles Police Department could confidently state that the "Chinese have no excuse for existence. They are

gamblers and dope fiends. They are a menace to our community." See Capt. Clyde Plummer, "Vice and Its Relation to Crime," in Vollmar, *Law Enforcement in Los Angeles, 1924*, p. 172.

91. One fascinating description of the "close to Nature" argument about Mexicans can be found in settlement house worker Amanda Mathews Chase's quasi-fictional *The Hieroglyphics of Love: Stories of Sonoratown and Old Mexico* (Los Angeles: Artemisia Bindery, 1906). See especially her associations of Mexican emotions and actions with a river's current, discussed at length in chap. 3 of this work. One of Chase's Mexican characters, a listless union man, is of course named "Juan Garcia." The author thanks Mike Davis for bringing this curious little book to his attention.

92. See George Lipsitz, *The Possessive Investment in Whiteness: How White People Profit from Identity Politics* (Philadelphia: Temple University Press, 1998). See also Bowman, "Brief Study," p. 124. Another LAPD officer concurred with admirable, if racist, succinctness: "The local problem is the Mexican." Lieutenant James Lyons, "Work of the Crime Crushers," in Vollmar, *Law Enforcement in Los Angeles, 1924*, p. 174.

93. "[Los Angeles] is no fool's paradise, nor boomer's dream. It has been done by the brains and energy of the typical American—here, for the first time in American history, fully free to expand to full potency, to work with Nature and not against her." Charles Fletcher Lummis in *Land of Sunshine*, June 1895, p. 48.

94. "Facts About Industrial Los Angeles, Nature's Workshop" (Los Angeles: Los Angeles Chamber of Commerce, 1926).

95. See Tom Ingersoll, "Los Angeles, Typical American City," in the *Los Angeles Examiner* monthly publication *What About Los Angeles*, December, 1922, p. 8. The author's thanks to Greg Hise for the reference.

96. "Typical Women" of Southern California are discussed beneath that heading in the *Los Angeles Times* "Annual Midwinter Issue," January 1, 1916.

97. The author expresses his gratitude to historian Doug Flamming of the Georgia Institute of Technology for his assistance in thinking through these ideas.

98. *Olvera Street News* 1 (August 1933): 1. Beneath a photograph of Olvera Street, the newspaper ran the following short poem: "Its way is narrow, and its passage brief; Around it throbs a clamoring, pulsing beat. Its crumbling fronts stand out in quaint relief—The mighty city's womb . . . Olvera Street!" See also Kropp, "Citizens of the Past?"

99. There's little doubt that Anglo Angelenos thought of Mexicans as racial others. There are examples of something else going on, i.e., census categories where Mexicans are white, but the overwhelming tendency, in pre-ethnicity days, was to characterize "Mexican" as a race. As pioneering Los Angeles sociologist Emory Bogardus wrote, in terms which emphasized both racial distinctions and Mexican typicality (not to mention gendered uniformity), "An under-

standing of the Mexican immigrant rests directly on knowing his culture traits, and on being able to diagnose the culture conflicts of Americans and Mexicans." Bogardus, *The Mexican Immigrant: An Annotated Bibliography* (Los Angeles: Council on International Relations, 1929), p. 3. It should be pointed out that Bogardus believed that social scientific and cultural knowledge of "the Mexican" would help alleviate what he called the pernicious "half-baked prescriptions of chauvinists."

100. A good example of Americanization's hold on the minds and campaigns of Progressive reformers in Los Angeles, especially as it relates to Mexicans, can be found in the opening lines of William Wilson McEuen's 1914 M.A. thesis from USC, written under the direction of Rockwell Hunt and Emory Bogardus. "Among the problems presented by the presence of foreign peoples in Los Angeles no one is greater than that of the Mexican population, and the difficulties encountered in its solution are greater than those met with in any other race problems in this city. These difficulties are of two distinct kinds: first, those arising because of numbers; and, second, those that spring from the character of the Mexican people." In a mere two sentences, McEuen obliterates history and, as swiftly, Anglo or class culpability in the creation of the "Mexican problem." McEuen, "A Survey of the Mexicans in Los Angeles." A thoughtful overview of Progressive-Era attitudes toward Mexico, Mexicans, and Mexican Americans as found in the American press is Mark C. Anderson, "'What's to Be Done with 'Em?': Images of Mexican Cultural Backwardness, Racial Limitations, and Moral Decrepitude in the United States Press, 1913–1915," *Mexican Studies/Estudios Mexicanos* 14 (winter 1998): 23–70.

101. Oxnam journal entry, February 26, 1913, Bromley Oxnam Papers, Library of Congress.

102. Oxnam journal entry, April 28, 1913, Oxnam Papers.

103. Oxnam journal entry and newspaper clipping, April 30, 1913.

104. Knights of the Round Table rules in Oxnam journal, April 30, 1913; see also *Los Angeles Express*, May 13, 1913. See also Mark Reisler, "Always the Laborer, Never the Citizen: Anglo Perceptions of the Mexican Immigrant during the 1920s," *Pacific Historical Review* 45 (May 1976): 231–254, and, more generally, Reisler, *By the Sweat of Their Brow;* also Martha Menchaca and Richard Valencia, "Anglo-Saxon Ideologies in the 1920s–1930s: Their Impact on the Segregation of Mexican Students in California," *Anthropology and Education Quarterly* 21 (1990): 222–249.

105. See Alice Bessie Culp, "A Case Study of the Living Conditions of Thirty-Five Mexican Families of Los Angeles with Special Reference to Mexican Children," M.A. thesis, University of Southern California, 1921, p. 1. Culp's study, and many others of the period, have been usefully reprinted by R. and E. Research Associates of San Francisco. Neatness of cultural supposition did not necessarily mask ugliness of race prejudice. "In the United States they don't like the Mex-

icans," a migrant repatriate observed in the mid-1930s. "They treat them like niggers there." James Carl Gilbert, "A Field Study in Mexico of the Mexican Repatriation Movement," M.A. thesis, University of Southern California, 1934, p. 160. McWilliams quoted from Carey McWilliams, "Once a Well-Kept Secret," *Pacific Historical Review* 42 (1973): 309.

106. Patric, *A Study of the Housing and Social Conditions in the Ann Street District*, p. 7.

107. *California Commission of Immigration and Housing* report; author's files. Again: the pronounal hubris ("our gates," "with us to stay;" "we can mold them as we will"). We should perhaps recall that the other becomes increasingly troubling not solely through simple proximity: proximity can be negotiated, as it was in 1850s Los Angeles, by force or coercion. Matters become much more complex when "the other" threatens an assimilative proximity, when they get close enough (i.e., through Americanization's aims, if not results) to overlap socially, sexually, residentially, with that group which has been doing most of "the othering." The 1920s, which featured immigration restrictions against Europeans, but no Mexican quotas, exacerbated this kind of assimilation fear.

108. See Vernon McCombs to Bromley Oxnam, January 17, 1921, Oxnam Papers.

109. Realtor reports, "Race Relations of the Pacific Coast" collection, Hoover Institution Archives, Hoover Institution on War, Revolution, and Peace, Stanford University.

110. "Race Relations of the Pacific Coast."

111. George Clements, Manager of the Agriculture Department, Los Angeles Chamber of Commerce, quoted in McLean, *That Mexican!*, p. 130.

2. HISTORY ON PARADE

1. Ferd Rule, "Birth and Growth of La Fiesta," in *Los Angeles Herald*, May 6, 1903 (Fiesta edition), p. 5.

2. Z.Z., *A Business Venture in Los Angeles, or, A Christian Optimist* (Cincinnati: Robert Clarke, 1899), quoted at p. 168.

3. Unnamed newspaper editorial, ca. November, 1900; from La Fiesta Scrapbook, 1900–1901, Southwest Museum.

4. Louise Doissy was "Z.Z."

5. Z.Z., *Business Venture in Los Angeles*, see pp. 168–215.

6. I have developed some of these ideas in cooperation with my colleague Doug Flamming; see our essay "Race, Rhetoric, and Regional Identity: Boosting Los Angeles, 1880–1930," in John Findlay and Richard White, eds., *Power and Place in the North American West* (Seattle: University of Washington Press, 1999).

7. In 1910, as part of a pro-labor campaign that included the dynamiting of

the *Los Angeles Times* building, at least one high-ranking M & M official would be targeted for assassination by labor saboteurs.

8. See Marco R. Newmark, "La Fiesta de Los Angeles of 1894," *Historical Society of Southern California Quarterly* 29 (March 1947): 100–111. Max Meyberg later recalled that the first Fiesta had in part been organized to refocus the city's attention away from an outbreak of smallpox. See the clipping from the *Los Angeles Times* for January 13, 1926, in the Max Meyberg Scrapbook, Seaver Center, Los Angeles County Museum of Natural History; hereafter Meyberg Scrapbook.

9. The various committees are all mentioned in *Los Angeles Times* stories devoted to the coming of the Fiesta during the first week of April 1894.

10. Max Meyberg, undated statement on La Fiesta de Los Angeles (ca. 1930 or 1931), Meyberg Scrapbook.

11. On children, see *Los Angeles Herald*, April 12, 1894. See also "circular order" stationary in Meyberg Scrapbook. As to opposition, the *Los Angeles Times*, presided over by the combative General Harrison Gray Otis, a man as fond of the military and its pomp as anyone in Los Angeles (or the West, for that matter), sniffed that "the fiesta needs a business manager, rather than a generalissimo, major domo or director-general"; *Los Angeles Times*, September 6, 1895. On discipline as a public way to consolidate authority, see David Glassberg, *A Sense of History: The Place of the Past in American Life* (Amherst: University of Massachusetts Press, 2001), p. 65.

12. From Los Angeles City Council Minutes, March 19, April 2, April 9, 1894, and Petition # 255 (March 27, 1894), Los Angeles City Archives.

13. *Los Angeles Times*, April 8, 1894, quoted in Isabel C. Wielus, "Las Fiestas de Los Angeles: A Survey of the Yearly Celebrations, 1894–1898," M.A. thesis, University of California, Los Angeles, 1946, p. 24; hereafter Wielus, "Las Fiestas."

14. See *Los Angeles Times*, April 8, 1894.

15. See *Los Angeles Times*, April 3, 1894.

16. Much of the following discussion of La Fiesta events is drawn from Christina Wielus Mead, "Las Fiestas de Los Angeles: A Survey of the Yearly Celebrations 1894–1898," in *Historical Society of Southern California Quarterly* 31 (June 1949): 63–113; hereafter Mead, "Las Fiestas." See also the slightly earlier Isabel C. Wielus, "Las Fiestas," and Tommy Tomlinson, "Bowers of Flowers," *Westways* 75, no. 12 (December 1983): 35–37, 77.

17. Quoted in Mead, "Las Fiestas," p. 69.

18. See Marshall Stimson, *Fun, Fights, and Fiestas in Old Los Angeles* (Los Angeles, privately printed, 1966), p. 58.

19. See Mead, "Las Fiestas," p. 73.

20. Harris Newmark, *Sixty Years in Southern California, 1853–1913* (New York: 1913), p. 608, quoted in Mead, "Las Fiestas," p. 74. *Philadelphia Record*, May 18, 1897; all newspaper references, unless noted, come from the La Fiesta Scrap-

books, Charles Fletcher Lummis Collection, Southwest Museum. See also Max Meyberg's statement [1930 or 1931] pasted into the Meyberg Scrapbook.

21. See, for instance, Davis, *City of Quartz*, p. 26.

22. Lummis in "La Fiesta of 1896," *Land of Sunshine*, April 1896, p. 234.

23. See, for instance, Stimson, *Fun, Fights and Fiestas*, pp. 38–55, for descriptions of the exoticism of fandangos in such places as El Monte. Jackson, *California and the Missions*, p. 174. "All the young people of California were literally cousins," journalist Harry Carr wrote of pre-statehood times, and these cousins "danced all the time." See Carr's introduction to Ana Begue Packman, *Leather Dollars: Short Stories of Pueblo Los Angeles* (Los Angeles: Times Mirror Press, 1932).

24. Bancroft, from *California Pastoral* (1888), quoted in Wielus, "Las Fiestas," p. 1; William Wallace diary, December 18, 1856.

25. Dana, *Two Years before the Mast*, p. 137. One representative version of the "happy, pre-capitalism natives" genre should suffice. Prominent attorney Jackson A. Graves noted in his autobiography (in a chapter called "The Passing of the Dominant Race") that "native Californians . . . led a pastoral life. . . . a happy care-free life. They loved the fiesta and the fandango. . . . They were careless of money, spent it freely when they had it, and did not hesitate to borrow it when they did not have it." Graves, *My Seventy Years in California*, pp. 134–135. See also Gary Kurutz, *Benjamin C. Truman*, for Truman's "dancing people" remarks.

26. See *San Bernardino Times-Index*, August 6, 1895; clipping found in La Fiesta Clippings Scrapbook, Southwest Museum. What makes the San Bernardino version of La Fiesta all the more interesting, and worthy of further investigation, is the Mormon history of the place.

27. Franklin Walker, *A Literary History of Southern California* (Berkeley and Los Angeles: University of California Press, 1950), p. 122.

28. From the *Los Angeles Evening Express*, April 5, 1894, quoted in Wielus, "Las Fiestas," p. 27.

29. Recall that it was tinsmith and nurseryman O. W. Childs who rode to El Monte in search of reinforcements during the "excitement" of 1856. See chap. 1.

30. From the *Los Angeles Times*, April 8, 1894, quoted in Wielus, "Las Fiestas," pp. 29–30; pronunciations from *Los Angeles Evening Express*, April 13, 1895, quoted in Wielus, "Las Fiestas," p. 49. See also *Los Angeles Record*, April 7, 1896.

31. A thoughtful reading of the complexity of urban public memory is John Bodnar, *Remaking America: Public Memory, Commemoration, and Patriotism in the Twentieth Century* (Princeton: Princeton University Press, 1992); see also Glassberg, *Sense of History*, especially chaps. 3 ("Celebrating the City") and 7 ("Making Places in California"). Glassberg's brief discussion on pp. 183–185 highlights the continuities between California commemorations of the regional past and the historical touchstones of colonial New England; see also pp. 193–202. For a discussion of public memory in the recent past, see George Lipsitz, *Time*

Passages: Collective Memory and American Popular Culture (Minneapolis: University of Minnesota Press, 1990); an especially intriguing chapter is "Mardi Gras Indians." David Wrobel's *Promised Lands: Promotion, Memory, and the Creation of the American West* (Lawrence: University Press of Kansas, 2002) is an especially insightful analysis of western regional memory and regional identity.

32. Meyberg from *Land of Sunshine*, "La Fiesta de Los Angeles," July 1894 issue, at p. 34; W. C. Patterson, "La Fiesta de Los Angeles," *Land of Sunshine*, April 1898. pp. 243–248, quote at p. 248.

33. Rule, "Birth and Growth of La Fiesta," p. 5.

34. Glassberg, *A Sense of History*, pp. 62, 63.

35. Frank Van Vleck, "La Fiesta de Los Angeles, 1895," *Land of Sunshine*, April 1895, p. 83.

36. Clipping from the *Los Angeles World*, April 15, 1894, Meyberg Scrapbook.

37. See Rule, "Birth and Growth of La Fiesta." The men got their pay.

38. Joseph Crawley to Max Meyberg, April 14, 1894, Meyberg Scrapbook.

39. Undated [1894] clipping, Meyberg Scrapbook.

40. See Los Angeles City Council Petition # 174, February 18, 1895, Los Angeles City Archives.

41. Van Vleck, "La Fiesta de Los Angeles, 1895," p. 84.

42. Lummis in *Land of Sunshine*, April 1895, unsigned editorial; "A Lost Art Found."

43. Lummis, *Land of Sunshine*, April 1895.

44. Meyberg apparently raised $19,436.50 in subscriptions for La Fiesta 1895; see Meyberg Scrapbook.

45. Francis letter from the Merchants' Association minutes, meeting of June 20, 1895, quoted in Wielus, "Las Fiestas," p. 63. The First National Bank of Los Angeles advanced the Fiesta Committee enough money to balance their 1895 books with a six-cent profit. See Meyberg Scrapbook.

46. *California Voice*, August 29, 1895.

47. See *Los Angeles Express*, April 11, 1896.

48. Charles Dwight Willard to Samuel Willard, October 27, 1895, C. D. Willard Papers, Huntington Library; hereafter Willard Papers.

49. Charles Dwight Willard to Samuel Willard, December 19, 1897, Willard Papers.

50. Charles Dwight Willard, *The Herald's History of Los Angeles* (Los Angeles: Kingsley-Barnes & Neuner, 1901), p. 282.

51. Charles Dwight Willard to Sarah Willard Hiestand, March 28, 1896, Willard Papers.

52. "La Fiesta de Los Angeles," *Land of Sunshine*, April 1896, pp. 269, 271. Eastern concerns quoted in *Los Angeles Record*, February 11, 1896.

53. Wielus, "Las Fiestas," p. 75, quoting from *Los Angeles Evening Express*, April 22, 1896.

54. See, for instance, the *Express* of April 18, 1896 (as well as all throughout the Fiesta week). In early twentieth-century San Francisco, the organizers of the Portolá Festival opted for a sexualized Latina, cigarette in hand, as their festival "mascot." See Glassberg, *A Sense of History*, pp. 74–75.

55. *Los Angeles Record*, April 11, 1896.

56. See *Los Angeles Record*, April 11, 1896. Portions of Miller's essay were also reprinted in the *Los Angeles Tocsin*, April 17, 1896. He also opposed the coronation of a Fiesta queen as a monarchical throwback.

57. *Los Angeles Record*, April 18, 1896.

58. *Chicago Evening Post*, April 21, 1896.

59. See *Los Angeles Express*, March 12, 1896.

60. Music for the "La Fiesta March" (dedicated to John F. Francis, president of the 1896 event) can be found in the Sam de Vincent Collection at the National Museum of American History, Smithsonian Institution. Thanks to Phoebe Kropp for finding the sheet music.

61. See *Santa Paula Chronicle*, May 1, 1896. Indicative, too, of La Fiesta's ethnic and racial teachings was the fact that non-parade events—like the Fiesta Ball, for instance—had only white attendees. See *Los Angeles Capital*, May 2, 1896.

62. *Pasadena Star*, March 20, 1896; *Riverside Enterprise*, April 24, 1896.

63. See *Los Angeles Record*, April 18, 1896. Philip Deloria's *Playing Indian* (New Haven: Yale University Press, 1998) is a thoughtful reflection upon the ways in which "Indian-playing" reveals racial attitudes through American history.

64. Lummis in *Harper's Weekly*, May 16, 1896, from Wielus, "Las Fiestas," p. 84.

65. *Los Angeles Times*, April 26, 1896.

66. *Santa Paula Chronicle*, May 1, 1896.

67. *Colton Chronicle*, March 21, 1896. Compare this notion of the "foreignness" of Spanish-language words with actress Mary Pickford's comments thirty years later that Spanish place-names on the Los Angeles landscape "tasted good in the mouth." See Greg Hise and William Deverell, *Eden by Design: The 1930 Olmsted-Bartholomew Plan for the Los Angeles Region* (Berkeley and Los Angeles: University of California Press, 2000), p. 33.

68. See *The Tidings*, May 2, 1896. This was a journal published by the Archdiocese of Los Angeles.

69. *California Voice*, April 18, 1896.

70. *Los Angeles Record*, April 18, 1896.

71. For a useful discussion of the discrimination aimed at the Chinese in Los Angeles in the period, see Armond, "Legal Dimensions of the Chinese Experience in Los Angeles."

72. *Los Angeles Record*, April 21, 1896.

73. *Los Angeles Non Partisan*, May 9, 1896.

74. "La Fiesta de Los Angeles," *Land of Sunshine*, April 1896, pp. 268–269. In

his book *No Place of Grace: Anti-Modernism and the Transformation of American Culture, 1880–1920* (New York: Pantheon, 1981), the historian T. J. Jackson Lears writes of the Anglo-American discovery of physical culture and exuberant outdoor activities in this period. I suspect that Lummis's enthusiasm springs from a similar well, with the added inducement that such activity in Southern California allows Anglos to play at being culturally or racially "primitive."

75. See Wielus, "Las Fiestas," p. 87.

76. Wielus, "Las Fiestas," p. 91, from Minutes of the Chamber of Commerce, May 20, 1896.

77. See Executive Committee minutes, January 7, 1897, and February 12, 1897; "La Fiesta Minutes Book, September 1896–May 1897," Southwest Museum; hereafter "La Fiesta Minutes Book, 1896–1897." Behymer's part in La Fiesta marked the beginning of the energetic promoter's many decades of labor on behalf of local boosterism and Spanish myth-making; he would move from La Fiesta promotion to pushing John Steven McGroarty's *Mission Play* in the new century.

78. Wielus, "Las Fiestas," p. 97; *Los Angeles Times*, April 6, 1897, and see all issues for first two weeks of April. Presumably adding to the ire of local moralists, a "souvenir sporting guide" to Los Angeles brothels was published for Fiesta 1897. See W. W. Robinson, *Tarnished Angels: Paradisiacal Turpitude in Los Angeles* ([Los Angeles], privately printed, 1964). My thanks to Tom Sitton for pointing this out to me.

79. *Los Angeles Evening Express*, April 25, 1896. Wielus, "Las Fiestas," p. 105.

80. John Vance Lauderdale, journal entry, April 20, 1897, John Vance Lauderdale Papers, Beinecke Library.

81. For representative sentiment along these lines, see the *Los Angeles Record* of June 1 and June 2, 1897. The event's most vociferous critic seems to have been the acerbic editor of the *Colton Chronicle*.

82. *Los Angeles Evening Express*, May 18, 1897; Wielus, "Las Fiestas," p. 108.

83. See minutes of March 30, 1897, "La Fiesta Minutes Book, 1896–1897."

84. See *Colton Chronicle*, November 20, 1897.

85. See, for instance, *Los Angeles Citizen*, February 19, 1898; *Los Angeles Record*, February 22, and 28, 1898; *California Voice*, February 24, 1898 .

86. *California Voice*, February 24 and March 4, 1898; Whittier Register [clipping, no date].

87. *East Side News*, March 5, 1898.

88. *Los Angeles Record*, March 10, 1898.

89. *Los Angeles Times*, March 13, 1898.

90. Quoted in *Los Angeles Record*, April 9, 1898.

91. *Colton Chronicle*, April 8, 1898.

92. *San Bernardino Sun*, April 21, 1898.

93. "Committee of Thirty" declaration from an untitled and undated pamphlet (incomplete) on the 1898 La Fiesta, Max Meyberg Scrapbook.

94. "Committee of Thirty" statement from undated, untitled pamphlet in Meyberg Scrapbook. See also *Los Angeles Capital*, April 9 and April 30, 1898.

95. *Fallbrook Observer*, May 13, 1898.

96. W. C. Patterson, "La Fiesta de Los Angeles," *Land of Sunshine*, April 1898, pp. 243–248, quote p. 243.

97. Lummis, "La Fiesta of 1896," *Land of Sunshine*, April 1896, p. 234.

98. *East Side News*, October 13, 1900.

99. The move away from the past, and from Latin references, is nicely symbolized by this line from the La Fiesta minutes of October 4, 1900: "The question of a name for the festival was then discussed and on motion of Mr. Montgomery seconded by Mr. Barkley it was decided that the festival shall be known as La Fiesta de Flores, if that name is grammatically correct." La Fiesta Minutes, 1900–1902, Southwest Museum.

100. *Los Angeles Independent*, November 15, 1900; see also unnamed newspaper editorial, ca. November, 1900 (cited in n. 3): "our fiestas should conform more to the American than the Spanish idea of fiestas."

101. See Gayle Gullett, *Becoming Citizens: The Emergence and Development of the California Women's Movement, 1880–1911* (Champaign: University of Illinois Press, 2000), pp. 124–127; *Los Angeles Times*, April 21, 1902.

102. From P. Maurice McMahon, *Fiesta Poems* (Los Angeles, privately printed, 1895).

3. REMEMBERING A RIVER

1. Charles Fletcher Lummis, editorial comment in *Land of Sunshine*, February 1896, p. 141.

2. Los Angeles River Pollution Committee, "Progress Report for the Period May 1948–April 1949," typescript, Water Resources Center Archives, University of California, Berkeley.

3. From the album *broken toy shop*, by E, Polygram Records, 1993.

4. Amanda M. Chase's official report is "Home Teacher Report," from California Commission of Immigration and Housing, Report on an Experiment Made in Los Angeles in the Summer of 1917 for the Americanization of Foreign-born Women (Sacramento: Commission of Immigration and Housing, 1917), p. 21. According to historian Matt Garcia, Chase was at the front lines of the Americanization assault in Southern California as the first home teacher in Los Angeles. See Garcia, *A World of Its Own*, p. 66.

5. Chase, *The Hieroglyphics of Love*, pp. 14–15. Chase published the collection under the name Amanda Mathews.

6. Chase, *The Hieroglyphics of Love*, pp. 70–71.

7. The great Mexican boxer Jose Ybarra, who lived against the Los Angeles River as a young man, took his professional name precisely because of such asso-

ciations. Asked by an Anglo gym owner, who had trouble pronouncing Ybarra's last name, where he lived, the boxer answered and thus became "Joe Rivers." See Greg Rodriguez, "'Palaces of Pain'—Arenas of Mexican-American Dreams: Boxing and the Formation of Ethnic Mexican Identities in Twentieth Century Los Angeles," Ph.D. diss., University of California, San Diego, 1999, pp. 34–35.

8. Henry Miller, *The Tropic of Cancer* (New York: Grove Press, 1961), p. 318.

9. See, for instance, the *Los Angeles Times* calendar section, August 21, 1994, in which local radio personalities Ken Minyard and Roger Barkley joke that "We think the L.A. River may become a raging torrent. And if it does, we're ready for it." See also Judith Coburn, "Whose River Is It, Anyway? More Concrete versus More Nature: The Battle over Flood Control on the Los Angeles River Is Really a Fight for Its Soul," *Los Angeles Times Magazine*, November 20, 1994, p. 18; Robert A. Jones, "A River without a Chuckle," *Los Angeles Times*, October 20, 1991. A very thoughtful piece on the river is D. J. Waldie, "The Myth of the L.A. River," *Buzz Magazine*, April 1996.

10. See, for instance, flood season stories in the city's local papers, i.e., "Rescue Crews Keep Keen Eye on L.A. River," *Los Angeles Times*, February 20, 1993. Los Angeles County has even made a video warning schoolchildren of the river's winter dangers; on average six people drown in the county each winter from river flooding.

11. Lawrence Clark Powell, "Strictly Local," *Southern California Quarterly* 47 (December 1965): 347–355; quoted at p. 348.

12. Michael DiLeo, "Can the River of Concrete Live Again?" *American Way*, June 15, 1992, p. 70.

13. This isn't a new publicity device. Early urban planning documents, particularly regarding railroads, mention the possibility of running track in the riverbed. Los Angeles pols have been making the "river as freeway" equation since the early 1920s at least. By the mid-twenties, the river occupied the interest of many who want to throw truck traffic off major thoroughfares and into the "River Truck Freeway." By the mid-1940s, the phrase "Los Angeles River Freeway" was a common one in city planning documents. For a modern version, see Assemblyman Richard Katz's plan as depicted in the *Los Angeles Times*, August 4, 1989.

14. Gabrielino Indians themselves had stories and folk legends about the river. One concerned a cocky coyote who challenged the little stream to a race. The Porciuncula agreed and, several miles downstream, the exhausted coyote had learned his lesson. See Cheri Gaulke, *The Los Angeles: River inside a River* (Los Angeles: Cheri Gaulke, ca. 1991).

15. Crespi and de Neve quoted in John Caughey and Laree Caughey, *Los Angeles: Biography of a City* (Berkeley and Los Angeles: University of California Press, 1976), pp. 49–54 and 63–66. See also J. N. Bowman, "The Names of the Los Angeles and San Gabriel Rivers," *Historical Society of Southern California*

Quarterly 29 (March 1947): 93–99; Raymund F. Wood, "Juan Crespi: The Man Who Named Los Angeles," *Southern California Quarterly* 53 (September 1971): 199–234. The single most comprehensive study of the Los Angeles River is Blake Gumprecht, *The Los Angeles River: Its Life, Death, and Possible Rebirth* (Baltimore: Johns Hopkins University Press, 1999). I am grateful to him for sharing his work with me in various forms.

16. Charles Franklin Carter, trans. and ed., "Duhaut-Cilly's Account of California in the Years 1827–28," *California Historical Society Quarterly* 8 (September 1929): 214–250; quoted at p. 246. See also Mary Mooney, "Side-Lights on Old Los Angeles," in Historical Society of Southern California, *Proceedings* 6 (1903–1904): 43–48.

17. See Ana Begue Packman's collection of local folktales, *Leather Dollars*, for a description of one such occasion.

18. This mill became the headquarters for Capitol Milling, still present in the flatlands just northwest of Union Station. An adobe wall from Stearns's day still sits inside the Capitol Milling operation.

19. A Works Progress Administration writer from the 1930s wrote that one of the first presses in Los Angeles was water-powered with Los Angeles River water. See Index of American Design materials, Huntington Library, folder 6.

20. Surely it is far more than coincidence that these two orienting features of Los Angeles are more associated with the Latino "what once was" than the Anglo "what will be."

21. Vincent Hoover diary entry, February 16, 1850, Huntington Library.

22. James Clarke to [his brother], December 6, 1854, Huntington Library. Clark's use of "+" signs for "and" has been changed.

23. Campbell's report can be found in Lieutenant A. W. Whipple's volume III of the United States *Reports of Explorations and Surveys to Ascertain the Most Practicable and Economical Route for a Railroad from the Mississippi River to the Pacific Ocean* (Washington: Beverley Tucker, Printer, 1856).

24. Testimony to the confidence city boosters had in the river's capabilities is found in such documents as *The Herald Pamphlet for 1876: Containing A Complete Description of Los Angeles County* (Los Angeles: Herald Publishing Company, 1876), which unequivocally states that "the water supply of Los Angeles is abundant for present requirements and ample to meet the rapid expansion that is going on. The waters of the Los Angeles River are under municipal control, and all waste prevented by stringent regulation." Even into the 1890s and the new century, city engineers were convinced that the Los Angeles River could alone supply the water needs of the city; see, for instance, Joseph Henry Dockweiler, quoted in the *Los Angeles Times*, December 30, 1891. Such certainty would fade in the crush of population explosion and lead to increasing demands that the city divert the Owens River, two hundred and fifty miles away, essentially into the Los Angeles River. See Elisabeth Mathieu Spriggs, "The History of the Domes-

tic Water Supply of Los Angeles," M.A. thesis, University of Southern California, 1931. As late as 1926, one student of the river imagined that it could supply the water needs for one quarter of a million people. See Don Jackson Kinsey, *The Romance of Water and Power: A Brief Narrative, Revealing How the Magic Touch of Water and Hydro-electric Power Transformed a Sleepy, Semi-arid Western Village into the Metropolis of the Pacific* (Los Angeles: Department of Water and Power, 1926).

25. *Los Angeles Star*, February 5, 1859.

26. For additional indication of the extent of localized cartographical and property markers in the region, see Edward M. Boggs, "A Study of Water Rights on the Los Angeles River, California," in Elwood Mead, *Report of Irrigation Investigations in California, U.S. Department of Agriculture Bulletin No. 100* (Washington: Government Printing Office, 1901), esp. pp. 332–334. See also, in general, Edwin C. Kelton, "History of Past Floods; Coastal Streams of Southern California, 1811–1939 and List of Prior Reports on Floods, Precipitation, Need for Flood Control Improvements, etc., Los Angeles and San Gabriel River Basins," United States War Department, Corps of Engineers, typescript, December 15, 1939, Water Resources Center Archives, University of California, Berkeley; hereafter, Kelton, "History of Past Floods." Even E. O. C. Ord's famed Los Angeles village survey of 1849 utilized large stones or other such quaint markers to establish geometric orientation; see W. W. Robinson, *Maps of Los Angeles* (Los Angeles: Dawson's Bookshop, 1966), p. 5.

27. See the testimony of Henrique Abila in William Maxwell Evarts, *In the Matter of the Survey of the Rancho "Tajauta," California; Arguments and Evidence for Claimants* [N.P. : n.p., 1869?].

28. Richard Bigger makes this statement in his fine study of Los Angeles flood control (see below). One author has counted eight major area floods from 1815 to 1876, inclusive, and another nine from 1884 to 1938 (the arbitrary periodization is apparently to mark a transition from "less concerned about flood control" to "more concerned about flood control"). See Anthony F. Turhollow, *A History of the Los Angeles District, U.S. Army Corps of Engineers 1898–1965* (Los Angeles: U.S. Army Engineer District, n.d), p. 146. Thanks to Doug Flamming for pointing this book out to me. Richard Bigger, who has done the most comprehensive work on Los Angeles basin flood control, estimates that there were twenty-one floods in the period 1811–1954; see Bigger, *Flood Control in Metropolitan Los Angeles* (Berkeley and Los Angeles: University of California Press; University of California Publications in Political Science, vol. 6, 1959).

29. The Los Angeles River was, she noted, "a very different river in summer." See Sarah Bixby Smith, *Adobe Days: Being the Truthful Narrative of the Events in the Life of a California Girl* (Cedar Rapids, Iowa: Torch Press, 1925; rpt. Lincoln: University of Nebraska Press, 1987). Young Los Angeles photographer Henry Workman Keller noted that the Los Angeles River was "a typical California

river, having little water on the surface but much under the sand." Keller, "The Amateur in Los Angeles" (manuscript scrapbook and journal, ca. 1885), Huntington Library.

30. See J. Gregg Layne, "Annals of Los Angeles: Part I; From the Founding of the Pueblo to the American Occupation," *California Historical Society Quarterly* 13 (September 1934): 195–234.

31. On the 1825 flood, see J. J. Warner (himself a student of Los Angeles rain and flood history) to the *Los Angeles Times*, August 6, 1882; Don Jose del Carmen Lugo, "Life of a Rancher," trans. Thomas Savage, *Historical Society of Southern California Quarterly* 32 (1950): 185–236, quoted in Gumprecht, *The Los Angeles River*, p. 141. See also Kelton, "History of Past Floods." That 1825 flood receded very slowly from local memory. In 1853, Judge Benjamin Hayes made note of it in his diary, as he just visited Luis Vignes, a prominent orchardist and vintner who had profited from the flood. The river's change of course pushed it to the other side of Vignes's house and, in the process, added considerably to his landholdings. See Wolcott, *Pioneer Notes from the Diaries of Judge Benjamin Hayes*, p. 97. See also the testimony of former Los Angeles alcalde Rafael Gallardo in Evarts, *In the Matter of the Survey of the Rancho "Tajauta."*

32. From *Three Memoirs of Mexican California by Carlos N. Hijar, Eulalia Perez, Agustin Escobar*, transcribed by Thomas Savage [originally transcribed, 1877] (Berkeley: Friends of the Bancroft Library, 1988), p. 80.

33. Scientist William Brewer noted in his journal the intensity of the 1862 floods. "At Los Angeles, it rained incessantly for twenty-eight days—immense damage was done—one whole village destroyed." Brewer, *Up and Down in California* (Berkeley and Los Angeles: University of California Press, 1966), p. 243. See also W. H. Workman "Olden Time Holiday Festivities," in Historical Society of Southern California, *Proceedings* 6 (1903–1904): 22–24. The wedding of Ascension Sepulveda y Avila to Thomas Mott on December 21, 1861, occurred in the midst of one of the heavy storms; stranded guests and musicians missed the once-a-month San Pedro steamer because so many roads had been washed out. See Sister Mary Ste. Therese Wittenburg, "A California Girlhood: Reminiscences of Ascension Sepulveda y Avila," *Historical Society of Southern California Quarterly* 64 (Summer 1982): 133–139. "Noachian deluge" quote from Kelton, "History of Past Floods" (quoting in turn, it appears, from J. M. Guinn's statement in Flood Control Interviews).

34. For instance, in a piece published in the *Los Angeles Times* on July 30, 1882 (titled "A Warning"), J. J. Warner reminded Angelenos about the volatile nature of the region's rivers: "A faint idea of what would be the condition of no inconsiderable part of Los Angeles city in case of a flood may be had by knowing and considering what past floods have done." A few months later, Warner wrote a four-part series on the river virtually demanding that the city take stronger action in order to prevent flooding and loss of property. See *Los Angeles Times*,

November 14, 15, 16, 17, 1882; my thanks to Professor Ralph Shaffer for bringing this series to my attention.

35. See Alfred Moore to the *Los Angeles Times*, August 2, 1882. Warner responded to Moore's cocksure insistence that riverbank residents had little to fear from the Los Angeles River: "I believe that a majority of all those who witnessed the flood in this city twenty years ago, upon considering the present condition of the waterway of the river, the many obstructions which since then have been placed therein, will concur in the opinion that the recurrence of such a flood would destroy a large part of the property situated in that part of the city before mentioned." See J. J. Warner to *Los Angeles Times*, August 6, 1882. Thanks to Professor Ralph Shaffer for pointing these letters out to me.

36. Los Angeles *Daily Times—Extra*, February 18, 1884 ("2:45 O'Clock P.M."). Thanks to Professor Ralph Shaffer for pointing out this special edition, as well as other *Times* pieces cited below.

37. See Bascom A. Stephens, ed., *Resources of Los Angeles* (Los Angeles: Sprague & Rodehaver, 1887), esp. pp. 4–5; *Los Angeles Express*, March 10, 1884.

38. See letter to the *Los Angeles Times* by "R.M.M.," December 22, 1885. Another letter writer, "West Side," complained that the city-sponsored levee work seemed focused upon the east side riverbank properties belonging local elites ("rich men all"). See *Los Angeles Times*, January 16, 1885. "On a bender" phrase comes from M. S. Baker to the editor of the *Los Angeles Times*, January 24, 1886.

39. See Abraham Hoffman, "The Controversial Career of Martin Aguirre: The Rise and Fall of a Chicano Lawman," *California History* 63 (fall 1984): 295–304.

40. In Allen's words, "visitations whose comings are not foreshadowed by the usual course of events, and must be laid to the account of Providence, whose dealings, though they may afflict, wrong no one." Quoted in William Webb Clary, *History of the Law Firm of O'Melveny & Myers, 1885–1965*, 2 vols. (Los Angeles: privately printed, 1966), 1: 132–133.

41. William Harper interview, from "Research Los Angeles County Flood Control 1914–1915," Huntington Library ; hereafter Flood Control Interviews. Kelton, in "History of Past Floods," notes that the 1861–1862 floods, for instance, carried driftwood down from the mountains "and furnished fuel to the poor people of the city for several years."

42. *Herald Pamphlet for 1876*, p. 42.

43. See C. P. Heininger, *Album of Los Angeles & Vicinity* (San Francisco: C. P. Heininger, ca. 1888); see also *Herald Pamphlet for 1876*, p. 27.

44. See letter to the editor, *Los Angeles Times*, July 24, 1889.

45. See "Pro Bono Publico" to the editor of the *Los Angeles Times*, December 6, 1887.

46. United States Department of the Interior, Report on the Social Statistics

of Cities, Part II (Washington, D.C.: Government Printing Office, 1887), p. 782; the same report suggests that 50 animals are disposed of in this way annually, which seems a remarkably low estimate for a city of more than 10,000 people.

47. From Kenderdine, *California Revisited*, p. 162.

48. The first edition of the *Los Angeles Star*, May 17, 1851, noted several murders recently committed. A woman had been hacked to death, the body tossed into the San Gabriel River; a Mexican had been beaten to death; and an Indian had been apparently beaten to death as well, his body then tossed into one of the *zanjas* fanning from the Los Angeles River.

49. Early resident John Welsh remembered a river of brushy banks and shacks, a place where a suspected felon could escape a cordon of twenty police officers by racing from a shanty, guns blazing, and disappearing into the reeds and willows alongside the river not far from downtown Los Angeles, never to be seen again. See Welsh's reminiscences of California in the manuscript collection of the Huntington Library.

50. See "Observer" to the editor of the *Los Angeles Times* (the letter is titled "Boys in the Brush"), October 14, 1886.

51. See Norval Nance Edwards, *Samson and Utie's Elderly Son: An Autobiographical Study of Seven Generations of an Obscure, Unhistoric American Family* (Los Angeles: University Press, 1972), p. 138. See also John Vance Lauderdale Journal, February 1, 1897, Lauderdale Papers, Beinecke Library.

52. This riverbed suggestion can be found in the transportation planning report issued by Chicago engineer Bion J. Arnold (1911); it is referred to as well in a preliminary copy of the report sent to Los Angeles progressive leader Thomas Gibbon; see Bion J. Arnold to Thomas Gibbon, October 18, 1911, Gibbon/Bergman Collection, Huntington Library.

53. Los Angeles Ordinance 17135, New Series.

54. The basin's other rivers created borders as well; in 1921, the African American weekly *The New Age* ran a story about the dangers an unchecked San Gabriel River posed to the "Race colony" in the town of Duarte. See *The New Age*, June 10, 1921; thanks to Professor Doug Flamming of Caltech for this reference. See also Sanchez, *Becoming Mexican American*, p. 138.

55. Oxnam diary entry. Note here that "east" Los Angeles traditionally meant both east of the river and also east of Main/Macy. With the industrialization of the river as backdrop, east Los Angeles is increasingly thought to be east of the river, by default. The association, then, is clear: the river increasingly becomes the dividing line between downtown (Anglo) and East (Mexican) Los Angeles, a division which continues to this day.

56. Los Angeles civic leader Marshall Stimson started a housing tract near Elysian Park in 1913 for Mexican occupants only, people who had been living in the dry riverbed; Stimson, *Fun, Fights, and Fiestas in Old Los Angeles* p. 58. See also untitled report of B. B. Bolton, Secretary of the El Monte Welfare Associa-

tion, August 1, 1918, in the Workman family papers, Loyola Marymount University. By 1920, industrialists in Los Angeles argued that the Los Angeles riverbed was "essentially industrial property." The attorney for one major concern inquired of the City Council: "I think it is a fair question if I ask, where will you locate your industries if they are not to be permitted along the Los Angeles river bed?" See Richard Culver, attorney for the Simons Brick Company (discussed in chap. 4), to the Los Angeles City Council, Petition 1163, May 7, 1920, Los Angeles City Archives.

57. See Bartlett, *The Better City*, esp. pp. 32–34.

58. See the biographical sketch of Joseph Mesmer in *From Pueblo to City: Eighteen Hundred and Forty-Nine–Nineteen Hundred and Ten* [no overall author] (Los Angeles: LeBerthon, [1910]). Architectural historian John Crandell calls Mesmer the Robert Moses of Los Angeles. The comparison is an exaggeration, especially given the role of later regional engineers, but it is nonetheless clear that Mesmer is a little-studied but important figure in the history of land use and planning in Los Angeles. See John William Crandell, "Visions of Forgotten Angels: The Evolution of Downtown Los Angeles, 1830–1910," M.A. thesis (Architecture), University of California, Los Angeles, 1990, p. 124.

59. The slogan was used on Chamber of Commerce pamphlets sent out from the city to parts east and abroad.

60. Bromley Oxnam, diary entry, February 24, 1913, Bromley Oxnam Papers, Library of Congress.

61. See Board of Directors Stenographic Minutes, Los Angeles Chamber of Commerce, April 13, 1924. Chamber directors estimated that the floods did $14 million damage.

62. See Bigger, *Flood Control in Metropolitan Los Angeles,* esp. pp. 2–4. As he notes, in reference to this period early in the century, "Lands which historically have been seriously menaced were purchased by those—especially newcomers—who thought that the climate of Los Angeles was all sunshine and warmth."

63. Donald Worster, *Rivers of Empire: Water, Aridity, and the Growth of the American West* (New York: Pantheon 1985), quote on p. 7.

64. See Los Angeles County, Board of Engineers, *Reports of the Board of Engineers, Flood Control* (Los Angeles: n.p., 1915), p. 275. Hereafter *Reports of the Board of Engineers.*

65. "Mr. Mesmer says his memory of early times is much brighter, than of recent times, owing to incidents and facts coming into his life that made them indelible." Mesmer was also composing a history of Los Angeles at this time, a work that unfortunately never got beyond the notecard stage. Joseph Mesmer, Flood Control Interviews. See also the Joseph Mesmer Papers, UCLA Special Collections (for his notes).

66. As Reagan himself later remembered: "I was a stranger in the county at the time, and I sent two very careful men out to search for the old residents, and

I told them not to bother about taking statements from any person who had come to Los Angeles County later than 1885, but to get the earlier ones. And I instructed them to take down the person's statement in their own language, even though it was irregular and ungrammatical, to take it down in their own language." From San Gabriel River Commission, "Reporter's Transcript," vol. 6, March 10, 1926, National Archives Record Group 49, document 033824, National Archives branch, Laguna Niguel, California. My thanks to Jared Orsi for sharing this document with me.

67. See *Reports of the Board of Engineers*, p. 275.

68. The early society had a single Latino officer, the ubiquitous R. F. Del Valle. See inaugural address of J. J. Warner, January 7, 1884, and address of President Ira Moore, 1887, in *Publications of Historical Society of Southern California* 1 (1884–1891); Moore quoted at pp. 12 of 1887 proceedings.

69. See Ford A. Carpenter, "Flood Studies at Los Angeles," *Monthly Weather Review* 42 (June 1914): 385–389.

70. See *Reports of the Board of Engineers*, p. 144.

71. Interestingly, even hydrologic or meteorologic accounts of the region's floods calibrated their destructiveness through reference to anecdotal or local knowledge; many statistical representations of the basin's flood history included remarks that noted what washed away in the floodwaters, what kinds of structures were damaged, etc. Local knowledge of this type was part and parcel of scientific reckoning, but the river's engineers simply did not have it deep enough or far enough back. See Carpenter, "Flood Studies at Los Angeles," esp. p. 388.

72. As Blake Gumprecht points out, engineers believed that the floods of 1862, 1884, and 1889 were larger than 1914; Gumprecht, *The Los Angeles River*, p. 177. McEuen quoted from "A Survey of the Mexicans in Los Angeles."

73. *Los Angeles Times*, July 12, 1914; see also report of H. Hawgood in *Reports of the Board of Engineers*.

74. Flood Control Interviews, Judge G. Sepulveda.

75. Jose Ruiz, Flood Control Interviews.

76. S. B. Reeve, Flood Control Interviews. John Slaughter echoed Reeve: "The people that are coming in here in these later days think that the old timers do not know anything of the floods, but unless something is done soon there will be a great loss of life and property in the next flood." John Slaughter, Flood Control Interviews.

77. The interviewer noted carefully that "Mr. Bernal's aunt remembered the location because she remembered an incident in those days that fixed it clearly in her mind." Joe Bernal, Flood Control Interviews.

78. William Crain and F. Z. Vejar, Flood Control Interviews. Crain had come to Los Angeles in 1858.

79. J. Frank Burns, Flood Control Interviews.

80. Mrs. Lopez, Flood Control Interviews.

81. Jesse Hunter, Flood Control Interviews.

82. J. R. Ramirez, Flood Control Interviews.

83. See *Reports of the Board of Engineers*, p. 3.

84. See *Reports of the Board of Engineers*, [i].

85. McWilliams, *Southern California Country*, pp. 65–66.

86. For preliminary discussion of strategies and plans, see Los Angeles County Flood Control District, "Report of J. W. Reagan," Filed with the Board of Supervisors of the Los Angeles County Flood Control District and Adopted January 2, 1917; copy in Millikan Library, California Institute of Technology. Reagan estimated that the bonding needs would be $4.5 million.

87. "Unsophisticated" flood control measures from early in the twentieth century generally included pilings and great bags of wire filled with stone (called "riprap") to hold in banks. Plans usually included encouragement of bank vegetation, such as willows, to hold and divert water as well. Given the ambition of the project—to "control the river"—such methods would prove unsatisfactory and, more and more, concrete came into favor.

88. *Los Angeles Times*, May 11, 1924.

89. There were exceptions to this certainty, most notably long-time county Supervisor John Anson Ford and his loyal supporters within civil and hydraulic engineering ranks. One such supporter, Donald Baker, wrote that he firmly believed flood control more a problem of "economics and human nature, with construction and hydraulics secondary." See Donald Baker to Herbert Legg, December 13, 1934, in John Anson Ford Papers, Huntington Library. Ford was equally concerned and doubly prescient. He feared that excessive flood control measures necessarily gave short shrift to erosion concerns in the mountains and were merely a kind of here-and-now stopgap, the consequences of which few cared to contemplate. In a thoughtful letter to Henry Wallace, Ford wrote that overzealous control of California waters "relates to the sort of social engineering in which real estate men have little interest. Indeed, the general short focus which results from the ordinary commercial incentives of our present economic set-up, so concentrate our attention on immediate sales and production that we make no provision against ultimate disaster." See John Anson Ford to Henry Wallace, September 2, 1936, John Anson Ford Papers, Huntington Library.

90. Woody Guthrie, "Los Angeles New Year's Flood" copyright 1964 Guthrie Children's Trust Fund. Others put the death toll at half of Woody's estimate. Frances Camareno, who lived in downtown Los Angeles in the Utah Street barrio, remembered that the river had been, before the big flood, "really nice. The neighborhood boys spent most of their time at the river. We had picnics there under the trees. The water was clean and pretty, except for at the Cudahy meat packing house—their water was really dirty. Then after the flood, they covered the river up." As quoted in Cuff, *The Provisional City*, pp. 133–134.

91. Some estimates put the death toll from the 1938 flood much higher;

Gumprecht's estimate of eighty-seven seems more appropriate. See Gumprecht, *The Los Angeles River*, p. 217.

92. See *Parks, Playgrounds, and Beaches for the Los Angeles Region* (a report by the landscape and planning firms Olmsted Brothers and Bartholomew and Associates, distributed in less than 200 copies to the Citizens' Committee on Parks, Playgrounds, and Beaches, 1930); quoted at p. 129. See also Hise and Deverell, *Eden by Design*, and Gumprecht, *The Los Angeles River*, pp. 265–269.

93. John Anson Ford captured his concerns in a phrase; the Corps, he wrote, "are primarily channel builders, not conservationists." What would happen to the mountain watersheds if the sole objective was to run water quickly to the sea? See John Anson Ford to Charles Dunwoody of the California State Chamber of Commerce, July 21, 1937, John Anson Ford Papers, Huntington Library.

94. It did not help the project much, either, when the St. Francis Dam tumbled down in front of a 180-foot-high wall of water in 1928. The public, and the engineering community, gained a little perspective following this tragedy, which killed some four hundred people.

95. Quoted in Coburn, "Whose River?" p. 22.

96. For instance, the very important legal case brought against the city of San Fernando by the city of Los Angeles over the so-called pueblo rights in the late 1960s prompted a judicial finding regarding the distinction between the Los Angeles River's previous incarnation as a river ("the former river") and the concrete channel put into place largely between the late 1930s and the late 1950s. See "Findings of Fact and Conclusions of Law" in the Los Angeles City Water Rights collection at the Huntington Library.

97. Index of American Design materials, Huntington Library.

98. See E. A. Tuttle to Homer Hamlin, December 6, 1907, in Los Angeles City Engineer's Reports, Los Angeles City Archives. It isn't long until the city designates, for planning purposes, an official bed of the Los Angeles River (they had tried for an official channel in the mid-1880s) and official banks as well. That level of municipalization must necessarily threaten the river's continued existence as a river. Even so, the bureaucratic move toward an official bed itself incorporated aspects of an older local knowledge. For instance, an 1890 ordinance describing surveying sequences mentioned a point at which "the official bed is intersected by the ledge of rocks." See Ordinance adopted November 15, 1890; copy in the Solano Reeve Collection; Huntington Library.

99. From a Board of Supervisors request to the Regional Planning Commission, February 1941, in Los Angeles Regional Planning Commission materials, Huntington Library.

100. Los Angeles Regional Planning Commission, *Summary of Report on Feasibility of Los Angeles River Freeway* (Los Angeles: Regional Planning Commission, 1943).

101. "The favorable aspects of the project as a whole are so outstanding as to

be shown almost obvious. There should be nothing surprising in the conclusion that the Los Angeles River forms an effective and superior route for a major artery of communication. For while the city was originally located near the river for the sake of a water supply, and the mouth of the river became an industrial harbor, the urban development has for the most part avoided the immediate banks because of flood hazards. Consequently, the river, penetrating to the industrial and commercial heart of the metropolis from two directions, fortunately preserves throughout most of its length the space necessary for such an artery." *Summary of Report on Feasibility*, p. 9.

102. See Waldie, "The Myth of the L.A. River." As he remarks, "Some decisions about the river cannot be unmade, including the century-old decision of Anglo L.A. to divide the county between upstream and down, and between eastside and westside." In other words, despite contemporary perceptions of the river's meekness, or thoughts that the concrete flood control efforts can be retracted in order to "rediscover" the Los Angeles River, the city and the river are beholden to history.

103. Withers, "Problems of Mexican Boys," p. 23.

104. See Coburn, "Whose River?" for a description of one encounter with a man in search of medicinal herbs at the river's edge.

4. THE COLOR OF BRICKWORK IS BROWN

1. Alejandro Morales, *The Brick People* (Houston: Arte Publico Press, 1988), p. 45.

2. De Schweinitz, "Social Work with Families in Los Angeles," chap. 4 of Young, "Family Case Work."

3. Adele O'Melveney, "The San Gabriel Mission," in *Sierra Madre Vista*, October 1883.

4. "Queer outside stair-case," quoted from the *San Francisco Argonaut* in *Sierra Madre Vista*, July 1881.

5. Edwin Baxter, "Leaves from the Last Decade," *Publications of the Historical Society of Southern California* 3 (1893–1896): 74–79, quoted at p. 79.

6. Mayo, *Los Angeles*, p. 41.

7. Guinn, "Los Angeles in the Adobe Age," *Publications of the Historical Society of Southern California* 4 (1898); see also his "Passing of the Old Pueblo," in which he also marks change by the transitions from adobe to brick. Another temporal link with building material is the classic Sarah Bixby Smith memoir *Adobe Days*.

8. Gonzalez, "Searching for the Feathered Serpent," p. 21.

9. Keller, "The Amateur in Los Angeles." Similarly, Angeleno Joseph Pomeroy Widney, in his quirky *Life and Its Problems, as Viewed by a Blind Man at the Age of Ninety-Six* (Hollywood, Calif.: Joseph P. Widney Publications, 1941), noted the

racialization of ephemeral construction material. "Thus far in his [the Latin's] long racial march, while he built great earthen mounds, and community dwellings, these were of broken stone or of dried earth—the adobe brick of the Mexican" (p. 112).

10. None was more important to the revitalization effort, which did not gain momentum until the 1890s, than irrepressible editor Charles Fletcher Lummis. For a representative Lummis view, see his "Lesson of the Adobe," in *Land of Sunshine*, March 1895, pp. 65–67. Despite his respect for the material and the symbolism it provoked, Lummis nonetheless felt compelled to ask, "what, then, are the lessons the Superior Race might profitably learn from the adobe?"

11. Journal entry, April 10, 1897, John Vance Lauderdale Papers, Beinecke Library. Lauderdale actually transposed the "old Mexican" and "the indian [*sic*] of free and easy ways of living" in his note to himself, as if the two were similar enough to stand in for each other. These transitions that observers like Lauderdale wished to pin on Social Darwinism or racial progression did, of course, have roots in the transitions in the region's political economy and the loss of a *Californio* land base through the 1850s and 1860s. A clear illustration of such change, as it relates to the symbolic role of adobe, can be found in the repetition of adobe structures in the city's delinquent property tax roles. See, for instance, the *Los Angeles Star*, February 5 and 12, 1859.

12. By the early years of the twentieth century, greater Los Angeles had more than twenty brick or pressed brick firms. See, for instance, the *Manufacturers Directory* of 1914 (Los Angeles: Los Angeles Chamber of Commerce) for a listing of firm names. My thanks to Greg Hise for bringing this publication to my attention.

13. *Los Angeles Times*, June 6, 1907. The Simons Brick Company was incorporated in California on March 10, 1900. The Simons family, prior to that, had engaged in brick making in Southern California for about fifteen years, starting out in bustling Pasadena in the late 1880s. See Cecelia Rasmussen, "Brick Firm Cemented Lives, Communities," in *Los Angeles Times*, November 6, 1995.

14. Only a few years after construction of workers' homes at Simons, and not far away, landscape architect Frederick Law Olmsted Jr. sketched out plans for the multi-industry (skilled labor) company town of Torrance for three major industrial firms of Los Angeles and the Dominguez Land Company. For a discussion of Torrance's checkered history, see Margaret Crawford, *Building the Workingman's Paradise: The Design of American Company Towns* (London: Verso, 1995), pp. 89–93, and Robert Phelps, "The Search for a Modern Industrial City: Urban Planning, the Open Shop, and the Founding of Torrance, California," *Pacific Historical Review* 64 (1995): 503–535.

15. A contemporary description of railroad *colonias* can be found in John Kienle's 1912 University of Southern California master's thesis, "Housing Conditions among the Mexican Population of Los Angeles."

16. Crawford, *Building the Workingman's Paradise*, p. 2. For local context, see Phelps, "The Search for a Modern Industrial City."

17. From the diary of Rev. Leo Gariador, O.S.B., October 31, 1905; original manuscript housed in Saint Gregory's Abbey, Shawnee, Oklahoma. My thanks to Rev. Joachim Spexarth for his assistance in bringing this volume to my attention.

18. Thanks to notes supplied to me by genealogist Patti Murray, it appears that two different, and perhaps unrelated, English-born men by the name of Reuben Simons, both of whom migrated to Los Angeles from Iowa, arrived in the late 1880s and went into the brick business. Reuben Garrett Simons was affiliated with the Seventh Street Brick Works and the Capital Brick Company; from genealogical records and notes in author's files. See also Rockwell Hunt, *California and Californians*, 4 vols. (Chicago: Lewis, 1926), 4: 185. Novelist Alejandro Morales, whose Guanajuato parents migrated to Simons in the prewar era, wrote his fascinating novel *The Brick People* about the yard and those who lived and worked there.

19. According to a local paper, the Simons brothers at one point faced charges of excessive cruelty to their mules. See Pasadena *Star News*, August 15, 1931.

20. Pasadenan Beth Broadway (born 1893), remembered the Simons yard running from El Molino to Lake Avenues: "You always saw it when you went on the streetcar." She also remembered that "the only house on Madison in the 1890s was the little brick house, just below California, which the [Simons family] built for the honeymoon cottage of their daughter." From *Talking about Pasadena: Selections from Oral Histories* (Pasadena: Pasadena Oral History Project, 1986), p. 12.

21. See *Architect and Engineer of California* (June 1907): 95.

22. Building permit statistics based on notice about 1922 figures from *Brick and Clay Record* 61 (November 14, 1922): 744.

23. See "Homes of the Spanish Type," published by the Common Brick Manufacturers' Association of America (but produced by Cleveland Publications, Los Angeles), n.d. [ca. 1920]. The publication listed twenty-five models, some designed for working-class incomes, some very large and ornate.

24. The author's thanks to Greg Hise for the simile.

25. Walter Simons quoted in a public health document: H. O. Swartout, M.D., "Survey—Simons Brick Yard," 1944, copy in the John Haynes Papers, Box 252, Special Collections, UCLA. Thanks to Greg Hise for this reference. Hereafter Swartout, "Simons Survey."

26. *Los Angeles Times*, June 6, 1907.

27. Ray Ramirez interview with author, April 14, 1996. Ramirez suggests that a brickyard worker named Jesus Morales from Guanajuato attempted to organize the brick workers. Mexican labor activity in prewar Los Angeles is a subject in need of much more scholarly scrutiny. We know very little about the ties between Simons employees or other Mexican workers in Los Angeles and the ris-

ing Mexican and Mexican American civil rights movement of the late 1930s and 1940s. At the very end of the Depression, for example, the first gathering of the National Congress of Spanish-Speaking Peoples, a wide-ranging civil, political, and labor rights organization for Latino peoples, met in Los Angeles. Participants at that meeting, drawn from over a hundred organizations, discussed common concerns about labor practices, housing, discrimination, and civil rights. Careful reconstruction of the meeting and its concerns would almost certainly reveal connections to the Simons workforce at one plant or another.

For general introductions to the topic of prewar Mexican labor in Los Angeles, see Sanchez, *Becoming Mexican American*, and Devra Weber, Luis Arroyo, and Juan Gomez-Quinones, "The First Steps: Chicano Labor Conflict and Organizing 1900–1920," *Atzlán* 3 (1972): 13–49. A recent and helpful discussion of race and labor in eastern Los Angeles County can be found in Garcia, *A World of Its Own*. See Gutiérrez, *Walls and Mirrors*, for a good introduction to the Congress of Spanish-Speaking Peoples, esp. pp. 110–116.

28. Samuel Clover, *Saturday Night*, December 19, 1925. *Saturday Night* was an elite social magazine of Los Angeles in that era.

29. As Douglas Monroy notes, "the labor market kept twentieth century Mexicans in their place, unlike their more physically restrained forebears." See Monroy, "Like Swallows at the Old Mission: Mexicans and the Racial Politics of Growth in Los Angeles in the Interwar Period," *Western Historical Quarterly* 14 (October 1991): 435–458; quoted at p. 445. For a fuller discussion of Mexican labor in the period, see also Monroy, *Rebirth*.

30. *Los Angeles Times*, June 6, 1907.

31. Many former Simons residents recall that no rent was charged during the winter months. No doubt this feature of the industrial town worked in the company's favor. It was at once compassionate, given the rainy season slowdowns in brick making, and it was clever. Workers were more apt to stay put if they did not have that monthly rental fee of $4 or $5.

32. The memory is that of John C. Clausen, who installed a telephone in one of the houses in the 1930s that was used by as many as forty families. From Charles Elliott, *City of Commerce: An Enterprising Heritage* (Los Angeles: Hacienda Gateway Press, 1991), p. 108.

33. Carlos Almazan tended crops early in the morning, worked a brickyard shift, and then went back to his crops at night. He did this for over a year before quitting the brickyard. See pp. 87–91 in Gamio, *Life Story of the Mexican Immigrant*.

34. Ismael Vargas interview with author, August 22, 1996.

35. Already by the mid-1880s, Baldwin employed over one hundred Mexicans, Indians, and Chinese at his rambling estate; a contemporary noted that Baldwin "wisely" separated these ethnic groups "into little colonies by themselves." Cited in Monroy, "Like Swallows at the Old Mission," p. 443.

36. Walter Malone Jr. recalls that his father would occasionally dismiss yard

workers, who would simply wait until Malone drifted away before they resumed work.

37. Ismael Vargas remembers the Malone brothers as "without prejudice"; Ismael Vargas interview with author, August 22, 1996.

38. Isidrio Osorio was speaking of general laboring work in the United States, not specifically work at the brickyard. See Gamio, *Life Story of the Mexican Immigrant*, pp. 42–45. Penjamo is in the southeastern corner of Guanajuato and, in the mid-1930s, had a population of about 10,000 people. See Gilbert, "A Field Study in Mexico of the Mexican Repatriation Movement," esp. chap. 3. By the mid-1930s, repatriation from the United States had swelled Penjamo's population and increased an unemployment problem.

39. Ray Ramirez interview with author (Ramirez organized a Simons reunion in the 1980s), April 14, 1996; Ernestina Macias interview with author, August 2, 1996.

40. Morales, *The Brick People*, p. 300.

41. Ramirez interview with author, April 14, 1996. See also Clover discussion in *Saturday Night*. Workers' letters, Clover wrote, "did much to counteract German propaganda inimical to our interests." In encouraging immigration from Mexico, the Simons brothers operated from a common position among brick-making capitalists. See, generally, *Brick and Tile Record* 61 (November 28, 1922).

42. Former Simons workers Jess Garcia and Ismael Vargas remember tensions between Mexican-born and U.S.-born Simons residents. The Mexican immigrants "wanted us to be like them," Garcia recalled. From interview with Ismael Vargas and Jess Garcia, October 7, 1996; see also Swartout, "Simons Survey."

43. Ismael Vargas interview with author, August 22, 1996; Ernestina Macias, interview with author, February 16, 1996. See also Gamio, *Life Story of the Mexican Immigrant*, pp. 145–149, for Berzunzolo's interview.

44. Ruth Ewald, "A Survey of the Spanish-Speaking Peoples of the Chaffey Union High School District," M.A. thesis, Pomona College (Romance Language), 1922.

45. See Carlos Almazan interview, pp. 87–91 in Gamio, *Life Story of the Mexican Immigrant*. The name, as with other Gamio informants, is a pseudonym.

46. See pp. 25–28 of Gamio, *Life Story of the Mexican Immigrant*.

47. Subsistence expenditures estimate made by "I. Corralles," foreman of Simonds [*sic*] Brick Company; see McEuen, "A Survey of the Mexicans in Los Angeles," p. 31.

48. Jess Garcia, interview, October 7, 1996.

49. See Gamio, *Mexican Immigration to the United States*.

50. "Old Brickyard Housed Own Community," *Montebello News*, December 21, 1978.

51. Later, when Jack Malone became a sheriff's deputy, he occasionally dropped by Simons for reinforcements when he had a difficult arrest to make.

Ismael Vargas and Jess Garcia interview with author, October 7, 1996; Walter Malone Jr. interview with author August 23, 1996.

52. Ismael Vargas interview, October 7, 1996. A general sense of the danger of brickyard work can be gleaned from the pages of the *Brick and Clay Record*, which regularly reported on yard accidents. See, for instance, the issue of November 28, 1922, with an article entitled "Lost Left Arm Last Year; Now Right," about a brickyard worker in Iowa.

53. Jess Garcia recalls this divide with some frustration, but he also points out that "we didn't like [the white truck drivers] anyway." Jess Garcia interview, October 7, 1996.

54. H. B. Howarth quoted in *Brick and Clay Record* 61 (August 8, 1922): 191.

55. Ramirez interview with author, April 14, 1996. By the 1930s, the baseball team had been replaced by a company softball team.

56. *Los Angeles Times*, June 6, 1907.

57. George Armer, telephone interview with author, August 31, 1996.

58. See Joseph F. Murphy, *Tenacious Monks: The Oklahoma Benedictines, 1875–1975; Indian Missionaries, Catholic Founders, Educators, Agriculturists* (Shawnee, Okla.: Benedictine Color Press, 1974), chap. 10, esp. pp. 264–271.

59. Ismael Vargas interview with author, August 22, 1996.

60. Interview with Alejandro Morales, cited in Julio Martínez and Francísco Lomeli, eds., *Chicano Literature: A Reference Guide* (Westport, Conn.: Greenwood Press, 1985).

61. Jess Garcia interview, October 7, 1996.

62. A mid-1940s survey of the Simons yard noted, "a few children are permitted to attend the Greenwood School in the City of Montebello." See Swartout, "Simons Survey," p. 6. Swartout also notes the prevalence of sickness among the Simons youth, especially during the winter months when their poorly insulated and damp homes would have been germ factories.

63. Ismael Vargas, interview with author, September 11, 1996.

64. Swartout, "Simons Survey," p. 7. Jess Garcia and Ismael Vargas, interview October 7, 1996, also made this point.

65. See W. E. Roop to Harry B. Allen, March 5, 1927, in "Survey of Race Relations" Papers, Hoover Institution Archives, Stanford University.

66. See Stephen A. Privett, "Robert E. Lucey: Evangelization and Catechesis among Hispanic Catholics," Ph.D. diss., Catholic University, 1985, p. 17.

67. From *Proceedings Sixth Annual Convention of Common Brick Manufacturers' Association of America* (Cleveland, [1924]): 7. Hereafter *Proceedings Sixth Annual Convention*.

68. *Proceedings Sixth Annual Convention*, p. 5.

69. See *Southwest Builder and Contractor*, February 15, 1924, pp. 42–43. See also *Los Angeles Times*, February 13 and 14, 1924; also remarks of architect Knickerbacker Boyd, *Proceedings Sixth Annual Convention*, p. 34.

70. Morbidity statistic from G. Bromley Oxnam, "The Mexican in Los Angeles" (Los Angeles: Los Angeles City Survey, 1920), p. 10. See also Reisler, "Always the Laborer, Never the Citizen." A 1925 Los Angeles Health Department report also declared that infant mortality rates for Mexican infants were three times that of whites. Cited in Scott, "The Mexican-American in the Los Angeles Area, 1920–1950," p. 77. There are other instances of this "delayed citizenship" idea for Mexican children; see, for instance, the photographs captioned "the future citizens" in Kienle, "Housing Conditions among the Mexican Population in Los Angeles." On the other hand, it could be argued that contemporary understandings of citizenship simply made it age-specific: age of consent, age of suffrage, age of adulthood, etc. But the recurrence of "future citizen" identifications of Mexican children leads me to believe that there was something else going on beyond mere recognition of chronological immaturity.

71. This is the image of Walter Simons that Ismael Vargas remembers from the early 1930s. Ismael Vargas interview with author, August 22, 1996.

72. By the early 1930s, the gates were gone, but the name, "el puerton," stayed.

73. See Ira Hancock, "A Survey of Public Health Activities in Los Angeles County," [1928] typescript, pp. 41, 43, 45. These statistics suggest that the Progressive-Era "rule of thumb" calculation, that Mexican infant mortality was three times that of white statistics, was conservative. In 1918, for instance, at the height of the flu epidemic, Mexican infant mortality was registered at nearly 350 of 1000 births, five times that of white babies. The report goes on to suggest, though without statistical support, that the rate for Mexican infant mortality could be, in certain times or districts apparently, as much as *eight times* that of whites. This is at virtually the same time in which the tourist-encouraging "All Year Club" is claiming, "in California infant mortality is lower than elsewhere in the nation." See the All Year Club's 1920s pamphlet "Southern California through the Camera."

74. See *Municipal League of Los Angeles Bulletin*, February 6, 1925, p. 3. The other five firms were the Davidson Brick Company, the Southern Pacific Railroad, the Los Angeles Gas and Electric Company, Griffith Engineering Company, and the Los Angeles Street Railway.

75. Ismael Vargas interview with author, August 22, 1996. The irony of this was that, during the 1930s, when numerous Mexicans were sent across the border during the repatriation movement, the language tables could be turned. As one Guanajuato boy, raised in Los Angeles, stated regarding his use of English in Mexico. "They call us Northerners and we attract attention because we always talk English among ourselves. One time a cop heard us talking English and he called us over and bawled us out. He asked us what nationality we were and we said 'Mexicans.' 'Well,' he said, 'why don't you talk Spanish? When you are in Mexico, talk Spanish!' . . . He said he would put us in the can if he heard us talk-

ing English, but shucks, we walk past him about every day talking English and he hasn't said a word. A lot of people don't like it when they hear us talking English among ourselves, but we don't care. If they don't like it, they can go ——." Gilbert, "A Field Study in Mexico of the Mexican Repatriation Movement," p. 152.

76. Ernestina Macias, interview with author, February 23, 1996. See also Gamio, *Life Story of the Mexican Immigrant*, pp. 87–91.

77. In the baptismal records of Our Lady of Mount Carmel, dating from the 1920s, the Simons addresses are rendered in Latin, as "Simons Domus No. 12," "Simons Domus No. 16," etc., or the simple directional location "Simons prope Rio Hondo [River]." Our Lady of Mount Carmel baptismal record, housed at St. Benedict's Church, Montebello. The author's thanks to Fr. Timothy Malone for his assistance in accessing these records.

78. According to brick manufacturer's figures, Los Angeles brick production rose from approximately fifty million in 1919 to 250 million by 1923. See *Southwest Builder and Contractor*, February 15, 1924. The firm that made Plymouth Locomotives advertised their use in the brickyard, printing a testimonial from Walter Malone that the engines worked well on the brickyard's short-gauge rail line. See, for instance, *Southwest Builder and Contractor*, April 25, 1924.

79. See Richard Culver to the City Council of Los Angeles, Petition 1163, May 7, 1920, Los Angeles City Archives. An excellent overview of pre–World War II Los Angeles industrialization is Greg Hise, "Industry and Imaginative Geographies," in Tom Sitton and William Deverell, eds., *Metropolis in the Making: Los Angeles in the 1920s* (Berkeley and Los Angeles: University of California Press, 2001).

80. For insight into the daily life of the yard, see Morales, *The Brick People*.

81. J. B. Ransom Organization, *Montebello Park—The Model Community of the New East Side* (Los Angeles: J. B. Ransom Organization, 1925). Page 11 of the report proudly displays a photograph of the Simons brickyard and, if I am not mistaken, page 15's photograph of "one of Montebello's beautiful residences" is the brick, faux-Tudor home of Simons yard general superintendent Walter Malone. "Splendid workers" quote from "Facts About Industrial Los Angeles—Nature's Workshop" (Los Angeles: Los Angeles Chamber of Commerce, 1926). See also "Special Report by Industrial Department, Los Angeles Chamber of Commerce," April 1930, 2 vols., Huntington Library. As this report summarized, the "common labor situation of a community is a true test of its skilled labor conditions, and Los Angeles is one of the best common labor markets in the United States, whether it be in the construction or manufacturing industry." For further discussion of the imposition of a dual labor system in the Southwest, see Gutiérrez, *Walls and Mirrors*; Albert Camarillo, *Chicanos in a Changing Society*; Romo, *East Los Angeles*; Almaguer, *Racial Fault Lines*; and Barrera, *Race and Class in the Southwest*.

82. J. B. Ransom Organization, *Montebello Park*; see also Montebello Chamber of Commerce, *You'll Like Montebello* ([Montebello: The Chamber], 1924). Also helpful is David Firman, "Montebello, California: Some Geographical Aspects of a Satellite City in the Los Angeles Basin," M.A. thesis, UCLA, 1949. In classic Southern California style, Montebello briefly changed its descriptive title in the late 1920s to "The City of Flowers with an Oil Well Payroll" and, later, to "The City of Flowers and Suburban Homes." Firman, "Some Geographical Aspects," pp. 35–36.

83. William Fox, "Seven Decades of Planning and Development in the Los Angeles Region: General William J. Fox" (UCLA Oral History, 1989), p. 99.

84. George Armer, telephone interview with author, August 31, 1996.

85. Ismael Vargas interview, September 11, 1996.

86. See *Brick and Clay Record* 78 (May 5, 1931): 483–484, and 82 (April 1933): 127–128.

87. Jess Garcia interview, October 7, 1996. Walter Malone Jr. tells of a time when INS agents asked a well-known Simons worker if he had any relatives in the United States. His reply, "yes, my Uncle Sam," apparently satisfied them, and they left him alone. Malone's father then asked him who this uncle was, and he was told that he was "the same Uncle Sam as your Uncle Sam." Malone interview, August 23, 1996. On repatriation, see Abraham Hoffman, *Unwanted Mexican Americans in the Great Depression: Repatriation Pressures, 1929–1939* (Tucson: University of Arizona Press, 1974), and Neil Betten and Raymond A. Mohl, "From Discrimination to Repatriation: Mexican Life during the Great Depression," *Pacific Historical Review* 42 (August 1973): 370–388.

88. "Ernie" Macias and Walter Malone have suggested this to me in several different interviews, as has Jess Garcia (October 7, 1996). Ray Ramirez remembers that the Simons workers walked off the job for a month. A scholarly overview of labor organizing among Mexican workers in Los Angeles and the agricultural hinterland in the period is Devra Weber, "The Organizing of Mexicano Agricultural Workers: Imperial Valley and Los Angeles, 1928–1934, An Oral History Approach," *Atzlán* 3 (Fall 1972): 307–347.

89. At least one late 1930s case of typhus originated in Simons, prompting fumigation of Simons houses and quarantine of the victim. See Swartout, "Simons Survey," p. 5.

90. From Swartout, "Simons Survey," citing the 1940 report of Health Inspector U. Troiano.

91. Attorney Stanley Hahn, who helped to settle the Simons land sale, remembers that burning the old Simons homes was an emotional event for many former residents. Stanley Hahn interview with author, April 2, 1996. For a scholarly analysis of "lost places" in twentieth-century Los Angeles (like Simons Brick Yard No. 3), see Cuff, *The Provisional City*.

92. See the *Los Angeles Times*, August 9, 1952; January 16, 1953; and Novem-

ber 9, 1954 for these stories and the obituary of Walter Robey Simons; see also the *Los Angeles Examiner*, April 8, 1953. Judge's remark recalled by Stanley Hahn; Stanley Hahn interview with author, April 2, 1996. See also the *Los Angeles Examiner*, April 8, 1953. Mrs. Simons left an additional amount of money in trust, approximately $40,000, for some of the longtime Simons workers.

93. Gamio, *Mexican Immigration*, p. 84.

94. Ismael Vargas interview with author, August 22, 1996. Likewise, Ernestina Macias remembers Simons as a place free from everyday acts of discrimination and prejudice, precisely because the community was effectively closed to non-Mexicans. Ernestina Macias, interview with author, August 2, 1996.

5. ETHNIC QUARANTINE

1. Quoted in *Los Angeles Times* story ("Southwest Has Big Advantages"), May 27, 1923. Rosenthal also repeated that chestnut of Los Angeles boosterism: "We have no slums." Like all others who claimed the same, Rosenthal was dead wrong.

2. Monica Highland [pseud.], *Lotus Land* (New York: Coward-McCann, 1983), p. 112. This book is a remarkable fictional account of the Los Angeles plague outbreak.

3. Charles Dwight Willard, booster *extraordinaire*, started the *Land of Sunshine* in 1894. The journal eventually became less boosterish in tone and content, especially once Charles Fletcher Lummis took over editorial duties and changed the magazine's name to *Out West*. In its earlier life, however, the journal was little more than a Chamber of Commerce megaphone. See chap. 2 for additional discussion of the journal.

4. For insightful readings of regional boosterism in the period, see, among others, Norman M. Klein and Martin J. Schiesl, eds., *20th Century Los Angeles: Power, Promotion and Social Conflict* (Claremont, Calif.: Regina Books, 1990), esp. chap. 1; Clark Davis, "From Oasis to Metropolis: Southern California and the Changing Context of American Leisure," *Pacific Historical Review* 61 (August 1992): 357–386; Starr, *Inventing the Dream,* and Starr, *Material Dreams: Southern California through the 1920s* (New York: Oxford University Press, 1990), esp. chap. 5; Robert Fogelson, *The Fragmented Metropolis: Los Angeles 1850–1930* (Berkeley and Los Angeles: University of California Press, 1993); Davis, *City of Quartz*, esp. chaps. 1 and 2; see also William Deverell, "Privileging the Mission over the Mexican: The Rise of Regional Consciousness in Southern California," in David Wrobel and Michael Steiner, eds., *Many Wests: Place, Culture and Regional Identity* (Lawrence: University Press of Kansas, 1997).

5. Some sense of the degree to which typicality informed the ways in which Los Angeles constructed and understood all kinds of cultural categories can be gained even by examination of non-Anglo promotional vehicles. The typicality

trope crossed racial bounds, and it was present as well among the African American community. For instance, the proud pamphlet "Western Progress," published in 1928 by two African American entrepreneurs, highlighted the "economic and social advancement in Los Angeles" through these now-familiar images. Businesses, homes, sunshine, flowers, etc. all were exhibited as representative images of African American life in the city. The Conner-Johnson Funeral Home, for instance, "typifies so well the progressive west" and Nickerson's Drug Store stood as "an excellent example of the new idea in western business." See Louis Tenette and B. B. Bratton, *Western Progress: A Pictorial Story of Economic and Social Advancement in Los Angeles, California* (Los Angeles: Tenette & Bratton, 1928). African American boosterism, and its relationship to Anglo boosterism, has been discussed in William Deverell and Douglas Flamming, "Race and Regional Identity: Black and White Boosters in Los Angeles, 1880–1930," in Richard White and John Findlay, eds., *Power and Place in the North American West* (Seattle: University of Washington Press, 1999), pp. 117–143.

6. "Facts About Industrial Los Angeles—Nature's Workshop" (Los Angeles: Los Angeles Chamber of Commerce, 1926). For an earlier depiction of the reflex, see *Los Angeles California, Queen City of the Angels* (Los Angeles: M. Rieder, ca. 1907) with its pamphlet depictions of the city's "typical Mission residence" and "typical cottage house" (both extremely large). Someone who saw through the typical trope, who saw it merely as "whooping it up for the sunshine and glorious Southern California," was the prominent Socialist newspaperman Frank Wolfe. Of "typical" workingmen's homes, Wolfe said that the proud imagery always failed to indicate "the mortgages on those homes " which "would reach from here to Santa Barbara." See testimony of Frank Wolfe in U.S. Senate, Report of the Commission on Industrial Relations, "Open and Closed Shop Controversy in Los Angeles," 1914, quoted at p. 5847. The author's thanks to Mike Davis for this last reference.

7. For representations of Mexican typicality see, for instance, Kienle, "Housing Conditions among the Mexican Population of Los Angeles." As he wrote of his research design (p. 2), "the idea was not to have the investigations confined to one locality or any particular type of construction, but to cover the vast area dotted with Mexican homes, thus endeavoring to select those in each community, which, in my judgment, were typical of the rest." Kienle had opened his discussion with an apparent nod to diversity among the Mexican population in Los Angeles, pointing out that "there are many Mexicans in Los Angeles, who are divided into different classes." Two pages later, however, he points out that "there are three classes of Mexicans."

8. From "Plague in Los Angeles, 1924–25," bound manuscript produced by the California State Board of Health, copy in the Huntington Library, subchapter 1, p. 49; hereafter "Plague in Los Angeles." Other sources I have found helpful include James H. Jones, *Bad Blood: The Tuskegee Syphilis Experiment*

(New York: Free Press, 1981), esp. chap. 2; Hans Zinsser, *Rats, Lice and History: The Biography of a Bacillus* (Boston: Little, Brown, 1934); Alan Brandt, *No Magic Bullet: A Social History of Venereal Disease in the United States since 1880* (New York: Oxford University Press, 1987); Nayan Shah, *Contagious Divides: Epidemics and Race in San Francisco's Chinatown* (Berkeley and Los Angeles: University of California Press, 2001); Alan M. Kraut, *Silent Travelers: Germs, Genes, and the "Immigrant Menace"* (Baltimore: Johns Hopkins University Press, 1994); and Natalia Molina, "Contested Bodies and Cultures: The Politics of Public Health and Race within Mexican, Japanese, and Chinese Communities in Los Angeles, 1879–1939," Ph.D. diss., University of Michigan, 2001. See also Highland, *Lotus Land,* esp. pp. 100–120.

9. Clara Street is directly behind the Terminal Annex Post Office on Alameda Street (not yet built in 1924), within sight of downtown Los Angeles. A penal complex today dominates the little bit of Clara Street still in existence.

10. See Helen Martin, *The History of the Los Angeles County Hospital (1878–1968) and the Los Angeles County–University of Southern California Medical Center (1968–1978)* (Los Angeles: University of Southern California Press, 1979), chap. 15: "The Plague Epidemic." Years later, a Los Angeles physician tracked down Luciana Samarano's midwife, who had not contracted plague. The midwife verified that Luciana had delivered a stillborn child on the very day that she died. See John Emmett to Alexander Langmuir, July 17, 1952, in miscellaneous correspondence files, Communicable Disease Division, City and County of Los Angeles Health Services Department. *El Heraldo de Mexico,* November 4, 1924, listed Luciana Samarano's age as thirty-eight.

11. Brualla is buried in the clergy burial plot at the San Gabriel Mission.

12. Martin, *History of the Los Angeles County Hospital,* p. 68.

13. Emil Bogen, "The Pneumonic Plague in Los Angeles," typescript, author's copy, p. 9; hereafter, Bogen, plague typescript. See also Bogen, "The Pneumonic Plague in Los Angeles," *California and Western Medicine* (February 1925): 175–176.

14. Maria Valenzuela was sent to the county hospital on October 31, just as the Belvedere Gardens quarantine got underway. Her mother, however, was not. One of the county physicians wrote that Guadalupe Valenzuela, along with her son and another daughter, were "appreciably under the influence of liquor" and that he "was not concerned regarding her condition." She died on November 3; see the narrative of county plague response, "Plague," in miscellaneous correspondence files, City and County Health Services. The author of this document was probably county public health officer Dr. J. L. Pomeroy.

15. Highland, *Lotus Land,* p. 105.

16. The Jimenez brothers' landlady on Date Street said later that she thought they had moved in on October 28. See California State Board of Health, Special Bulletin 46, *Pneumonic Plague: Report of an Outbreak at Los Angeles, California,*

October–November, 1924 (Sacramento: California State Board of Health, 1925), p. 8.

17. The Mercurochrome solution was "30 cubic centimeters of a 1 per cent solution," administered several times over the course of a week. It is difficult to determine how old Raul Samarano was at the time of the epidemic. Some texts (e.g., Martin, *History of the Los Angeles County Hospital*) argue that Raul was the fourteen-month-old son of Luciana and Guadalupe. Eyewitness accounts suggest that he was older, somewhere between six and nine years old. A photograph in "Plague in Los Angeles" indicates that Raul was a young boy, and he himself verified this years later. A 1960 story in the *Los Angeles Examiner* about the plague brought about an impromptu reunion of Raul Samareno [*sic*] and Dr. Elmer Anderson, one of the physicians who had first responded to the Macy Street quarter illnesses. After the epidemic rendered him an orphan, Raul lived with relatives, became a ward of the state in foster homes, worked for the Civilian Conservation Corps in the thirties, joined the Navy, and ended up with a position in the Army Corps of Engineers in Los Angeles County. See *Los Angeles Examiner*, March 14, 1960. Bogen, in plague typescript, p. 9, refers to Raul as an eight-year-old. The death grip of disease was actually the work of two different strains of plague: most of the cases were diagnosed as the more deadly and contagious pneumonic plague, a few others were identified as bubonic plague. According to a graph in *Pneumonic Plague: Report of an Outbreak at Los Angeles, California, October–November, 1924*, the plague outbreak (both strains) killed the following thirty-three individuals, spelling maintained as printed: Francisca Lujon, Lucena Samarano, Guadalupe Samarano, Jessie Flores, Ruth San Ramon, Josephe Christenson, Peter Hernandez, Roberto Samarano, Gilberto Samarano, Victor Samarano, Marie Samarano, Alfredo Burnett, Father Brualla, Urbano Hurtado, Joe Bagnolio, Juliano Herrera, Fred Ortega, Arthur Gutierrez, Horace Gutierrez, Efren Herrera, Jesus Valenzuela, Juana Moreno, Refugio Ruiz, Guadalupe Valenzuello, John McLoughlin, Mike Jimenez, Jose Jimenez, Tomasa Vera, Lujo Peralta, Frank Perinlo, Maria Rodriguez, Mercedo Rodriguez, and Martin Hernandez [Abedannio]. In some cases, I have checked spellings in the 1924 Los Angeles City Directory; in others I have relied on the documentation within "Plague in Los Angeles." All plague victims except for ambulance driver McLauthlin died at General Hospital. McLauthlin died at St. Vincent's. There remains some confusion as to the identity of the four Samarano brothers; I suspect that one of them was named Victor (Raul, Roberto, Gilberto, and Victor). This would mean that the disease killed two Victor Samaranos: the young boy and his uncle. The other, equally plausible scenario given the poor record keeping of the period, is that there were actually only three Samarano brothers, not four as eyewitness accounts suggest. See also Dr. Emil Bogen's plague typescript, author's copy. Bogen writes that the disease killed thirty-four individuals (thirty

from pneumonic plague, four from bubonic). My thanks to Dr. Bogen's daughter, Dr. Ellen Alkon, for making this typescript available to me.

18. Bogen, plague typescript, p. 5.

19. Walter Dickie to William Lacy, November 15, 1924; copy in City Council Petition 7340, Los Angeles City Archives.

20. One radical labor group in Chicago predicted that plague would be the result of class, race, and ethnic segmentation in Los Angeles. Just a month before the outbreak, the *Industrial Pioneer* ran a cartoon depicting California as a capitalist rattlesnake, spitting venom of crime and disease. The cartoon, which urged a complete boycott of California products until it released political prisoners, blasted the state as "the land of rattlesnakes and plague, earthquakes and volcanoes, poverty and grasping greed. Out of it come like a miasma, hoof and mouth disease, botulism, poisoned celery, typhoid fever, and occasionally the Asiatic scourge, the dread bubonic." This was, certainly in part, a reference to the plague outbreak in San Francisco at the beginning of the century, but it does predict events in the Macy Street district of Los Angeles only weeks later. Cartoon reprinted in a Better America Federation flyer entitled "Usual Tactics of Misrepresentation," n.d., Better America Federation Collection, Bancroft Library.

21. As historian George Sanchez has noted with particular reference to Los Angeles, "Americanization programs are an important window for looking at the assumptions made about both Mexican and American culture by progressive Californians during the 1920s." For studies of local Progressive reform, see Mary Odem, *Delinquent Daughters: Protecting and Policing Adolescent Female Sexuality in the United States, 1885–1920* (Chapel Hill: University of North Carolina Press, 1995); William Deverell and Tom Sitton, eds., *California Progressivism Revisited* (Berkeley and Los Angeles: University of California Press, 1994); and Sanchez, *Becoming Mexican American,* esp. chap. 4, quoted at p. 106.

22. Quoted in Arthur Viseltear's excellent essay, "The Pneumonic Plague Epidemic of 1924 in Los Angeles," *Yale Journal of Biology and Medicine* 47 (March 1974): 40–54, quoted at p. 41. The author's thanks to his father, Dr. William Deverell, for help in finding and interpreting Viseltear's essay.

23. Quoted in Viseltear, "Pneumonic Plague Epidemic," p. 41. Viseltear also notes that both the *New York Times* and the *Washington Post* quickly picked up the story.

24. "Plague in Los Angeles," subchapter 12, p. 11. Retired Los Angeles physician Edward Shapiro remembers riding the Pacific Electric to his weekly violin lesson during the epidemic and hearing the conductor yell for everyone to stay on the train as it sped through quarantined neighborhoods. Author phone interview with Edward Shapiro, August 7, 1996.

25. "Plague in Los Angeles," subchapter 12, p. 7. An informed discussion of the Los Angeles civic and commercial elite can be found in Starr, *Material*

Dreams, chap. 6; see also Davis, *City of Quartz,* esp. chaps. 1 and 2; and Jaher, *The Urban Establishment.*

26. "Plague in Los Angeles," subchapter 1, p. 27.

27. Delivery of food proved absolutely critical, as some families, caught as they were in the quarantine nets, ran out of food very quickly. See *El Heraldo de Mexico,* November 4, 1924.

28. "Plague in Los Angeles" listed Belvedere's Mexican population caught in the quarantine as five hundred (a figure that seems absurdly low). At other times, health officials admitted that the entire Mexican population of Belvedere ranged from seven to twenty thousand. The truth is that no one knew how many people lived there (or in any other poor neighborhood of Los Angeles). Census records are notoriously unreliable. Los Angeles journalist Timothy Turner wrote a short story about a Mexican couple from the neighborhood in which he describes the area's poverty. "Pepe and Encarnción lived in that part of Los Angeles that had the elegant name of Belvedere Gardens. The street they lived in was one of squalor, scented with aromatic chile and decorated with silk lamp-shades and bright advertising calendars." Turner, *Turn off the Sunshine: Tales of Los Angeles on the Wrong Side of the Tracks* (Caldwell, Idaho: Caxton, 1942), p. 37.

29. One guard, evidently seeking a promotion up through the ranks, pointed out that he had been in charge of the "general cleanliness + disinfection of a German Prisoner of War camp in France." See E. Teasdale to Carl Williams, November 9, 1924, in "Applications" file, City and County Health Services. The $5-a-day wage would have made guards among the highest paid people within the quarantine boundaries, plague or no plague.

30. Ethnic quarantine was old news in Los Angeles by the 1920s. The region had even seen local resolutions passed in some communities that expressly prohibited access by Mexicans and Native Americans during, especially, smallpox epidemics. El Monte did so in 1863; a worried Anglo noted a "resort to arms" in the process. See King, "El Monte." See also Ronald C. Woolsey, "Rites of Passage? Anglo and Mexican-American Contrasts in a Time of Change: Los Angeles, 1860–1870," *Southern California Quarterly* 69 (1987): 81–101. An 1880s smallpox outbreak had been "introduced by the clothing of some visiting Mexicans," a contemporary pamphlet claimed; H. S. Orme, *Smallpox in Los Angeles in 1887* (Los Angeles?, [1888]). This outbreak of smallpox claimed at least fifteen lives, and local authorities were so convinced that the disease vector ran as a straight line directly to/from Mexico (and Mexicans) that they began checking rail cars for Mexican immigrants. Pomeroy admitted that he had gone home before establishing much of the quarantine perimeter on October 31 because "the hour was late." Of yet another quarantining incident, he wrote ominously that, despite "considerable resistance from the Mexicans . . . military quarantine soon brought them to terms." See J. L. Pomeroy's report for 1924 in miscellaneous correspondence files, City and County Health Services. See also the narrative description of county

response, "Plague," in miscellaneous correspondence files. While it is most likely that the author of this latter document was county chief Pomeroy, there is a slight chance that it was one of the quarantine's other physicians, a Dr. Roth.

31. The totals for one of the details ran to twenty-six dogs, eighty-five cats, five chickens, and a goat killed in eleven days of quarantine labor. See C R. Williams to J. L. Pomeroy, November 17, 1924, miscellaneous correspondence files, City and County Health Services Department.

32. See "Claims—Damages, etc." file in City and County Health Services Department.

33. The food, which, presumably, quarantine guards either ate or threw away, included hundreds of large and small tamales, 90 pounds of chili, and 75 pounds of mixtamel [sic]. See Benigno Guerrero to Pomeroy, November 11, 1924, and Guerrero to Los Angeles County Board of Health, n.d.; "Claims—Damages, etc." file.

34. Cyanide and monoxide treatments may have come into use primarily once the United States Public Health Service took over much of the rat killing in the summer of 1925. See the *Annual Report of the Surgeon General of the United States Public Health Service, 1926* (Washington, D.C.: Government Printing Office, 1926), pp. 80–81. See also Walter Dickie, transcription of remarks before the City Council of Los Angeles and Board of Directors, Los Angeles Chamber of Commerce, November 15, 1924, in City Council petition #7340. I cannot find any contemporary suggestion that raising houses off the ground and above their foundations was a bad idea in earthquake country. San Francisco public health authorities seem to have pioneered this idea. See the photograph on page 37 of Frank Morton Todd, *Eradicating Plague from San Francisco: Report of the Citizens' Health Committee and an Account of Its Work* [San Francisco, ca. 1909]. See also Guenter B. Risse, "'A Long Pull, A Strong Pull, and All Together': San Francisco and Bubonic Plague, 1907–1908," *Bulletin of the History of Medicine* 66 (Summer 1992): 260–286. See also *Annual Report of the Los Angeles County Department of Health, 1924* (Los Angeles: County Department of Health, 1925). The quotation "destroy a large part of Los Angeles" comes from a retirement notice for plague detail member Charles Stewart, *Los Angeles Herald Examiner*, October 17, 1958. For analysis of the continuation of such destructive practices in the name of urban renewal in 1940s and 1950s Los Angeles, see Cuff, *The Provisional City*, esp. chaps. 16–22.

35. See Dickie transcription, November 15, 1924; see also *Annual Report of Department of Health of the City of Los Angeles California for the year ended June 30, 1925* (Los Angeles, n.p., 1925), p. 60; hereafter *Annual Report 1925*.

36. At his retirement, it was noted that former plague sanitary detail commander Charles Stewart alone superintended the destruction of over three thousand buildings. See Health Department press release, October 17, 1958, "Plague Reference" file; City and County Health Services Department.

37. In one month alone, apparently, 600,000 pieces of poisoned bait were distributed in the industrial and commercial district down by the Los Angeles River. Charles Stewart, one of the foremen of a rat-killing detail, remembered years later that he "couldn't sleep at night. . . . Small children in the district often attempted to eat our 'rat sandwiches.' More than once I slapped a piece of poisoned bread out of a kid's hand." Stewart said no children ingested any of the poison, an assertion somewhat difficult to believe given the sheer amount of "rat molasses" spread around the various neighborhoods. See Health Department press release (marking Stewart's retirement), October 17, 1958, in "Plague Reference" file, Health Services Department; also undated newspaper clipping "City in Nightmare: How L.A. Battled Plague," by Ben Zinser, same file. The "dainty poison crouton" label comes from San Francisco; see Todd, *Eradicating Plague from San Francisco.* See also the Annual Report of the United States Public Health Service, 1926.

38. The operation, militarized and beholden to perceptions of ethnicity, has a certain "La Fiesta gone crazy" feel to it. By May 1925, the number of rats killed by the program was estimated to be over one hundred thousand. Of these, 182 tested positive for plague.

39. See "L.A. Tenement Problem and the Bubonic-Pneumonic Plagues: Report of Survey by Representatives of Nine Leading Organizations," *Municipal League of Los Angeles Bulletin* 7 (February 1925): 2–6. On the tendency of the dominant culture to create dichotomies between "native Americans" and "Mexicans," see the insightful discussion in Haas, *Conquests and Historical Identities in California,* chap. 5.

40. See "Los Angeles and the Plague," in *California and Western Medicine* 23 (February 1925): 191.

41. "Plague in Los Angeles," subchapter 1, p. 52.

42. Bogen, plague typescript, p. 9. Viseltear notes that the maker of the plague serum wasted no time in advertising the company's role (which was actually negligible) in stamping out the Los Angeles plague. See Viseltear, "Pneumonic Plague," pp. 43–44.

43. Dickie's remarks transcribed in Stenographer's Reports, Board of Directors meeting, Los Angeles Chamber of Commerce, November 6, 1924; Regional History Center, University of Southern California.

44. Health officials nonetheless declared the Los Angeles harbor "plague infected" at the end of the year, despite the fact that no disease-laden rodent had been discovered there. See Viseltear, "Pneumonic Plague," pp. 49–51.

45. *Los Angeles Herald Examiner,* November 16, 1924.

46. See Stenographer's Reports, November 26, 1924. The Chamber of Commerce had earlier appointed a new health and sanitation committee, composed of "physicians, health officers, business men, city editors and local publishers and charity and school organizations." "Plague in Los Angeles," subchapter 12, p. 8.

47. Dickie, in a letter to Los Angeles mayor George Cryer, wrote that the "rapidity with which this epidemic was brought under control has been accomplished only by the cooperation of Federal, State, County and Municipal departments, and by the assistance given by the Chamber of Commerce and the local publishers." See Dickie to Cryer, December 8, 1924, in "Plague in Los Angeles," *Los Angeles Realtor,* December 1924, (Los Angeles: The Los Angeles Realty Board), p. 7. Chamber of Commerce members agreed in mid-November that they ought to get the word out regarding "the absolute truth of this little flare up of the plague." Stenographer's Reports, November 13, 1924.

48. See W. B. Knox, "Los Angeles' Campaign of Silence," *Nation* 121 (1925): 646–647. A later *Nation* article regretted Knox's hyperbole but stood by the assertion of a concerted public relations campaign to mask the true details of public health problems in Los Angeles. See "Los Angeles and Its News," *Nation* 122 (1926): 272.

49. See Stenographer's Reports, Board of Directors meetings of the Los Angeles Chamber of Commerce, October 30, 1924.

50. In the first weeks of 1924, the city faced a serious smallpox outbreak that the Board of Directors of the Chamber of Commerce wanted kept quiet ("it would be poor policy to publish it in the newspapers"). See Minutes of the Board of Directors, Los Angeles Chamber of Commerce, January 9 and January 31, 1924.

51. See Minutes of the Board of Directors, Los Angeles Chamber of Commerce, November 13, 1924; telephone interview with Edward Shapiro, August 7, 1996. Mr. Shapiro remembers his father as a regular reader of the *Los Angeles Times* as well. Several years after the epidemic, Morrow Mayo, who certainly knew the local scene, wrote in mock seriousness that it was "considered very unpatriotic in the City of Angels for any journalist to spread abroad unpleasant news, such as a hoof-and-mouth disease, a tainted-water scandal, an infantile-paralysis epidemic, a tax trap, or an outbreak of bubonic plague." Mayo, *Los Angeles,* p. 320.

52. *El Heraldo de Mexico,* November 4, 1924. Robert McLean, in his reformist tract *That Mexican!* (p. 150), chastised the white press for publishing news of the plague outbreak "in the columns on the back pages of the newspapers—columns which are reserved for the stories of the earthquakes." He added, in an apparent jibe at the quarantine practices, which he may have thought more people-centered than rodent-centered, that "infected rats cannot read the quarantine regulations, and move with perfect freedom from one quarter of the city to another."

53. Minutes of the Board of Directors, Los Angeles Chamber of Commerce, November 13, 1924.

54. Transcription of Walter Dickie's remarks, November 15, 1924, is in the petitions of the Los Angeles City Council #7340 held at the City Archives of Los Angeles.

55. Mexican consul Almeda registered protests with the city and the Chamber of Commerce over these dismissals. The Chamber of Commerce agreed to work toward the reinstatement of those workers who did not live within the quarantined districts. Those that did were out of luck.

56. Dickie transcription, November 15, 1924, emphasis added. It is illustrative that despite earlier concerns about other poor and predominantly ethnic neighborhoods housing Russians, Asians, and others, Dickie's explicit reference regarding autopsies is to Mexicans, and only to Mexicans. The suggestion is, I think, that plague transmission had become a supposed vector of ethnicity and not of class. Acting Health Commissioner Elmer Pascoe quoted in the *San Francisco Chronicle*, November 2, 1924.

57. Dickie transcription, November 15, 1924. Of course getting the Chamber members to go to Macy Street would have been a problem even if plague weren't whipping around the poor neighborhood. These are the very same business leaders who had been chastised by a fellow member of the Chamber only months before for not even bothering to look at flyers or leaflets calling for additional public expenditure, on social reform, homes for wayward girls, that sort of thing. See Board of Directors, Los Angeles Chamber of Commerce, Stenographic Minutes, May 8, 1924, comments of Frank Wiggins.

58. Dickie transcription, November 15, 1924.

59. Dickie transcription, November 15, 1924. It was not as if no one saw the potential for trouble well before the epidemic. Lillian Simpson, for instance, of the Los Angeles City Department of Health wrote of conditions in Maravilla Park, just east of the city limits (and a plague vector neighborhood) a year and a half before the outbreak. "The conditions which prevail are appalling due to lack of proper housing and sanitation which is a result of cheap lots marketed to these people who are too poor to do more than make an initial payment and buy a few boards and nails, and these together with what boxes they can collect represent the type of average 'home.'" Lillian Simpson to J. J. McGinnis, March 28, 1923, Archival Center. "Largest Mexican school" quote comes from Stenographer's Reports, November 26, 1924.

60. In later months, when the United States Public Health Service took over some of the plague suppression activities, it was noted that the policy of destroying homes willy nilly was "expensive, time consuming, and devoid of any great benefits." See *Annual Report of the Surgeon General, 1926*, p. 80. This sentiment, to be sure, was a case of too little, too late.

61. [George Parrish], *Annual Report of Department of Health of the City of Los Angeles California for the Year Ended June 30, 1925* (Los Angeles, n.p., 1925).

62. In a small pamphlet published about a year after the outbreak, the Los Angeles County Medical Association celebrated both "the limited number of deaths" and absence of "a money loss, which, while running into the millions,

could have been, five, or ten or twenty times as great!" Los Angeles County Medical Association, "The Bubonic and Pneumonic Plague: Some Questions and Answers in Regard Thereto" (Los Angeles, [County Medical Association, 1926?]). According to the pamphlet's author, "only a Kind Providence, and extremely prompt action by the health and other authorities of the city of Los Angeles, and the State of California, enabled our city of Los Angeles to come out of that experience with a limited number of deaths."

63. "Plague in Los Angeles," subchapter 12, p. 4. The Chinatown plague of 1900, according to one physician who studied it, was "one of the darkest pages in the history of North American medicine" in that an effort was made by business and political leaders to cover up the outbreak and silence medical personnel. In addition, some city physicians refused to endorse the findings of plague by others. The outbreak arguably lasted four years. See Silvio J. Onesti Jr., "Plague, Press, and Politics," *Stanford Medical Bulletin* 13 (February 1955): 1–10, quoted at p. 1; see also Henry Harris, *California's Medical Story* (San Francisco: Grabhorn Press and J. W. Stacey, 1932). Harris notes succinctly, in reference to the Chinatown outbreak: "such news was bad, for business and capital, always timid and jumpy, were fearful of sick rats and Chinamen." See also Risse, "'A Long Pull, A Strong Pull,'" and Shah, *Contagious Divides*, passim.

64. There is one tantalizing mention of rebellion by the "inmates" of the Macy Street quarantine in the newspaper record. The unsubstantiated story, which appeared decades after the outbreak, mentions LAPD officers wielding shotguns at angry residents who demanded that the quarantine be broken. See Zinser, "City in Nightmare."

65. I found several helpful sources in this regard, including Reisler, "Always the Laborer, Never the Citizen"; Monroy, "Like Swallows at the Old Mission"; and Monroy, *Rebirth*. See also McWilliams, *Southern California Country,* esp. chap. 15; Gutiérrez, *Walls and Mirrors,* esp. chap. 3; Haas, *Conquests and Historical Identities*, esp. chap. 5; and Sanchez, *Becoming Mexican American.*

66. This is precisely the connection made in the California Development Association's 1928 *Survey of the Mexican Labor Problem in California* (San Francisco?, 1928) in describing Mexican "greasers" as "sizzling with disease" (p. 11). The report drew heavily on "findings" by George Clements of the Los Angeles Chamber of Commerce.

67. "Plague in Los Angeles," subchapter 12, p. 43.

68. See remarks of William Lacy, Stenographer's Reports, November 6, 1924, Regional History Center, University of Southern California. An earlier investigation of the Mexican outbreak that took place in Mazatlàn estimated that nearly 1,200 homes were burned. See anon., "The Foreign Colony at Mazatlàn and the Bubonic Plague," in Doheny Foundation, "Notes, 1917–1919," typescript, Stanford University Libraries.

69. Stenographer's Reports, November 6, 1924. A still-useful discussion of the "Mexican problem" is Carey McWilliams, *North from Mexico: The Spanish-Speaking People of the United States* (New York: Lippincott, 1949), chap. 11.

70. Kienle, "Housing Conditions among the Mexican Population of Los Angeles," p. 1. Kienle later became a city housing official.

71. Such association was by no means new or limited to Los Angeles. Assumptions about Mexicans' role in disease susceptibility and transmission had long been staples of American medical, not to mention political, thought. For a representative version of this ideology, albeit slightly later, see Benjamin Goldberg, "Tuberculosis in Racial Types with Special Reference to Mexicans," *American Journal of Public Health* 19 (March 1929): 274–286. "We seem, throughout the United States," Goldberg wrote, with specific reference to Chicago, "to be asleep to the menace of the immigrant Mexican." It is especially intriguing that Goldberg distinguished the health risks posed by urban African Americans from those posed by Mexicans. The former, he argued, had a more legitimate claim upon citizenship and its benefits (including, presumably, health care) than the latter. I am grateful to David Gutiérrez for bringing this article to my attention. See also Howard Markel, *Quarantine!: East European Jewish Immigrants and the New York City Epidemics of 1892* (Baltimore: Johns Hopkins University Press, 1997). Shah's work on San Francisco is germane here as well.

72. Photographs at pp. 67 and 69, respectively, in "Plague in Los Angeles," subchapter 12; other citations, italics added, subchapter 12, pp. 19 and 29.

73. Such presumptions stuck. Four years after the plague outbreak, a public health survey of Los Angeles noted that "certain of the foreign groups constitute distinct health problems. The tremendous problem of overcrowding, and spread of certain communicable diseases among the Mexicans . . . increase the responsibilities of the health department." Mexicans and Japanese were singled out as particular health challenges in this report. See Ira V. Hiscock, "A Survey of Public Health Activities in Los Angeles County, California," typescript prepared for the Committee on Administrative Practice, American Public Health Association, 1928, pp. 13, 45. The report went on to point out that unincorporated sections of Los Angeles (like Belvedere) were populated by "a large Mexican population of low type, with no regard for public health." In other words, the perennial Mexican problem had its own subset in the mid-1920s: the "Mexican health problem."

74. See Samuel Holmes, "An Argument against Mexican Immigration," in *Transactions of the Commonwealth Club of California* 21 (March 23, 1926): 23. A more progressive opinion was offered at about the same time by Methodist minister and missionary Vernon McCombs in his book *From over the Border*: "It is not the Mexicans alone who pay the price for these unfortunate conditions, nor are they chiefly responsible for them. Gradually we are coming to see that the community itself is responsible, and that the conditions which exist are a peril

to everyone. A striking illustration of that is the pneumonic plague which broke out in the fall of 1924." McCombs, *From over the Border* (New York: Council of Women for Home Missions and Missionary Education Movement of the United States and Canada, 1925), p. 36.

6. THE DRAMA OF LOS ANGELES HISTORY

1. See *West Coast Magazine* 12 (June 1912): 335.

2. *Los Angeles Times*, April 21, 1912.

3. Willard Huntington Wright, "The Mission Play: A Pageant-Drama of the History of the Franciscan Missions in California," *Sunset* 29 (July 1912): 93–100.

4. I have developed some of these ideas in "Privileging the Mission over the Mexican," in Wrobel and Steiner, eds., *Many Wests*. I am grateful to historian Matt Bokovoy for sharing with me his thesis chapter on the San Diego Pageant of 1911 (which was the city's first cultural volley in the Panama-Pacific Exposition of 1915), at which John Steven McGroarty played an important role; Bokovoy, "The Cultural Contradictions of the San Diego Pageant of 1911," author's files.

5. *Los Angeles Times*, April 28, 1912.

6. See Wright, "The Mission Play."

7. Jordan quoted in Franklin Walker's underappreciated *A Literary History of Southern California* (Berkeley and Los Angeles: University of California Press, 1950), p. 4.

8. Years later, a glowing tribute to Miller would claim an even larger role for him in the invention of the Mission Play. When Miller read McGroarty's first effort, writes Samuel Clover in *Constructive Californians*, "he said to Mr. McGroarty that the idea and the structure were far too fine and great to be used in the simple way that it would have been presented at the Inn, and encouraged him to make it larger and to give it a setting in a big way, in a place where all the world might see it, so through Mr. Miller's encouragement and personal enthusiasm, the Mission Play has come to be one of the annual events of Southern California which every traveler makes a point of seeing." Samuel T. Clover, *Constructive Californians: Men of Outstanding Ability Who Have Added Greatly to the Golden State's Prestige* (Los Angeles: Saturday Night Publishing, 1926), p. 138.

9. McGroarty's biographer disagrees with the timetable later offered up by various Mission Play publications and ephemera. She claims that the playwright actually worked on the script for three years. See Mary Eleanor Craggs, "The Career of John Steven McGroarty," M.A. thesis, Catholic University of America, San Rafael, California, 1958, pp. 12–13. McGroarty took out his first copyright for the play on August 15, 1911. It seems likely that later claims about McGroarty's production of *The Mission Play* in so short a time were exaggerated for effect.

10. For a recent discussion of mission revivalism and the preservation movement, see Kropp, "'All Our Yesterdays.'"

11. John Steven McGroarty to Fr. Zephyrin Englehardt, August 12, 1910, from copies of original. The author's thanks to Viola Carlson for providing me copies of this correspondence, the originals of which are housed in Mission Santa Barbara.

12. Zephyrin Englehardt to John Steven McGroarty, August 15, 1910, quoted in Craggs, "Career of John Steven McGroarty," p. 25.

13. John Steven McGroarty to Zephyrin Englehardt, September 11, 1911, from copies of original.

14. McGroarty to Englehardt, September 16, 1911, quoted in Craggs, "Career of John Steven McGroarty," p. 25; copy in author's files. "But, be sure, I shall see the whole thing go by the board sooner than offend," McGroarty assured Englehardt. Nonetheless, Englehardt later wrote to Charles Fletcher Lummis: "Having had such very unpleasant experiences in connection with the miscalled Mission Play, I determined to be fortified against further deception and unworthy treatment." And in an aside that seems also aimed at McGroarty, Englehardt wrote that "anyone out for filthy lucre, is constitutionally unfit to have a hand in the matter." Englehardt to Charles Fletcher Lummis, July 4, 1916, Lummis Collection, Southwest Museum; hereafter Lummis Collection.

15. Charles Fletcher Lummis to John Steven McGroarty (written just days before *The Mission Play* opened), April 7, 1912, Lummis Collection.

16. Carey McWilliams writes, and Kevin Starr echoes him, that McGroarty was a converted Catholic.

17. For McGroarty's early life, see Craggs, "The Career of John Steven McGroarty." See also Francis J. Weber, *John Steven McGroarty: From the Green Verdugo Hills* (San Diego: San Diego Historical Society, 1974). McGroarty deserves a full-length biography.

18. Starr, *Inventing the Dream*, p. 87.

19. Bertha Hirsch Baruch, "Problem of the Emigrant: The Serious Question Which the Pacific Coast Must Soon Answer," *West Coast Magazine* 12 (June 1912): 291–297; Arthur Hinton, "The Mexican Problem," *West Coast Magazine* 12 (May 1912): 167–170.

20. The Association borrowed a significant amount of money. A letter from W. E. Hampton of the Association to Bishop Thomas Conaty in 1915 makes mention of a $20,000 loan made by a local bank in 1913 (Conaty co-signed one of the two $10,000 notes). See Hampton to Bishop Conaty, July 30, 1915, Archival Center, Archdiocese of Los Angeles, Mission San Fernando; hereafter Archival Center.

21. The Catholic journal *The Tidings* saw in the ground-breaking great signs for the faith. "Mr. McGroarty has brought to bear not only his full knowledge of the history of these matchless missions and their heroic work in Christianiz-

ing savage Indians, but his Catholic faith has given him a deeper insight into the spiritual significance of their building, and his poetic nature has added a charm of romance to the scenes depicted, that will go far towards making the play both popular and instructive." *The Tidings*, February 9, 1912. McGroarty offered the bishop a cut of his profits, but it is unclear if the church accepted the proposition. Conaty did suggest that *The Mission Play* "will be the means of throwing the proper light upon the history of early California." See McGroarty to Bishop Thomas Conaty, April 4, 1911, and Conaty to George Wharton James, June 5, 1912, Archival Center.

22. "Old monastic refectory" line from Henry Van Dyke, untitled story, *Century Magazine* [1913], from scrap clipping in the Western History Collection, Denver Public Library.

23. See Elizabeth Murray, "A Sketch of the Play's Creation and History," *West Coast Magazine* 12 (June 1912): 372–374.

24. Of the play and her sister's performance (she played Ramona herself), the Princess later wrote that "it enshrined in words and songs and dances, in its characters and episodes, the poetry and chivalry of those early Spanish days, as well as the comedy and tragedy and religious fervor of the times, the center of which was mission life." See Princess Lazarovich-Hrebelianovich, *Pleasures and Palaces: The Memoirs of Princess Lazarovich-Hrebelianovich* (New York: Century Company, 1915), p. 308.

25. See "Statement of Mission Play Association," July 17, 1912, which notes a ten-week payroll for the Princess at $4,419.80 and almost $27,000 for the rest of the troupe.

26. *Los Angeles Times*, April 21, 1912.

27. See back cover of vol. 13, January 1913 issue of *West Coast Magazine*; see also *The Tidings*, May 3, 1912; Burton quoted in a 1915 Mission Play playbill; copy in the Huntington Library.

28. Van Dyke fragment, *Century Magazine*, p. 179.

29. Willard Huntington Wright, "An American Oberammergau," *West Coast Magazine* 11 (March 1912): 537.

30. Ruth Comfort Mitchell, "The Mission Play," *West Coast Magazine* 12 (June 1912): 369–372. That this review appeared in the journal McGroarty himself edited of course should be pointed out; but other reviews elsewhere sing similar songs of *Mission Play* praise; see also Percival Carroll, "The Mission Play," *West Coast Magazine* 12 (June 1912): 275–282.

31. See *The Tidings*, October 17, 1913.

32. Mary Austin to John Steven McGroarty, January 8, 1913, Happy Book, vol. 1, Archival Center. McGroarty's "Happy Books" are two volumes of clippings and letters housed at the center.

33. Oxnam wrote that "some people feel that these men because they were Catholics did not know God. Oh they did." Oxnam diary entry (with tipped-

in lithograph of Benjamin Horning as Serra), April 25, 1913; Bromley Oxnam Papers, Library of Congress. Robert Graham to John Steven McGroarty, April 4, 1922, Happy Book, vol. 1.

34. McGroarty would later rewrite Act 3 so that the play closed with a more exuberant call for contemporary mission restoration.

35. For a brief biographical portrait of Lucretia del Valle, see Wallace Smith, "The Last of the Señoritas," *The Californians,* March/April 1986, pp. 39–43. The *Los Angeles Times* put Lucretia del Valle on the cover of its January 1, 1914, Midwinter edition, a tourist vehicle, above a caption reading "A Native Daughter." As Smith points out in his article, del Valle's grandmother had been portrayed in Helen Hunt Jackson's *Ramona* as the cruel wife of General Moreno; now the granddaughter had, in *The Mission Play*, restored *Californio* dignity to the family legacy. Historian Matt Garcia, in his recent book *A World of Its Own*, discusses ethnic identity and theatrical performance in reference to the Padua Hills players of eastern Los Angeles County from the 1930s forward; see especially chap. 4, "Just Put on That Padua Hills Smile."

36. See the June 1912 issue of *West Coast Magazine*. In a 1915 letter to Charles Fletcher Lummis, McGroarty complained of a $50,000 debt hanging over the Mission Play since its 1912 birth; that debt had been nearly cleared, he said, "but at what sacrifice of nerves and flesh and blood, nobody on this earth will ever know." John S. McGroarty to Charles Fletcher Lummis, November 22, 1915, Lummis Collection.

37. See Mission Play Association to Reginaldo Francisco del Valle, June 4, 1913, Huntington Library manuscript collection (this document is signed from "Frank," most likely Frank Miller). Ticket receipts are included in this letter. McGroarty variously claimed to have been between $50,000 and $100,000 in debt at this point.

38. John Steven McGroarty to Bishop Thomas Conaty, April 29, 1914, Archival Center.

39. McGroarty to Charles Fletcher Lummis, June 24, 1916, Lummis Collection. Some indication that the play had financial difficulties even at this early stage can be gleaned from Hampton to Conaty, July 30, 1915, Archival Center.

40. From a review in the *Kansas City Star News-Press*, November 12, 1916, quoted in Craggs, "Career of John Steven McGroarty," pp. 31–32. *Los Angeles Times* critic quoted in Smith, "The Last of the Señoritas," p. 42. In St. Louis, *The Mission Play* faced a pageant rival. St. Louis business leaders put on the elaborate *Pageant and Masque of St. Louis* beginning in 1914, a *Mission Play*–like drama extolling the city's progression from Mound Builders to modern civilization; see Glassberg, *A Sense of History,* p. 71.

41. See Frederic Warde, *Fifty Years of Make-Believe* (Los Angeles: Times-Mirror Press, 1923), pp. 312–313.

42. George Searle to John Steven McGroarty [n.d., 1922], Happy Book, vol. 1.

43. Mission Play program, 1920, Archival Center.

44. From John S. McGroarty, "California's Boulevards—and Historic Old Missions," *Touring Topics*, March 1921, pp. 40–41, quoted from p. 40.

45. A contract for the season after the disastrous trip outside the state, for instance, binds actress Jessica Dixon to the show in theaters wide and far (for a salary advance of $1) and allows McGroarty's Mission Play Association to determine the length of the season. Dixon was to receive $40 a week, unless the season were interrupted by "strikes, lockouts, fire, accident, riot, act of God, or the public enemy." See "Artist's Contract," August 21, 1916, L. E. Behymer Papers, Huntington Library.

46. John Steven McGroarty, *The Golden Scroll* ([San Gabriel, Calif.]: The Mission Play Foundation, ca. 1927), p. 5.

47. See Walter Malone to John Steven McGroarty, April 18, 1925, McGroarty Collection, Archival Center.

48. Pomona Bulletin, September 25, 1923, clipping in Happy Book, vol. 2.

49. Nothing so illustrates this as the letter McGroarty received from Jeanne Johnson, who wrote to say that the journalist's columns saved her from suicide. See Jeanne Johnson to McGroarty, n.d., Happy Book, vol. 1; see also John T. Flynn to McGroarty, March 5, 1923, Happy Book, vol. 1.

50. See Harry Peterson to Bishop Thomas Conaty, June 19, 1913, Archival Center; W. E. B. Du Bois to McGroarty, April 12, 1923, Happy Book vol. 1.

51. Maisie Marjenhoff to John Steven McGroarty, May 4, 1922, Happy Book, vol. 1; C. A. Pugsley to John Steven McGroarty, April 12, 1924, Happy Book, vol. 2.

52. McGroarty's honorary doctorates came from the University of Southern California (Literature, 1925) and the University of Santa Clara (Law, 1928).

53. Stoughton Cooley, a Los Angeles writer on taxes and finance, to John Steven McGroarty, July 30, 1923, Happy Book, vol. 2.

54. A. N. Palmer to John Steven McGroarty, August 11, 1922, Happy Book, vol. 1.

55. Reynold Bright to John Steven McGroarty, May 18, 1923, Happy Book, vol. 1.

56. Charles Fletcher Lummis to McGroarty, May 28, 1926, Lummis Collection.

57. Ella S. Rebard to John Steven McGroarty, March 26, 1922, Happy Book, vol. 1. See also John Steven McGroarty to William Hughes, March 6, 1922, Archival Center.

58. John D. Gordon, Pastor of Tabernacle Baptist Church, to John Steven McGroarty, February 26, 1925, Happy Book, vol. 1. See also, for example, McGroarty's piece in the *Los Angeles Times*, February 12, 1909.

59. See *Highland Park Herald* clipping, April 24, 1925, Happy Book, vol. 2. McGroarty did write many history texts during his career, including *Riverside County: The Story of the Upbuilding of the Empire County of California* (Los Ange-

les: Western Historical Society, 1910?); *California: Its History and Romance* (Los Angeles: Grafton, 1911); *A History of Southern California* (Los Angeles: Southern California Panama Expositions Commission, 1914); *History of Los Angeles County*, 3 vols. (Chicago: American Historical Society, 1923); and *Los Angeles from the Mountains to the Sea* (Chicago: American Historical Society, 1921).

60. Amado Chávez to John Steven McGroarty, April 4, 1923, Happy Book, vol. 1. For a perceptive and thorough analysis of the ethnic and racial complexities in New Mexico of this period, consult Montgomery, *The Spanish Redemption*.

61. See *Los Angeles Times* clipping, June 3, 1923, Happy Book, vol. 2.

62. Mission Play program, 1923 season, Archival Center.

63. See Conor Ford to L. E. Behymer, February 2, 1925, and F. A. Shaw to L. E. Behymer, May 26, 1926, Behymer Papers. Interestingly, as architectural historian Richard Longstreth has pointed out, early designs for the new playhouse included "a ceremonious automobile entrance and large parking lot." Though this feature was not part of the final design, Longstreth suggests that it was one of the first efforts to link car and theater in Los Angeles, several steps ahead of the drive-in movie theater. See Longstreth, "Don't Get Out: The Automobile's Impact on Five Building Types in Los Angeles, 1921–1941," *ARRIS* 7 (1996): 32–56, quoted at p. 36.

64. As Peck wrote to McGroarty in 1925, "I would be a very ungrateful wretch . . . had I not taken the Mission Play matter to the Chamber of Commerce after Charlie Pyke told me your trouble. . . . and I hope we can bring matters about so that you will be able to carry on the Mission Play and have your name associated with it in a way that will bring to you much happiness." See T. C. Peck to John Steven McGroarty, November 23, 1925, Happy Book vol. 2.

65. See 1926 document in the Behymer Papers, Box 4.

66. See F. A. Shaw to L. E. Behymer, May 26, 1926, quoting A. G. Arnoll, secretary of the Los Angeles Chamber of Commerce to the "Commercial Secretaries of Southern California," January 27, 1926, Behymer Papers.

67. "No profits made in producing the play will go to any individual or corporation and any profits made will be used in restoring old California landmarks, including old missions in which religious services are not held." This accords strangely with the Chamber's arrangements for the new corporation. They must be talking about no profits after they, in effect, take profits, at 7 percent. See D. W. Pontius, "Adding to the Mission Play House," *Southern California Business* 6 (April 1927): 30.

68. See Mission Playhouse Corporation [John Steven McGroarty] to Henry E. Huntington, June 1, 1926, Huntington manuscripts, Huntington Library.

69. See Mission Playhouse Corporation [John Steven McGroarty] to Henry E. Huntington, June 15, 1926, Huntington manuscripts.

70. George I. Cochran to W. I. Hollingsworth, June 23, 1926, Behymer Papers.

71. See 1926 document in the Behymer Papers, Box 4.

72. Mission Playhouse Corporation [W. I. Hollingsworth] to Henry E. Huntington, December 28, 1926, Behymer Papers.

73. Los Angeles Chamber of Commerce *Bulletin*, March 7, 1927, p. 2.

74. See L. E. Behymer to Mr. Pyke, January 13, 1926, and Behymer to Conor Ford, February 20 [1926], Behymer Papers. As Behymer wrote in late 1926, "Personally it matters not who is the manager of the Mission Play or who plays the leading role. I stand for the OBJECT, the advertising for Southern California and the historical significance of the pageant. . . . The Mission Play is bigger than individuals." Behymer to John Mott, October 4, 1926, Behymer Papers. Lummis quote from Charles Fletcher Lummis to John Steven McGroarty, May 28, 1926, Lummis Collection.

75. See L. E. Behymer to W. I. Hollingsworth, February 21 [1926], Behymer Papers; see also Behymer to Frederick [*sic*] Warde, February 17, 1926, and F. A. Shaw to Behymer, May 26, 1926, Behymer Papers. See also R. F. del Valle to John Steven McGroarty, May 6, 1926, Happy Book, vol. 2.

76. See L. E. Behymer to W. I. Hollingsworth, January 29, 1926, Behymer Papers.

77. See L. E. Behymer to W. I. Hollingsworth, February 15, 1926, Behymer Papers.

78. Behymer to, for instance, Lyman Johnson, February 4, 1926, Behymer Papers.

79. See L. E. Behymer to Conor Ford, February 20 [1926]; a few weeks later, Behymer warned Ford that he was in no position "to allow long dead wood to be drawing income from the Mission Play." Behymer to Ford, March 12 [1926]; and see Behymer to W. I. Hollingsworth, February 15, 1926, Behymer Papers.

80. L. E. Behymer to C. L. Gerstner and J. W. Broxholme, February 9, 1926, Behymer Papers.

81. Behymer to President, American Casualty Company Convention, Alexandria Hotel, Los Angeles, February 2 [1926], Behymer Papers.

82. These postcards can still be found at regional flea markets and swap meets. The Archival Center of the Archdiocese of California has a small collection, including one from 1915, addressed to Winifred Roe from her husband J.W.: "Finest ever 4620 people on the stage I only wish dearest you were here."

83. Behymer to Robert Hurd of Anthony Radio, February 24, 1926; see also Behymer to L. A. Tripp, March 1, 1926 (both in Behymer Papers) in which he complains that radio station KFI wished to charge him a fee to read the advertisement over the air; Behymer pointed out that he himself was doing his Mission Play work free, and that other stations "are pleased to be of assistance in this great advertising medium of cultural Southern California."

84. See Department of Publicity and Excursions: The Mission Play, March 1, 1926 report, Behymer Papers.

85. See L. E. Behymer to John Steven McGroarty, February 15, 1926, Behymer Papers.

86. See Francis A. Shaw to L. E. Behymer, May 26, 1926, Behymer Papers. In Shaw's words: "If we made errors in selling out the Playhouse, not under our control, have you all forgotten McGroarty's famous 'Nigger Night' and the unpaid admissions[?]"

87. See L. E. Behymer to M. L. Schoenthal of the Riverside Chamber of Commerce, March 12, 1926, Behymer Papers.

88. L. E. Behymer to John Kemp [and Directors of the Mission Play Corporation], December 1, 1926, Behymer Papers. There are notes and clippings in McGroarty's Happy Books that relay stories of Angelenos who had seen the Mission Play fifty times. See also Behymer to Ellen Scripps, July 10, 1926, Behymer Papers.

89. See the reports of the Department of Publicity and Excursions: The Mission Play, for March 1 and March 6, 1926, Behymer Papers.

90. See L. E. Behymer to W. I. Hollingsworth, October 4, 1926, and Behymer to John Kemp [and Directors, Mission Play Corporation], December 1, 1926, Behymer Papers.

91. Haldeman was an architect of the rabidly right-wing Better America Federation and also knee-deep in the Julian Petroleum scandal. See L. E. Behymer to W. I. Hollingsworth, April 24 [1926], Behymer Papers.

92. See L. E. Behymer to H. N. Partridge, Jr., July 15, 1926, Behymer Papers.

93. The Mission Play Corporation was located in the Hollingsworth Building in downtown Los Angeles in the mid-1920s.

94. W. I. Hollingsworth to L. E. Behymer, June 19, 1926, Behymer Papers.

95. See L. E. Behymer to W. I. Hollingsworth, August 18, 1926, Behymer Papers..

96. See L. E. Behymer to Harry Chandler, November 12, 1926, and Behymer to W. I. Hollingsworth, November 12, 1926, Behymer Papers.

97. Behymer to John Steven McGroarty, February 10, 1927, Behymer Papers.

98. Even McGroarty's hometown newspaper in Wilkes-Barre covered the playhouse opening; see clippings in vol. 2 of the Happy Book.

99. Mission Playhouse Corporation [W. I. Hollingsworth] to Henry E. Huntington, December 28, 1926, Behymer Papers.

100. Behymer to D. W. Pontius, March 8, 1927, Behymer Papers. See also Pontius, "New Home of the Mission Play," *Southern California Business* 6 (April 1927): 30.

101. Enna C. Hampton to John Steven McGroarty, [ca. May 1927], Happy Book, vol. 2.

102. See Amalie Parr, "The Mission Play," *The Mentor,* January 1928, pp. 41–45.

103. Harry Chandler to L. E. Behymer, December 6, 1926, Behymer Papers.

104. See, for instance, L. E. Behymer to Harry Chandler, March 31 and April 9, 1927; Norman Chandler to L. E. Behymer, April 15, 1927, Behymer Papers.

105. See L. E. Behymer to Norman Sprowl, February 28 [1927], and L. E. Behymer to D. W. Pontius, June 27, 1927, Behymer Papers.

106. D. W. Pontius to L. E. Behymer, June 30, 1927; W. I. Hollingsworth to L. E. Behymer, July 23, 1927, Behymer Papers.

107. Roy Cloud to John Steven McGroarty, April 25, 1928; Lt. Commander H. G. Gatlin to McGroarty, April 5, 1928; Happy Book, vol. 2.

108. See "Adding to the Mission Play House," p. 46.

109. A Los Angeles Unified School District typescript from 1933 makes a weak curricular tie to *The Mission Play*, asking teachers to consider "pageants in the vicinity that may lead to interests in reading, such as the Ramona Pageant, the Mission Play." From "Seventh and Eighth Grade Course of Study," typescript in the Edward Doheny Library, University of Southern California.

110. See L. E. Behymer to Harry Chandler, March 4, 1936, Behymer Papers.

111. See Stenographer's Reports, Board of Directors, Los Angeles Chamber of Commerce, August 20, 1936.

112. *Pasadena Post*, September 17, 1939; from Curtis Melton Scrapbooks, Pasadena Public Library.

113. See L. E. Behymer to Francis A. Shaw, July 28, 1945, Behymer Papers.

114. For instance, the 1947 program depicts Josepha Yorba in a strapless gown, as a kind of nineteenth-century pin-up; a slightly earlier program depicts a Franciscan friar blessing a native girl in what to modern eyes looks to be an eroticized, even violent, way. It is reminiscent of similar patterns a bit earlier on the Los Angeles landscape, such as the Los Angeles–based "Mexican Girl Mining Company" of the early part of the century, with its "Mexican Girl" mine in Sonora. See *Greater Los Angeles Illustrated*, pp. 152–153. Images advertising the San Francisco Portolá Festival underwent similar change at the same time; see Glassberg, *Sense of History*, chap. 3.

115. The phrase is, I think, Behymer's. See L. E. Behymer to Alfred Human, February 10, 1926, Behymer Papers.

CONCLUSION: WHITEWASHED ADOBE

1. From *Publications of Historical Society of Southern California* 1 (1884–1891); Moore quoted at p. 12 of 1887 proceedings.

2. Joan Didion, "The Golden Land," *New York Review of Books*, October 21, 1993, p. 91.

3. Charles Victor Hall Scrapbooks, 2 vols., Huntington Library.

4. See Davis, *City of Quartz*, 33–34. See also Sarah L. Schrank, "Art and the

City: The Transformation of Civic Culture in Los Angeles, 1900–1965," Ph.D. diss., University of California, San Diego, 2002.

5. Weston quoted in Michael Dawson, "South of Point Lobos: Photography in Southern California, 1890–1950," in Victoria Dailey, Natalie Shivers, and Michael Dawson, *LA's Early Moderns: Art, Architecture, Photography* (Los Angeles: Balcony Press, 2003).

Page references followed by *fig* indicate a photograph; those followed by *m* indicate a map.

Abila, Henrique, 100

Adamic, Louis, 34

adobe houses, 134–35

adobe making, 134*fig*

Aguirre, Martin, 106

Aliso/Los Angeles Streets (1886), 27*fig*

Allen, Matthew, 106

All Fools' Nite (1897), 80, 81, 83–84, 85

Almazan, Carlos, 147

Americanization, 45–46, 272n.100

Ames Brothers, 238

Anglo society: cultural/physical boundaries created by, 31; defined by Anglo Saxonism, 44; intermarriage between *Californio* families and, 29–31; Mexican space/stereotypes recast by, 31–48, 59–61; mutual hostility between Mexicans and, 14–16; racial attitudes toward Mexicans by, 271n.99; response to plague outbreak (1924) by, 201–5

Anthony Radio, 239

APA (America Protective Association), 77

"Arizona Colonization Society," 18–19, 24

Arizona Republican, 193

Armer, Thomas, 152, 166

Army Corps of Engineers, 122, 123–26

Arnold, Carlos, 148

Arrowsmith (Lewis), 195

Austin, Mary, 218

Baker, Arcadia de, 153

Balch, A. C., 234

Baldwin, E. J. "Lucky," 144

Ballard, R. H., 231

Bancroft, Hubert Howe, 60, 121

Baptist Mission church, 184, 185*fig*, 193

Bartlett, Rev. Dana, 44, 110, 200

Barton, Clara, 143

Barton, James R., 19, 20

Barton murders (19th century), 22–23

"Bath of the Virgins" ceremony, 97

"Battle of the Mesa" (1847), 98

Bear Flag Rebellion, 12

Behymer, Lyndon Ellsworth: asked to resuscitate *The Mission Play,* 235–36; contacted to sell the official Fiesta program, 80; financial support of *The Mission Play* by, 234; last appeals

Behymer, Lyndon Ellsworth *(continued)*
regarding *The Mission Play* by, 246–47,
248; publicity blitzkrieg by, 237–38,
239–40, 241–45, 317n.83
Bell, Horace, 11, 12, 13–14, 21, 260n.26,
261n.35
Belvedere Gardens operation (1924):
plague quarantine around, 185–86,
304nn.28, 30; property damage during,
187–88, 190–95; strategies used during,
186–87; urban renewal efforts following,
200–201
Benton, Arthur, 242, 244
Bernal, Joe, 118
Berzunzolo, Juan, 129, 147
The Better City (Bartlett), 110
Bogardus, Emory, 8, 44, 117, 203
Bogen, Emil, 176–77, 182
Boyle Heights, 97
Brewer, William H., 13
The Brick People (Morales), 129
Brook, Harry E., 53, 59
Brown, Benjamin, 183
Brualla, Father Medrano, 178
bubonic plague epidemic (1924): analysis
within social/cultural context, 201–5;
attention paid to Macy Street district
during, 199–200; Baptist Mission
church as plague abatement headquarters, 184, 185*fig*, 193; Belvedere Gardens
operation during, 185–88, 190–95, 200–
201, 304nn.28, 30; demographics of
mortality due to, 182, 205; efforts to
minimize news of, 197–98; impact
on selling of Los Angeles, 196–97;
isolation of plague patients, 193, 195;
Mercurochrome treatment of, 182, 203,
302n.17; Mexican district quarantine
due to, 183–87, 304nn.28, 30; novelist's
description of, 179; origins and initial
spread of, 176–82; plague abatement
wrecking crew, 188*fig*, 190*fig*, 191–95,
192*fig*; plague prevention work during,
191–95, 193*fig*; property destruction due
to, 187–88, 190–91, 193, 194*fig*; as reinforcing isolation of Mexican neighborhoods, 182–83; rodent eradication pro-

grams during, 191, 193, 197–99, 306n.37;
tied to ethnicity, 201–5, 303n.20,
310n.73; treatment methods used
during, 182, 195; urban renewal efforts
following, 200–201
Bullocks Department Store, 241
Bureau of Housing and Sanitation, 196
Burnett, Alfredo, 179
Burns, J. Frank, 119
*A Business Venture in Los Angeles, or, A
Christian Optimist*, 49, 50

Calhoun, Eleanor (Princess Lazarovich-
Hrebelianovich), 215, 216
Calhoun, Ezekiel Ewing, 215
Calhoun, Virginia, 215
California: Its History and Romance
(McGroarty), 209, 214
California Common Brick Manufacturers'
Association, 155
"California under Four Flags" (Hamilton
lecture), 238
California Voice, 71, 77, 83
Californios: described, 17; increasingly
consigned to the past, 134; intermarriage
between elite Anglos and, 29–31; loss
of land and power by, 41; offense over
Severance remarks by, 88–89. *See also*
Mexican population
Camacho, L. S., 186–87
Campbell, Albert, 99
Carmen Lugo, José del, 13, 101
Carr, Harry, 34, 36
Carson, Kit, 98
Chandler, Harry, 3, 197, 234, 243, 246, 248
Chase, Amanda Mathews, 92, 93
Chávez, Amado, 230
Chicago Evening Post, 75
Childs, Mrs. O. W., 64
Childs, Ozro, 18
Chinatown siege (1870s), 108
Chinese community: La Fiesta participa-
tion by, 61, 68, 69*fig*, 75; response to
plague outbreak by San Francisco, 201,
309n.63
"The City of Destiny" (McGroarty), 2
City Hall of Los Angeles, 244–45, 246

"City of Los Angeles" poetry contest
(1920s), 3
City of Quartz (Davis), 3
The City That Grew (Workman), 1
Civilian Conservation Corps, 166
Clara Street homes (Los Angeles), 177*fig*,
179, 180*fig*
Clarke, James, 98–99
Clark, Eli, 234
Cloud, Roy, 247
Clover, Samuel T., 129, 157, 158, 159, 160–61
Cochran, George I., 234, 248
Colton Chronicle, 85
Coma, Perdona, 104
Committee of Safety, 18
Conaty, Archbishop Thomas J., 214, 223
Copp, Angeleno Andrew, 27
Coronel, Manuel, 99
Costello, Mary, 180–82
Crabb, Henry A., 18, 19, 23, 24, 32
Crabb invasion (1850s), 23–25, 260n.29
Crain, William, 119
Crawford, Margaret, 137, 141
Crawley, Joseph, 67
Creel, "Queen Ann," 143
Crespi, Juan, 95, 96
Cryer, George, 155, 184

Daily News, 196
Dana, Richard Henry, 11, 27, 60
Davis, Mike, 3, 5
Debs, Eugene, 58
del Valle, Lucretia, 222, 223
De Schweinitz, Karl, 129
Dickie, Walter, 182, 184–85, 187, 188, 195,
198, 199, 200
Dixon, James Main, 44
Doheny, E. L., 234, 242
Dominquez, Manuel, 72
Du Bois, W. E. B., 228, 229
Duhaut-Cilly, Auguste Bernard, 97
Dunham, Mr., 80

E. 6th Street, 189*fig*
East Side News, 82, 87–88
Ecology of Fear (Davis), 5
El Dorado myth, 69

El Heraldo de Mexico, 197
El Monte, 18, 19, 23
El Pueblo de Simons, 136
Engelhardt, Fr. Zephyrin, 207, 210–11
Espinosa, Jose Jesus, 23
Estudillo, Francisco, 57
ethnic hatred: link between Manifest
Destiny and, 12, 18, 33; vigilante violence
of 1850s and legacy of, 25–33, 261n.34
ethnicity: disease linked to, 201–5, 303n.20,
310n.73; infant morality rates (1925–1926)
by, 206
ethnic violence: Barton murders, 22–23;
Crabb's invasion, 23–25, 260n.29; Dave
Brown's hanging, 261n.36; ethnic hatred
legacy of 1850s, 25–33; "Louis Mesmer
Dictation" incident of, 261n.35; overview
of 19th century, 17–25
Evening Express, 80–81
Ewald, Ruth, 147

"Facts About Industrial Los Angeles—
Nature's Workshop" (Chamber of
Commerce), 43, 174–75
Fallbrook Observer, 86
Fiesta Association, 79–80
Fiestas de Las Flores, 89
Flagons and Apples (Jeffers), 213
Flores, Jessie, 180
Flores, Juan, 19, 22, 23
Ford Motor Company, 240
foreign miner's tax, 13
Forsyth, John, 24
Fox, William, 166
Francis, John, 71, 72
Free Harbor Jubilee (1899), 87
Free Harbor League, 73
Frémont, John C., 12, 29

Gadsden Purchase, 18
"Gadsden Purchase settlers," 23
Gamio, Manuel, 8, 149
Garbutt, R. P., 47
Garcia, Jess, 167
Garcia, Juan (*That Mexican!* character):
Census ethnic identification of, 41;
stereotype characterization of, 36, 38–41;

Garcia, Juan (continued)
  as synonymous with Mexican ethnicity,
  43; as unquestioned EveryMexican, 41;
  urban living space allowed, 46, 47–48.
  See also Mexican stereotypes
Garcia, Manuel, 136
Gatlin, H. G., 247
Getman, William, 17
Glassberg, David, 65
Gonzalez, Michael, 133
Graves, Jackson A., 28, 31
"Greasers in Embryio" (1907), 40fig
Greater Los Angeles, 86
Guadalupe Hidalgo Treaty (1848), 12, 13–
  14, 18, 258n.17
Guinn, James Miller, 13, 25, 29, 133
Gullett, Gayle, 88
Guthrie, Woody, 123
Gutiérrez, David, 15
Gutiérrez, Horace, 178

Haldeman, Harry, 242
Hall, Victor, 250
Hamilton, R. Hayes, 238
Hampton, Enna M., 245
Hayes, Benjamin, 14, 17, 19
Hearst, William Randolph, 216
Herald Examiner, 191
Hiawatha (play), 243
Hidalgo, Miguel, 36
Highland, Monica, 172
Historical Society of Southern California,
  29
Hoak, E. K., 224, 248
Hollingsworth, W. I., 168–69, 232, 234,
  242–43, 245, 246, 247, 248
Holmes, Samuel, 203
"Homes of the Spanish Type" (publica-
  tion), 138–39
Hoover, Vincent, 98
Horning, Benjamin, 215, 216, 222
"Housing Conditions among the Mexican
  Population of Los Angeles" (Bogardus),
  203
Howarth, H. B., 151
How to See a Play (Burton), 216
"How to Whitewash" instructions, 250–51

Hunter, Jesse, 119
Hunter, Sherley, 1
Huntington, Henry E., 1, 233–34, 245
Hunt, Rockwell, 8, 44

The Indispensable Enemy (Saxton), 9
infant mortality rates by race/ethnicity
  (1925–1926), 206
intermarriage: between Californio families
  and elite Anglos, 29–31; shame associated with, 258n.15

Jackson, Helen Hunt, 60, 214, 215
Janss, Harold, 244
Jeffers, Robinson, 213
Jenkins, Williams, 17
Jimenez, Jose, 180
Jimenez, Mike, 179, 180
J. M. Hale & Co., 55–56
Johnson, Reginald, 156
Jones, E. W., 30
Jordan, David Starr, 210
Just California (McGroarty), 212

Kabierske, Henry, 215
Keller, Henry Workman, 134
Keller, Matthew, 105
Kenderdine, Thomas, 31
Kienle, John, 203
Knox, William Boardman, 196

Lacy, William, 196, 202, 203
La Fiesta Committee of Thirty, 82, 86
La Fiesta de Los Angeles: as boosterim
  tool, 82–83; canceled in 1899, 87;
  Chinese participation in, 61, 68, 75;
  Civil War reconciliation incident at
  1896, 77; continued expansion of, 72–
  84; criticisms of, 68–69, 71, 83–84;
  establishment as annual affair, 71–72;
  events of 1896, 73–79; evidence of
  cultural game plan in, 62, 64–67;
  excesses/revelers during, 66–67, 80–81,
  83–84; financial success of second, 71;
  founding and development of, 52–72;
  function of, 58–59; funding problems
  of 1898, 82; as Manifest Destiny celebra-

tion, 64; Mexican space perpetuated by, 59–61; Mexican stereotypes perpetuated by, 60–61; planning for 1897, 79–82; planning and promotion of, 53–58; racial rapprochement through diversity of, 57–58; response to Spanish American War by, 84–88; "Sir Knights of La Fiesta" of, 80; specific events of week-long, 56; white attendees of non-parade events, 277n.61; Z.Z.'s description of, 50–52

La Fiesta de Los Angeles controversies: over All Fools' Nite (1896), 80–81, 83–84, 85; over Chinese participation, 68; response to Spanish American War, 84–88; over Severance color line remarks, 88–89

La Fiesta de Los Angeles parade: Caballeros in, 61*fig*; children marching in 1894, 57*fig*; Chinese dragon in, 69*fig*, 75; float (1894) of, 55*fig*; historical progression represented in, 69–70, 75–76; Native Americans in, 67*fig*, 69–70; participants in 1894, 56*fig*; planning for floats and, 56–58; troops marching (1894) in, 51*fig*

La Fiesta poster (1896), 63*fig*
La Fiesta's Committee on Public Morals, 80
La Fiesta's Historical Day, 66
La Golodrina (McGroarty), 230
Lajun, Francisca Concha, 176, 202
Land of Sunshine (magazine), 53, 72, 73–74, 173
Lauderdale, John, 134–35
League for Better City Government, 73
Letts, Arthur, 244
Lewis, Sinclair, 195
"Life in the Feudal Era" racial types (19th century), 33*fig*
"Lion's Den" column (Lummis), 213
Los Angeles: bird's-eye view of, 107*m*; bubonic plague epidemic (1924) in, 176–95; building of (1910), 37*fig*; literature on urban destiny of, 1–3; Mexican workers in downtown, 38*fig*; multicultural future of, 5–6; photographic representation of "typical" ethnic traits in, 175*fig*; race/

ethnicity ideas leading to maturation of, 6–8; rewriting history of, 26–27; simple images/symbols of, 173–75; "typical" postcard view of, 173–74, 174*fig*; white-washing of, 250–52

Los Angeles: Capital of the Third World (Rieff), 4
"Los Angeles: Metropolis of the Future?" symposium, 3
Los Angeles Brick Exchange, 155
Los Angeles Builders Exchange, 155
Los Angeles Chamber of Commerce: Chinese village established by, 42; end of plague reported to, 195–96; enlisted to help with decline of *The Mission Play*, 231–38, 248; ephemeral publications produced by, 42–43; on Mexican district living conditions and plague outbreak, 202; publications/productions promoting LA by, 174; reporting on unskilled wage rates, 164; role in plague-carrying eradication programs, 191; typical Spanish village established (1920s) by, 41–42

Los Angeles Chamber of Commerce's Publicity Committee, 196
Los Angeles Citizen, 83
Los Angeles County Charities, 184
Los Angeles County infant mortality rates (1925–1926), 206
Los Angeles Examiner, 43
Los Angeles Express, 72, 74
Los Angeles Herald, 87
Los Angeles Independent, 84
Los Angeles Non Partisan, 78
Los Angeles Realtor, 196
Los Angeles Record, 74, 76, 77–78, 83
Los Angeles River: channelization (1930s) of, 124*fig*; city beautification efforts for, 108–9; as city water source, 107; contemporary state of, 94; evolves as industrial boundary, 109; flood damage (1880s) by, 105*fig*; history of, 93–99, 95*fig*, 96*fig*; localized culture developing around, 99–100; Miller's requiem of, 93–94; north from Seventh Street Bridge, 112*fig*; postal workers/Charles

Los Angeles River *(continued)*
Puck following flooding (1916), 113*fig;*
"river as freeway" equation of, 280n.13;
Salt Lake Railroad at, 112*fig;* used as
sewage/trash dump, 107–8; under
municipal control, 281n.24; undesirable
areas/populations around, 108, 109–10;
zoning ordinances around the, 110
Los Angeles River flooding: Army Corps of
Engineers role in controlling, 122, 123–
26; changing patterns of river and, 100–
106, 102*m,* 104*fig,* 111, 113–15; concerns
over excessive controls over, 288n.89;
concrete project proposed to control,
110–11; interviews/reports on measures
to control, 115–27; *Los Angeles Times* on,
103, 106, 117, 122; on New Year's Day
(1934), 122–23, 288n.90
Los Angeles River paving: Army Corps of
Engineers role in, 123–26; ethic boundaries demarcation by, 130; interviews/
reports taken prior to, 115–27; proposed
to control flooding, 110–11
Los Angeles Star, 17, 21, 99
Los Angeles Times: "American" themes on
cover (1901), 88; on city of Los Angeles,
49; La Fiesta adopted as boosterism
tool by, 82–83, 85; La Fiesta editorial/
advertisements in, 55–56; on Los Angeles
River floods, 103, 106, 117, 122; masthead
of the, 2; on *Mission Play* cast and performance, 216, 224; on rat eradication
program, 197–98; reporting on Simons
company by, 136, 140–43, 152, 158, 168
"The Los Angeles of Tomorrow?"
(Matson), 172
"Louis Mesmer Dictation," 261n.35
Lummis, Charles Fletcher, 59, 66, 70, 76,
78, 79, 87, 207, 211, 223, 229

M & M (Merchants and Manufacturers
Association): La Fiesta founded by, 52–
53; meeting on continuation of La Fiesta
(1897), 81–82; Merchants Association
origins of, 52; merging to create (1897),
79
McEuen, William, 117

McGarry, D. F., 203
McGroarty, Ida Lubrecht, 212, 218, 224
McGroarty, John Steven: California history
dramatic trilogy attempted by, 230;
comments about *The Mission Play* to/by,
207, 225, 245; commissioned to write
The Mission Play, 210–11; early life and
writing career of, 212–14; fame/riches
made from *The Mission Play,* 212; fan
mail to, 226, 227–29, 247; financial
difficulties of, 222–24; growing disassociation from *The Mission Play* by, 236,
239–40; "Happy Book" scrapbooks of,
227; as *Los Angeles Time* column writer,
226–27, 229; photograph of, 213*fig;* as
public figure, 226–27; racial attitudes
of, 230; *Titanic* eulogy by, 208. See also
The Mission Play (McGroarty)
Macias, Constancio, 167
Macias, Ernestina, 151, 159*fig*
Macias, "Wildman," 167
McKinley, William, 88
McLauthlin, Emmett, 180
McLean, Robert, 36
McWilliams, Carey, 8, 9, 28, 31, 45, 60, 121,
122
Macy St. district, 199
"Major Traffic Street Plan" (Traffic
Commission), 122
Malone, Jack, 151
Malone, Walter, 144–45, 150, 153, 155, 167,
226
Malone, Walter Jr., 147, 151, 170*fig*
Maner, George, 178
Manifest Destiny, 12, 18, 26, 33, 64
Maravilla Park housing, 308n.59
Marjenhoff, Maisie, 228
Marshall, James, 81
Marshall, Thomas R., 225
Martinez, Lupe, 169
Matson, Clarence, 172, 199
May Department Store, 241
Mayo, Morrow, 133
May, Robert, 12
Merchants Association, 52, 68
Mercurochrome treatment, 182, 203,
302n.17

Mesmer, Joseph, 110–11, 114, 116, 122
Mesmer, Louis, 23
Meusel brothers, 152
Mexican boys (1907 photograph), 40*fig*
Mexican population: Americanization of, 45–46, 272n.100; Anglo Angelenos racial attitudes toward, 271n.99; Anglo creation of space around, 31–48; attempts to deMexicanize, 43–44; disappearance of old settlements of, 30–31; disease linked to ethnicity of, 201–5, 303n.20; diversity/classes among, 300n.7; falling proportion to white of, 26; Guadalupe Hidalgo Treaty (1848) on citizenship of, 15–16; Manifest Destiny and racial hatred of, 12, 18; metaphorical connections between water and, 92–93; "Mexican" descriptor of, 270n.88; mutual hostility between Anglos and, 14–16; response to plague epidemic (1924) by, 201–5; Sonoratown population of, 16; white resentment and size of, 27–28. See also *Californios*
"Mexican problem" source, 27–28
Mexican Revolution, 145–46
Mexican shack (N. Alameda St.), 189*fig*
Mexican space: housing allowed within created, 46–47; perpetuated by La Fiesta, 59–61; recast by Anglo society, 31–48; redlining as part of, 47
Mexican stereotypes: analysis of plague outbreak in context of, 201–5; La Fiesta perpetuation of, 60–61; recast by Anglo society, 31–32; Simons Brick Company Yard No. 3 use of, 139–41. *See also* Garcia, Juan (*That Mexican!* character)
Mexican workers: building of Los Angeles (1910) by, 37*fig*; Chamber of Commerce report on unskilled wages of, 164; in downtown Los Angeles, 38*fig*. *See also* Simons Brick Company workers
Mexico. *See* Republic of Mexico
Meyberg, Max, 53, 54, 55, 62, 65, 67, 68
Miller, A. P., 74–75, 77
Miller, Frank, 36, 209–10, 214, 234

Miller, Henry, 94
Million Dollar Theater, 152
Minister's Association, 78
The Mission Play (McGroarty): Act 1 of, 218*fig*, 219–20; Act 2 of, 220–22; advertisements of, 222*fig*, 227*fig*; anticipation for opening of, 215–16; attraction of attending, 152, 156; audience responses to, 208–9, 217; Behymer's public relations activity for, 241–43; California Catholic history enacted in, 132, 209–12, 225–26; Chamber of Commerce enlisted to help with, 231–38, 248; commercial advertising using, 231; corporate support/wealthy patrons solicited to support, 233–41; critic response to, 216, 218, 224; declining popularity of, 231–40; development as institution, 225–26, 228–31; end of the run for, 245–49; failure of 1916 road trip, 223–25; Fiesta scene of, 221*fig*; growing disassociation of McGroarty from, 236, 239–40; La Fiesta as model for, 89; new playhouse built to house, 244–45; as part of tourist experience, 226; proposed merger with *Hiawatha,* 243
The Mission Play (or Playhouse) Association, 169, 214, 223, 234
Mission Play (or Playhouse) Committee, 232, 233, 246
mission-to-mission tour diary, 35*fig*
Montebello Hills, 132, 136, 138, 148–49
Montebello Park, 166
Montgomery, Charles, 17
Mooney, Angeleno Mary, 31
Moore, Alfred, 103, 104
Morales, Alejandro, 129, 146
Moreno, Mrs. Pasquale, 186, 187
Mount Carmel (*Monte Carmelo*), 153–54
"Mr. and Mrs. Los Angeles," 34–36, 40

Nation, 196
National Horse Show Committee, 238
Native Sons of the Gold West, 214
de Neve, Felipe, 96, 97
Newmark, Harris, 58
New Year's Day flooding (1934), 122–23, 288n.90

Nixon, Richard, 83

Obregon, Alvaro, 33
Olvera Street News, 43
Osburn, George, 225
Otis, Harrison Gray, 82, 83, 85, 86, 212
"Our Mexican" label, 33
"Our Mexico" claims, 32–33
Out West (magazine), 213
"Owl Drug Company Fashion Show," 239
Oxnam, G. Bromley, 44, 45, 46, 91, 109, 218

Palmer Method of Penmanship, 228
Palmet, A. N., 228–29
Parra, Concepcíon, 104
"The Passing of the Dominant Race"
    (Graves), 28
Patterson, W. C., 86–87
Peck, T. C., 231
Peralta, Eulogio, 180
Perez, Eulalia, 101
Petsch, Adolph, 53
Philadelphia (man-of-war), 75
Philadelphia Record, 58
Phillips, J. J., 104
Pickwick Stage Company, 238
Pico, Andres, 22, 29
plague epidemic. *See* bubonic plague
    epidemic (1924)
Pomeroy, J. L., 186, 203
Pontius, D. W., 234, 246
Porcupine, 82
Porter, Giles, 176
Portolá, Gaspar de, 219
postcard views, 173–74*fig*
Power, Patia, 224
Power, Tyrone Sr., 224
Prado, Genaro "Henry," 144, 145, 169
Prado, Walter Leon, 171
Pugsley, C. A., 228
Pullman strike (1894), 58

racism: early incidents (19th century) of
    violence and, 17–25; of foreign miner's
    tax, 13; link between Manifest Destiny
    and, 12, 18, 26; reports on historic, 13–
    14
Ramirez, J. R., 119–20

Ramona (Jackson), 214, 215, 238, 249
Rand, Charles Edward, 25
Ransom Company, 164
Ransom, J. B., 164, 165–66
Reagan, J. W., 115, 116, 120
Rebard, Ella, 229
redlining, 47
Redondo, José Maria, 24
Reeve, S. B., 118
Reisler, Mark, 43, 158
Republic of Mexico: Crabb invasion of,
    23–25, 260n.29; historians on outcome
    of war against, 12–13; Manifest Destiny
    and war against, 12; Mexican Revolution
    of, 145–46
"Research Los Angeles County Flood
    Control 1914–1915" report, 115–16
Retail Merchants Association, 234
Rieff, David, 4
Rivers of Empire (Worster), 115
Robinson, Charles Mulford, 114
Robinson, Henry M., 234
rodent eradication programs (1924), 191,
    193, 197–99, 306n.37
Rodriguez, Richard, vii, 252
Roman Catholic Church: financial support
    of McGroarty by, 223; *The Mission Play*
    enactment of California and, 132, 209–
    12; *The Mission Play* response by, 217
Romo, Francisco, 144
Rosenthal, Bernard, 172
Ruiz, Antonio, 17
Ruiz, Jose, 118
Rule, Ferd K., 49

Samarano, Gilberto, 179
Samarano, Guadalupe, 178, 180
Samarano, Luciana, 176, 178, 182
Samarano, Raul, 181*fig,* 182
Samarano, Roberto, 178–79
Samarano, Victor, 178, 179
Sanchez, George, 28
San Gabriel Mission, 21, 135, 156, 214
Saturday Night (Clover), 129, 157
"Science of Early California Life"
    (Calhoun), 215
Scott, Joseph, 242
Sea Bird (steamer), 18

Searle, George, 225
Semi-Tropical California (Truman), 26
Sepulveda, Ygnacio, 118
Serra, Father Junipero, 159, 215, 216, 219–20, 223, 225, 229, 230
741 Clara Street (Los Angeles), 180*fig*
742 Clara Street (Los Angeles), 177*fig*, 179, 202
Severance, Caroline, 88
Severance controversy, 88–89
Simons Brick Company: baby bonus program of, 136, 146; brickyard/town of Simons sold by, 168–69; building industrial Los Angeles together (poster) on, 165*fig*; compared to Mexican hacienda arrangement, 163; decline of, 166–68; expansion of, 135–37; groutlock brick patented by, 166; interplay of culture with commerce in, 138–39; as one of the largest employers in Los Angeles, 160–61; vision of, 163–64
Simons Brick Company workers: Christmas presents passed to children of, 157–58; company rules governing, 152–54; history of specific, 144–45; housing conditions of, 143–44, 156, 168; leisure activities of, 152, 162; numerous company bands played in by, 152, 157*fig*; photograph of, 131*fig*; religious arrangements made for, 153–54; response to Mexican Revolution by, 145–46; working conditions/wages of, 147–51. *See also* Mexican workers
Simons Brick Company Yard No. 3: contributions to growth of Los Angeles by, 169; described, 138, 139; use of Mexican stereotypes by, 139–41; photograph of, 140*fig*; selling of, 168–69; trucks ready to haul at, 167*fig*
Simons brothers: brick making/labor management experience of, 137–38; brickyard expansion by, 135–37; chain migration encouraged by, 146; impact of, 132; *Los Angeles Times* reporting on, 142–43; migration of family in 1880s, 133
Simons company band, 152, 157*fig*
Simons (company town): conditions of,

143–44, 156; LA County Health Department order on, 168; *Los Angeles Times* reporting on, 103, 106, 117, 122; reflections on irony of, 169–71; selling of, 168–69
Simons, Elmer, 135, 138
Simons, Joseph, 135, 138
Simons, Reuben, 137–38
Simons, Walter: big heart/generosity of, 157–59; death of, 169; on groutlock brick, 166; lavish lifestyle enjoyed by, 161; partnership with brothers, 135, 138; photograph of, 159*fig*; racial paternalism of, 155–56; on reasons for building Simons, 141; *Saturday Night* reporting on, 157
"Sir Knights of La Fiesta," 80
Sixty Years in Southern California (Newmark), 58
Sleepy Lagoon murder trials, 252
Smith, Jack, 227
"Social Work with Families in Los Angeles" (De Schweinitz), 129
Sonoratown (1870s), 16*fig*
Southern California (ca. 1850), 20*m*
Southern California Country (McWilliams), 9, 121
Southern California Retail Hardware Association, 238
Southern Pacific Railroad, 26
Spanish American War, 84–88
Spellmire, Verona, 155
Spurlock, E., 47
Starr, Kevin, 212
Stearns, Abel, 98
Stevens, George, 176
Stewart, Charles, 47
Stockton, Robert, 29
Stoltz, George, 104
"Summary Report on Feasibility of Los Angeles River Freeway" (1943), 126
Sunset Club, 73
Sunset (Southern Pacific Railroad), 173
Sutter, John, 70, 81

That Mexican! (McLean), 36
Tidings (Catholic journal), 216, 217

Tile and Mantle Contractors Association of America, 238
Titanic disaster (1912), 207–8
Titanic eulogy (McGroarty), 208
Traffic Commission, 122
Treaty of Guadalupe Hidalgo (1848), 12, 13–14, 18, 258n.17
Troiano, U., 168
Tropic of Cancer (Miller), 94
Truman, Benjamin, 13, 26, 27
Tuttle, E. A., 126

Ubaldo, 219, 221
United States Weather Bureau, 116
U.S. Census Bureau, 41

Valenzuela, Guadalupe, 179
Valenzuela, Jesus, 179
Valenzuela, Maria, 179, 301n.14
"The Value of Property and Sentiment in the Real Estate Business" (McGroarty), 222
Van Dyke, Henry, 210
Van Vleck, Frank, 66
Vargas, Ismael "Mayo," 147, 154, 162, 169
Vejar, F. Z., 119
Vera, Thomas, 180
violence. *See* ethnic violence

Waldie, D. J., 126
Walker, Franklin, 62
Wallace, William: on the *Californians*, 11; on Crabb invasion, 18, 19, 25; on difficulties of Mexicans exercising voting

rights, 16; journal kept by, 44; on joy of dancing, 60; on the old California, 14–15; predictions of civil unrest by, 17; on the trial of Juan Flores, 23
Wander Songs (McGroarty), 212
Warde, Frederic, 225
water, as Mexican metaphor, 92–93
West Coast Magazine, 213, 222
Weston, Edward, 252
White, Thomas Jefferson, 103
Why Los Angeles Will Become the World's Greatest City (Hunter), 1
Widney, Joseph P., 7, 104
William E. Hampton Company, 234–35
Willard, Charles Dwight, 72–73
Willhardt, Louis, 103
Withers, Charles, 127
Woman's Christian Temperance Union (WCTU), 78, 80
Woman's Home Missionary Society of Southern California, 80
Wood, Frederick, 53
Workman, Boyle, 1
Workman, William, 115
Works Progress Administration, 166
Worster, Donald, 115
Wright, Willard Huntington, 217

Yeats, William Butler, 3
Yorba, Josepha, 221–22, 319n.114

Zimmermann telegram, 146
Zoot Suit riots, 22, 252
Z.Z., 50–51

Compositor:	BookMatters, Berkeley
Indexer:	Sylvia Coates
Text:	11.25 / 13.5 Adobe Garamond
Display:	Adobe Garamond
Printer and binder:	Maple-Vail Manufacturing Group